ISBN 0-275-95693-8

90000>

EAN

9 780275 956936

HARDCOVER BAR CODE

Commercial Banking
in an Era of Deregulation

Commercial Banking in an Era of Deregulation

Third Edition

Emmanuel N. Roussakis

Westport, Connecticut
London

Library of Congress Cataloging-in-Publication Data

Roussakis, Emmanuel N.
    Commercial banking in an era of deregulation / Emmanuel N.
Roussakis.—3rd ed.
        p.   cm.
    Includes bibliographical references and index.
    ISBN 0–275–95693–8 (alk. paper)
    1. Bank management.   2. Banks and banking—United States.
I. Title.
HG1615.R68   1997
332.1'2'068—dc20   96–33187

British Library Cataloguing in Publication Data is available.

Library of Congress Catalog Card Number: 96–33187
ISBN: 0–275–95693–8

First published in 1997

Praeger Publishers, 88 Post Road West, Westport, CT 06881
An imprint of Greenwood Publishing Group, Inc.

Printed in the United States of America

The paper used in this book complies with the
Permanent Paper Standard issued by the National
Information Standards Organization (Z39.48–1984).

10 9 8 7 6 5 4 3 2 1

Copyright Acknowledgment

Every reasonable effort has been made to trace the owners of copyright
materials in this book, but in some instances this has proven impossible. The
author and publisher will be glad to receive information leading to more
complete acknowledgments in subsequent printings of the book, and in the
meantime extend their apologies for any omissions.

To George, Marina and Lucas,
Nicholas and Angela, and George

Contents

Tables and Figures

FIGURES

Preface

As noted by the author in the previous editions, this book examines commercial banking in the framework of the U.S. financial services industry. This industry is currently in a state of dynamic change that is rapidly transforming the role of commercial banks and the entire financial system. The 1990s are a period of dramatic transition for the commercial banking industry, one in which the nature of the banking industry is changing more rapidly than at any other time in its history. The combined forces of deregulation, electronic data processing, and telecommunications are altering both the nature of commercial banks and the competitive environment within which they operate. These forces have broken down the traditional barriers that both restricted the activities in which banks could engage and protected their position within the prescribed areas of activity. As a result, banks can now offer a wide array of services and pay competitive rates of interest; at the same time, they now compete directly with a variety of other financial and nonfinancial institutions for savings and loan customers. And as more of their corporate clients have dealings and operations abroad, banks have expanded their international operations and their presence in foreign financial markets. In addition, computer-mediated information transfer is bringing banking services into customers' offices and homes and altering traditional mechanisms of payment.

The increasingly competitive environment makes skill and efficiency in bank management more important than ever. Indeed, it is efficient management that underlies the effectiveness of commercial banks in meeting the demands of the society, and hence in stimulating the development and growth of the economy. It is essential, therefore, that bank management be prudent, safe, and profitable if there is to be a strong and adaptable banking system capable of meeting the needs of a growing society. As in the previous editions, this book reviews the management aspects of commercial banks, with special attention to the challenges presented by the ongoing changes in the financial marketplace.

The third edition of this book represents a substantial revision of the material contained in the second edition. The changes made go beyond the updating of numbers, tables, and graphs. The revisions reflect the experience of the author from use of the book in the classroom, numerous comments from students and colleagues, and, last but not least, the dynamic changes in the financial services industry, in which commercial banks operate.

The major change made for this new edition is a substantial revision of the majority of chapters. Many chapters have been revised and expanded to incorporate new developments and, where applicable, new regulations. For example, Chapter 3, "The Banking Industry in Transition," incorporates the new interstate banking powers of commercial banks and in addition reflects the effects on the banking industry of technological developments, changes in laws and regulations, and market forces. Similarly, Chapter 5, "Bank Capital and Its Management," elaborates on recent changes in international capital standards to deal with interest-rate risk. Chapter 6, "Deposits," was expanded to include the pricing strategy of banks offering deposit services and the effects of the Truth in Savings Act. Chapter 9, "Solvency," provides additional insights into the management of risk. Chapter 10, "Income," has been revised to reflect the current state of bank profitability. Chapter 12, "Bank Lending," has expanded coverage of securitization of loans and loan sales. Chapter 16, "International Banking," is a new chapter that provides insights into this aspect of banking activity. As in the revisions of other chapters, the attempt has been made to make the discussion as current as possible, and at the same time to provide perspectives on major trends that are affecting commercial banks, their management, and their regulation. The relevant laws and regulations are discussed in detail in various parts of the book, as are their implications for commercial banks and other depository institutions.

Like the previous editions, this book is designed for both academics and professionals, as well as for anyone interested in the fundamentals of commercial banking from a management perspective. As a college textbook, it is intended for use in banking courses at either the undergraduate or the graduate level. It has purposely been designed so that students can follow the presentation without need for prerequisites. Tables and figures clarify and strengthen major points covered in each chapter, and use of mathematical formulas is kept to a minimum.

This book has been written with the objective of providing professionals and students alike with a description and an analysis of the problems faced in the management of banks. In principle, the problems bank managers face can be easily identified and rationally considered. In practice, however, solutions are anything but watertight. Indeed, in the real world in which the banker operates, application of the principles discussed in this book becomes an exercise in informed judgment. The principles presented therefore must be viewed as guidelines that will assist the banker in the systematic evaluation of the relevant facts.

This book does not provide the final answers, which vary among banks, and even for the same bank, over a period of time.

The organizational structure of the book has remained the same. The material is divided into five parts. Part I provides an overview of the U.S. commercial banking system and the financial environment in which banks operate. Part II deals with the sources of bank funds, and Part III with the policy objectives in the employment of bank funds. Part IV examines the uses of bank funds and describes the character of bank assets. Part V deals with international banking. Because of the quasi-public character of commercial banking, pertinent laws and actions by regulatory bodies are given due consideration throughout the book.

This edition is an extension of the original work; several individuals made contributions to either the two previous or the current third edition, or both. I am particularly indebted to my colleagues Professors A. J. Prakash and R. Daigler for their helpful comments and suggestions. A special debt is also due to Caroline Ciancutti and Ana-Maria Figueredo for valuable editorial assistance. For her editorial assistance on the present and previous books published by Praeger, I am grateful to Elizabeth I. Wilson.

Finally, I am deeply indebted to my wife, Sophie, for her unfailing love, patience, and support.

Part I

Overview of the U.S. Commercial Banking System

Chapter 1

Scope of Commercial Banking

The U.S. financial system includes a variety of financial institutions, the oldest of which are the commercial banks. The first modern type of bank was chartered in 1781 at Philadelphia, and many of those established in the nineteenth century are still in operation. Perhaps because of this head start, banks have grown to be by far the most important intermediaries. Indeed, with assets in excess of $4 trillion, they constitute the largest type of U.S. financial institution. Banks perform a variety of functions. Although lending and investing have been the epicenter of commercial banking, the last few years have witnessed a general surge in bank services. This surge has reflected the expansion of both the types and the volume of services that banks extend to the communities or markets served. This surge has been induced in part by government regulation, but most importantly by competitive pressures. This chapter describes the major functions performed by banks and reviews some salient features of bank financial statements.

FUNCTIONS OF COMMERCIAL BANKS

Commercial banks perform many functions, some central to their main role in the economy and others more peripheral. The three main functions of commercial banks are interrelated: the creation of money, accomplished through lending and investing activities; the holding of deposits; and the provision of a mechanism for payments and transfer of funds. They all relate to the banks' critical role in the overall management of the flow of money and credit through the economy.

Other services are offered primarily to draw customers by providing complete money management and ancillary services through a single institution. Some of these services, such as trust management and leasing, may themselves be profitable; others may be loss leaders offered solely to attract depositors to the institution.

Money Creation

Banks are unique among financial institutions in their ability to create money.* When banks extend credit in the form of loans and investments, they create demand deposits that result in an increase in the supply of money. Banks hold almost all business deposits and the majority of individual and government deposits. Thus, although thrift institutions offer demand deposits, the banks' supremacy in this area remains unchallenged.

Money creation is performed within the framework provided by law and regulation. The process of lending and investing builds up deposits against which banks must maintain sufficient reserves to comply with the requirements of the Federal Reserve System. Ultimately, expansion in the total deposits of the banking system is dependent upon the willingness of the Federal Reserve System to permit creation of additional reserves in order to stimulate economic growth.

The ability of banks to create money in this way results in a flexible credit system that is critical to the functioning of the economy. Without the provision of this credit, much economic activity either would become impossible or would be dependent on the ability of producers to amass capital from past sales before undertaking expansion or the production of goods for future sale. The existence of such a credit mechanism allows much economic activity to be financed through loans in anticipation of repayment from future proceeds. It also obviates the need for individual business to maintain large working balances at all times to meet changing needs for available funds.

Beyond the needs of individual businesses or other entities for flexible credit, the banks' role in credit creation is an essential component of the Federal Reserve System's objective of controlling the supply of money for the economy as a whole. The Federal Reserve System attempts to maintain a money policy consistent with stable prices, sound economic growth, and minimal unemployment, and thus to avoid both inflation (which results when increases in money supply surpass increases in production of goods and services) and deflation (which results when the money supply increases at a slower rate than production).

*The Federal Reserve's most recent definition of the supply of money in its narrowest sense, M_1, includes currency outside the Treasury, Federal Reserve banks, and the vaults of commercial banks; traveler's checks of nonbank issuers; demand deposits at all commercial banks other than those due to domestic banks, the U.S. government, and foreign banks and official institutions, less cash items in the process of collection and Federal Reserve float; and negotiable order of withdrawal (NOW) and automatic transfer service (ATS) accounts at banks and thrift institutions, credit union share-draft (CUSD) accounts, and demand deposits at mutual savings banks.

Payments and Transfers of Funds

An important function of banks, one that provides an invaluable service for depositors, is the provision of a mechanism of payment and transfer of funds. Transferring balances among accounts is an activity that banks perform when directed to do so—that is, upon receipt of checks issued by deposit holders. Banks provide a payments and collection mechanism primarily to attract deposits.

Providing for a payments mechanism is a costly activity. Indeed, managing the payments mechanism can absorb up to a third of total bank costs. Cost items include wages for tellers and bookkeepers, computer purchase and maintenance, advertising, and substantial amounts of equipment and supplies. A large portion of employee time is spent performing the payments mechanism function. Service charges do not cover all of these expenses; in fact, competition for customers at times when interest rates are high (meaning high yields for invested and loaned deposits) leads many banks to offer free checking services.

The procedures for effecting the actual transfers of funds are undergoing rapid change with the introduction of technological advances in the storage and transfer of information. Transfers of funds at the local level occur primarily through clearinghouse arrangements for the exchange of checks. These are citywide within individual cities. Transfers between cities are routed either through large banks in major cities or through regional banks of the Federal Reserve System. Transfers of funds between banks are also done electronically through the Fedwire, which handles more than 300,000 transfers per day, amounting to about $1 trillion. The Fedwire is a wholesale wire transfer system operated by the Federal Reserve that links all 12 Federal Reserve banks, their branches, and those U.S. depository institutions eligible to join. In addition to the transfer of funds, this communication system is used for the transfer of bank entries representing purchases and sales of government securities, and the transfer of financial information.

The expansion of computerized payment systems promises to reduce the employee time and paperwork involved in transferring funds. The introduction of automatic teller machines (ATMs) has heralded the inauguration of computerized systems that permit 24–hour banking services, such as electronic withdrawal of cash from one's deposit account, making deposits and loan payments, and transferring funds between accounts. Highly advanced ATMs offer customers such additional services as access to their mutual fund accounts, purchase or sale of stocks, payment of utility and store bills, and printouts of bank statements. A recent study by the Bank Administration Institute determined that 55 percent of all retail banking transactions in the United States take place at ATMs or over the telephone.

Developed in Britain, the ATM spread to Europe before its introduction in the United States in 1969 by the Philadelphia National Bank. Since then, ATMs have been installed by banks in cities all over the country. They are usually set up outside bank premises and at other convenient locations, such as airports, malls, and university campuses.* To further expand their retail services over a broader geographic area, banks throughout the country joined forces to share their ATM facilities. This led to the growth of two nationwide ATM networks, Cirrus (owned by MasterCard) and Plus (owned by Visa). In 1990 the two systems—accounting jointly for over 100,000 ATMs—agreed to provide access for each other's customers, thereby enormously enhancing the usefulness of ATMs. Expansion of the Cirrus and Plus systems abroad has enabled the connection of foreign banks to these interbank networks. As a result, Cirrus or Plus cards have been issued for their customers by banks in Canada, Japan, Singapore, Thailand, Hong Kong, Australia, New Zealand, and several European and Latin American countries. The internationalization of both ATM networks enables customers whose banks are affiliated with either card system to receive cash from any participating institution in a foreign country, at the day's exchange rate. The transaction takes six seconds to complete—that is, from the moment the customer punches in his or her secret code until the computer approves the transaction and funds are made available in the local currency.

Another related electronic development has been the trend toward in-home banking. In-home banking enables a customer to communicate with the bank via a computer terminal linked to the bank's computer. This represents another dimension of electronic funds transfer (EFT) systems, and consequently of paperless banking. In-home banking enables a customer to transact business from the home or place of work, at a convenient time. It is generally viewed as the dominant delivery system of banking services in the foreseeable future.

Early experiments go back to 1980, when Banc One in Columbus, Ohio, began transmitting banking information into homes. Since then, several banks have offered their customers in-home banking services. One such institution is Citibank, which offers its customers checkbook balancing, transferring money between accounts, bill paying, electronic messages to and from the bank as well as between customers, and electronic statements. Banks see an enormous potential in this field, based on studies indicating that by the year 2005, 75 percent of the U.S. household market will be using in-home services. Wider use of these services will take people out of the bank, reduce the paperwork load, and drive down costs. In 1994, the average teller transaction cost Banks $1.07; ATM transactions cost just 27 cents. A PC bank transaction is expected to cost banks even less, according to analysts. While banks have to pay for ATMs, customers pay for their PCs, a fact that will save banks countless dollars.

Providing Credit

The extension of credit is the central activity of a commercial bank. Not only is it the primary source of bank income, but it provides financing for productive

---

*A court ruling in 1984 that an ATM does not qualify as a branch ensured that the installation of ATMs at distant locations would not be hindered by interstate banking laws.

activity throughout the economy. Virtually every phase of the manufacture and transport of industrial products benefits from the availability of commercial bank credit. The purchase of raw materials and equipment, the manufacturing process itself, and the transport of goods must all be financed in advance of the sale of the goods, and this is frequently done through bank loans. When goods are to be stored for future sales at times of high demand (such as the Christmas season for many retail products), the lag between expenditure and sales revenue is even longer and the need for credit is greater.

The agricultural industry, through improved transport, processing, and storage of foods, has freed man from dependence on seasonal availability of foods and has mitigated the impact of climatic and other damage to harvests. Food production is a lengthy process, in terms of the time it takes to realize a return on the agricultural investment. This industry illustrates well the role of bank credit in financing productive activity through loans against its future revenues. The farmer, the processor, the transporter, the wholesaler, and the retailer all rely on bank credit to finance their activities.

Bank loans are also used to finance growth and expansion, to start new businesses, and to pull businesses through periods of unexpected loss or reversals. Finally, banks make loans to consumers for major purchases, such as homes and automobiles. Consumer loans allow individuals to improve their standard of living in the present by borrowing against future earnings.

Many government activities are financed through bank loans and through bank purchase of bonds issued by municipalities, states, or the federal government. Short-term loans are issued to government bodies to cover cash-flow contingencies. When banks buy bond issues, they help finance government capital development in the form of construction, purchase of capital equipment, and other activities.

Depository Function

Banks are in the business of borrowing money, principally in the form of deposits; therefore they offer deposit accounts in a variety of forms. Commercial banks hold deposit funds in the form of transaction (demand) accounts and nontransaction (time and savings) accounts. The purposes for which funds are deposited with banks vary. One of the primary reasons for holding bank balances is to use the payment facilities of the banking system. Balances held for this purpose take the form of demand deposits. Predictable daily cash-flow needs obviously call for immediately available funds in a checking account. Because of the purpose for which they are held, balances in these accounts are referred to as transaction or working balances.

In other cases, deposits are used as a reserve against contingencies. Whether maintained by individuals or businesses, these precautionary balances can take the form of demand, time, or savings deposits. For example, individuals may hold balances for the possibility of an unexpected emergency, to provide for retirement, or for other, nonspecific needs. Businesses maintain such balances to offset disruptions in production caused by strikes or recession. Many companies do well in periods of prosperity, but in periods of recession their incomes decline and their capital may dissipate.

Funds may be placed in demand, time, or savings deposit accounts to fund future expenditures. Such funds are usually accumulated by individuals for a planned purchase of a big-ticket item or service, and by businesses to finance acquisition of fixed assets or a new facility.

Funds may also be deposited in commercial banks simply because the depositor chooses this form of claim over other financial assets. Some of these assets may be money-market instruments—instruments of less than one year maturity, such as commercial paper, bankers' acceptances, or government securities; other assets may be capital-market instruments—longer-term debt instruments and stocks; still others may be in the form of claims on other financial intermediaries. The choice of a bank deposit over other options is affected by a number of considerations, including the saver's expectations regarding changes in economic activity, interest-rate trends, and movements in the general level of prices. For example, in periods of recession savers might prefer bank deposits to equity and debt instruments because of declining interest rates and depressed stock market activity. By contrast, when the economy enters the recovery phase, savers might prefer stocks to deposits, in anticipation of increased stock market activity.

Last, funds may be deposited with banks because of a compensating-balance requirement. Banks require businesses to carry a deposit balance with them in order to be considered for the extension of credit. After all, businesses carry a deposit balance somewhere, so why not with the lending institution?

From the bank's point of view, accumulation of deposits expands reserves, which in turn enables the bank to make loans and investments and, in the process, to create money. Clearly, banking policy must determine what portion of deposits must remain available for withdrawal upon demand and what portion can be considered reserves.

Trust Services

For a great variety of reasons, individuals or corporations may desire a reliable outside entity to administer their assets. To meet this need, and to attract large depositors, banks offer trust services. As wealth in the United States has increased, the need for trust services has grown. Management of trusts involves both investing the funds for growth and carrying out specific instructions regarding them.

Personal trust services are available through many banks, and the assets held in trust in some cases exceed those of the bank. Estate planning and serving as executor/trustee under a will are the most common forms of trust service; others include administering funds for a minor or someone judged incapable of managing his or her own financial affairs, holding securities, and collecting interest or dividend income. Ancillary services such as tax counseling and tax return preparation may also be offered.

Although corporate trust services are becoming more common, they are still offered primarily by large banks in major metropolitan areas. Management of pension funds and profit-sharing plans is a leading function in this area. Banks may administer bond issues for corporations. Besides receiving the funds from the corporation and making the necessary interest and principal payments, the bank also must ensure that the corporation meets all the obligations created through the issuing of the bonds. Banks may act as stock transfer agents, maintaining stockholder records and carrying out transfers. Again, the bank assumes responsibility for the corporation's obligation, seeing to it, for example, that the stock is not overissued. A related function is the administration of corporate stock-purchase plans intended to allow one corporation to gain a controlling interest in another or to absorb it altogether. Funds are deposited with the bank, which uses them to purchase the desired shares from stockholders.

International Services

The postwar decades have been a period of rapid development for international trade. This growth has produced a derived demand for higher levels of international banking services. Initially most of these services were offered by relatively few money-center banks, and a large part of this business was conducted through foreign correspondent banks. The rapid growth in the demand for international banking services prompted money-center banks as well as regional banks to establish a presence abroad and expand the scope of the services offered.

At the present time approximately 160 U.S. banks have international banking departments and maintain a large network of branches, subsidiaries, and affiliates throughout the world. The number of U.S. banks having correspondent relationships with foreign banks is in the thousands. With their international network of offices and correspondent relationships, these banks are prominent suppliers of a host of international services. Liberalization of trade restrictions on a global basis and the opening of the markets of Eastern Europe and the republics of the former Soviet Union have induced many U.S. companies to expand their business internationally through exports or through direct foreign investments. It is of great value to such companies to obtain up-to-date information on issues like foreign market conditions, availability and cost of financing abroad, investment incentives offered by foreign countries, plant location sites, and foreign regulations. Some banks have established a trade-development unit to help customers find new markets and new sources of supply. The fact that a bank has a worldwide network of offices and correspondent banks puts financial information and services at its fingertips and at the disposal of its customers.

Country and marketing intelligence is just one of the many services that banks extend to their customers. Others include foreign collections, letters of credit, short-term financing of exports and imports, transfer of funds, foreign exchange, and assistance with mergers and acquisitions.

Safekeeping

Banks maintain vaults and elaborate security systems to safeguard their own stores of cash, securities, and other negotiable instruments. A traditional bank service has been to make this security available to customers for the safekeeping of their valuables. These services are of two types: safe deposit boxes and safe-keeping.

Safe deposit boxes are metal compartments stored within the bank vault and rented to individual customers. This arrangement gives the customer both control over access to the stored valuables and privacy. The bank protects the goods from theft or damage, and guarantees that only the customer or authorized representatives shall have access to the box. The customer's right to the privacy of the safe deposit box is guaranteed by law: the bank may open the box only by court order following the death of the boxholder.

Safekeeping, by contrast, calls for the bank to exercise custodial functions over the valuables and to act as agent for the customer. Securities such as stocks and bonds are the items most commonly held under this type of arrangement. Individuals or corporations owning large amounts of securities commonly keep them in banks. Securities pledged as loan collateral are frequently held by banks.

Leasing

Many large banks, primarily through their holding companies, are involved in the leasing of equipment to customers. Although this consists mainly of leasing transportation equipment or heavy machinery to businesses, some banks lease automobiles to individuals.

The leasing arrangement benefits both the bank and its business customers. Businesses are able to acquire the use of equipment without making the capital investment necessary to purchase it; thus they realize a financial benefit and increased flexibility. Since banks are able to obtain funds at lower interest rates than those available to their business customers, the interest component of equipment purchase is less when the bank does the buying. The lessee realizes this saving by bearing the reduced interest cost through the lease arrangement. The leasing expense is wholly tax-deductible; there is no need to calculate interest payments or depreciation schedules.

The bank, meanwhile, benefits from ownership of the equipment. In case of default by the lessee, the bank can reclaim the equipment without going through the legal steps involved in foreclosing on a purchase loan.

Other Functions

Banks offer many other services in addition to those discussed above. To consumers, for example, banks offer credit cards, traveler's checks, and investment products (annuities and mutual funds), which provide the prospect of higher yields than are currently available on conventional banks deposits but entail more risk. Annuities are insurance products that enable banks to earn fee income from commissions. Essentially they are tax-deferred, long-term savings plans that promise the holder payment of a stream of income at scheduled intervals, beginning on a designated future date (e.g., upon retirement). Mutual funds (formally open-end investment companies) are professionally managed investment programs that pool funds from their shareholders in stocks, bonds, and other securities in accordance with their announced objectives (e.g., to maximize income or attain long-term capital appreciation). With mutual-fund shares representing competing investment alternatives to bank CDs and time deposits, many banks have entered this market. Since the Federal Reserve's authorization in 1992, some banking firms have organized subsidiaries to market these services (e.g., Citicorp's Investment Services), while others have expanded into this service area through acquisition of existing mutual funds (e.g., Mellon Bank purchased Dreyfus) or establishment of joint ventures with security firms (e.g., NationsBank and Dean Witter). In 1995, bank-managed funds accounted for over 15 percent of all mutual funds' assets. This record establishes banks as major players in the mutual funds business.

To their business customers, banks provide credit information, account reconciliations, inventory-control accounting, billing, lockbox plans, counseling on the investment of corporate funds, and business and financial advice on a wide range of matters, including foreign markets. For example, for companies that want to develop export activity, banks provide information about quotas, duties, health regulations, legal problems, and related issues associated with selling in specific countries. They can also provide market information on incomes, tastes, and existing competition in these markets. If the business customer is interested in establishing a physical presence overseas, banks can offer advice on locating plants or even purchasing foreign companies.

Apart from their services to consumers and businesses, commercial banks cater to the needs of the government by underwriting security offerings. Some large money-center banks, acting singly or in combination, frequently underwrite federal government issues and general obligations of state and local governments. In addition, they may make a market in such securities, standing ready to buy or sell particular issues at established bid and ask quotations. Beginning in the late 1980s, the Federal Reserve expanded the activities of several money-center banks by authorizing their holding companies to set up subsidiaries to engage in the underwriting and trading of such issues as commercial paper, corporate bonds, municipal revenue bonds, and securities backed by mortgages and consumer debt. Repeal of the Glass-Steagall Act of 1933, which mandated the separation of commercial and investment banking, will further enhance the investment banking activities of commercial banks.

To their underwriting and marketing activities many banks have added a complementary function, brokerage service (they execute trades without offering investment advice). Over 2,000 banks now act as brokers for their customers (buy and sell stocks, bonds, and options), offering discount rates for the service. Bank holding companies that are authorized by the Federal Reserve to engage in underwriting through a special subsidiary are permitted to offer full-service security brokerage (including providing customers with investment advice).

In addition to investment banking and brokerage services, U.S. banks provide their corporate customers with a variety of merchant banking services. These include identifying companies for possible merger or acquisition, financing takeovers, offering hedging services against fluctuating interest rates and foreign-exchange rates, and guaranteeing customers' debt issues to ensure low-cost financing from the open market or other lending institutions.

Some of the services discussed above are provided by banks directly, while others are offered indirectly, through holding company subsidiaries and affiliates that enable banks to enter product and geographic markets from which they are barred by laws and regulations. Banks have used these vehicles to provide their customers with data-processing services, courier services, travel services, factoring, mortgage banking, and management consulting. Until enactment of broader reforms, banks devised still another vehicle for expanding the scope of services offered to their customers without running afoul of the law. In the mid-1980s, Chemical Bank, for example, rented the lobby space of some of its branches to one of the nation's largest marketers of real-estate and other tax-shelter investments. In a similar move, BankAmerica rented branch space to an insurance company. Other banks followed the lead of these institutions. Although there is considerable pressure to allow banks to encompass both the insurance and real-estate-related activities among their functions, currently they are able to offer only a limited set of these activities—those that involve brokerage rather than underwriting or ownership.

Even more significant are the services that banks offer abroad, where they are permitted a much wider scope of activity. Thus, through foreign subsidiaries and affiliates, banks engage in direct equity investments, commodity trading, insurance operations, and an array of other services that, though prohibited in the United States, are permissible in foreign countries.

BANK FINANCIAL STATEMENTS

Many of the commercial banking functions discussed above are reflected in a bank's report of condition (balance sheet). However, since size is an important determinant of the magnitude and variety of functions performed by a bank, rather than review the individual asset and liability items of a single bank, it is more meaningful if such examination is based upon an aggregate, all-inclusive balance sheet, such as the one presented in Table 1.1, which identifies the magnitude and scope of activities of all insured commercial banks in the United States. Since many of these activities are income-generating, no balance-sheet analysis can be complete without a corresponding review of the aggregate income statement. Brief explanation of the various items included in both statements will contribute to better understanding of the U.S. banking system and will highlight much of the material presented in the succeeding chapters. The following sections provide a brief description of the various items in the balance sheet and income statement of all banks, referring to 1995 data for U.S. insured commercial banks.

Balance-Sheet Items

As shown in Table 1.1, the assets, liabilities, and equity of all insured commercial banks are composed of many categories, each of which encompasses subcategories.

The first component of the combined balance sheet for all insured commercial banks is "cash and due from banks." This category, also referred to as "cash assets," is the most liquid of the assets held and goes to meet banks' working and legal reserve requirements. It includes checks that are drawn on other banks and are in the process of being presented to those banks for payment. As indicated earlier, in connection with the payments mechanism, these checks may be cleared through a local clearinghouse, a correspondent bank, or the district Federal Reserve bank. Increasing use of electronic transfer will significantly reduce the number of checks in process of collection. Other items considered as cash assets are coins and currency kept in the vault to meet the needs of depositors, demand balances kept with domestic correspondent banks, other balances with U.S. depository institutions and foreign correspondent banks, and balances that law requires banks to maintain at the district Federal Reserve bank.

"Securities" is the next category of items, and the second major class of assets after loans. It includes both debt instruments and stocks. As implied by the term, debt instruments are evidences of indebtedness issued by borrowers and acquired by banks either at the time of issue or later, by purchasing them from other investors. Because of the variety of borrowers and their differing needs, a bank's investment portfolio contains debt issues that differ by issuer, maturity, stated rate of interest, and marketability. Debt issues are generally classified into obligations issued by the U.S. Treasury, federal agencies, state and local governmental units, and other.

U.S. Treasury issues are the direct debt of the U.S. government. Because these obligations are virtually free from risk of default, they are generally considered of prime quality. Federal agency issues include the obligations of a number of agencies, such as the Federal National Mortgage Association (FNMA or Fannie Mae), the Federal Home Loan Mortgage Corporation (the Mortgage Corporation or Freddie Mac), the Federal Home Loan Banks, and the Farm Credit System.

Table 1.1
Aggregate Balance Sheet of All Insured Commercial Banks, September 30, 1995

Item	Amount (millions of dollars)	Percent of Total
ASSETS		
Cash and due from depository institutions	$275,113	6.5
Securities	818,749	19.4
Federal funds sold and securities purchased under agreements to resell	155,700	3.7
Loans and leases, net	2,502,700	59.2
Plus: allowance for losses	52,875	1.3
unearned income	6,054	.1
Loans and leases, gross	2,561,629	60.6
Real estate	1,070,946	25.3
Commercial and industrial	647,434	15.3
Consumer	518,475	12.3
Other loans	272,265	6.4
Lease-financing receivables	52,509	1.2
Assets held in trading accounts	223,940	5.3
Bank premises and fixed assets	60,955	1.4
Other real estate owned	7,632	.2
Other assets	184,639	4.4
Total assets	$4,229,427	100.0
LIABILITIES AND EQUITY		
Total deposits	$2,931,386	69.3
Demand	778,671	18.4
Savings	750,697	17.7
Time	952,359	22.5
Deposits in foreign offices	449,659	10.6
Federal funds purchased and securities sold under agreements to repurchase	330,924	7.8
Subordinated notes and debentures	43,724	1.0
Other liabilities	579,308	13.7
Total liabilities	$3,885,342	
Equity capital	344,085	8.1
Total liabilities and equity	$4,229,427	100.0

Note: Details may not add to totals due to rounding
Source: Federal Deposit Insurance Corporation, *Call Report*, September 30, 1995.

State and local obligations, often called municipals, account for the largest portion of commercial bank investment portfolios. Their major attraction is that the interest is exempt from federal income tax. This is especially important for commercial banks, which have relatively high marginal tax brackets compared with other financial intermediaries (such as pension funds and thrift institutions). The item ''all other securities'' includes obligations of domestic corporations, foreign governments, international institutions (such as issues of the International Bank for Reconstruction and Development), and foreign corporations. Also part of "all other securities" are bank holdings of stock. When a bank joins the Federal Reserve System, it is required to purchase stock in its district Federal Reserve bank in an amount determined by its capital. Other stock holdings include shares in subsidiary corporations (such as safe deposit companies and affiliated banks) and shares acquired as a result of borrower default on a loan for which those shares served as collateral. In the latter instance the stocks must be disposed of within a reasonable time.

Another component of the "all other securities" category is trading-account securities. Securities held in trading accounts are customarily those federal and municipal securities (general obligations) that large money-center banks underwrite; issues in which banks make a market—that is, they stand ready to buy or sell at established bid and ask quotations; and various securities that banks buy and sell in a nondealer capacity.

"Federal funds sold and securities purchased under agreements to resell" involve very-short-term loans of funds to other banks and securities dealers. A bank sells federal funds when it lends another bank its excess reserves on deposit with the Federal Reserve bank. Except for weekends and holidays, a federal-funds transaction is normally for one day, which means that a bank experiencing an unexpected outflow of deposits may enter the market on an overnight basis to adjust its reserve position. A similar transaction is the lending of federal funds to other banks and U.S. government securities dealers through the purchase of securities under a repurchase agreement. Under this agreement the seller (borrower) makes a commitment to repurchase these securities on a particular future date for a specified sum. The repurchase agreement thus makes the entire transaction functionally equivalent to collateralized borrowing.

"Loans" is the largest category of assets held by commercial banks and the main source of their income. Although loans may be classified in a number of ways (by security, by maturity, by repayment), their most commonly employed classification is by type of borrower or purpose for which the funds are used. The largest and most important type of loan is secured by real estate (e.g., residence, farmland, and large multifamily, commercial, and industrial property). Other important types are loans to individuals, commercial and industrial loans, and loans to finance agricultural production. Finally, banks hold a variety of miscellaneous loans, among which are loans to financial institutions and to individuals or firms purchasing or carrying securities. Two accounts customarily reported with loans are "allowance for loan losses" and "unearned income on loans." The former reflects the amount of reserves set aside for possible loan losses; the latter, the unearned interest on loans that were recorded on the banks' books in amounts including such interest. Eventually, as interest is earned, appropriate transfers are made out of this account and into the current income.

"Lease-financing receivables" reflects the size of the banks' direct lease-financing activity (banks usually engage in lease financing indirectly, through leasing subsidiaries).

"Bank premises and fixed assets" represents the depreciated value of the bank building, furniture, fixtures, and equipment used in the conduct of the banking business. Although many banks own their building and equipment and depreciate them over time, some banks—especially those in bigger cities—prefer to lease part or all of the fixed assets they use. Bank ownership of "other real estate" may represent property that was foreclosed to protect against greater losses on bad real-estate loans. In other instances it may represent purchases of property that was intended to become a bank's new site or to open a branch or otherwise to expand operations (for instance, to establish drive-in facilities). Sometimes a bank's ownership of real estate may take the form of shares in subsidiaries formed to hold titles to the bank's premises, parking lot, and other real estate, in which case such ownership would be reported under "securities."

Banks providing international banking services usually include in their balance sheet the item "customer liability on acceptances." This represents claims of banks against their customers arising from bank acceptance of drafts and bills of exchange, generally issued in connection with foreign trade. Lack of individual reference to this item in Table 1.1 implies that it has been incorporated in the "all other assets" category. This is a catchall category found on any balance sheet, and covers assets that defy classification in any of the groups mentioned above. Typically it includes prepaid expenses and accrued items.

On the liability side of the balance sheet, the largest item is "deposits." Deposits are accounts representing the different forms through which funds are placed with a bank. Demand deposits are deposits that may be drawn upon or transferred at any time, without prior notice. Since withdrawals or transfers are usually effected by check, these deposits are also referred to as checking accounts. This type of account is customarily sought by depositors who wish to maintain an account for transaction purposes. Savings deposits, also known as passbook savings, legally require the depositor to give the bank advance notice prior to any withdrawal, although banks hardly enforce this requirement. Time deposits, as the name implies, are funds left with the bank for a specified period of time. Banks offer a range of time-deposit accounts to individuals, businesses, and governments. One popular form of time deposit is the certificate of deposit (CD), which derives its name from the fact that it is evidenced by a certificate. CDs, especially the larger negotiable ones (over $100,000), have become an important part of the U.S. financial system in recent years.

"Federal funds purchased and securities sold under agreements to repurchase" is the reverse of "federal funds sold and securities purchased under agreements to resell." This item represents borrowing to cover a reserve deficiency or to acquire additional funds to lend. Its size is always larger than its counterpart on the asset side, because bank borrowing may be done not only from other banks but also from securities brokers and dealers, and from corporations that possess temporarily idle funds.

In recent years banks have been raising funds by relying increasingly upon the issuance of subordinated notes and debentures. These are intermediate- or long-term debt instruments subordinate in priority of payment to payment in full of all deposit and nondeposit liabilities. "Other liabilities" consists of a number of items that, for the purpose of our analysis, may be distinguished into two subgroups: "other borrowings" and "all other liabilities." "Other borrowings" reflects funds borrowed by banks for short periods from such nondeposit sources as the Federal Reserve discount window, a bank's overseas branch network (Eurodollar borrowings), and commercial paper (short-term, unsecured promissory notes). "All other liabilities" represents such diverse items as taxes and other expenses that, though incurred before the end of the accounting period, have not yet been paid. As these items are paid, new accruals replace them.

"Equity capital" is a composite of the following capital accounts: preferred stock, common stock, surplus, undivided profits, reserves for contingencies, and other capital reserves. The sum of these items, excluding preferred stock (if any), is significant to holders of a bank's common stock. This figure, divided by the number of shares of stock outstanding, gives the book value of each share, which relates to the price at which shares may be bought or sold.

Income Statement Items

In performing their various functions, banks generate revenues and incur expenses. Over time, the flows of these revenues and expenses determine the profitability of bank operations and the rate of return on capital accounts. Just as with any other business, so with a bank: unless it is profitable and provides a reasonable return on capital, it will be unable to continue as a going concern. Hence the importance of income statements in appraising the financial position of banks. Table 1.2 identifies the income and expense items of all insured commercial banks, and the profitability of their operations, in 1995.

The single largest source of operating income for banks is interest and fees on loans. Indeed, as Table 1.2 shows, interest on loans provides more than half of the operating income for insured banks. The relative importance of this source is generally attributed to the large volume of loans made by banks and the rates charged, which in the course of the last few years have increased significantly. Another source of income is interest on balances with banks, which is essentially interest on loans. This income is derived primarily from the redepositing (placement) of Eurodollars with other banks. This item is of importance especially to large banks that have international operations. Income on federal funds sold and securities purchased under agreements to resell is realized from the lending of excess reserves and the purchase of securities under resale agreement. Since both transactions technically involve the lending of bank funds, here, too, the income earned is basically interest on loans.

Investment income is the second most important source of income for banks. Interest from U.S. government, state, and local obligations accounts for most of

Table 1.2

Aggregate Income Statement of All Insured Commercial Banks, September 30, 1995

Item	Amount (millions of dollars)	Percent of Total
OPERATING INCOME		
Interest and fees on loans	$165,510	57.9
Interest on balances due from depository institutions	4,667	1.6
Income on federal funds sold and securities purchased under agreements to resell	7,639	2.7
Income on investment securities	38,447	13.4
Interest income from assets held in trading accounts	6,296	2.2
Trading account gains and fees	2,649	.9
Income from lease-financing receivables	2,683	.9
Income from fiduciary activities	9,052	3.2
Foreign-exchange and other foreign-transaction income	2,119	.7
Service charges on deposit accounts	11,991	4.2
Other noninterest income	35,000	12.2
Total	$286,053	100.0
OPERATING EXPENSES		
Salaries and employee benefits	47,361	16.6
Interest on deposits	78,255	27.3
Expense of federal funds purchased and securities sold under agreements to repurchase	13,909	4.9
Interest on other borrowed money	15,462	5.4
Interest on subordinated notes and debentures	2,348	.8
Net occupancy expense	14,679	5.1
Provisions for loan and lease losses	8,804	3.1
Other noninterest expenses	49,143	17.2
Total	$229,961	80.4
Income before income taxes	$56,092	
Gains (losses) on securities not held in trading accounts	440	
Applicable income taxes	19,674	
Income before extraordinary items	36,858	
Extraordinary items, net	24	
Net income	$36,882	

Note: Details may not add to totals due to rounding.
Source: Federal Deposit Insurance Corporation, *Call Report*, September 30, 1995.

the banks' investment income. Clearly, the total income derived from investments at any one time depends upon such factors as size of the investment portfolio, security mix, and rates of return on the various types of issues. A related item is interest income earned on securities that banks deal in and/or underwrite. ''Income from lease financing'' identifies the amount of income that banks realized from their involvement in the leasing business. Because of the growing popularity of this form of financing, the importance of this source of income should increase significantly in the years ahead. Fiduciary activities and foreign exchange constitute additional sources of income for banks.

Service charges on deposit accounts are imposed by banks on demand deposits to cover the cost of handling these accounts. The faster growth of time and savings deposits, as against demand deposits, and the trend toward lower or no service charges by banks in competing for demand deposits, have generally contributed to a reduction in the importance of this source of income. "Other noninterest income" is a catchall category for all other sources of operating income. This broad category includes commissions, charges, and fees associated with collection of checks, promissory notes, and other matured items; sale of bank drafts; acceptance of bills of exchange; servicing real-estate mortgages; data-processing services; safe deposit boxes; and loan commitments.

On the expense side, "salaries and employee benefits" refers to payment of salaries, wages, and fringe benefits by banks. This item constitutes the second largest category of bank expenses after interest on deposits. As Table 1.2 indicates, the largest source of bank expenses by far is interest on deposits. The size of this expense reflects the higher rates that banks have been paying to attract funds, especially time deposits.

As banks obtain funds from sources other than deposits, several interest expense items figure prominently in their income statement. The item "expense of federal funds purchased and securities sold under agreements to repurchase" represents the interest expense that banks sustained in purchasing federal funds and selling securities under repurchase agreements. "Interest on other borrowed money" comprises the amounts of interest paid by banks for short-term borrowing from the Federal Reserve discount window, a correspondent bank, or the Eurodollar market, or by issuing their own commercial paper. "Interest on subordinated notes and debentures" is the interest that banks paid to holders of their notes and debentures. "Net occupancy expense" includes depreciation of furniture, fixtures, office machines and equipment, rental expenses, maintenance and repairs, and related items. "Provisions for loan losses" represents current revenues commercial banks have diverted from profits to raise or replenish their reserves for loan and lease losses. "Other expenses" include items not elsewhere classified, such as cost of the examinations conducted by supervisory agents, premiums to the Federal Deposit Insurance Corporation for the insurance of deposits, other insurance premiums (for risks associated with the nature of the banking business), office supplies, and advertising.

"Income before income taxes" is arrived at by deducting operating expenses from operating income. This amount, adjusted for gains (losses) for securities transactions, is subject to federal income taxes. Banks—like all other business corporations—are profit-oriented institutions, and thereby are subject to federal income taxes. The resulting after-tax income, adjusted for extraordinary income, determines net income. Banks usually distribute part of their net income as dividends and retain the remainder.

Off-Balance-Sheet Items

In the mid-1980s significant attention began to be devoted to a number of fast-growing items that—under current accounting rules—are not directly included on bank balance sheets or income statements. Instead, they are reported in footnotes to the financial statements; hence the reference to them collectively as "off-balance-sheet items." The forces responsible for the phenomenal growth in these items were essentially (1) the stringent capital requirements which prescribed that banks must back up their assets with capital, and (2) the lower bank profitability stemming from a rise in the number of both domestic and foreign nonbanking firms offering traditional banking services. These pressures forced banks to seek new ways of maintaining or boosting their profitability. Thus, in an effort to bolster their rates of return on equity, and on assets, banks began to explore methods of moving their activities off the balance sheet, thereby avoiding capital requirements while earning fee income. The importance of these activities increased considerably, especially for large money-center banks. In 1988, the off-balance-sheet activities of the five largest banks (Citicorp, BankAmerica, Chase, Morgan, and Manufacturers Hanover) amounted to approximately $1.2 trillion, which was more than twice the combined total assets of these institutions.

Off-balance-sheet items are essentially contingent claims or contracts that legally bind a bank to lend or provide funds should the contingency be realized. For example, banks offer as regular services advance commitments to lend or to provide backup credit. This kind of potential obligation does not affect a bank's balance sheet until the contingent claim is activated and a loan is created that must be funded. Whereas off-balance-sheet activities may effectively mitigate a customer's risk, at the same time they expose a bank's balance sheet, or portfolio, to ongoing risks. Because the off-balance-sheet activities of several institutions ran into billions of dollars, federal regulators subjected them in 1989 to capital adequacy requirements phased in at year-end 1992, as discussed in Chapter 5. In today's rapidly changing financial services environment, the types of off-balance-sheet transactions undertaken by commercial banks are continually expanding. Some of the more common off-balance-sheet activities of commercial banks include loan commitments, commercial letters of credit, standby letters of credit, investment-related commitments, and commitments to buy and sell foreign exchange. The following paragraphs briefly describe these activities and their associated risks, which are discussed further in later chapters of this book.

Loan commitments represent a major off-balance-sheet activity of commercial banks. In fact, most of the commercial and industrial loans extended by banks are made under loan commitments. The purpose of the commitment is to provide some insurance to the borrower that the funds will be available if and when they are needed. In effect, the bank agrees to accept a credit exposure at some future date. Several types of commitments may be agreed upon by borrowers and commercial banks. One major type, referred to as an open line of credit, is an informal agreement between a bank and a borrower whereby the bank stands ready to extend an agreed amount of credit, usually at a stipulated rate, for a specified period of time. It is not uncommon for such an agreement to be in a written form. Banks try to honor most such agreements because their reputation is at stake, but this type of agreement is not enforceable in court, and banks can legally refuse to honor it. A more binding and exacting financial arrangement is the standby commitment. The loan agreement is quite detailed, containing provisions about the time availability of funds and such lending terms as security, interest rate, and liquidation of the loan. In addition, banks generally require the borrower to pay a fee for this commitment.

Unlike a standby commitment and an open line of credit, which do not customarily exceed one year, a revolving credit is a medium-term loan commitment. A revolving credit is a formal agreement which guarantees that funds may be borrowed, repaid, and borrowed again over an extended period, which may run from three to five years. The bank assumes a considerable risk in a guarantee of this type because the borrower's financial condition may deteriorate in the meantime and undermine his ability to service the debt. As a result, the commitment fee charged is generally higher. A note issuance facility is another type of medium-term loan commitment (for instance, three to seven years) whereby the underwriting bank agrees either to purchase any notes a borrower cannot sell or to provide standby credit at a predetermined spread over a reference rate, such as LIBOR. The notes are typically short-term (e.g., of three to six months' maturity) and are issued in amounts of $100,000 or more. They are customarily placed by the underwriting bank with smaller banks and nonbank investors, such as insurance companies, money-market funds, and businesses. There is no active secondary market for these notes; most of them are held to maturity. Under such an arrangement, the borrower not only is assured of the funding that might be needed at some future date but also gains flexibility as business conditions change. For the bank involved, the risk of this transaction is the same as with revolving credit—potential deterioration in the borrower's financial condition and inability to service the debt. In other words, the bank is exposed to credit risk (risk of default) that is inherent in virtually every loan.

Commercial and standby letters of credit function like a surety bond in that the issuing bank guarantees the performance of another party in fulfilling the terms of a contract. A commercial letter of credit, often used in international trade, is a financial instrument issued by a bank, on behalf of one of its customers, that authorizes a third party (an individual or business firm) to which it is addressed to draw drafts on the bank for its account under certain conditions in the document. In essence, the letter of credit is a commitment that legally binds the bank to pay the drafts if the terms specified in the document are met. If the letter of credit provides for payment through a time draft, acceptance of such a draft creates an unconditional liability for the bank regardless of whether the buyer reimburses the bank. The purpose of the letter of credit is to substitute the financial strength or credit of the bank for that of its customer because the credit of the bank may be more substantial and more widely known. A standby letter of credit is a similar document with an important difference: the bank is obligated to pay a third party *only if* the customer (in whose favor the letter is issued) cannot meet the terms and conditions of his contractual agreement with the third party. Traditionally, standby letters have been used as backup lines of credit to support commercial paper offerings or municipal securities, to meet margin requirements on commodity exchanges, or to guarantee performance on construction contracts. Other applications, such as their use for mergers and acquisitions, are emerging. Because the commitment is relied on chiefly for credit enhancement or as an emergency source of funds, it is essentially a loan of a bank's credit rating rather than of its funds. Ideally, banks would provide this kind of insurance only for the obligations of customers in sound financial condition, or where the likelihood of nonperformance is virtually nil. Banks attempt to protect themselves from cases where there is a probable default or poor performance by securing collateral interests from the borrower. In return for providing these letters, banks receive a fee, and interest income should the credit be extended. Because they view these letters as guarantees, and not as loans, banks have followed the practice of not reporting them in their balance sheets. The phenomenal growth of this item, combined with the collapse of a large issuer of standby letters (Penn Square Bank in Oklahoma City), prompted regulators to consider the subjection of off-balance-sheet items to capital adequacy guidelines.

Investment-related commitments are another major category of off-balance-sheet items. These are essentially commitments to undertake interest-rate risk through forward, futures, and options contracts and interest-rate swap agreements. Forward and futures contracts represent a commitment to buy or sell a specific instrument in the future, while options involve a commitment to purchase the right (but not the obligation) either to buy some financial instrument from or to sell the same to the contract seller at an agreed-upon price. Regulations allow banks to engage in these transactions for hedging purposes only. Banks may also engage in interest-rate swaps to hedge their exposure to interest-rate risk, or they may act as intermediaries in arranging swap transactions for third parties. Even though they are designed to reduce interest-rate risk, derivative instruments entail risks—credit risk (failure of the other party to fully perform its contractual obligations) and liquidity risk (the possibility that a position cannot be eliminated quickly either by liquidating it or by establishing offsetting positions). In recognition of these risks, regulators have required banks to list on quarterly call reports their total obligations for both the future delivery of securities and the purchase or sale under option contracts.

Commitments to buy and sell foreign exchange are a dominant contingent liability for many money-center banks. These banks are major participants in foreign-exchange markets and provide their customers with a variety of services that involve different types of guarantees and exchange rates. For example, if a customer has a future need for a foreign currency, the bank may provide a forward commitment to sell him this currency at a specific price in the future. For a fee, the bank will assume the customer's risk of an unfavorable exchange-rate movement, but at the same time it will cover its position through a forward or futures contract that provides for a deferred purchase of the foreign exchange at current prices.

As might be expected, not all banks with off-balance-sheet items have the same profiles of commitments. For example, some banks (e.g., Citicorp and J.P. Morgan) have relatively heavy commitments in futures, options, and foreign currency, while others (e.g., Chase) have heavier exposure in loan commitments. Until recently, compiling this type of data and making comparisons across commercial banks was a hard task because there was no uniform accounting system for commitments and disclosure information was limited. Since 1994, however, both the issuance of a new accounting standard by the Financial Accounting Standards Board and the introduction of expanded reporting requirements by the Federal Reserve have increased the level of detail and clarity of annual-report disclosures about the derivative activities of commercial banks. Under the new accounting standard (SFAS 119), a bank is required to differentiate in its disclosures between derivatives used for trading purposes and those used for hedging or other risk-management purposes. Moreover, it must describe how it reports derivatives in its financial statements and give certain details about gains or losses being deferred. The bank must also disclose quantitative information that would be useful to readers of its financial statements in evaluating its activities in the context of risk management. A bank that deals in derivatives must report the fair value of derivatives' positions and disaggregate the share earned from derivatives from the trading revenues.

The Federal Reserve's expanded reporting requirements call, among other things, for a more detailed breakdown of the notional or principal amounts of contracts and—for larger banks—the fair market values of derivative instruments according to broad risk exposure and management objectives. Fair market value, sometimes referred to as the replacement cost or current credit exposure, is for off-balance-sheet derivatives subject to risk-based capital standards. The derivative holdings of the top ten U.S. dealer banks, as disclosed in their 1994 annual financial reports, are presented in Table 1.3.

Table 1.3
**Ten U.S. Banks with the Largest Notional Amount of Derivative Contracts
Outstanding, December 31, 1994 (amounts in billions of dollars)**

Institution	Notional Amount	Fair Market Value
Chemical Banking Corp.	3,182	18
Citicorp	2,665	27
J.P. Morgan & Co.	2,471	31
Bankers Trust New York Corp.	1,982	26
BankAmerica Corp.	1,376	14
Chase Manhattan Corp.	1,367	10
First Chicago Corp.	622	7
NationsBank Corp.	511	2
Republic New York Corp.	239	2
Bank of New York Co.	80	1

Source: Federal Reserve Bulletin, September 1995, p. 825.

SUGGESTED REFERENCES

Baughn, William H., and Charles E. Walker, eds. *The Banker's Handbook*. 4th ed. Home-
   wood, Ill.: Business One Irwin, 1990.
Cooper, Kerry, and Donald Fraser. *The Financial Marketplace*. 4th ed. Reading, Mass.:
   Addison-Wesley, 1993.
Rose, Peter. *Money and Capital Markets: The Financial System in the Economy*. 5th ed.
   Homewood, Ill.: Richard D. Irwin, 1994.
Rose, Peter, James Kolari, and Donald Fraser. *Financial Institutions: Understanding and
   Managing Financial Services*. 4th ed. Homewood, Ill.: Richard D. Irwin, 1993.

Chapter 2

Evolution of the U.S. Banking Industry

To understand the current state of the U.S. banking system, we must look at how banking has evolved into its present form. In Chapter 3 we focus on the banking industry—its structure and the diverse vehicles through which banks may expand, and hence change their organizational form. This chapter will review the history of banking in the United States and examine some of the salient features of the U.S. banking system. We will review how legal and historical developments have influenced the chartering of banks and discuss conditions for entry into the banking industry. Our discussion will highlight the number and relative size of banks in the industry and examine the development of correspondent banking, through which banks maintain reciprocal relations with banks in other cities.

We will begin our discussion by looking into the historical background of the U.S. banking industry.

U.S. COMMERCIAL BANKING: ITS ORIGINS AND DEVELOPMENT

Early History of Banking

Though moneylending and money changing are very old activities (there are records of loans by Babylonian temples as early as 2000 B.C.), the early beginnings of commercial banking may be traced to the growth of Italian coastal cities as maritime powers and the rise of Italian merchant banking houses that dominated high finance from the twelfth through the fifteenth centuries. These family-owned and -managed firms are generally viewed as the direct ancestors of modern commercial banks. Italian banking houses accepted deposits; financed foreign trade; made a market in foreign exchange; met the short- and medium-term credit needs of entrepreneurs, rulers, noblemen, and the clergy; and invested in industrial and commercial ventures.

As the winds of economic prosperity moved further north in Europe, German merchant banks grew in importance and dominated banking and finance throughout the sixteenth century. The discovery by the Portuguese of the trading routes to the Indies and the opening of the markets of southern Asia brought a shift in European trading patterns from the Mediterranean to the Atlantic seaboard. This shift led to the rise of Antwerp, and subsequently of Amsterdam, as important financial centers that contributed further to the development of banking.

During Amsterdam's economic dominance, two distinct types of banking activity began to emerge—acceptance credits and loans to foreign governments. In the conduct of international commerce, Dutch merchants relied extensively upon commission merchants, agents who resided in commercial centers and sought out customers without owning the commodities in which they traded. In the course of the eighteenth century it became a practice among these merchants to ask established houses to endorse their trade bills and enhance their acceptance by exporters or bankers at home and abroad. In essence, these houses were asked to assess credit risk and offer their guarantee. Bills guaranteed in this way came to be known as ''acceptances,'' and the houses that guaranteed them as ''acceptance houses.'' Development of this practice played an important role in the growth of trade financing in nineteenth-century England.

The wealth of Amsterdam also contributed to the development of another financial activity, that of lending to foreign governments. Indeed, in the course of the seventeenth and eighteenth centuries the Dutch loaned substantial sums to finance the needs of foreign kings and governments. Initially these loans were taken almost entirely by the lenders for their own accounts; gradually, however, other merchants and wealthy individuals were recruited to share in the financing of these loans. This process of syndication was further refined in the second half of the eighteenth century and developed into a specialized financial activity of international stature. A case on record is that of the leading Amsterdam firm of Hope and Company, which floated ten loans for the Kingdom of Sweden (1767–1787) and eighteen loans for Russia (1788–1793). The loan contractors of the late eighteenth century also assumed the responsibility to retail the bonds to investors not only on the Amsterdam stock exchange but also throughout Europe. This pioneering technique of syndicating risk and distributing securities flourished in nineteenth-century England and evolved into modern-day securities underwriting.

The history of international trade reveals that the center of commerce never stayed long in one place. Thus, in the early eighteenth century Great Britain, which had begun to flourish through the growth of large-scale industry and capitalistic enterprise, started challenging Holland for economic leadership of the world, and sometime during the second half of that century, London emerged as the financial and banking center of the world. This development was of no little consequence in the evolution of banking activity. In fact, it was in Great Britain that the term "commercial" bank came into wide usage because of the general belief that banks accepting demand liabilities should limit their lending to highly liquid, short-term commercial loans.

Banking During the Colonial Period

As Western European nations were transforming themselves from agrarian societies into complex economies with thriving industry and commerce, colonial America was experiencing financial stringency as a result of a severe shortage of money in circulation. Much of the gold and silver coinage brought by the early settlers gradually found its way back to Europe in payment for imports. The shortage of money became so severe that barter transactions were quite common. Thus, in 1618 tobacco became legal tender in Virginia, and in 1641, corn in Massachusetts.*

The first bank to be established in the colonies was started in Massachusetts in 1671 by Rev. John Woodbridge.[2] This bank and several that followed it became known as land banks, which were private associations that made loans by issuing banknotes on the security of real estate. Land banks were unincorporated, were usually formed to finance specific needs, often lasted only for the lifetime of the loan, and did not accept deposits. They justified their operations on the ground that they remedied the shortage of specie from which the colonies allegedly suffered. In time many of these banks failed because of the unsound manner in which they operated and the limited liquidity of land, which constituted the security for their loans.

An important stage in the early banking history of the United States came in December 1690, when the General Court of Massachusetts empowered a committee of individuals to establish a public bank. The purpose of this bank, the first such bank in the colonies, was to provide the means to meet the expenses of the ill-fated expedition the colony had mounted against Quebec at the urging of King William III. The Provincial Bank of Massachusetts was formed and issued "bills of credit" to cover the £40,000 cost of the expedition. A large portion of this amount was to be paid to the soldiers, who were to have been paid in loot. The bills were issued in anticipation of tax revenues and promised payment in hard coins. Although initially many of these notes were called in by the payment of taxes, eventually they proved such a tempting expedient that many new issues followed, and by 1704 the policy of postponing their payment

---

*In Virginia during the administration of Governor Samuel Argall, the value of tobacco was set at 3 shillings per pound. His administration went to great lengths to define commodities both in specie and in tobacco. The list included wine, vinegar, cider, beer, bread, butter, cheese, fish, corn, and meal—and the price of young women brought from England to become wives of local planters. Initially the price of a wife was set at 100 pounds of tobacco; as the number of wives decreased, the price was raised to 150 pounds of tobacco. Any debt incurred in the purchase of a wife had precedence over all other debts.[1]

was adopted.[3] By 1713 these notes had become accepted as a medium of exchange and a store of value, thus qualifying as the first paper money to be introduced in the colonies and, for that matter, in the British Empire. From then on, it was only a matter of time before other colonies followed the Provincial Bank's example and issued their own bills of credit to fund government expenditures.

As the colonial period drew to a close, the banks in existence were both public and private, the latter consisting of land banks, merchandise banks, and specie banks, depending upon the nominal base against which notes were issued. None of these banks were commercial in nature; their only function was the issuance of notes.

The Emergence and Growth of Commercial Banking

The first commercial bank to be established in the United States was the Bank of North America, which was chartered by the Continental Congress in December 1781 and opened for business in Philadelphia the following month. Questions regarding the legal power of the Congress to charter a banking institution led the bank to obtain a charter from the state of Pennsylvania, and later from other states as well. Within a few years the Bank of North America was a financial success. It accepted deposits and made loans to the general public and the government (e.g., the national government and the state of Pennsylvania during the closing phases of the Revolutionary War). The bank rendered an important service by issuing a high-quality currency that was redeemable in specie on demand. In 1863 the Bank of North America joined the National Banking System, on the ground that it already had a national charter.

Shortly after the establishment of the Bank of North America, several states, including Massachusetts, New York, and Delaware, followed the example of Pennsylvania in making provisions for the state chartering of banks. As a result, within two and a half years of the opening of the Bank of North America, two state-chartered banks were formed: the Bank of Massachusetts in March 1784, and the Bank of New York in June of the same year. The lead of these early institutions was soon followed by a large number of state-chartered banks.[4] They were all banks of deposit and issue, and were located predominantly in states along the Atlantic seaboard. Many of these banks were quite successful and most are still in operation, either under the original name or under a different one as a result of merger, addition of trust activities, or reincorporation under the National Banking System.

The federal government entered the bank-chartering field in 1791 with the issuance of a 20–year charter for the establishment of the Bank of the United States. The bank's creation was promoted by Alexander Hamilton, first Secretary of the Treasury, who intended this institution to have central banking powers and to function as a fiscal agent of the government. Since the bank was meant to be of national character, it opened branches in the leading cities in addition to its head office in Philadelphia. The bank was capitalized at $10 million, one-fifth of which was subscribed by the government, which thus became the bank's largest stockholder. The government raised the $2 million by borrowing it from the bank and agreeing to repay it in ten annual installments.

Although the bank was charged with a variety of duties (including such commercial banking activities as accepting deposits and making loans to individuals and businesses), its greatest contribution was regulating the amount of money in circulation and controlling inflationary pressures. This it did in its capacity as a fiscal agent of the government. As depository of the government, the bank received on deposit tax revenues, which it held for disbursement by the Treasury. Since these revenues were paid in notes of different state banks, it followed the practice of presenting these notes to the banks of issue for redemption in gold or silver. By reducing the specie that the state banks held as reserves against their notes, the bank was able to control the quantity of notes they issued.

Despite the bank's aloofness from politics and its success as a banking institution, Congress refused renewal of its charter when it expired in 1811. Criticism of the bank came from various quarters. Some critics attacked the bank on constitutional grounds by questioning the authority of Congress to issue a charter for a national bank. State banks opposed it for restricting their note issuing and controlling their freewheeling. Agricultural interests denounced it for failing to pursue a liberal extension of credit. Most detrimental, however, was the criticism of those who opposed the extent of the bank's foreign ownership, which had grown to almost three-quarters of the total stock. Although foreign investors could not vote their shares, national feeling ran high and was quite powerful in public affairs. This state of events led the officers of the bank to apply for a charter from the state of New York and thereafter to operate the bank as a state institution.

The lapse of the charter of the Bank of the United States led to a quick deterioration of economic conditions. The number of state-chartered banks increased significantly (from 88 in 1811 to 246 by 1816), contributing to a rapid increase in the amount of notes in circulation and a concomitant depreciation in the value of those notes. The War of 1812 compounded the country's economic problems by forcing most banks, except for those in New England, to suspend redemption of their notes in specie. These developments set the stage for the reestablishment, with almost unanimous support, of a national bank, which was expected to restore an orderly currency and contribute to the growth and stability of the economy. In 1816 the second Bank of the United States was established by a federal charter that ran for 20 years.

The bank had a total capital of $35 million, one-fifth of which was subscribed by the government and the remainder by the public. The bank's charter provided for essentially the same functions performed by the first bank. Despite some difficulties and significant mismanagement in its early years, it achieved great success by 1823, when Nicholas Biddle became its president. Its success was such that by 1825 it had as many as 25 branches and controlled one-third of the country's bank assets. Unfortunately, this success incurred the wrath of the same forces that had been responsible for the demise of the first bank. As a result, when a bill was enacted in 1832 to extend the bank's charter, which was due to expire in 1836, President Andrew Jackson vetoed it. The following year Jackson arranged to have all government deposits with the bank transferred to various state banks, referred to as "pet banks." This move ended the bank's role as the fiscal agent of the government and virtually deprived it of its central banking powers. Upon expiration of its federal charter in 1836, the bank was able to secure a charter from the state of Pennsylvania and to continue in business until 1841, when it failed.

A review of the banking conditions in the pre–Civil War years reveals that the banking system, consisting of the separate state systems, was in chaos. All the state systems suffered, although unequally, from defects in banking law, supervision, and practice, with conditions being especially bad in the South and West. More than half of the states continued to cling to the practice of chartering banks by special acts of the legislature, while the rest had adopted free banking acts that permitted the chartering of banks upon compliance with certain general provisions of law. But even among the states that had passed free banking laws, there was a considerable difference in chartering requirements. For example, to protect depositors, the bank charters of some states called for a maximum ratio of bank liabilities to capital (generally between 3:1 and 5:1), while other charters made no mention of such provisions. (The practice of stipulating capital requirements was borrowed from the charter of the Bank of England.) Some state charters required specified amounts of specie reserves (gold and silver) against notes issued, but others only provided for certain types of bonds.

This general lack of uniformity among states was not limited to requirements for entry into the banking field but also extended into the relationship between banks and states. Specifically, some banks were privately owned, others were wholly owned and operated by states, while still others were owned jointly by state and private interests. Wide variation was also encountered in the responsibilities of the privately owned banks to their chartering state. In some states, for example, bank chartering was just a matter of compliance with the various provisions of the banking law. In other states, however, chartering was also conditional upon the bank's commitment to finance certain projects that the state legislature viewed as of utmost importance (canal companies, railroads, and other enterprises).

Equally chaotic during the pre–Civil War years was the country's currency condition. Although the banking system comprised both private (unincorporated) and state-chartered banks, only the latter had the note-issuing privilege, and hence supplied the country with paper money. With some 1,600 state-chartered banks in operation by 1861 and each of these banks issuing its own currency in different denominations, the country had a currency mosaic. One estimate places the total number of different types of notes issued by these banks at about 10,000. Since these issues varied in size, material, and design, distinguishing the degree of protection to the note holder presented a serious problem. The issues of northeastern banks were generally of good quality, whereas many of the notes issued by western banks were of questionable value. Some shrewd promoters in the West had established banks in remote areas, rendering it virtually impossible for note holders to redeem their notes. This practice became known as wildcat banking from the fact that in the area where these institutions were located, there were more wildcats than bank customers. Apart from wildcat currency, note holders were exposed to counterfeits, notes of banks that had ceased to exist, and notes that, although issued by solvent banks, had depreciated in value. The situation became so bad that in time specialized publications, known as banknote detectors, appeared, purportedly to provide note holders with up-to-date information on the quality of the currency in circulation.

This state of the country's currency, along with the need to finance the Civil War, led to the passage of the National Bank Act of 1863. This act, repealed and superseded by a law of similar title in 1864, became the banking code of the United States until substantially replaced by the Federal Reserve Act of 1913. By providing for the granting of national charters by the Office of the Comptroller of the Currency, which was set up under the Treasury Department, it marks the beginning of the National Banking System. The provision for incorporation of banks under the National Bank Act established the dual banking system, in which banks have a choice between a national and a state charter. The intention of this legislation was to form a system of national banks that, under the supervision of the federal government, would issue a safe and uniform currency to replace that of state banks; assist in the financing of the war by purchasing government bonds, which were to be used as security against their national banknotes; and provide a reliable depository for government funds. When initial hopes for bank conversions from state to national charters proved disappointing, Congress moved in 1865 to impose a 10 percent tax on any individual or bank using or paying out notes of state-chartered banks. This tax, by rendering the note-issuing privilege of state banks unprofitable, proved effective in inducing many state banks to join the National Banking System—so much so that between 1864 and 1866, the number of national banks swelled from 139 to 1,582, while that of state banks decreased from 1,089 to 297. From then on, the formation of national banks progressed rapidly, providing the country with a safe, uniform currency: the national banknotes. These notes remained in circulation until the creation of the Federal Reserve System in 1913, when they were supplanted by Federal Reserve notes. Thus, until 1913 the chartering and supervision of national banks constituted the means through which the Comptroller of the Currency controlled the amount of money.

Despite loss of the money-issuing privilege, state banks did not disappear; instead they developed as banks of deposit. Realizing that they did not have to issue notes to operate profitably, they started accepting demand deposits—merely an alternative form of obligation—which they used in the funding of their loans. National banks shared in the growth of deposit banking because of statutory limitations on their note-issuing privilege. Deposit banking grew significantly in subsequent decades, and so did the number of state banks, which benefited from essentially less stringent requirements than those for national banks. By 1890 state banks, after a strong comeback, took the lead over national banks and have maintained it.

Prior to the passage of the National Bank Act, the United States had a good number of private banks along with state-chartered banks. Many of these private banks engaged in limited commercial banking activities that were conducted from frontier mercantile stores. Their activities included accepting deposits, buying banknotes at a discount and then presenting them to the banks of issue for payment, and extending credit. Some of these private banks obtained state charters to enjoy the note-issuing privilege. The National Bank Act and the 10 percent tax levy forced many of them to join the National Banking System, and limited the activities of those that remained. Subsequent legislation further restricted the activities of private banks, and their formation is no longer feasible because of the formal chartering requirements for newly organized banks.

Consolidation of the Commercial Banking Industry

From 1838 on, one state after another began to adopt free banking acts, which provided that charters would be issued almost automatically to any group of individuals capable of meeting certain minimum legal requirements. The chartering process instituted by these acts made entry into the banking business easy, and resulted in the establishment of thousands of commercial banks. By 1920 there were 30,000 banks in the United States, operating 1,300 branches. Much of this spectacular increase was a product of the rapid economic development experienced from the latter part of the nineteenth century on. These were years of rising productivity in agriculture and increasing efficiency in industry that propelled the United States, just before the outbreak of World War I, into the position of the world's principal economic power. These conditions were responsible for the unprecedented increase in the number of banking facilities, most of which were unit banks located in farming regions.

This expansion in the number of banks suffered important setbacks during the 1920s and early 1930s resulting in significant consolidation of the industry. (see Figure 2.1). Mergers and, most important, failures during 1921–33 were responsible for the disappearance of about 15,000 banks and losses to depositors in excess of $2 billion. Sizable losses were also sustained by the owners of bank stock, who in addition to loss of their investment often paid voluntary assessments to meet claims of bank creditors, in an effort to avert the closing of their bank.

Available data indicate that many of the banks which failed during this period were small unit banks in the agricultural and rural regions of the country. The sharp postwar deflation of 1920–22 and the recession of 1923–24 caused a general retrenchment in economic activity that hit the agricultural sector espe-

Figure 2.1
Number of Banks and Branches, 1911–88

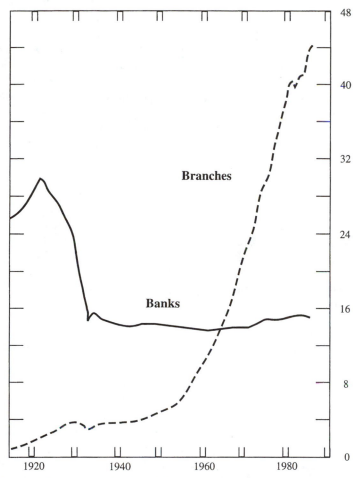

Source: Board of Governors of the Federal Reserve, *Historical Chart Book* (Washington, D.C.: Federal Reserve System, 1988), p. 82.

cially hard. As a result many banks suspended operations, with the greatest number of bank failures registered in the agricultural states of the Midwest, Southeast, and Rocky Mountains. The renewed collapse of agricultural prices in 1929–30, accentuated by severe drought, accelerated the pace of bank failures in farming areas. These failures tended to undermine further the depressed state of economic activity, precipitating a general distrust of banks and widespread panics. On March 4, 1933, declaration of a national bank holiday by President Franklin D. Roosevelt restored public confidence in banks and averted the collapse of the banking system.

The poor performance of the banking system during the 1920s and early 1930s convinced legislators of the need to eliminate free banking and subject the activities of commercial banks to extensive government controls. As a result, near the bottom of the depression, Congress passed the Banking Act of 1933 (Glass-Steagall Act), which was followed two years later by an equally comprehensive piece of legislation, the Banking Act of 1935. Some of the key provisions of the former included the introduction of a temporary plan of federal deposit insurance; prohibition of interest payment on demand deposits and the setting of maximum interest rates on time and savings deposits (Regulation Q); subjection of branching by national banks to state legislation and on the terms applicable to state banks; and the strengthening of the control of the Federal Reserve System over diversion of commercial bank funds to speculative and investment uses.

The Banking Act of 1935 addressed issues that covered virtually every aspect of banking. For example, it provided for the organization of the Federal Deposit Insurance Corporation (FDIC) on a permanent basis and granted it supervisory authority over all insured banks that were not supervised by a federal agency (the comptroller of the currency or the Federal Reserve System). This meant the extension of federal regulatory standards over all state-chartered banks that did not opt for Federal Reserve membership. Other provisions of the Banking Act of 1935 changed the legal title of the Federal Reserve Board to Board of Governors of the Federal Reserve System; revised the structure and functions of the Federal Reserve System; increased the control of the Federal Reserve System over commercial banking activity; and strengthened the influence of the government over the Federal Reserve System.

As the effects of the depression began to fade and economic recovery set in, the banking structure emerged at the end of 1934 with about 15,400 banks and 3,000 branches. During the next two decades, as shown in Figure 2.1, structural changes in the banking industry were characterized by a gradual decline in the number of banks and a rapid increase in the number of branches as their operations became increasingly important. The bank attrition was essentially due to mergers, which accounted for part of the branch-banking growth of this period. The phenomenal expansion in branching activity was a product of various developments, the most important of which were the liberalization of state banking laws on branching, population shifts from rural areas to urban centers, movement of industry out of central cities, and growth of suburbs. Bank attrition did not reverse itself until the early 1960s, when the Office of the Comptroller of the Currency (OCC), recognizing the stimulus that new banks would provide to competition, adopted a more liberal entry policy that increased the number of OCC-chartered banks. A similar liberalization of chartering requirements by state banking authorities in the early 1970s contributed to a gradual increase in the number of banks throughout that decade.

The 1980s and 1990s witnessed another era of consolidation for the banking industry, as a result of which the number of independently owned banks has

Table 2.1

Classification of U.S. Commercial Banks and Branches, 1994

Type of Bank	Number of Banks	Number of Branches
National banks	3,075	28,558
State-chartered banks	975	8,390
Total members of the Federal Reserve System	4,050	36,948
Nonmember state-chartered banks	6,400	18,196
Total FDIC-insured banks	10,450	55,144

Source: Federal Deposit Insurance Corporation, *Statistics on Banking* (Washington, D.C.: FDIC, 1994), pp. B-2, B-3.

decreased while the average size of individual banking firms has increased. Indeed, this period witnessed the acquisition of many small banks by holding companies as well as the merger of some of the largest banks in the industry (e.g., Bank of New York and Irving Trust, NCNB and C&S/Sovran, Bank-America and Security Pacific, and Chemical Bank and Manufacturers Hanover). Moreover, many states have opened up their markets to banking firms from contiguous states, and in 1994 the federal government enacted legislation that removed all restrictions on nationwide banking. According to the Riegle-Neal Interstate Banking and Branching Efficiency Act of 1994, effective June 1, 1997, holding companies may consolidate their interstate banks into a branch network, and freestanding banks may branch interstate by merging with another bank across state lines. The end result will be a dramatic increase in branching activity in the late 1990s and a sizable decrease in the number of independently owned banks. At the end of 1994 there were 10,450 FDIC-insured commercial banks in the United States operating 55,144 branch offices.

CLASSIFICATION OF BANKS

From a regulatory perspective, banks may be classified on the basis of different characteristics: origin of charter, membership in the Federal Reserve, and insurance coverage by the FDIC. Table 2.1 identifies the number of U.S. banks falling into each of these classifications.

Of the 10,450 banks in operation in 1994, 7,375 were state-chartered banks and 3,075 held national charters. National banks, on average, are larger institutions and account for the majority of bank assets. Although the United States still has a dual banking system, differences in the powers and responsibilities of banks, which were so pronounced in the late nineteenth century, have been greatly reduced as state banking regulations have been patterned after federal legislation. An important factor in this respect has been the freedom of banks to switch charters from one regulatory agency to the other. This fact has exerted significant pressure toward more uniformity in bank regulation between national and state banking authorities. However, a more significant factor favoring standardization of banking practices among state and national banks is that virtually all commercial banks have come under federal authority through the influences of the Federal Reserve and the Federal Deposit Insurance Corporation. The only area left completely to the discretion of individual states is whether, and to what extent, to permit bank branching within their jurisdiction. State regulations on this point apply to both federally and state-chartered banks.

The distinction between state-chartered and nationally chartered banks is but one of the several ways of classifying banks. They may also be classified as members or nonmembers of the Federal Reserve System. Federal Reserve membership is required for national banks but optional for state banks. State banks may become members of the Federal Reserve System upon the approval of the Board of Governors, which considers such factors as financial history and condition of the applying bank, general character of its management, the adequacy of its capital structure and earnings, and whether its corporate powers are consistent with the purposes of the Federal Reserve Act.

An important characteristic of membership is that each member bank is required to buy stock in its regional Federal Reserve bank by paying in 3 percent of its capital stock and surplus, with another 3 percent being subject to call. Ownership of Federal Reserve bank stock entitles the member bank's stockholders to receive an annual 6 percent statutory dividend on the paid-in capital stock. Beyond this stipulated rate of return, however, member banks' rights as shareholders are subject to important limitations. For example, Federal Reserve bank stock is nontransferable; it entitles a member bank to a single vote, regardless of the number of shares owned; and voting is conducted only once every three years for the election of directors of the district Federal Reserve bank.

Until enactment of the Depository Institutions Deregulation and Monetary Control Act of 1980 (DIDMCA), a bank's decision to be a member of the Federal Reserve System was primarily influenced by reserve requirements against deposits. Although in many states the percentage reserve requirements for nonmember banks were comparable with those for Federal Reserve members, their definition of the form of reserves was generally more liberal. In many states the reserves required of nonmember banks could be in the form of correspondent balances or even of certain earning assets, such as short-term government securities. The consequence of this differential was that during the 1970s many newly formed state banks chose not to join and an increasing number of members withdrew from the system.

This development raised serious questions as to the effectiveness of the Federal Reserve's control over the monetary aggregates and led to calls for regulation. As a result, the DIDMCA extended reserve requirements to all banks, requiring them to maintain reserves against their deposits in the nonearning forms of cash and balances with the Federal Reserve bank of their district. Nonmember banks and thrifts were given an eight-year phase-in period, which ended in 1987, to build their reserves up to the requirements applied to members. The provision for uniform reserves has resulted in greater equity and allowed the Federal Reserve System to implement monetary policy more effectively. At year-end 1994, Federal Reserve member banks numbered 4,050, 76 percent of which were national banks and 24 percent were state banks. These banks, though accounting for almost 39 percent of all commercial banks in the United States, held 77 percent of all bank assets.

Banks may also be classified as insured or noninsured, depending upon whether their deposits are insured by the FDIC. Membership in the FDIC is mandatory for all national banks and those state-chartered banks that are members of the Federal Reserve System. Nonmember state-chartered banks interested in federal deposit insurance are also eligible to join the FDIC, as long as they are willing to subject themselves to its supervision. At year-end 1994, 6,400 nonmember state-chartered banks were insured by the FDIC, for a total of insured banks of 10,450.

The Glass-Steagall Act, which established the FDIC, provided for annual insurance premiums amounting to 1/12 of 1 percent of total deposits. These assessments, to be remitted semiannually, were to provide funds for operating costs as well as maintenance of an insurance fund. The concept of a uniform assessment for all banks was abandoned in 1991 with enactment of the Federal Deposit Insurance Corporation Improvement Act (FDICIA). This law directed the FDIC to relate deposit insurance rates to risk-taking, so that low-risk institutions do not subsidize high-risk institutions. As a result, on January 1, 1993, FDIC set its premiums for the strongest institutions at 23 cents per $100 of domestic deposits and for the weakest institutions at 31 cents. Premiums for other institutions varied within this range, depending upon their capital (adequacy) levels and supervisory ratings.

The FDICIA also restricted the ability of the FDIC to protect uninsured deposits (those over $100,000 and those overseas) in the event of bank failure ("too-big-to-fail" doctrine), and restrained the Federal Reserve from propping up failing banks with long-term loans unless the stability of the banking system is threatened. Another key feature of this act is the requirement for the FDIC to close an institution when it reaches a critically undercapitalized position (prompt corrective action). This issue is presented in Chapter 5, which addresses bank capital and regulatory requirements. Other important provisions of this act are listed in Table 2.2.

Classifying U.S. banks by origin of charter, Federal Reserve membership, and insurance helps to identify their regulatory status. However, we can further enhance our understanding of the structure of the commercial banking industry by examining banks in terms of another important characteristic, size. The U.S. banking system differs from all others in that there is enormous variation in the size of banks, with the large majority falling into the small category. This is

Table 2.2
Key Provisions of the Federal Deposit Insurance Corporation Improvement Act (FDICIA) of 1991

Restricts insurance coverage of brokered deposits only at well-capitalized institutions
Directs FDIC to institute risk-based deposit insurance premiums
Limits the use of "too-big-to-fail" doctrine for bailouts of large banks
Recapitalizes the Deposit Insurance Fund
Limits Federal Reserve's authority to provide extended credit to banks in trouble
Provides for early intervention (prompt corrective action) when a bank's capital falls below
    minimum levels
Requires foreign banks that accept small U.S. deposits to obtain deposit insurance
Provides greater authority for regulators to accept or deny new charters for foreign banks
    and order their closings

---

readily apparent in Table 2.3, which categorizes all insured commercial banks according to asset size. On September 30, 1995, 1,851 banks had assets of $25 million or less, whereas 679 banks had assets in excess of $500 million. Stated differently, banks having less than $25 million in assets accounted collectively for only 0.7 percent of all bank assets, while banks having over $500 million accounted for 81 percent of all bank assets. This pattern of asset distribution is largely accounted for by the prevalence of unit banking, which gives rise to a proliferation of small banks. This pattern will change from 1997 on, as more states change their laws to permit interstate branching, for such a move will result in fewer banks with many offices. However, sentiment in favor of small, locally run banks persists, because they offer customers personalized service.

CORRESPONDENT BANKING

The correspondent banking system has been the dominant form of interbank relations for most of U.S. history, and it continues to play an important role. Correspondent banking involves a small bank's maintaining deposits with a larger bank in exchange for a variety of services. The larger bank may, in turn, have as correspondents larger banks in money-market centers. By means of this pyramidal structure banks throughout the country are linked in an informal network. The chief, but by no means only, service provided by correspondent banks is the clearing of checks. In the nineteenth century, prior to the creation of the Federal Reserve System, correspondent banking flourished because of the need for banks to maintain funds with other banks for the redemption of banknotes. Later, as maintenance of deposits became an acceptable practice, the major service performed was check clearance. Although smaller banks received services in exchange for maintaining deposits with their correspondents, in the nineteenth century the correspondents also paid interest on the deposits they held for other banks. During the 1930s the payment of interest on these deposits was prohibited; additional services replaced the interest compensation.

The National Bank Act of 1863 allowed national banks to include balances

Table 2.3
Size Distribution of Insured Commercial Banks

Asset Size	Number of Banks	Assets		
		Total per Category (billions of dollars)	Percent of Total	
Less than $25 million	1,851	30.3	0.7	
$25 to 50 million	2,432	89.2	2.1	
$50 to 100 million	2,547	182.2	4.3	
$100 to 300 million	2,150	352.1	8.3	
$300 to 500 million	395	151.4	3.6	
$500 million to $1 billion	271	188.6	4.5	
$1 to 3 billion	210	350.7	8.3	
$3 to 10 billion	129	716.1	16.9	
$10 billion or more	69	2,168.8	51.3	
Total	10,054	4,229.4	100.0	

Source: Federal Deposit Insurance Corporation, *Statistics on Banking* (Washington, D.C.: FDIC, 1995). Data are as of September 30, and were derived from *Call Report.*

with correspondents in their required reserves. With creation of the Federal Reserve System, this practice was prohibited for member banks, although many states continued to allow it for their nonmember, state-chartered banks. Then the enactment of DIDMCA in 1980 extended the Federal Reserve System's control over reserve requirements to nonmember banks and other depository institutions, including foreign banks.

The chief function of correspondent banking has been to provide a channel for check clearing. Prior to the creation of the Federal Reserve System, virtually all checks written on one bank and deposited in another were cleared through exchanges among correspondent banks in an informal network that often involved roundabout routing of checks. Even after the Federal Reserve offered this service, many banks continued to rely on their correspondent banks for check clearing, since this channel was often considerably faster. In the early 1980s the Federal Reserve began charging for its check-clearing services, reinforcing the preference for correspondent banks.

Correspondent banking allows small banks to overcome many of the limitations imposed by their size. First, it enables small banks to offer their customers services that would otherwise be prohibitively expensive. Second, it provides direct services to the small banks themselves.

A small bank in effect purchases from its correspondent services that are too expensive for it to offer on its own. If a customer wishes a larger loan than a small bank is permitted (or considers wise) to make, the small bank may share the loan with its correspondent in an arrangement known as loan participation. Small banks may also participate in loans originated by their correspondents. In addition, the correspondent relationship makes it more economical for a small bank to extend to its customers services, such as trust management or international banking, that it lacks the expertise and funds to provide.

The correspondent bank relationship also helps small banks perform many internal functions in which economies of scale can be realized. At any particular time a small bank may have a relatively small amount of cash to place in the federal funds market or may need a small amount of funds. Trading in small volumes is expensive, however, and by going through its correspondent, the small bank can participate in this market more effectively. Banks may also loan to or borrow from each other, or buy and sell earning assets from each other. This service is especially important to banks that wish to avoid borrowing from the Federal Reserve System. In addition, the correspondent may provide management and investment counseling. It may help the small bank manage its assets and acquire capital. It may share credit information, evaluate loans, perform audits, purchase and hold securities, or, through electronic data systems, process the small bank's installment loans, deposit accounts, and other information. Some of these services are similar to those provided by a home office for its branches. However, the correspondent bank system provides the advantages of communication and pooled resources without creating a risk of over-centralization.

Maintaining a profitable correspondent bank relationship requires careful management by both parties. Payment for the services rendered by the correspondent may be through direct fee or through maintenance of compensating balances. In the latter case the level of balance required fluctuates with changes in the interest rate, since the cost of the services the correspondent bank provides must be covered by the dollars of interest the deposited funds earn for the correspondent. Alternatively, the respondent bank may receive fewer services in times of low interest rates and more services when interest rates are high.

The correspondent banking system provides an elaborate web of communication among U.S. banks. New York banks may act as correspondents to hundreds of banks in cities across the country because of New York's importance as the leading financial center of the country. Banks in other cities may have as customers many smaller banks in their region. In addition, many U.S. banks have correspondent relationships with banks in foreign countries. They maintain accounts with these banks in order to facilitate conversion of currency for their customers who travel or conduct business abroad. The correspondent bank network is thus an integral part of the U.S. banking system.

NOTES

1. Herman E. Krooss, ed., *Documentary History of Banking and Currency in the United States.* 4 vols. (London and New York: Chelsea House and McGraw-Hill, 1969), II, pp. 838–39.

2. Adolph Oscar Eliason, *The Rise of Commercial Banking Institutions in the United States* (New York: Burt Franklin, 1970), p. 9.

3. Ibid., p. 12.

4. Krooss, op. cit., pp. 857–60.

SUGGESTED REFERENCES

Friedman, Milton, and Anna Schwartz. *A Monetary History of the United States, 1867–1960*. Princeton, N.J.: Princeton University Press, 1963.

Hammond, Bray. *Banks and Politics in America from the Revolution to the Civil War*. Princeton, N.J.: Princeton University Press, 1957.

Knight, Robert E. "Correspondent Banking. Part I, Balances and Services." Federal Reserve Bank of Kansas City, *Monthly Review*, November 1970, pp. 3–14.

———. "Correspondent Banking. Part II, Loan Participations and Fund Flows." Federal Reserve Bank of Kansas City, *Monthly Review*, December 1970, pp. 12–24.

Studenski, P., and Herman E. Krooss. *Financial History of the United States*. 2nd ed. New York: McGraw-Hill, 1963.

Chapter 3

The Banking Industry in Transition

The structure of the U.S. commercial banking system is undergoing changes of unprecedented magnitude. Several factors are responsible, including changing laws and regulations, technological developments, globalization of banking services, and the growing importance of foreign banks in this country. Whatever the driving forces, these changes constitute a revolutionary departure from the past. They are transforming the structure of the banking industry and bringing about the integration of the U.S. financial system.

Specific aspects of this transformation will be highlighted in this chapter as we examine some key characteristics of the banking industry. We will first consider the diverse vehicles through which banks may expand, and hence change their organizational form. These vehicles include branching, merging, and group banking. Since the different aspects of banking activity are subject to regulatory control, we will also examine the structure of bank supervision and the scope and character of bank regulation. In recent years banks have been experiencing increased competition from other financial institutions. We will therefore describe the competitive environment in which banks operate and identify current developments and emerging trends in the financial services market. Last, we will review the activities of foreign banks in the United States and the various organizational forms under which they operate.

THE MOVE TOWARD NATIONWIDE BRANCHING

Unlike most other countries in the world, which have long experienced nationwide branching, in the United States this will become a reality after June 1997. Legal barriers to intrastate and interstate branching affected the development of the U.S. commercial banking system and accounted for a low level of banking services per capita vis-à-vis banks in Western European countries. The evolution of regulation of bank branching and its ramifications for commercial banks are traced below.

Intrastate Bank Branching

The U.S. Constitution granted powers of incorporation to the states, and each state, in turn, chartered banks that were authorized to operate within its borders. In addition, the federal government, through the Office of the Comptroller of the Currency, has chartered banks in many areas. This had led to a proliferation of banks in the United States, in contrast with most countries, where only a few banks exist and are permitted to branch nationwide. Throughout much of U.S. history, branching has not been allowed in most states. Fear of banking monopoly by the large northeastern banks, some of which were branch institutions, led most states to prohibit branching—so much so that by 1910, only 12 states permitted it. As a result, the vast majority of state banks were single-office institutions (unit banks).

National banks enjoyed no better status than state banks. Indeed, because the National Bank Act of 1863 did not address the branching issue, officials believed that it prohibited it. Moreover, the Federal Reserve Act of 1913 did not authorize national banks to establish branches; but it did not prohibit the state banks that joined the system from operating existing branches. It was not until 1922 that a ruling by the Office of the Comptroller of the Currency led to the issuance of individual permits that allowed national banks to establish branches only within their home cities, provided state banks already operated branches in the same cities. This authorization was legalized in the McFadden Act of 1927. The collapse of the banking system in the early 1930s led to reevaluation of the prevailing antibranching sentiment. As a result, when the McFadden Act was modified by the Banking Act of 1933, national banks were placed under the same restrictions regarding branching that governed state banks. Thus the U.S. Congress placed determination of the branching activities of national banks in the hands of state authorities. Subjecting national banks to state branching laws prevented these banks from branching widely within and across state lines.

It was not until after World War II that a substantial number of states changed their laws to permit branching. Based on their branching legislation, states fell into three broad categories: states that prohibited their banks (whether state or federally chartered) from opening any branches (''unit-banking'' states); states that limited the branching abilities of individual banks to a portion of the state (''limited-branching'' states); and states that permitted individual banks to branch statewide (''branch-banking'' states). Unit banking was entrenched in states where a combination of tradition, vested interests, and special customer demands kept unit-banking laws in place. It predominated in the Midwest and was generally well suited to states with small, homogeneous, and far-flung communities. Improved transportation and communication, the growth of businesses, and a more mobile and convenience-conscious population forced unit banking to give way to limited-branch banking. In mid-1988, 6 states prohibited full-service branches, 22 states allowed limited branching, and 22 states and the District of Columbia permitted statewide branching. By 1995, no unit-banking states remained, and only two states provided for limited branching.

States that provided for limited branching used different criteria to confine branching. Frequently they subjected branching to geographical limits (e.g., a bank was allowed to branch within the city or county in which its head office was located or within a certain distance of its home office). Sometimes capital requirements, population considerations, or both were used to restrict branching. States permitting branching allowed banks to branch statewide subject to certain conditions, such as capital requirements, population size, and limits on the number of branches.

Interstate Bank Branching

Growth of statewide branching came very slowly and was a product of many and varied forces. Some of the more important forces included the movement of individuals and businesses from the city to the suburbs and the need for city banks to follow their customers; the emergence of sizable corporations and the consequent rise in corporate financing demands, which prompted banks to reach out into many local markets and pool small deposits into large-volume loans; and the regulatory-induced acquisition of failed banks by healthier institutions and their conversion into branches of these institutions.

Branching made it possible for banks to benefit in a number of ways. Branching generally allows for better management (more resources to invest in training), promotes specialization, provides for greater asset diversification, and expands the consumer deposit base, thereby reducing the likelihood of a run. Moreover, there are arguments regarding improved service to customers—for instance, that branch offices can be established in new areas quickly and can offer services in areas that are not economically strong or active enough to support individual banks. Banks with branches can take advantage of economies of scale and pass these savings along to their customers.

The deregulation climate of the early 1980s elevated the branching issue from the statewide to the nationwide level. A number of banks saw interstate banking on the horizon and took steps to place themselves in a favorable position when this development would occur. Growing acceptance of the regional banking concept in the mid-1980s enabled banks in one state to own banks in another. Bank bills approved by the legislatures of several contiguous states promoted regional banking on a reciprocal basis. New England states led in this development, which was soon duplicated in other parts of the country and contributed to the emergence of regional compacts in the Southeast, the West, and the Midwest. The original intent of the regional compacts was to promote the development and growth of superregional banks to rival in size the country's largest banks. The Supreme Court upheld the constitutionality of regional banking in 1985.

By the late 1980s, most states had passed some form of interstate banking deregulation. Prospects for market growth and the need for recapitalization of an increasing number of troubled institutions prompted these states to take a stance in favor of interstate banking. The most liberal state laws (e.g., of Alaska, Arizona, Texas, Oklahoma, and Maine) allowed entry by banking organizations from any state in the nation, while other laws provided for such entry only on a reciprocal basis (e.g., Kentucky, New York, Washington, and West Virginia). Still other states enacted laws that authorized entry for special-purpose facilities such as credit-card operations (e.g., South Dakota and Delaware) or for the acquisition of troubled or failing institutions.

Another factor that spurred states to relax their interstate restrictions was the need of federal regulators to sell troubled thrifts* at the least cost to the Savings Association Insurance Fund (SAIF), the thrift deposit insurance fund. The U.S. Congress had provided in 1989 for the establishment of the Resolution Trust Corporation (RTC) to dispose of the assets and liabilities of failed thrifts. In mid-1990, in a case involving a New Mexico thrift institution, a federal appeals court upheld the RTC's right to allow acquiring banks to convert failed thrifts into branches even if such a move was contrary to state branching laws. In May 1992, the Office of Thrift Supervision (successor regulator to the Federal Home Loan Bank Board) allowed nationwide branching for all thrift institutions. Thus, thrift institutions gained interstate branching rights five years ahead of banking organizations.

Deregulation of interstate banking gave important impetus to the growth of bank holding companies as a vehicle for banking organizations to expand geographically. Thus, to operate across state lines many banks formed holding companies and purchased banks in other states. Although this approach moved the country toward nationwide banking, for the expansion-minded banking organizations it entailed costly duplication of capital and management. In 1994, to reduce these costs and offer consumers greater access to banking services across state borders, Congress passed the Riegle-Neal Interstate Banking and Branching Efficiency Act. Important provisions of this act are listed in Table 3.1. This law authorized a bank holding company in a safe and sound condition (i.e., adequately capitalized and adequately managed) and with a favorable community reinvestment record to acquire a bank in any state within a year from its enactment. For the transaction to be approved, however, the resulting institution must not control more than 30 percent of the deposits in the state or more than 10 percent of nationwide deposits.

Beginning June 1, 1997, bank holding companies may consolidate their interstate banks into a branch network, and freestanding banks may branch interstate by merging with another bank across state lines. Such mergers would be

*Savings and loan associations and mutual savings banks are designated as thrift institutions.

Table 3.1
Key Provisions of the Riegle-Neal Interstate Banking and Branching Efficiency Act of 1994

Permits bank holding companies to acquire (effective September 30, 1995) banks in any state and stipulates the terms and conditions for such acquisitions

Authorizes bank holding companies to convert (effective June 1, 1997) their banks in other states into branch offices unless the states involved "opt out" of the interstate branching provisions of this law. Banks in such states cannot participate in interstate banking acquisitions

Asserts the right of states to permit *de novo* interstate branching

Allows the U.S. subsidiary corporations of foreign-owned banks to acquire banks and branches across state lines subject to the conditions applying to U.S. banks

Stipulates that foreign-owned banks acquiring domestic banks subject to the Community Reinvestment Act must comply to all the provisions of said Act subject to the same safety and soundness, community reinvestment, and concentration requirements stated above. States were given until June 1, 1997 to decide. They were allowed to prohibit (opt out of) interstate branching by merger before June 1, 1997, or to authorize it earlier (opt in). If a state chose to opt out, then its banks could not engage in interstate mergers. De novo branching (i.e., branching other than by merger with an existing bank) must be specifically authorized by individual states. Branch offices established across state lines to take deposits must provide an adequate volume of loans to meet the credit needs of local communities; interstate branches used "primarily for deposit production" are prohibited and may be closed down by regulators. Same terms and conditions apply to the interstate branching of subsidiary corporations of foreign banks.

Interstate branches of national banks will be subject to the laws of the host state regarding consumer protection, intrastate branching, community reinvestment, and fair lending, unless the Comptroller of the Currency determines that federal law preempts such state laws or that they would have a discriminatory effect on national bank branches. Interstate branches of state-chartered banks are subject to all of the laws of the host state and also are under the jurisdiction of the chartering state.

Enactment of the Riegle-Neal law has triggered a wave of mergers that is restructuring the commercial banking industry. For the first time in the history of this country, banks may follow their customers and expand the scope of their operations across state lines. For some banks the spread of automation offers entry in distant markets electronically with ATMs and telecommunications equipment, a much cheaper way to broaden the size of their markets than building a brick and mortar facility.

BANK MERGERS

A merger occurs when a bank ceases to exist as a distinct entity because of its acquisition by another bank. A related type of arrangement is consolidation. This term is used when a number of banks combine to form a new bank, with each of the combining banks giving up its corporate identity. Although "merger" has a technical meaning, it will be used here to mean any form of combination in which two or more banks join to form a single bank under a single management.

There is no single reason for bank mergers. In fact, a variety of factors have been responsible for bank mergers in the United States. First, relaxation of restrictions on intrastate and, more recently, on interstate branching has provided an important impetus for mergers. Mergers have allowed banks to follow their customers into new markets in a manner far less expensive than chartering new banks or establishing new branch offices. Large banks seeking to expand their operations geographically may merge with smaller institutions that then function as branches of the acquiring banks. If the new markets have a different economic profile than those the bank already serves, *geographic diversification* is attained. This tends to stabilize the acquiring bank's cash flow and earnings.

Second, if a bank wishes to offer a new form of service (for instance, trust services), merger may be the most expeditious way to acquire the facilities to do so. It is frequently more economical to buy a going concern with the desired area of expertise and an established market than to build such an area from scratch, recruit the necessary personnel, promote it, and operate it profitably. A merger of this type creates a *product-line diversification*, which also contributes to the stabilization of the acquiring bank's cash flow and earnings.

Third, economies of scale provide a motive for mergers. Spreading overhead costs over a larger volume of business reduces unit costs.

Fourth, mergers allow banks to increase their capitalization and deposits. This is significant because legal limits on the size of loans made to one borrower are based on the size of the bank's capital and surplus (15 percent to any single borrower on an unsecured basis and, under certain conditions, an extra 10 percent on fully secured loans). With a merger the newly enlarged bank has a larger capital base and can make larger loans. Since growth in the size of businesses has increased the size of the loans they wish to negotiate, these larger maximum loan limits based on expanded capitalization are important.

Finally, other factors motivating banks to merge include the urge to accelerate growth, the desire to improve earnings, and the need or desire to provide better service to existing businesses.

On the other side of the transaction, there are a number of reasons why banks may find it advantageous to be absorbed by larger ones. If a bank encounters difficulty in acquiring capital it needs, or if it faces failure, merger may provide the solution. Indeed, many mergers in the 1980s and 1990s were encouraged by the FDIC and other regulatory agencies in order to prevent the failure of banking organizations. The Garn-St. Germain Depository Institutions Act of 1982 and the Competitive Equality Banking Act of 1987 introduced an important departure from previous practices—they permitted failing banks and thrift institutions to be acquired by bank holding companies across state lines. The Financial Institutions Reform, Recovery, and Enforcement Act (FIRREA) of 1989 went one step further; it allowed even healthy thrifts located anywhere in the country to be acquired by holding companies, subject to regulatory approval.

Another very important reason for agreeing to be absorbed has been the problem of management. Small banks are often at a disadvantage in trying to attract highly trained and skilled management personnel. As current executives reach retirement age, merger or absorption by a larger bank may seem the best way to secure top-quality management skills. Stockholders in small banks may desire mergers in order to trade their shares for those of the larger bank, which often yield better earnings and sell for higher prices.

Although acquisition of banks has been a recurring phenomenon in the banking history of the United States, the 1950s saw a wave of mergers, almost 1,600, that aroused congressional concern over preservation of competition in banking. This concern culminated in the Bank Merger Act of 1960, which assigned authority over bank mergers to federal banking agencies and introduced specific standards for exercising this authority. This act requires approval of the Comptroller of the Currency if the acquiring bank is a national bank, of the Board of Governors of the Federal Reserve System if the acquiring bank is a state member bank, and of the FDIC if the acquiring bank is an insured nonmember bank. In deciding on merger requests, each agency is to consider the financial history and condition of the merging banks, the adequacy of their capital, the banks' earning prospects, the character of management, the convenience and needs of the community served, and the effect of the merger on competition. Each agency is also required to consider the advisory opinions of the other two agencies and of the Department of Justice, which may challenge in court any merger that attempts to monopolize or lessen competition in any industry. This authority of the Department of Justice stems from the Sherman Antitrust Act of 1890 and the Clayton Act of 1914, the country's federal antitrust legislation.

Before long it became apparent that certain provisions of the Bank Merger Act of 1960 lacked clarity or were too general. For example, the act did not assign relative weights to the individual criteria that regulatory authorities were to apply to merger applications. As a result, federal banking agencies emphasized banking factors, convenience, and community needs, whereas the Justice Department stressed competition. This conflict became evident in the first bank merger case to come up, that of the Philadelphia National Bank and the Girard Trust Corn Exchange Bank. Their merger was opposed by the Justice Department, although it had been approved by the Comptroller of the Currency.

A series of Supreme Court decisions* and the need to reconcile differences between the courts and the banking agencies led to the enactment of the Bank Merger Act of 1966, an amendment to the act of 1960. This act assigned greater weight to the competitive factors than did the 1960 act. Under its terms, each federal agency reviewing a merger application must give top priority to the competitive effects of the proposed merger on the local community. Mergers with moderate anticompetitive effects are likely to win regulatory approval, while mergers with high anticompetitive effects are likely to be rejected. Even then, however, antitrust authorities may not challenge a proposed merger if the institutions involved agree to divest some of their affiliated banks and overlapping branch offices, or if the proposed merger entails significant public benefits. Qualifying scenarios of public benefit would be the extension of banking services in areas where none are conveniently available and the rescuing of a troubled depository institution whose failure may place an undue burden on the public welfare.

United States v. Philadelphia National Bank et al., 210 F. Supp. 348 (1962), 83 S. Ct. 1715 (1963); *United States v. First National Bank and Trust Company of Lexington et al.*, 208 F. Supp. 457 (1962), 84 S. Ct. 1033 (1964).

Merger Guidelines

To assist them in their decision process, regulatory agencies employ the merger guidelines of the Department of Justice (revised in 1984 and 1992). These establish a level of market concentration that the Justice Department is likely to challenge as anticompetitive unless there are extenuating circumstances. The degree of concentration in a market is measured by the share of assets or deposits controlled by the depository institutions serving that market. If that share is substantial, it suggests concentration in the local market among providers of depository services; this implies reduced competition, and hence damage to the public from excessive prices and poor service quality. Regulatory guidelines require calculation of the Herfindahl-Hirschman Index (HHI), which measures concentration in local banking markets and in markets in other industries. The HHI calls for identifying the percentage of market share held by each depository institution competing in a given market, then squaring these numbers and summing the results. If all the assets or deposits in a market are controlled by a single banking organization (a monopoly position), the HHI would be 10,000 (that is, 100^2). As the number of firms increases, the index decreases toward its lower bound of zero; as the number of firms decreases, the index rises.

For example, if there are seven banking firms in a given market, and two hold a share of 15 percent each and the rest hold 10 percent each, the index would be 950: $(15)^2 + (15)^2 + (10)^2 + (10)^2 + (10)^2 + (10)^2 + (10)^2$. If two of the firms holding 10 percent each are seeking to merge, the index in the postmerger period would increase to 1,150: $(15)^2 + (15)^2 + (10)^2 + (10)^2 + (10)^2 + (2 \times 10)^2$. Any merger that would (a) change the value of the index by less than 200 or (b) increase the total index by less than 1,800 is not likely to be contested by the Department of Justice. Standard benchmarks are that a market with an HHI below 1,000 is unconcentrated, a market with an index between 1,000 and 1,800 is moderately concentrated, and a market with an index above 1,800 is highly concentrated. In the latter case, the Department of Justice may challenge the proposed merger in federal court unless there is evidence of extenuating circumstances. The mitigating factors may include ease of entry into the market by new firms, conduct of existing firms in this market, and type and character of buyers in the given market.

In recent years there has been a substantial increase in the number of bank mergers and acquisitions in this country. Indeed, during the 1980s and 1990s, the pace of these transactions reached a level not seen in at least 50 years. Although some of these mergers were induced by the regulators and involved failing institutions, the majority were between healthy organizations. This merger momentum was encouraged by two forces: first, the desire of banking organizations to position themselves in anticipation of interstate banking and, second, the relaxed antitrust standards of the Department of Justice. The latter has been effected by considering the importance of local thrift and nonbank financial institutions when analyzing the competitive effects of proposed bank acquisitions and mergers. Specifically, by incorporating local savings and loans, credit unions, and other financial institutions into the analysis, the market share of each bank in the local market will be lower, and hence the effect of a proposed merger or acquisition on the HHI will be more moderate. As the damage to competition becomes restrained, the prospects for a merger transaction to gain regulatory approval increase.

Relaxation of antitrust standards has encouraged many acquisition-minded banks to pursue *horizontal mergers* (mergers between banks offering similar services in the same locality). However, the most frequent type of merger has been the *market extension merger*, which involves banks operating in different markets and hence not in direct competition with each other (e.g., a wholesale bank [catering to a corporate clientele] merging with a smaller retail bank). Generally, bank mergers have been of the friendly type, enjoying the consent of the relevant parties. A case of a hostile takeover was that of Irving Trust by Bank of New York in 1988. Opposition by Irving's management stalled the takeover process until the courts cleared the way for the merger to be effected.

GROUP BANKING

Ownership or control of two or more banks by an individual, group of individuals, or corporation is called group banking. When an individual or a group of individuals controls more than one bank, the term "chain banking" is used. Bank control may be exercised in varying degree by majority stock ownership, common directors, or any other manner permitted by law. A bank holding company is a corporation that owns one or more banks. These categories and their many subdivisions, as they have evolved over the years, are charted in Figure 3.1.

Chain banking first appeared in the late nineteenth century in northwestern and southern agricultural states. It developed primarily where branching and multibank holding companies were not permitted. Chain banking is usually fairly localized, involving a few small banks in a region. Often the chain includes one focal bank that is larger than the others. At times, chains may spread across state lines. The chain is built through acquisition in any legal manner of a controlling interest (ownership of 50 percent or more of common stock) in each member bank. The member banks retain their separate identities and boards of directors.

Although chain banking has been in existence for years, comprehensive statistics are few. However, it is clear that it is of small significance as a form of bank ownership. Chain banking is regulated under the Bank Control Act of 1978 (Title VI of the Financial Institutions Regulatory and Interest Rate Control Act of 1978). Any transfer of 25 percent or more of a bank's voting stock to an individual or a group of individuals acting together comes under regulatory review.

Figure 3.1
Types of Group Banking

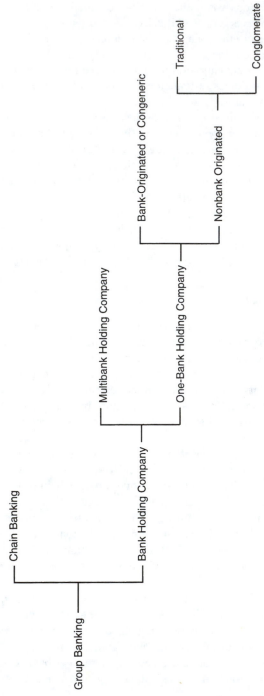

Source: Prepared by author.

Unlike chain banking, bank holding companies are a dominant industry feature. This form of bank ownership has evolved in response to the increasingly complex competitive environment in which banks operate and to increase public demand for varied banking and financial services. In addition, bank holding companies represent a response to legislation prohibiting branching and regulations limiting growth of individual banks.

The growth of bank holding companies and the extent of their importance in the banking industry are reflected in the following data. At the end of 1957, there were 50 bank holding companies registered with the Federal Reserve System, and they held 7.5 percent of all bank deposits. At the end of 1994, there were 5,264 bank holding companies, and they held 92.9 percent of all FDIC-insured deposits in the nation. By contrast, independent banks amounted to 2,634 firms and accounted for 7.1 percent of deposits.

Just as in chain banking, each bank owned by a bank holding company retains its own name and its own board of directors, which is responsible to the stockholders and to supervisory agencies for the functioning of the bank. Bank holding companies are generally divided into two categories: multibank holding companies and one-bank holding companies. The relative importance of each type is shown in Table 3.2. As shown in the table, although multibank holding companies trailed one-bank holding companies in number, they controlled 70.9 percent of all insured deposits. The scope of activities of each type of holding company and the factors responsible for their development are discussed below.

Multibank Holding Companies

As the name implies, a multibank holding company is a company that owns controlling interest in more than one bank. Multibank holding companies have been used as a substitute for branching in states that limit or prohibit branch banking. The individual banks may be run from above, much as branches are. They enable holding companies to extend throughout the state a full array of specialized banking services (such as trust and international services) that these banks individually would find economically prohibitive to offer even if there were a local demand for them.

Subsidiary banks enjoy certain operational efficiencies through their relationship with the holding company. For example, they benefit from centralized and computerized bookkeeping, auditing, advertising, marketing, purchasing of supplies, research, personnel recruitment, group insurance, retirement programs, tax guidance, investment counseling, and other advisory services. The economies of scale realized through their holding company affiliation could not be attained by the banks individually. Subsidiaries also benefit from the holding company's better access to capital markets for the raising of funds. As small independent banks they would be unlikely to receive a quality rating for their security issues. Moreover, holding companies facilitate mobility of funds through loan participations among members of the organization. In this way returns on the aggregate

Table 3.2
Banking Organizations and Volume of FDIC-Insured Deposits, 1994

Type of Institution	Number of Firms	Percent of Total	Deposits (billions of dollars)	Percent of Total	Mean Deposits per Firm (millions of dollars)
Independent banks	2,634	33.4	$ 170.0	7.1	$ 64.5
Holding companies					
One-bank holding companies	4,464	56.5	523.0	21.9	117.2
Multibank holding companies	800	10.1	1,689.6	70.9	2,112.1
	5,264	66.6	2,212.6	92.9	2,229.3
Total	7,898	100.0	$2,382.7	100.0	$ 301.7

Source: Federal Reserve Bulletin, January 1996, p. 5.

loans of the system are maximized. In addition, the returns on bank assets can be spread over all members of the holding company.

Although multibank holding companies date from the turn of the century, it was in the mid-1950s that federal legislation was enacted to regulate them. This legislation was prompted by the activities of a West Coast multibank holding company, the Transamerica Corporation. As early as 1948, the Board of Governors of the Federal Reserve System initiated antitrust proceedings against Transamerica, which controlled the Bank of America in addition to 46 other banks in a five-state area (Arizona, California, Nevada, Oregon, and Washington). When the court ruled in favor of Transamerica (instructing it to divest itself only of its Bank of America stock and allowing it to expand into other states), public pressure for regulation began to mount.

This pressure culminated in the Bank Holding Company Act of 1956, which provided for the registration of all multibank holding companies with the Federal Reserve Board and gave these companies the option of divesting themselves of all their nonbanking business or of all their banking business. All companies must submit to periodic examinations of their records by the Federal Reserve Board. Board approval is required prior to the formation of a bank holding company. It is also required for mergers among bank holding companies and for a company's acquisition of over 5 percent of the voting stock in a bank. In evaluating any of these actions, the Federal Reserve Board is required by law to consider the financial history and condition of the company or companies and the banks involved; the convenience, needs, and welfare of the community; and the degree of economic competition and concentration. Since the Bank Merger Act of 1966, with its emphasis on the competitive climate, this consideration has been of primary importance in evaluations of the acquisition requests of bank holding companies.

The objectives of the Bank Holding Company Act of 1956 were twofold: to prevent undue concentration of banks by bank holding companies, and to preserve the historical separation between banking and commerce. The act failed to achieve either objective. One reason for the act's failure was that it defined a bank holding company as any corporation controlling 25 percent or more of the voting stock of two or more banks. This definition contained a number of loopholes. Partnerships, trusts, and single individuals could control banks and remain outside the scope of the act. More important, it failed to bring under the purview of the act companies that own one bank or less than 25 percent of the stock of other banks. This loophole was a key factor leading to the spectacular growth of one-bank holding companies in the 1960s; it offered banks the opportunity to extend their operations to include insurance, real estate, and data processing.

Enactment of the Riegle-Neal Act will spur many multibank holding companies to convert their banking subsidiaries into branches and become one-bank holding companies.

One-Bank Holding Companies

Unlike multibank holding companies, which developed primarily in unit-banking and limited-branching states, one-bank holding companies have become a significant force on the banking scene. As the name implies, one-bank holding companies control a single bank. They fall into two types; bank-originated and nonbank-originated. The bank-originated one-bank holding company occurs when an existing bank creates its own holding company, thus placing itself in a subsidiary status. This type of one-bank holding company is also known as congeneric, since it is formed by a bank to engage in related financial activities such as mortgage banking and factoring. The nonbank-originated holding company does not draw its origin from the bank that it owns and controls. This type of holding company can be further divided into traditional and conglomerate. Traditional one-bank holding companies are corporations established to control a small bank; they may also be involved in real estate, insurance, and finance. Conglomerate one-bank holding companies are corporations that own a bank but engage in other activities or have subsidiaries that are nonfinancial. Examples include Hershey Foods, Goodyear Tire and Rubber Company, World Airways, charitable trusts, nonprofit foundations, and labor unions.

Of the different classifications of one-bank holding companies, the most important is the congeneric because it enables a bank, or a bank-originated holding company, to establish a nonbank subsidiary and enter product and geographic markets from which banks are barred. It was precisely this prospect that induced bankers to take advantage of the loophole in the Bank Holding Company Act of 1956 and launch, in the 1960s, a number of bank-originated one-bank holding companies. The bank-originated one-bank holding company offers bankers other advantages, such as greater flexibility in fund-raising. This aspect became significant during the tight money periods of the late 1960s. The holding company could raise funds by issuing its own commercial paper and then funneling these funds to the bank by purchasing loans from its portfolio or bank-issued stocks and bonds. This technique was advantageous because the holding company, which was not subject to interest ceilings, could pay higher returns than the bank could offer its depositors. In addition, these funds were not subject to reserve requirements and did not have to be insured.

The rapid growth of one-bank holding companies in the 1960s led to calls for control by competing firms. As a result, the Bank Holding Company Act of 1956 was amended in 1970 to cover one-bank holding companies. The 1970 amendments to the Bank Holding Company Act extended the definition of a bank holding company to include all companies (corporations, partnerships, business trusts, and associations). More important, the term ''control'' in the definition of a bank holding company was identified as an interest between 5 and 25 percent. The 1970 amendments called for the Federal Reserve to regulate the activities of these companies, including placing limits on the nonbank activities in which they can engage. These activities must bear a close relation to traditional banking functions. One of the first tasks of the Board of Governors of the Federal Reserve System was to approve a list of permissible activities in which one-bank and multibank holding companies may engage. This list has grown considerably over the years, and some of the most important activities included are the following:

1. Extensions of credit
    a. Mortgage banking
    b. Finance companies: consumer, sales, and commercial
    c. Credit cards
    d. Factoring
2. Operating an industrial bank, Morris Plan bank, or industrial loan company
3. Operating savings and loan associations
4. Operating a trust company
5. Investment or financial advising
6. Full-payout leasing of personal or real property
7. Investments in community welfare projects
8. Providing bookkeeping or data-processing services, including data transmission services, facilities, databases, or access to such by any technologically feasible means
9. Acting as insurance agent or broker primarily in connection with credit extensions
10. Underwriting credit life, accident, and health insurance for affiliates
11. Providing courier services
12. Management consulting to all depository institutions
13. Sale at retail of money orders, traveler's checks, and savings bonds
14. Performing appraisals of real estate
15. Arranging commercial real estate equity financing
16. Securities brokerage
17. Underwriting and dealing in government obligations and money-market instruments
18. Foreign-exchange advisory and transaction services
19. Futures commission merchant
20. Options on financial futures
21. Advice on options on bullion and foreign exchange
22. Consumer financial counseling
23. Tax planning and preparation
24. Futures and options advisory services
25. Check guaranty services
26. Collection agency and credit bureau services
27. Personal property appraisals

Examination of Board of Governors' rulings reveals the criteria used in approving or denying requests by bank holding companies to enter nonbanking activities. To determine whether certain activities are closely related to banking, the Board of Governors considers whether the proposed activities are similar to bank lending or operationally integrated into the lending process. Similar to bank lending are activities that involve extension of credit, such as factoring, leasing, and mortgage banking. Such activities as data processing and underwriting credit life insurance are judged to be operationally integrated into the lending process. There are other criteria as well, such as public interest and convenience, efficiency of management, conflict of interest, and competition versus concentration. The latter issue is an especially important consideration. De novo entries into new areas of activity are generally favored because they add another competitor to the scene. Thus, the Board of Governors might approve a holding company's application to create, rather than acquire, a factoring company. By contrast, moves to acquire existing concerns are rejected if they will have a negative impact on local competition. As a result, the acquisition of a small company would be favored over that of a large one.

Apart from charging the Board of Governors with regulating one-bank holding companies, the 1970 amendments include more substantive sections. One confers automatic approval on any application that the board has not acted on within 90 days following submission of all the requisite forms. Another, which spells out tie-in restrictions, reflects congressional concern that the spread of holding-company activities into nonbanking areas might adversely affect competition. These restrictions forbid any bank from making the availability of its services contingent on the customer's purchase of other services from the bank, its holding company, or its affiliates. In addition, a bank cannot require that its customers not do business with the bank's competitors, their holding companies, or affiliates. These restrictions do not apply to requirements intended to assure the soundness of loans or to traditional bank services such as deposits or trusts. Finally, a grandfather clause exempts some nonbanking subsidiaries acquired before June 30, 1968. However, the Board of Governors was given authority to review any subsidiary, even if acquired before this date, and call for its divestiture if it was judged to inhibit competition unduly.

One facet of the 1970 amendments to the Bank Holding Company Act of 1956 gives bank holding companies an avenue for significantly broadening their activities. Nonbanking activities of bank holding companies are not restricted geographically; that is, bank holding companies can operate nonbank subsidiaries engaging in the approved bank-related activities without geographic limits.

BANK REGULATION

The development of bank regulation has occurred largely in response to financial crisis rather than through constructive planning. The financial crisis of the Civil War gave rise to the National Bank Act; the Panic of 1907 led to the creation of the Federal Reserve System; and the Great Depression spawned the Banking Act of 1933 and the Banking Act of 1935. The last two pieces of legislation established the Federal Deposit Insurance Corporation, separated commercial banking from investment banking, and introduced interest-rate ceilings on deposits. These measures mark the point at which bank regulation was most aggressive in its efforts to protect the depositor and ensure the safety of banking.

By the late 1970s it became apparent that key regulatory provisions introduced during the Depression era were inconsistent with developments in financial markets. Price and product controls limited the rates depository institutions paid on deposits and restricted the scope of the services offered. Concern also existed about the exposure of savings and loans to interest-rate risk; the high interest rates of the late 1970s had caught thrifts in a bind of paying higher rates on savings deposits while collecting fixed, low-interest income from their mortgage holdings. Thrifts' severe profit and cash-flow squeezes prompted recommendations for expanding the scope of their assets and liabilities beyond the traditional ones of mortgages and savings deposits.

These concerns prompted the enactment of two major pieces of legislation in the early 1980s that sought to deregulate the activities of depository institutions and increase competition. The DIDMCA of 1980 and the Garn-St. Germain Depository Institutions Act (DIA) of 1982 reflect this intent. Table 3.3 highlights the main features of these acts. The DIDMCA provided, among other things, for uniform reserve requirements, access to the discount window by all depository institutions, pricing of Federal Reserve services, phaseout of interest-rate ceilings on deposit accounts (Regulation Q), offering of interest-bearing transaction (NOW) accounts by all depository institutions, and increased lending and investment powers for thrifts. The DIA dealt in some respects with the problems that had not been solved by the 1980 legislation. For example, it expanded the sources of funds for depository institutions, granted new powers to thrifts, and provided for emergency takeovers of failing institutions.

The new powers given to thrifts in the early 1980s gradually gave rise to credit-risk problems that by the end of the decade precipitated the S&L crisis that cost the federal government—according to experts' estimates—about $500 billion. To deal with the problems of the thrift industry and an insolvent deposit insurance fund (FSLIC), the U.S. Congress enacted the Financial Institutions Reform, Recovery, and Enforcement Act (FIRREA) of 1989. Key provisions of this law, listed in Table 3.3, restructured the regulatory framework for thrifts, reversed the deregulation of the earlier legislations, and imposed such stringent requirements that, according to some analysts, it signaled the end of thrift institutions as a separate industry.

Unlike the legislation of the 1980s, which deregulated and reregulated depository institutions, the Federal Deposit Insurance Corporation Improvement Act (FDICIA) of 1991 was intended to reform the financial system by transforming the role of commercial banks and streamlining bank regulation. A U.S.

Table 3.3
Principal Features of Banking Legislation Enacted in the 1980s

---

Depository Institutions Deregulation and Monetary Control Act (DIDMCA) of 1980

Introduces uniform reserve requirements, set by the Federal Reserve, for all depository institutions

Allows depository institutions to borrow at Federal Reserve discount window

Makes available the services of Federal Reserve to all depository institutions at prices based on its operating costs

Increases federal deposit insurance to $100,000

Provides for phaseout of interest-rate ceilings on deposits at depository institutions and overrides state limits on deposit rates

Authorizes depository institutions to offer interest-bearing negotiable orders of withdrawal (NOW) accounts

Allows thrifts to invest in commercial paper, corporate debt securities, consumer loans, and unsecured construction loans; issue credit cards; and offer trust services

Authorizes credit unions to issue share drafts

Garn-St. Germain Depository Institutions Act (DIA) of 1982

Allows regulators to arrange mergers and acquisitions for problem institutions across geographic and institutional markets

Authorizes thrifts to make commercial loans and overdrafts loans

Provides for depository institutions to issue money-market deposit accounts

Increases legal lending limit for any single customer as percentage of commercial bank capital and surplus

Financial Institutions Reform, Recovery, and Enforcement Act (FIRREA) of 1989

Restructures the regulatory framework of the savings and loan industry

Places a new deposit insurance fund for thrifts under FDIC control

Allows banks to take over sound thrifts and integrate them into their existing branch network

Brings capital requirements in line with those for banks and tightens the investment and lending powers of savings and loans

Increases the enforcement powers of regulators and the penalties for banking law violations

Creates the Resolution Trust Corporation to supervise the liquidation of insolvent thrifts

---

Treasury study—mandated under FIRREA and presented to Congress in early 1991—proposed fundamental structural changes that included full interstate banking, expansion of bank product lines into securities and insurance services, ownership of bank holding companies by commercial firms, and reorganization of bank supervision. Although these recommendations were included in the original bill, the enacted law incorporated only the part that dealt with deposit insurance proper (highlights of this law were presented in Table 2.2).

Most recently we have witnessed growing support for heavier reliance on market forces (e.g., the Riegle-Neal Act) and technological developments. Just as the technological advances of recent years are transforming many aspects of banking activity, so they are likely to speed up the process of regulatory change in the near future and increase the efficiency of bank regulation.

Scope of Bank Supervision

Commercial bank regulation today covers nearly every phase of banking activity. Although there is some degree of variation between federal and state regulation, the overall purpose—to ensure the soundness of the U.S. banking system—does not vary. Some of the more important regulatory activities include passing on applications for the chartering of new banks; issuing and enforcing laws and regulations; periodically examining the conditions, operations, and policies of individual banks; passing on applications for changes in banking powers, such as the offering of trust services; and passing on applications for branch offices, proposed mergers and consolidations, acquisitions by existing bank holding companies, and the formation of new holding companies. Other issues coming under regulatory purview include bank capital requirements, the maintenance of reserves against deposits, types and amounts of assets banks may hold, and liquidation of banks.

Evaluation of individual banks is carried out by means of the bank examination. Under the FDICIA of 1991, bank regulators generally must examine all banks on-site at least once each year. Examiners arrive unannounced at a bank and spend days or weeks, depending on the size of the bank, going over its operations. Bank examiners make sure that the bank is in sound condition and that it is in compliance with all applicable laws and regulations.

To provide a general framework for the evaluation of all federally insured depository institutions, regulators introduced in 1979 the Uniform Financial Institutions Rating System. This system identifies five distinct areas of bank operation and conditions for evaluation: Capital adequacy, Asset quality, Management and administration, Earnings quantity and quality, and Liquidity level. These are commonly referred to by the acronym CAMEL. Each of these areas is rated on a scale of 1 ("strong") to 5 ("unsatisfactory and in need of immediate remedial attention"). In addition, the bank as a whole receives a composite rating on this scale. Banks with composite ratings of 1 are examined relatively infrequently, while banks earning the 5 rating undergo continual scrutiny.

A similar system, known as BOPEC, is used to determine the corporate rating for a bank holding company. In this system, the corporate rating is a composite of the five components of the bank holding company: the Bank subsidiaries, Other (nonbank) subsidiaries, the Parent company, consolidated Earnings, and consolidated Capital adequacy; hence the acronym BOPEC. As with CAMEL, each component is assigned a rating on a scale of 1 to 5, in descending order of performance.

Between on-site examinations, regulators monitor financial institutions off-site, using computer-based systems. These monitoring systems typically analyze the financial information that each institution must report to regulators quarterly (*Call Report*). During the mid-1980s, the FDIC developed a surveillance system known as CAEL because it evaluates four of the CAMEL component ratings (the system does not provide a rating for management). A more sophisticated off-site bank surveillance system is the Financial Institutions Monitoring System (FIMS), introduced by the Federal Reserve in 1993. Although the Federal System has monitored the condition of banking organizations since the mid-1970s, FIMS is viewed as significantly more accurate than previous systems in identifying financially troubled institutions; for instance, it provides institutional estimates of the component ratings as well as the composite CAMEL ratings. FIMS is also used by the Federal Reserve in estimating the bank component of the BOPEC rating. The high correlation of the bank component rating with the composite BOPEC rating provides a reliable off-site assessment of a bank holding company's financial condition.

Although safety and soundness of operations is of primary concern to regulators, there are additional types of examinations that address specific aspects of banking activity. For example, compliance examinations seek to determine bank compliance with regulations introduced by federal legislation, (e.g., truth-in-lending, equal credit opportunity, and community reinvestment). Electronic data-processing (EDP) examinations evaluate every aspect of EDP operations to ensure adequacy of internal controls and safeguards. Trust examinations seek to determine whether trust operations are carried out in accordance with acceptable fiduciary standards, court orders, and laws and regulations of the state and federal governments.

The bank examination culminates in the preparation of a formal report, copies of which are placed in the files of the regulatory agency and submitted to the bank's directors. The report lists all problems or failings uncovered during the examination: instances of noncompliance with laws or regulations; problem loans; inadequacies in the capital base. In addition, the report may comment on specific management practices that are considered unsound or problematic. It is the responsibility of the directors to see that the report's recommendations are implemented. Regulatory agencies can, under expanded cease-and-desist authority granted by FIRREA, impose civil penalties against the bank for violating the law or regulations, or misstating financial information. Failure to comply can also result in the removal of the officers or directors involved and stringent criminal penalties for offenses. These enforcement powers seek to discourage fraud, which contributed to the failure of many thrifts.

Current Regulatory Structure

A distinctive feature of the American banking system is that supervisory and regulatory functions are carried out by a number of different agencies. Table 3.4 identifies the U.S. regulatory structure for all depository institutions. The agencies involved in commercial banking regulation are several. The Office of the Comptroller of the Currency is the chartering authority and principal regulator for national banks. The Federal Reserve System is the regulator for state-chartered commercial banks that are members of the Federal Reserve; this

Table 3.4
Primary Supervisors of Banks and Thrifts

Institution	Regulator
National banks	Office of the Comptroller of the Currency
State member banks	Federal Reserve and state authority
Insured nonmember banks	FDIC and state authority
Noninsured banks	State authority[1]
Insured federal savings associations	Office of Thrift Supervision
Insured state savings associations	Office of Thrift Supervision and state authority
Uninsured state savings associations	State authority[1]
Federal credit unions	National Credit Union Administration Board
State credit unions	State authority
Bank holding companies	Federal Reserve
Savings and loan holding companies	Office of Thrift Supervision

[1]The FDIC can intervene in the administration of these institutions to prevent a loss to the federal deposit insurance fund.
Note: The FDIC has some examination authority over all FDIC-insured institutions.
Source: Christopher Pike and James Thomson, "FDICIA's Prompt Corrective Action Provisions," Federal Reserve Bank of Cleveland, *Economic Commentary*, September 1, 1992, p. 3.

authority is shared at the state level with the appropriate regulator. The FDIC has authority over all insured nonmember state-chartered commercial banks, and that authority is shared with the state. The individual states are the principal regulators for all noninsured banks. As a result of the overlap in the jurisdiction of these agencies, state member banks, for example, are subject to the banking laws of the state in which they are chartered and operate, and to all applicable federal legislation by virtue of their membership in the Federal Reserve System and the FDIC. By the same token, national banks are supervised by their chartering agency, the Office of the Comptroller of the Currency, and, because of their national charter, are required to be members of the Federal Reserve System and the FDIC. In addition, national banks are subject to the laws of the state in which they operate.

The regulatory pattern for thrifts and credit unions is similar to that for banks except that here there is only one federal regulator for each type of depository institution. As shown in Table 3.4, the Office of Thrift Supervision, a federal regulator, has authority over all insured savings and loans but shares its authority with the state over those insured institutions that hold a state charter. Uninsured state-chartered savings and loans are subject to state authority. The National Credit Union Administration Board, a federal regulator, has authority over all federally chartered credit unions, while the state has authority over all state-chartered. The Federal Reserve Board must pass on all bank holding company transactions, and the Office of Thrift Supervision, on all savings and loan holding company transactions.

Over the years, the complexity of the U.S. regulatory system and the degree of overlapping jurisdictions have prompted a number of proposals aiming to reform it, consolidate it, and make it more efficient. Dating from the early 1960s, these proposals originated from a variety of sources, including administrative officials, committees, commissions, the U.S. Congress, and most recently the U.S. Treasury (1991) and the Clinton administration (1993). The common feature of these proposals is the assignment of the supervisory functions of the Federal Reserve, the Office of the Comptroller of the Currency, the Office of Thrift Supervision, and the FDIC to one federal agency. These proposals have been too sweeping to gain favor with the various regulators that are to be abolished or drastically altered under the proposed changes. Thus, as of 1996, none of these proposals has been enacted.

The only progress toward reform of bank regulatory authority at the federal level remains the enactment of the DIDMCA, which brought all depository institutions under uniform reserve requirements and provided them with access to the Federal Reserve discount window. Another important step toward consolidation of regulatory authority was the enactment of the Riegle-Neal Act. As banks proceed with interstate branching activity, national charters appear more advantageous. For a bank chartered in one state to establish branches in another, its branches will be subject to all of the laws of the host state while also under the jurisdiction of the chartering state. A national charter obviates these difficulties. This difference will further attenuate the dual banking system and will tend to increase the influence of the Office of the Comptroller of the Currency compared with that of the Federal Reserve and the FDIC. Such a shift is bound to result in the concentration of authority in a single agency.

COMPETITION IN FINANCIAL SERVICES

In recent years commercial banks have been facing increasing competition from other participants in the money and capital markets. In their attempts to attract funds, as well as to lend and invest these funds, banks have been competing with other financial institutions, nonfinancial businesses, and the government. On the liability side, banks must compete with the short-term and long-term debt instruments of financial institutions, nonfinancial corporations, and the government. In the mid-1970s a new competitor entered the fray in the form of the money-market funds. The money-market funds are mutual funds (formally known as open-end investment companies) whose objective is to invest the funds raised from the sale of their own stock in liquid instruments (e.g., negotiable CDs of large banks and commercial paper of large, well-known corporations).

To the consumer who wanted to earn a market return on liquid funds, money-market funds offered an instrument that paid a more attractive rate than did the time and savings deposits of bank and nonbank depository institutions, which were subject to interest-rate ceilings. In addition to the higher rate on funds, this instrument offered some checking privileges and required no minimum maturity period. These features of money-market fund shares were responsible for the spectacular growth of those funds from almost zero in late 1974 to a record $232 billion in assets by December 1, 1982. Most of that amount was drained from thrift institutions and medium-size and small banks. For big banks, by contrast, money-market funds were a source of funds, since they invested a major share of their assets in the negotiable CDs of those banks. To remedy this situation, the Garn-St. Germain Act permitted banks and thrifts to introduce, on December 14, 1982, a money-market deposit account that offered consumers the same features (limited checking privileges, no minimum maturity period, and no interest-rate ceiling) as money-market fund shares, plus the same insurance coverage (up to $100,000) as all other deposit accounts. This account enabled banks and thrifts to recapture some of the funds that they lost to money-market funds. Since the Federal Reserve's authorization in 1992, several banking organizations have expanded the scope of their products to include mutual funds. This move has enabled banks to retain customers and play an important role in this market.

On the asset side (lending and investing), banks compete with a host of institutional and corporate lenders. On the institutional level they compete with such financial intermediaries as insurance companies, pension funds, commercial factors, and finance companies. On the corporate level banks compete with large manufacturing corporations—such as auto or farm equipment manufacturers—whose captive finance companies (finance companies they own) have expanded their traditional equipment-financing function to offer receivable and inventory financing as well as leasing. However, while they are making the same kinds of loans that banks do, they are not subject to the same regulatory constraints that banks are. Firms like General Motors and General Electric may extend loans anywhere in the country, while banks must conform to branching laws. National retail concerns, like Sears Roebuck, are still another example of a nonfinancial contender in the financial services market. Sears Roebuck competes directly with banks by offering consumer credit throughout its nationwide chain of retail stores. Until recently, Sears owned a real-estate firm (Coldwell Banker), an insurance company (Allstate), a brokerage firm (Dean Witter), and a bank (Greenwood Trust Co., Delaware). Acquisition of the bank in 1985 enabled Sears to issue Discover, the first major general-purpose credit card to challenge Visa and MasterCard in a decade.

Until 1987, nonfinancial corporations could conduct banking activity across state lines by putting together corporate structures that did not meet the legal definition of banks, and thus were not subject to state branching laws. The Bank Holding Company Act defined a bank as any organization that offered demand deposits and made commercial loans. Hence, an institution that offered either demand deposits or commercial loans was a bank and yet not a bank—a nonbank bank. However, the Competitive Equality Banking Act of 1987 attempted to close the nonbank-bank loophole by defining a bank as any institution that offers federally insured deposits or that accepts demand deposits and also makes commercial loans. By extending the definition of a bank to all institutions with FDIC-insured deposits, this act in effect eliminated the future chartering of institutions that divest themselves of their commercial loan portfolios. The act "grandfathered" over 160 nonbank banks existing as of March 5, 1986. The "grandfathered" institutions circumvented interstate restrictions through subsidiaries that offered a more limited array of financial services than commercial banks. The first nonbank bank was established in 1980 by Gulf & Western when it acquired a bank and sold its commercial loan portfolio. Other institutions of various types quickly followed suit, creating similar limited-service banks. For example, Merrill Lynch set up Merrill Lynch Bank and Trust Company in New Jersey; it does not accept demand deposits but does accept insured time deposits and makes commercial loans. Insurance companies, like Prudential, were also among those setting up limited-service banks across state lines.

Nonbank and nonfinancial contenders in the financial-services market have become such a force that they are causing a structural change in financial markets that is permanently altering competitive relationships. Although in the past the dominant pattern was one of institutions concentrating in a limited service area, the trend has developed toward a broader range of services offered by fewer, larger institutions. In other words, a few firms now offer a full product line of financial services.

Why has this wave of new competitors been so eager to enter the banking business? The answer lies in the profitability of the commercial banking industry and the stability of its returns compared with those of other businesses. The net earnings of banks grew steadily throughout the 1970s and 1980s.

More important, the return on assets (ROA) for commercial banks held steady at about 1 percent throughout the 1970s and 1980s, exhibiting very low volatility compared with the wider swings in the annual returns of different types of financial institutions (e.g., securities companies, insurance firms, and real-estate companies). With the returns of various industry groups moving in the opposite direction to the returns of banks (negative correlation) during this period, banking presented an attractive diversification alternative.

The multidimensional competition that banks have been facing will no doubt intensify in the years ahead. At the same time, differences among depository institutions are quickly disappearing. Banks now compete with savings and loans and credit unions in providing basic banking services. Although the long-run implications of growing competition will be positive for the U.S. financial system, in the transitional stage it promises significant challenges for most of the nearly 10,000 commercial banks and 14,000 other depository institutions. As nonbank competitors close in, three major scenarios appear likely for banks and other depository institutions: electronic banking, specialty banking, and the financial supermarket. These approaches may be employed singly or in combination.

Electronic Banking

Many of the tedious tasks that bankers once loathed are now done electronically, and one of the chief beneficiaries of the electronic revolution in banking is the bank customer. The growing use of electronic funds transfer systems (EFTS) combines both cost savings and increased convenience to customers. The most visible effects of EFTS are occurring in the payments mechanism. In recent years a growing number of banks, concerned with the declining profitability of additions to their brick-and-mortar branch networks, have developed extensive systems of automatic teller machines (ATMs) to substitute for full-service, fully staffed branch offices. Recently some 35 banks have started offering personal loans (between $500 and $10,000) through automated loan machines (ALMs) located in supermarkets, shopping malls, and bank branches. Additional types of consumer loans (e.g., car loans and home-equity loans) were added in 1996. Borrowers do not have to be customers of the bank to obtain a loan through the bank's ALM.

Point-of sale (POS) banking is another EFTS application at the consumer level. POS facilities enable a customer to pay for purchases by means of a direct transfer of funds from his or her account to that of the merchant through a debit card. Clearly the POS system has several key advantages over the use of cash and checks: it reduces the need to carry substantial amounts of cash, reduces the amount of paperwork, and eliminates the possibility of a bad check being written. Several regional debit card networks are already in place, and there are plans to set up nationwide networks.

A more dramatic breakthrough for customer convenience is the advent of in-home banking. A number of banks are actively extending services to their clients through two-way cable television hookups. Telephones may also link the home or office computer with that of a bank. The ability to conduct banking transactions without leaving home appears more attractive, despite the reduced personal contact with bank employees. Bank costs, meanwhile, are shifting, to some extent, from salaries to the substantial fixed costs involved in acquiring and maintaining electronic equipment. Since large numbers of transactions are necessary to bring the cost per transaction to a profitable level, the trend toward electronic banking favors large banks over smaller ones. Thus electronic banking represents one more force in the trend toward fewer, larger banks in the United States. Citicorp offers an example of a banking organization that has already invested heavily in electronic technology with the view that before too long, all types of financial service transactions will be conducted electronically.

Along with Citicorp, a number of banks are attracting computer-savvy customers by offering them on-line access. The most secure channel is through a direct link with the bank, using either the bank's proprietary software or a third party's software (e.g., Intuit's Quicken or Microsoft's Money). Alternatively, the customer may gain access to the bank via the Internet. Its huge client base (a market of over 30 million people, estimated to be growing by 10 percent a month) and the need to stop existing customers from being lured away by competing institutions have led a growing number of banks to connect themselves to the Internet. Indeed, from none in 1989, about 500 banks and other financial-services groups were on the network at year-end 1995. Most of the banks provide information and advertising about the range of their services. Some banks already let customers order statements, apply for products, and make credit-cared purchases on the Internet. A handful of banks are working on more sophisticated strategies for the products they plan to offer on the network, with success depending upon developing methods to improve security. Whatever the degree of involvement, these banks constitute Internet's banking pioneers.

Specialty Banking

Deregulation of financial institutions and increased competition for financial-service companies will prompt some banks to take a path chosen by firms in other deregulated industries, such as airlines and trucking. These banks, rather than offering a wide variety of financial services over a large geographic area, may choose to retrench from their full-service offerings and concentrate on a more attractive product or customer segment of the market. This move will mark the emergence of specialty banks, institutions that will compete aggressively in a narrower range of financial services or in specific segments of the market, usually segments with a high customer-service preference (such as developing special service packages to cater to the needs of high-income customers). Geographic boundaries will lose their significance as deregulation proceeds and electronic banking becomes more prevalent; thus geographically defined market niches will cease to provide security for banks.

Banks that wish to create a secure position by becoming specialty banks will selectively acquire competitors that will deepen rather than broaden their expertise, thus better equipping them to provide the more specific services on which they have chosen to focus. Commercial banking has been said to consist of five separate forms of business: retail, domestic wholesale, international wholesale, trading, and trust. Each of these is large enough to be considered an industry with room for a limited number of banks to emerge as leaders exercising substantial control in that area. Morgan Guaranty Trust Company and Bankers Trust of New York are examples of banks that are the farthest into investment banking, while State Street Bank and Trust Company of Boston has largely abandoned traditional banking in favor of trust business, which it dominates with assets under custody in excess of $1.2 trillion.

Financial Supermarkets

While some banks deal with the coming challenges by narrowing their service offerings or focusing on electronic in-home banking, others will enlarge and broaden themselves to create "financial supermarkets." These will aim to provide customers with a complete range of financial services from a single institution. Since mergers will be a central vehicle in building these large and diverse institutions, the trend to financial supermarkets will significantly reduce the number of depository and other financial institutions in the United States.

This structural change in the banking industry has already begun. Enactment of the Riegle-Neal Act is spurring more and larger interstate bank acquisitions and will result in the first truly national depository institutions in the nation's history. It can be reliably predicted that a continuing wave of mergers and acquisitions will bring about consolidation in the banking industry regionally and nationally; there will be fewer and larger banks.

In addition to providing for a stronger regional and/or national presence, holding companies have proved instrumental in the entry of banks into product markets from which they were traditionally barred. As stated earlier in this chapter, holding companies have enabled banks to acquire or establish businesses and diversify into related financial activities (such as mortgage banking, consumer finance, factoring, and leasing). Regulatory proposals for restructuring the banking system agree that bank holding companies should expand to include such financial services as investment banking, selling and underwriting insurance, and real-estate investment. Regulators feel that such restructuring not only would enhance the competitiveness of banks in financial markets but also would benefit consumers and businesses by reducing the cost of these services.

Perhaps the most important issue faced by regulators is whether bank holding companies should be permitted to offer nonfinancial services and products. The Federal Reserve System rejects this idea by adhering to the narrow view that banking should be kept separate from commerce. On the other hand, the FDIC, administrative officials, and members of congress have at various times taken the stance that bank holding companies should be free to offer a full range of financial and nonfinancial services, requiring separate subsidiaries for those services deemed especially risky. Strong "fire walls" (such as restrictions on intracompany loans) would protect the bank from any losses suffered by the commercial company. Under this plan, a bank holding company could engage, for example, in the automobile business. This example is not as unrealistic as it may originally appear. General Motors already sells cars and—through its financial subsidiary, GMAC—makes consumer loans. It could become a bank holding company either by acquiring an existing bank or by obtaining permission to offer insured deposits through its finance subsidiary. Thus, if General Motors could become a bank holding company, Citicorp could own an automobile factory. The debate on this issue continues.

Whatever the outcome of this debate, over 30 bank holding companies have been permitted by the Federal Reserve to operate investment banking subsidiaries. The Federal Reserve has interpreted Section 20 of the Glass-Steagall Act to allow bank holding companies to engage in investment banking through nonbank subsidiaries (also referred to as Section 20 subsidiaries). Banks have also made inroads in the insurance business. A 1916 federal banking statute authorized national banks in small rural communities to act as insurance brokers. Some banks have parlayed this right into a broader power by setting up a subsidiary in a small community and using it to market insurance nationwide. In the early 1990s several states (e.g., Delaware and Indiana) allowed the banks they supervised to underwrite and sell insurance nationwide. As a result, a number of major banks (e.g., Citicorp and Bankers Trust New York Corporation) set up subsidiaries in these states to take advantage of this opportunity. However, opposition by the insurance industry led the FDICIA of 1991 to bar states from granting any further insurance powers to banks.

Just as banks have been positioning themselves in the market for financial services, so have financial-service companies. The examples are numerous. American Express purchased E.F. Hutton Group (1987) and Centurion Bank (1987), adding commercial and investment banking to its financial services, which include traveler's checks and international banking. Acquisition of the Centurion Bank enabled American Express to introduce its Optima card, a revolving-credit card that complements its charge card, initially introduced as an entertainment and travel card only. Another case is that of Prudential Insurance, which in 1981 entered retail stockbrokerage through acquisition of Bache Halsey Stuart Shields. Since then, Prudential has built itself into a financial organization that includes savings and loan associations, commercial banks, and mortgage companies.

Still another example is that of Merrill Lynch and Company, Inc., which as early as 1972 established in London a wholly owned banking subsidiary that was renamed Merrill Lynch International Bank, Ltd., in 1976. This institution went on to establish a banking subsidiary, Merrill Lynch Bank (Suisse) S.A. A separate entity is Merrill Lynch Bank & Trust Company (Cayman), Ltd., which—through a representative office in Miami—has been catering to the banking needs of nonresidents. In 1994, Merrill Lynch initiated the conversion of its brokerage offices in Europe into branches of the London-based bank, offering both brokerage and banking services under one roof. In the domestic market, Merrill Lynch moved into the turf of commercial banks in 1994 by originating loans to medium-size and large companies and syndicating a large portion of these loans to other financial institutions. More important, once the Glass-Steagall Act is repealed, Merrill Lynch is expected to convert its 450 branches into integrated banking and brokerage offices, thereby evolving into perhaps the largest private bank in the country.

These and other examples indicate that the trend in the United States is toward a broader range of services offered by fewer, larger institutions. No one doubts the outcome of these developments; the end result will be the integration of financial markets across institutions and space. What will emerge from this integration process will be a financial supermarket offering a smorgasbord of financial services. "Supermarket banking," "supermarket of financial services," and "financial supermarket" are terms that have been used loosely in the last few years to describe one-stop shopping for financial services. Financial supermarkets will be no different from the *universal* banks of Germany and other European Community countries. The term universal bank is attributed to Deutsche Bank, and refers to a fully integrated conglomerate that engages in such services as deposit-taking, lending, investment banking, and insurance. In addition, universal banks are allowed to own equity holdings in commercial and industrial firms.

A comparison with the Japanese *keiretsu*, powerful commercial and financial organizations, suggests a possible future scenario for the banking industry as the financial supermarket trend continues to develop. *Keiretsu* (literally, business affiliations) binds together companies through such strategies as cross-ownership of a small block of shares (e.g., up to 5 percent of stock), interlocking directorships, and long-term business relationships. Descendants of the pre-World War II *zaibatsu*,* they include such giants as Mitsubishi, Mitsui, and Sumitomo. The *keiretsu* combine commercial, industrial, and financial activity and represent a major force in the Japanese economy. While there is nothing comparable in the United States, there are giant financial institutions that dominate significant markets. All but a few of the 100 largest mortgage-banking companies are controlled by commercial banks. Factoring is dominated by commercial banks. As the homogenization of financial intermediaries continues, we will see the emergence of giant concerns, each offering the gamut of financial services. And if bank holding company powers expand to include nonfinancial products, the new entities will, in many respects, resemble the *keiretsu* or the universal banks. Figure 3.2 illustrates a simplified structure of a bank holding company organization. If nonfinancial services were to be approved in the years ahead, they would become another important addition to this organizational structure.

FOREIGN BANKS IN THE UNITED STATES

A number of foreign banks operate in the United States alongside the domestic ones. In September 1995 there were 274 foreign banks in the United States, operating through various types of international banking offices and controlling approximately 26 percent of U.S. banking assets. These banks engage in a wide variety of activities in addition to commercial banking. For example, they provide investment-banking services, venture-capital financing, and real-estate development.

The presence of foreign banks in the United States is generally attributed to a variety of factors. One consideration prompting foreign banks to establish U.S. offices was the need to facilitate foreign trade and the flow of long-term investment between the United States and other countries. Another motive was to follow their domestic clients to the United States or to extend to the corporate headquarters of U.S. multinationals the relationship these banks had established

---

*Family-controlled holding companies that dominated the pre–World War II Japanese economy. The Japanese do not allow holding company structures for fear of re-creating the *zaibatsu*.

Figure 3.2
Bank Holding Company Organization

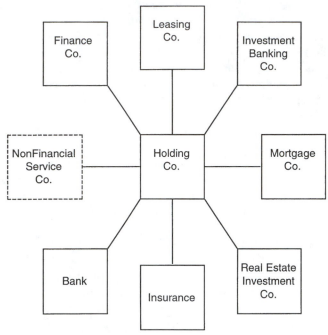

Source: Prepared by the author.

at home with the U.S. companies' local subsidiaries and affiliates. Other reasons for the presence of foreign banks include developing a retail banking business; gaining access to the largest money and capital market in the world; assuming the settling, or clearing, of all dollar transactions involving the foreign banks and their non-U.S. customers; and engaging in securities trading and under-writing activities.

Foreign banks may operate in the United States—and U.S. banks may operate abroad—under a variety of organizational forms. These include the representative office, the agency, the branch, the subsidiary, and the investment company. The form chosen is often dictated by what state banking laws permit.

The *representative office* is not really a bank, but simply an office that assists clients of the parent bank in doing business in the United States and solicits U.S. customers for the parent bank. It does not conduct any actual bank operations. This is the most restrictive form of foreign bank organization.

An *agency* can engage in limited banking activity—it can make local loans, but it cannot accept deposits from U.S. residents. The agency is well suited to foreign banks whose U.S. operations consist largely of trade financing, money-market operations, and wholesale banking. New York permits formation of *investment companies* by foreign banks; these function much as agencies do.

Foreign banks operating in the United States enjoy the most flexibility when they are permitted by state laws to establish *branches*. Branches may offer the full range of banking services. Like branches of domestic banks, they function as direct extensions of their home offices. Thus, while the loan limit for a subsidiary is based on its own capitalization, the limit for a branch is based on the broader capital base of the home office in the foreign country. Foreign-bank branches must comply with the same regulations as domestic branches.

Some states allow foreign banks to own *subsidiaries* in the United States. These are established banks wholly or partly owned by foreign banks or by foreign bank holding companies. Subsidiaries offer the full spectrum of banking services. Foreign banks are subject to the same regulations and procedures as domestic banks in creating or acquiring subsidiaries. One form of subsidiary is the *Edge Act corporation*. The Edge Act privilege was extended to foreign banks by the International Banking Act of 1978. Edge Act corporations have their origin in a 1919 amendment to the Federal Reserve Act, proposed by Senator Walter E. Edge of New Jersey, that expanded the original provisions of the act to allow the federal chartering of subsidiaries for the purpose of engaging in international or foreign banking. Edge Act corporations generally require a minimum capital investment of $2 million and have relatively broad powers to conduct international business. They are permitted to open branch offices, and a number of Edge Act corporations have offices in various cities. Major disadvantages of an Edge Act corporation, compared with an agency, are the smaller size of its loans (due to its smaller capital base, compared with that of the agency's parent bank) and the limitation of domestic lending ability to international or foreign business transactions. In addition to activities ordinarily considered incidental to international financing, an Edge Act corporation may invest in foreign financial organizations—such as foreign banks, finance companies, and leasing firms—and maintain branches abroad.

The geographic pattern of foreign banking activity in the United States has been determined largely by the particular types of activity in which the foreign banks have wished to engage and by the regulatory climate, both national and within individual states. Foreign banks wishing primarily to finance foreign trade or to participate in the U.S. money and capital markets have located in New York City and in some other major money centers, including other East Coast cities, Chicago, and San Francisco. New York City has been the chief site of foreign banking activity in the United States because of its central role in the U.S. money and capital markets. In addition, East Coast cities have traditionally provided international services more extensively than inland banks, and thus have attracted more foreign banks.

The regulatory climate also has played a significant role in the growth of foreign banks in the United States. Chartering of foreign banking institutions prior to the enactment of the International Banking Act of 1978 (IBA) was the sole prerogative of individual states. Although since enactment of the IBA foreign banks can operate under a national charter, state laws still determine the scope and organizational form of operation (for instance, Florida prohibits establishment of foreign branches). The principal states with foreign banks are New York and California. The laws of the state of New York allow foreign banks from reciprocating countries to accept both domestic and foreign-owned deposits and to make the same types of loans that domestic banks make. Since 1973 Illinois has allowed full-service branches of foreign banks in downtown Chicago if reciprocity is granted.

The absence of any federal legislation prior to 1978 contributed significantly to the growth in the number of foreign banks and in their assets in the United States. While the McFadden Act of 1927 did not allow domestic banks to engage in interstate banking, foreign banks were able to establish banking facilities across state lines. Moreover, they were permitted to underwrite and sell stocks in the United States, an activity prohibited to domestic banks by the Banking Act of 1933. Last, foreign banks were not required to join the Federal Reserve System. As a result, their reserve costs were much lower than those of domestic banks.

Armed with these competitive advantages, foreign banks flourished in some areas, competing successfully for domestic customers for such services as deposit holding and loan making. The International Banking Act of 1978 established specific federal regulation of foreign banks and attempted to limit inequities with domestic banks. This law required each foreign bank to select one state as its ''home state'' and subjected it, in terms of branching, to the same treatment as a U.S. bank chartered in that state. The act also extended to foreign banks most regulations that applied to domestic banks. A grandfather clause exempted foreign banks' existing out-of-state operations from the act's legal restrictions. A further effort to provide equal treatment of domestic and foreign banks came in 1980 with the DIDMCA, which subjected the domestic deposits of foreign banks to reserve requirements. More recently, the Riegle-Neal Interstate Banking and Branching Efficiency Act of 1994 subjected the U.S. subsidiaries of foreign banks to the same interstate branching conditions applying to U.S. banks.

The Foreign Bank Supervision Enhancement Act (FBSEA) of 1991 amended the IBA and imposed additional restrictions on foreign banks in response to the debacle of the Bank of Credit and Commerce International (BCCI). Established in 1972 by a Pakistani financier with support from Gulf Arab investors, BCCI was controlled by a Luxembourg holding company, with a principal operating subsidiary based in Grand Cayman. By 1991 it had branches in 69 countries with over $20 billion in deposits, and owned—through fronts—several U.S. banks, including First American Bancshares of Washington, D.C. In a coordinated sweep by regulators in several major countries, BCCI was closed down in 1991, allegedly for fraud and corruption.

It was against this background that FBSEA was enacted. The law mandates that in addition to any other approval or license required under state or federal law, foreign banks must obtain the prior approval of the Federal Reserve Board to establish banking offices in the United States. The Fed may withhold approval unless the bank's worldwide operations are subject to comprehensive supervision or regulation in its home country. Foreign banks must also seek the Federal Reserve's approval before acquiring more than 5 percent of the voting shares of a U.S. bank or bank holding company. No foreign bank can accept retail deposit accounts under $100,000 unless it secures FDIC insurance coverage. The Board can terminate the operations of a foreign bank in the United States if it violates U.S. laws, sound banking practices, or the public interest. The various provisions of FBSEA make it much less attractive for foreign banks to initiate or expand their operations in this country.

SUGGESTED REFERENCES

Berger, A., W. Hunter, and S. Timme. "The Efficiency of Financial Institutions." *Journal of Banking and Finance* 17 (1993): 221–49.

Berlin, Mitchell. "Banking Reform: An Overview of the Restructuring Debate." Federal Reserve Bank of Philadelphia, *Business Review*, July–August 1988, pp. 3–14.

Boyd, John, Stanley Graham, and Shawn Hewitt. "Bank Holding Company Mergers with Nonbank Financial Institutions: Effects on the Risk of Failure." *Journal of Banking and Finance*, February 1993, pp. 43–64.

Cole, Rebel A., and Jeffery W. Gunther. "FIMS: A New Monitoring System for Banking Institutions." *Federal Reserve Bulletin*, January 1995, pp. 1–15.

Federal Reserve Bank of Kansas City. *Banking Regulation*. 3rd ed. Kansas City, Mo.: Federal Reserve Bank, 1990.

Garcia, Gillian, et al. "The Garn–St. Germain Depository Institutions Act." Federal Reserve Bank of Chicago, *Economic Perspectives*, March/April 1983, pp. 6–12.

Hannan, Timothy, and Stephen Rhoades. "Future U.S. Banking Structure: 1990–2010." *The Antitrust Bulletin*, Fall 1992, 737–98.

Kohn, Meir. *Financial Institutions and Markets*. New York: McGraw-Hill, 1994.

Lemieux, Catherine. "FDICIA: Where Did It Come from and Where Will It Take Us?" Federal Reserve Bank of Kansas City, *Financial Industry Perspectives*, November 1993, pp. 1–14.

Rose, Peter. *The Changing Structure of American Banking*. New York: Columbia University Press, 1987.

Savage, Donald. "Interstate Banking: A Status Report." *Federal Reserve Bulletin*, December 1993, pp. 1075–89.

Part II

Formation of a Bank and Funds Gathering

Chapter 4

Establishment and Management of a Bank

A bank's subjection to regulatory control actually begins before its formal establishment and commencement of operations. The chartering process, whether at the state or the federal level, requires bank organizers to comply with legal and regulatory prescriptions. This chapter will review the process of forming a bank and describe the key characteristics of a bank's organizational structure. As a quasi-public institution, a bank must function within the constraints set by the many regulations affecting the banking industry. The organizational structure of a bank is in part affected by this regulatory environment. However, within these constraints there is considerable room for diversity of organization and of management policy that reflects the differing personalities and objectives of individual management teams.

ESTABLISHING A COMMERCIAL BANK

Establishing a commercial bank is a process that is considerably more involved than establishing any other type of business. Because of the serious effects attendant on bank failure, bank charter applications undergo close scrutiny to prevent the establishment of potentially weak or poorly managed banks. Bank failures not only injure individual depositors; they also affect the economic climate of their respective communities. One failure may spark a panic, spurring customers of other banks to withdraw their deposits. Under the fractional reserve system, in which total deposits exceed available reserves, excessive withdrawals can exert undue pressure on a bank having immediately to convert all its deposits into cash. In addition, large-scale withdrawal of deposits from banks reduces the nation's money supply, and this may retard economic activity.

A variety of motives may explain the interest in starting a new bank. The settlement of new territories has historically accounted for much bank formation in the United States, and population growth and shifts continue to create a need for new banks in individual communities. In addition, there may be dissatisfaction with existing bank services or the desire for more sources of loans to promote real estate and business development. More personal motives for wishing to be involved in the founding of a bank include the desire to share in expected earnings and the prestige associated with bank ownership. Bank organizers are usually businessmen interested in their community's economic development and possessing considerable financial and personal standing.

Filing of the Application and Preliminary Approval

Since the procedures for organizing banks under national laws are uniform throughout the United States, they can serve as the basis for a discussion of bank chartering in general. The National Bank Act stipulates that five or more individuals may apply for a national bank charter. The application must be submitted to the Regional Administrator of National Banks, the officer in charge of the field office of the Comptroller of the Currency in the region where the bank is to be established. The form is entitled ''Application to Charter a National Bank.'' It must indicate the proposed name of the bank, which should not duplicate that of another bank in the community and, moreover, should include the word ''national'' or the initials N.A. (for national association). Other information requested includes the location of the bank and its market area; existence of competing banks and financial institutions in that area; initial equity capital funds, which must be in excess of the minimum required, net of organizational expenses; pro forma financial statements for the first few years of operation; experience and integrity of the proposed directors and executive management; and other details, such as whether the bank will be operating out of rented or owned premises, and the expenditures for furniture, fixtures, and equipment. In order to supply this information, the bank organizers must make an economic or market survey of the area, estimate costs involved in securing and equipping a bank site, and obtain legal advice on a variety of matters.

The information requested serves to assure the Comptroller of the Currency that the applicants possess adequate capital, experience, and managerial ability to conduct banking operations safely and profitably. However, another factor enters into the chartering decision. The applicants must demonstrate that their community needs a new bank and that its entry into the area will not pose a threat to existing banks. This process ensures not only the viability of the individual bank but also the preservation of a climate of stability for the banking industry as a whole.

Upon receipt of the application, the Regional Administrator's office—through a national bank examiner—will conduct a thorough field investigation to verify and/or supplement the material submitted by the organizers and proposed directors (the organizing group). The resulting field investigation report, the application, and all supporting data become part of a public file (except for material deemed confidential). Members of the public have an opportunity to comment on the application during the 21 days following the publication by the organizers of the Regional Administrator's notice that the application has been accepted for filing. Besides making written comments, individuals may challenge the legality of an application by requesting a hearing, which may be granted by the Regional Administrator if it is determined that such a hearing would be beneficial to the decision-making process.

After review of all materials submitted by the applicants, interested members of the public, and office staff, the Regional Administrator may—under delegated authority—act on the case and grant preliminary approval for the proposed bank. It is important to note that occasionally the Regional Administrator's office may grant a preliminary approval and yet disapprove the participation of certain individuals (among those who submitted the application) as directors, officers, or shareholders of the bank, or altogether bar any affiliation of such individuals with the bank. A preliminary approval in essence authorizes the organizing group to take certain procedural actions that will lead, within 18 months, to final approval of the bank (a charter) and commencement of operations. These actions include establishing the bank as a body corporate with directors, articles of association, and bylaws.

Establishing the Bank as a Body Corporate and Securing a Charter

The process of establishing the bank as a body corporate is initiated through the filing with the Regional Administrator of two forms, the articles of association and the organization certificate. The articles of association contain information on the organization of the bank, largely drawn from the preliminary application papers. The organization certificate states the purpose of the organization; lists particulars regarding the bank's name, location, and capital stock; and states the net worth of shareholders and number of shares held by each. Acceptance of the articles of association and organization certificate by the Regional Administrator establishes the bank's corporate existence for the purpose of entering into contracts and performing all necessary actions other than the business of banking. The organizing group then meets to fix the number of interim directors and to elect to these positions the individuals approved by the Regional Administrator in the letter of preliminary approval. These interim directors are to serve until the bank's stock is sold and the stockholders are convened to elect the bank's board. In their first meeting the interim directors appoint the board's interim chairman, adopt bylaws, adopt a form of stock certificate, authorize the solicitation of stock subscriptions, designate an insured bank as depository of stock subscription funds, and authorize the purchase of fidelity insurance to cover the funds that will be raised from the sale of capital stock. Documents covering these items and the minutes of the meetings of the organizers and the interim board are forwarded to the Regional Administrator, in compliance with procedural requirements.

If they were not approved in the letter of preliminary approval, the interim board proceeds at this time to select the bank's executive officers: president, cashier, and senior officers. Their appointment must be approved by the office of the Regional Administrator after proper inquiry into the professional histories and backgrounds of these individuals. With at least the president in place, and an offering circular approved by the Regional Administrator, the organizing bank may proceed to solicit subscription offers for stock in the bank (see Figure 4.1). The selling price of the stock will be above its par value, so as to provide the bank with the necessary capital and an amount of surplus out of which organizational expenses are paid, even though, for regulatory purposes, they appear as charges to the undivided profits account (see Table 4.1). As the stock is being sold, the proceeds are deposited in an escrow account with a previously designated bank, to the credit of the organizing bank. The bank serving as an escrow agent will inform the Regional Administrator of the amount of money received and, under the provisions of the escrow agreement, will purchase government securities and indicate their maturities. The funds in escrow can be released to the interim board only after authorization of the Regional Administrator to the escrow bank. Some of the reasons for which releases can be made include the purchasing of fixed assets, payment of salaries, and other expenses necessary for preparing the organizing bank to conduct business.

Once the sale of capital stock has been completed and a list of shareholders has been submitted to—and approved by—the Regional Administrator, the first shareholders' meeting will be called. The agenda of this meeting will include the election of a board of directors consisting of the individuals set out in the offering circular and approved by the Regional Administrator; approval of all organizational expenses and commitments made, which are to be reimbursed or paid from the capital funds; and ratification of the articles of association, the organization certificate, and all the official acts of the organizers, interim directors, and officers. Following the shareholders' meeting, the board will convene to take such actions as executing the oath of national bank directors (that they will "diligently and honestly administer the affairs" of the bank), appointing all executive officers (who must have been approved by the Regional Administrator), and ratifying the bylaws. Once documents of the above actions and minutes of meetings are submitted to the Regional Administrator, the board and executive management should draft and adopt the policies of the bank (on loans, investments, and funds management), its organizational chart and job descriptions, internal control safeguards, and security devices.

When all preparations for opening are complete, a national bank examiner will be scheduled to visit the bank to conduct a preopening audit and to ascertain whether satisfactory operational procedures and policies have been established. Upon completion of this visit, the examiner will meet with the management to apprise it of his findings and the need for any corrective action. If the results

Figure 4.1
Sample Cover of Offering Circular

OFFERING CIRCULAR
FIRST BANK OF HIALEAH GARDENS, NATIONAL ASSOCIATION
(In Organization)

8200 N.W. 103rd Street
Hialeah Gardens, Florida 33016
(305) 528-2800

$2,600,000
COMMON STOCK

260,000 Shares

$5 Per Share - Par Value
$10 Per Share - Offering Price

THE MERITS OF THESE SECURITIES HAVE NOT BEEN PASSED UPON BY THE COMPTROLLER OF THE CURRENCY NOR HAS THE COMPTROLLER OF THE CURRENCY PASSED UPON THE ACCURACY OR ADEQUACY OF THE OFFERING CIRCULAR.

NO AGENT OR OFFICER OF THE BANK OR ANY OTHER PERSON HAS BEEN AUTHORIZED TO GIVE ANY INFORMATION OR TO MAKE ANY REPRESENTATIONS OTHER THAN THOSE CONTAINED IN THE OFFERING CIRCULAR, AND IF GIVEN OR MADE, SUCH INFORMATION AND REPRESENTATIONS SHOULD NOT BE RELIED UPON AS HAVING BEEN AUTHORIZED BY THE BANK.

THE ISSUANCE OF THE STOCK OFFERED HEREBY IS SUBJECT TO THE APPROVAL OF THE COMPTROLLER OF THE CURRENCY. THE BANK RESERVES THE RIGHT TO CANCEL ACCEPTED SUBSCRIPTION OFFERS AT THE DIRECTION OF THE COMPTROLLER OF THE CURRENCY UNTIL THE DATE THE BANK COMMENCES OPERATIONS. IF, FOR ANY REASON, THE BANK DOES NOT OPEN FOR BUSINESS OR IF FUNDS ARE RETURNED TO SUBSCRIBERS, ALL OF THE CASH PAID BY THE SUBSCRIBERS FOR THEIR SHARES WILL BE RETURNED, PLUS OR MINUS ANY PROFITS OR LOSSES INCURRED THROUGH INVESTMENT OF SUCH FUNDS IN UNITED STATES GOVERNMENT SECURITIES. ANY OTHER COSTS OR EXPENSES WILL BE BORNE BY THE ORGANIZERS.

	Price to Public	(1) Underwriting Commissions	(2) Expenses of the Offering	(3) Proceeds to Bank
Per Unit	$ 10.00	$-0-	$ .04	$ 9.96
Total	$ 2,600,000.00	$-0-	$ 10,400.00	$ 2,589,600.00

(1) These securities will be sold by the Organizers, and Directors of the Bank, who will receive no commission in connection with such sales, but who will be reimbursed for expenses, if any, in connection with such sales. The Bank has not employed, nor does it intend to employ, any professional underwriter, brokers or salespersons in connection with this Offering.

(2) All expenses consist solely of legal, accounting, printing, mailing, filing and similar expenses. Expenses of the Offering Circular are subject to approval by the Comptroller of the Currency before they are reimbursed to the Organizers.

(3) Does not take into account expenses incurred by the Organizers in obtaining the charter ("Organizational Expenses"), which Organizational Expenses will he reimbursed to the Organizers, subject to approval by the Comptroller of the Currency.

The Effective Date of this Offering Circular is February 9, 1983.

Source: Reprinted by permission of First Bank of Hialeah Gardens, N.A.

Table 4.1
Sample Pro Forma Statement of Capitalization, First Bank of Hialeah Gardens, N.A. (in organization)

Equity Capital		Pro Forma Capitalization
Common stock (par value $5.00 per share)		
260,000 shares authorized		
260,000 shares issued and outstanding		$1,300,000
Surplus[1]		1,289,600
Deficit accumulated during developmental stage[2]		
Organizational and preoperating expenses	($209,000)	
Less: Estimated investment income[3]	25,000	(184,000)
Total Equity Capital		$2,405,600

[1]Expenses of the offering circular are charged to surplus.

[2]Organizational and preoperating expenses, if approved by the Comptroller of the Currency, are charged to undivided profits when the bank opens for business.

[3]Subscription funds are held in escrow and invested in U.S. government securities. Income from these investments is estimated to be $25,000.

Source: Offering Circular, First Bank of Hialeah Gardens, N.A. (February 25, 1983), p. 5. Reprinted by permission of First Bank of Hialeah Gardens.

of the examination are satisfactory, the bank must proceed to subscribe to stock of the district Federal Reserve bank and submit evidence that it has paid an amount equal to 3 percent of its capital stock and surplus. This and other information, including the definite date for opening the bank, constitute the final preopening documentation submitted to the Regional Administrator.

Once all the required steps of the organizational phase have been completed, the Regional Administrator will submit to the Comptroller of the Currency the bank's complete file with a recommendation that a "certificate of authority to commence business" be issued (banks commonly refer to it as the "charter"). The Comptroller of the Currency will notify the bank accordingly, and mail the charter. At the time the bank commences business, FDIC insurance is immediately in effect, as is Federal Reserve membership.

After the bank opens for business, it is required to advise the Comptroller of the Currency of the date it commenced business as a national bank and of the amount of total deposits it took that first day. It is also required to issue its stockholders stock certificates. Another postcommencement requirement for the bank is to publish its new charter in a local newspaper at least once each week for nine consecutive weeks and return to the Comptroller of the Currency an affidavit to this effect, signed by the newspaper's publisher. Once issued, a charter is perpetual unless it is terminated by action of the bank's owners (dissolution) or a regulatory body (as in cases of insolvency or violation of law).

Proposed charters may be rejected, usually because the community need is not considered great enough, the capital base is deemed inadequate, or the applicants are judged unsatisfactory with respect to financial standing or character. In addition, many prospective bank organizers are discouraged at an early stage from pursuing their application. Applications unsuccessful at the national level may be submitted to state chartering bodies, but the latter use virtually identical criteria in judging the proposed new bank.

ORGANIZATIONAL STRUCTURE OF A BANK

A bank, like an institution, mobilizes human resources for a defined purpose. The organizational structure of a bank reflects the specific arrangements that have been devised to accomplish desired goals. This structure consists of three main elements: the shareholders, who have invested their capital in the bank in hopes of realizing a profitable return; the board of directors, which is responsible for setting bank policy and bears ultimate responsibility for the bank's performance; and management, which carries out the policies set by the board and conducts actual bank operations. The roles of each of these groups will be discussed in the following sections.

Shareholders

A bank's stock may be distributed in a number of ways. It may be owned by a single individual or it may be a closely held corporation with a small number of shareholders. In the latter case the shareholders may consist solely of the board of directors as a matter of policy. Other banks seek broad-based ownership through public sale of stock in small lots. The distribution of a bank's stock is one aspect of a bank's character. Closely held corporations are more directly related to the interests of a small group of people. Banks with large and diverse groups of shareholders are more independent in character, and change of ownership occurs as a matter of course. When directors must answer to large numbers of shareholders, they are more likely to be responsive to community needs and to adopt a public-service stance. The bank issues annual reports to its shareholders to inform them of the scope and profitability of bank activities.

Board of Directors

At the top of the bank's organizational chart is the board of directors. As noted above, this group sets policy for the bank, oversees its management, and is liable for the bank's activities and performance.

By law, national banks and state banks that are members of the Federal Reserve System must have at least 5, and no more than 25, board members. At least two-thirds of them must have resided for at least a year in the state in which the bank is located or within 100 miles of its main office, and must continue such residence during their term of office. These directors are elected to one-year terms by the shareholders. A majority of the directors must be U.S. citizens. Each director is required to own at least $1,000 worth of capital stock in the bank. Requirements for directors of state nonmember banks vary somewhat, but for the most part are similar to the federal requirements.

Although federal laws prohibit interlocking directorates among banks, the same individual may be a director of a bank and of another type of business as long as no conflict of interest occurs. Such a conflict would exist, for instance, if the other business is a competing financial institution. Thus the same individual would not be expected to serve as director of a bank and of a savings and loan association.

Duties and Responsibilities

The duties and responsibilities of the directors are many. They are in part determined by the directors' fiduciary responsibility to the bank's shareholders and customers and by banking statutes. Broadly speaking, they may be categorized as follows: setting bank objectives, formulating bank policies, selecting management, creating committees, providing supervision and counsel, and developing business for the bank.

Setting Bank Objectives. One function of the board of directors is to chart the bank's course, and this is generally done by setting goals and objectives toward which bank activities are directed. Goals and objectives are an integral part of any successful planning effort. Some of these goals are derived from projected financial statements that result from strategic planning. For example, a goal might be to capture a certain share of the local market (for instance, to hold 8 percent of a community's deposits) or to attain a target rate of return on assets or equity capital by a certain time.

More specific objectives are formulated to provide targets for particular areas of bank activity. Thus the board might decide that certain types of loans are in the bank's best interest, and set objectives in this regard that become the basis for the loan department's planning. Progress toward these objectives is continually monitored. In addition, such objectives are adjusted or revised as changing economic or market conditions warrant. Many boards set short-, intermediate-, and long-term profit objectives. Setting these objectives involves relying on a detailed plan that establishes targets for each type of activity in which the bank engages. The board receives regular reports on the profit performance of all bank activities and uses them to monitor progress toward the bank's overall goals.

It is useful for the organization to have its goals communicated briefly and specifically to the bank's entire staff. Besides building moral and a sense of teamwork among bank employees, such goals improve coordination and efficiency of bank activity because all bank operations are directed toward the goals.

Formulating Policies. To guide management in its progress toward defined goals and objectives, the board of directors formulates bank policies. These provide the framework for the specific types of activity that are to be undertaken. Liquidity and reserve levels, types of investment to pursue, kinds of loans to solicit, the establishment of branches, and the introduction of automation are matters of policy that allow managers to direct their efforts in coordinated fashion toward the stated objectives. Policies are also set regarding public relations, customer relations, and marketing strategies. In order not to straitjacket management, policies must be flexible and subject to periodic review and adjustment. Personnel policies represent a specific category of policy issues governing salaries and benefits, vacations and leaves, and other matters relating to bank staff.

Policies are not to be confused with rules. A rule is a statement that calls for a specific and definitive course of action in a given situation. For example, in the opening of a new account the officer is instructed to verify the identity of the depositor by requesting two pieces of identification, such as driver's license, current passport, and credit card. Another example would be the specific provisions that govern the different types of deposits (e.g., minimum balance requirement and fees).

Objectives, policies, and rules must be communicated to all bank employees. A major instrument for dispensing this information is the bank manual. In the case of rules, these would be classified under different headings, for each area of banking activity, such as tellers, commercial loan officers, trust officers, and auditors. Meetings, at the various administrative levels, constitute another important vehicle for dispensing information.

Selecting Management. Although one of a few board members may wear the dual hats of board member and senior bank officer, the directors do not run the bank. They recruit and hire officers and managers who are skilled in bank operations. Competition for managerial talent in banking is keen, and the board must keep salaries and benefits competitive in order to attract high-caliber management personnel.

Creating Committees. Most boards create committees that are charged with overseeing specific areas of bank operations. Committees serve several purposes. By focusing the ongoing attention of a few directors on a specific area of concern, they allow the board to stay in closer touch with a bank's diverse activities. They provide an excellent means of tapping the specialized skills and experiences of individual directors. In larger banks, committees help coordinate the activities of the different bank departments. Committees also serve the public interest because they provide the safety of group decision making in the handling of the deposits entrusted to the bank.

The most common standing committees are listed below. In addition, ad hoc committees may be formed to oversee specific, short-term matters, such as moving to a new building.

—Executive Committee. Decides on issues requiring action between board meetings; conducts studies and reports findings to the board

—Loan Committee. Ensures that the bank's loan policies are being carried out appropriately. Reviews interest rates, types, and amounts of loans to be made; passes on individual loans above a specified amount

—Investment Committee. Ensures that the bank's investment policies are being complied with; decides on types of investments and amounts to be placed in each

—Trust Committee. Oversees administration of the trust department and investment of trust funds. Large banks may have a separate committee for each of these functions

—Audit Committee. Conducts periodic unannounced audits similar to bank examinations. These may be conducted either by the members of this committee or by a hired accounting firm

—Salary and Employee Relations Committee. Reviews salaries and employee benefits, ensuring that they are competitive and otherwise appropriate.

Providing Supervision and Counsel. Although boards of directors vary considerably in terms of their direct involvement in bank activities, all are responsible for seeing that their bank is run in a sound and profitable manner, and is in compliance with the many regulatory requirements to which banks are subject. This supervisory function may be carried out, for instance, through periodic review of the loan and investment portfolios to ensure that they conform to bank policies in these areas. In addition, the directors stand ready to provide counsel to the bank's managers in many areas. Since bank directors are usually individuals with substantial business interests or high professional standing, and possess wide community contacts, they have many kinds of knowledge that will be valuable to the bank's managers. For example, a director's extensive knowledge of a particular industry may be useful to loan officers in the extension of credit to companies in that industry.

Developing Business. Again, because of their community contacts and standing, a board of directors drawn from a cross section of business and professional fields is in a good position to attract deposits and loan customers to the bank. Some boards set specific objectives in this regard for each member. In addition, directors are expected, in their other activities, to act as public relations agents for the bank.

Having reviewed the duties and responsibilities of bank directors, we may now look into their legal liabilities.

Liabilities

Bank directors are personally liable for a bank's operations under both criminal and common law. Thus, they may face prosecution under criminal law for participation in, assent to, or knowledge of bank activities that violate statutory requirements and prohibitions. Such legal restrictions include bans on falsification of records and entries, on loans to bank examiners or loans of trust funds to directors, and on political contributions. Theft or fraud by bank employees and misrepresentation of FDIC coverage are among criminal violations for which directors may be held liable. In addition, under common law they are liable for negligence if they fail to exercise ordinary care and prudence in overseeing the bank's activities.

Clearly, bank directorship is not a role to be undertaken lightly. In order to function adequately, a director must learn the rules and regulations under which banks operate, and must participate actively, so as to be aware of actual bank procedures and operations. Ignorance of bank activities is not accepted as a defense against a charge of negligence. Once one has decided to accept the challenge of bank directorship, with its responsibilities and liabilities, specific steps can be taken to minimize the risk involved. First, the directors establish procedures to ensure that they are receiving adequate information about bank activities. This is one purpose of internal auditing and ongoing supervision. Second, the risk can be transferred through the purchase of liability insurance to cover losses from criminal acts, burglary, theft, forgery, and errors. Because of its coverage of these and other risks involved in bank activity, this type of policy is frequently referred to as a blanket bond.

Management

The third component of a bank's organizational structure is the management team headed by the bank's senior executive officers. It is the job of management to carry out the policies set by the board of directors and to conduct the bank's day-to-day operations. However, policy is not simply handed down by the board of directors. In most banks management proposes policy. These recommendations are discussed, perhaps modified, and ratified by the board. Thus policy emerges from a dynamic interaction between senior management and the board of directors.

The management team of a bank is usually headed by the chairman of the board of directors, the president, and other officers. This group is the primary liaison between the bank's employees and the board. These individuals provide executive leadership for the bank. The chairman of the board is often the chief executive officer of the bank. Through this combined position he is responsible for harnessing the energies of the board of directors in the best interests of the bank. He is active in civic affairs and his stature in the community builds goodwill for the bank.

The president is the administrative head of the bank. In cases where the board chairman is not also a bank officer, he is the bank's chief executive officer. His duties are of two basic types: representing the bank in the community and overseeing bank operations. Usually one or the other of these roles is emphasized. Thus one bank president may spend much time developing business and goodwill for the bank, while another may devote most of his time to internal operations and planning. The latter case is more typical of smaller banks.

In the performance of his tasks the president is assisted by a number of officers. One of these, the cashier, is a traditional bank officer who, in small banks, works directly under the president and oversees the bank's internal operations. Once the board and the president have set bank policy, the cashier assumes responsibility for the actual transactions that implement it. His many functions include overseeing bank funds and investments; signing certificates of stock, cashier's checks, and bank drafts; endorsing notes and drafts to be submitted to other banks for collection; hiring junior staff members; and purchasing.

All banks except very small ones have a comptroller, who oversees the accounting department and makes statistical reports on bank activities to senior management and the board. These reports enable the board to gauge the profitability of bank activities and the soundness of current policies. In addition, the comptroller is responsible for seeing to it that bank operations are conducted as efficiently as possible. For instance, he might recommend increased automation or the elimination of unnecessary procedures. Finally, the comptroller drafts proposed budgets that serve as the basis for final budget adoption by the board.

The auditor has ongoing responsibility for assuring that bank operations are conducted in a manner that is consistent with generally accepted accounting practices, the policies of the bank, and the rules and regulations of supervisory agencies. To prevent or control fraud, the audit staff frequently verifies the bank's cash accounts and security holdings. In addition, it scrutinizes operating procedures to identify inherent weaknesses and enhance internal security. The auditor has the authority to examine every aspect of a bank's operations. This vigilance is designed to protect the bank against waste, misappropriation of funds, and unauthorized manipulation of bank assets. The activities of the auditor are independent of outside audits conducted by supervisory agencies and contracted accounting firms. The auditor reports directly to the board of directors. Any discrepancies found, or any suggestions for improvement are reviewed by the board, which may proceed to take appropriate action.

In branch banking each branch has an administrative head whose title may be manager or vice president. This individual reports to the branch supervisor at the bank's administrative headquarters.

Determinants of Bank Internal Structure

Although all banks possess shareholders, a board of directors, and management, there is important variation among banks in the extent of departmentalization. Organizing managerial functions by departments occurs in all but the smallest banks and serves several functions. Departmentalization means that individuals with particular talents or specialized knowledge can concentrate their efforts in areas where they have the most to offer. It allows banks to provide more complex services and thus to draw customers they could not otherwise attract. It promotes efficiency and growth.

As mentioned, many small banks do not have departments. Larger banks may have separate departments for one or a few major functions while grouping other functions in the hands of a single officer. In other words, departments tend to emerge as a given area of functioning outgrows one individual's capacity to manage it. Since banks range in size from those with fewer than five employees to those with several thousand, there is room for considerable variety in organizational arrangements. In addition, bank organization is affected by such factors as the personalities and abilities of individual managers and the relative scope of various bank activities.

Bank departments may also be organized along line and staff functions. Line functions are the bank's activities that are integral to attaining its objectives, such as lending, investing, accepting deposits, managing trusts, and issuing credit. Staff functions are the activities that support the performance of line functions, such as accounting, control, training, marketing, personnel functions, and building maintenance. In small or medium-size banks there may be a clear-cut division between line and staff activities, while in larger banks, with their more elaborate organizational structures, they may be somewhat intertwined.

The specific nature of a bank's organizational structure is largely determined by three factors: the kinds of markets the bank serves, the bank's size, and the prevailing statutes regarding branching.

The markets in which banks operate vary according to the types of economic activity prevalent in the community the bank serves and the geographic scope of the bank's operations (local, regional, national, or international). Thus, banks in the Detroit area may have departments that specialize in financing the automobile industry, while banks in rural areas may have departments focusing on agribusiness. Such specialized departments accumulate the knowledge to make wiser lending decisions in these areas; they also attract customers who will benefit from such specialization. In addition, banks may create departments according to types of service offered, thus having a trust department, an international department, or a leasing department. Finally, banks that offer specialized financial services on a nationwide basis may divide these departments according to geographic markets.

Size is another important determinant of a bank's organizational structure. As a bank grows, the number of people needed to do its work grows, and the job of coordinating its activities becomes more complex. At some point in a bank's expansion, growth and specialization feed each other. Growth creates the need and the capacity for greater specialization; the creation of specialized departments, in turn, promotes further growth in several ways. Highly talented and specialized managers increase bank productivity and efficiency. Service departments with in-depth knowledge of certain areas of investment or service attract customers whose needs could not be met by a smaller bank with less specialized knowledge. Meanwhile, growth affects the overall organizational structure of a bank. Whereas in a medium-size bank all departments may report directly to the president, in larger banks there may be several levels of administrative officers with broader authority to oversee the diverse areas of the bank's activity. The titles of these officers may range from executive vice president to assistant vice president to differentiate the level of authority. Executive vice presidents normally are in charge of groups or divisions; senior vice presidents, of divisions and/or departments; vice presidents may not necessarily have administrative duties but bear the title in recognition of hard work, diligence, and expertise; assistant vice presidents are young bankers showing great promise in a given area.

If a bank maintains branches, there is a need for some type of control and coordination of the individual branches from the head office. Several reporting methods are practiced. In some cases all branches in a particular geographic area report to a single officer—a regional administrator—at the bank's headquarters. In other cases the bank's smaller branches (as measured by deposits held and loans issued) report to one officer and larger branches report to another. A third reporting mechanism does not involve a single branch coming under the authority of a single individual at the head office. Rather, the branch's loan department reports to the main office's senior loan officer; the branch's deposit officer reports to his or her counterpart at the head office; and so on. In small branch banks each branch manager typically reports directly to the bank president.

A bank's organizational chart identifies the channels of administrative responsibility of the principal officers, the degree and kinds of departmentalization, the bank's committees, and the use of line and staff functions. Figure 4.2 shows a hypothetical organizational chart for a small unit bank. The bank is composed of two departments, loans and operations, each of which is headed by a vice president reporting to the president and chief executive officer of the bank. The loans department covers commercial, consumer, and other loans. The credit and

Figure 4.2
Hypothetical Organizational Chart of a Unit Bank

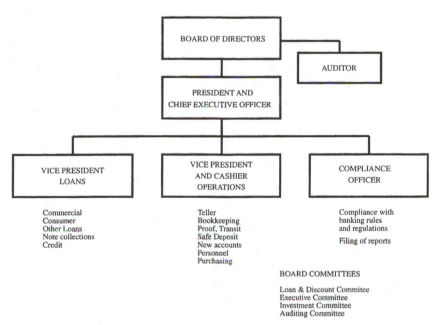

BOARD OF DIRECTORS

AUDITOR

PRESIDENT AND
CHIEF EXECUTIVE OFFICER

| VICE PRESIDENT LOANS | VICE PRESIDENT AND CASHIER OPERATIONS | COMPLIANCE OFFICER |

Commercial
Consumer
Other Loans
Note collections
Credit

Teller
Bookkeeping
Proof, Transit
Safe Deposit
New accounts
Personnel
Purchasing

Compliance with
banking rules
and regulations

Filing of reports

BOARD COMMITTEES

Loan & Discount Commitee
Executive Committee
Investment Committee
Auditing Committee

note collection functions are included under the vice president in charge of loans. Operations are covered by the vice president and cashier. The functions included in this department are many and varied; some are customer-oriented (e.g., tellers, safe deposit, and new accounts), while others are "housekeeping" in nature (e.g., bookkeeping, proof, transit, personnel, and purchasing). It is not uncommon for small banks to have some important tasks performed outside departmental lines. In this bank a designated officer is entrusted with compliance (e.g., filing the reports required by the regulatory and supervisory agencies), and an auditor is assigned the auditing function. The former reports to the president and the latter to the board of directors. Many small banks do not have an auditing department or an auditor; the function is performed annually by a private accounting firm under the supervision of the board. Other functions, though not explicitly identified in the organizational chart of a small bank, may still be provided through designated officers (e.g., the president may be handling bank investments) or the bank's city correspondent (e.g., trust services).

The bank is headed by the president, who is both the chief executive officer and a director. As officer-director the president is the liaison between the management and the board. His main task is to present to the board the various problems that confront the institution, so that it may determine the appropriate course of action and formulate policy.

Another important feature in the organization of this bank is its reliance on

Figure 4.3
Hypothetical Organizational Chart of a Large Branch Bank

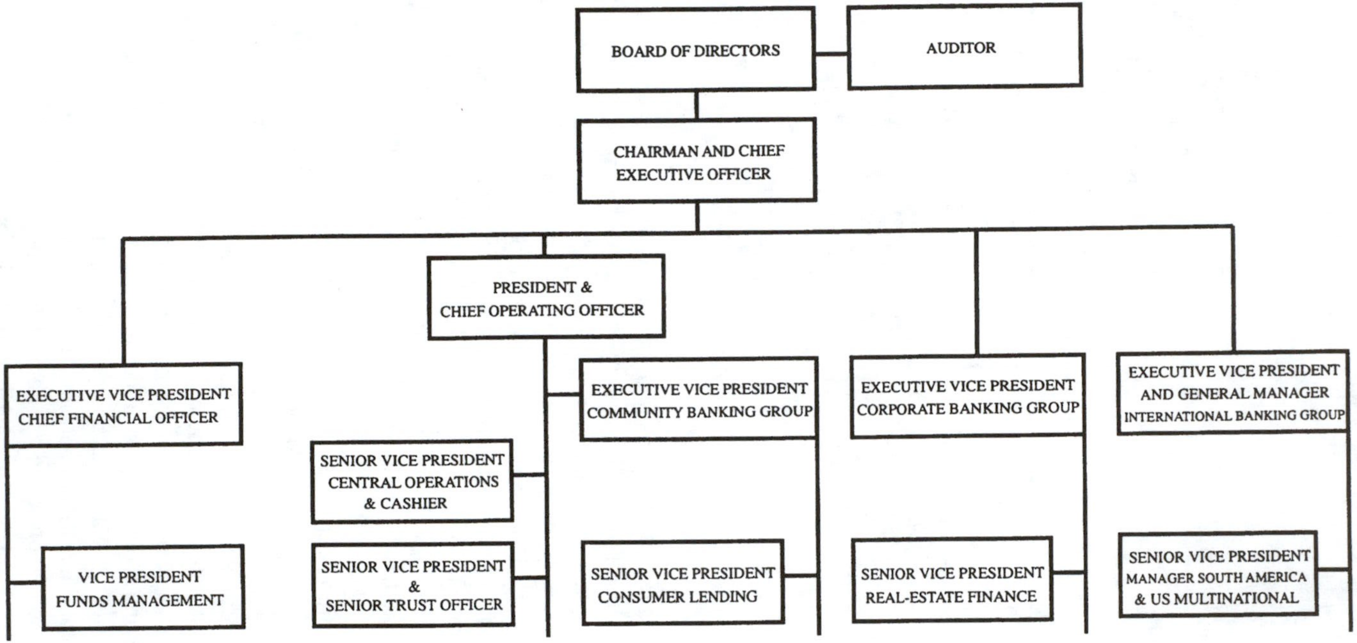

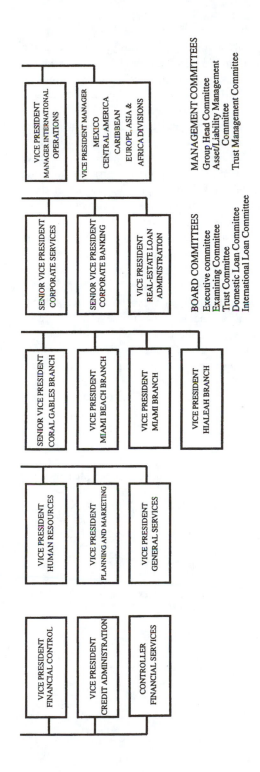

VICE PRESIDENT
MANAGER INTERNATIONAL
OPERATIONS

VICE PRESIDENT MANAGER
MEXICO
CENTRAL AMERICA
CARIBBEAN
EUROPE, ASIA &
AFRICA DIVISIONS

SENIOR VICE PRESIDENT
CORPORATE SERVICES

SENIOR VICE PRESIDENT
CORPORATE BANKING

VICE PRESIDENT
REAL-ESTATE LOAN
ADMINISTRATION

SENIOR VICE PRESIDENT
CORAL GABLES BRANCH

VICE PRESIDENT
MIAMI BEACH BRANCH

VICE PRESIDENT
MIAMI BRANCH

VICE PRESIDENT
HIALEAH BRANCH

VICE PRESIDENT
HUMAN RESOURCES

VICE PRESIDENT
PLANNING AND MARKETING

VICE PRESIDENT
GENERAL SERVICES

VICE PRESIDENT
FINANCIAL CONTROL

VICE PRESIDENT
CREDIT ADMINISTRATION

CONTROLLER
FINANCIAL SERVICES

MANAGEMENT COMMITTEES
Group Head Committee
Asset/Liability Management
Committee
Trust Management Committee

BOARD COMMITTEES
Executive committee
Examining Committee
Trust Committee
Domestic Loan Committee
International Loan Committee

board committees. This feature, typical of many banks, had its origin in the depression years and the need for sound judgment in a period of increased bank failures. As shown in Figure 4.2, the bank has a number of board committees. The duties of these committees are similar to those described earlier in this chapter.

Figure 4.3 is the hypothetical organizational chart for a large branch bank. The differences are quite striking. Since there is more to manage in a bank of this size, there is a wider range of titles and increased delegation of authority to the lower levels of management. All related functions are grouped together under five individuals who make up the bank's top management; one of these individuals (head of auditing) reports directly to the board of directors, while the other four report to the chairman of the board in his additional capacity as the bank's chief executive officer. One of these four individuals is the president, who oversees such basic aspects of the bank as branch banking, operations, marketing, human resources, consumer lending, trust, and general services (such as purchasing and telecommunications). Branch banking is identified by region and the branch executive in charge of it. Each branch executive is responsible for the branches in his region. The bank's other major activities are headed by three executive vice presidents: the chief financial officer, who covers such aspects as investments, asset/liability management, and accounting; an executive vice president covering corporate banking; and one in charge of international banking. In the latter instance the bank's international interests are readily identifiable by the regions covered and also by the seniority of the officers in charge of these regions.

SUGGESTED REFERENCES

Austin, Douglas, and Paul Simoff. *Strategic Planning for Banks.* Rolling Meadows, Ill.: Bankers Publishing Company, 1990.

Baughn, William H., and Charles E. Walker, eds. *The Banker's Handbook.* Rev. ed. Homewood, Ill.: Dow Jones-Irwin, 1978.

Burke, Ronald G. "Bank Directors Face Stronger Role." *Magazine of Bank Administration*, September 1978, pp. 28–31.

Chaps, B. D. "If I Were a Bank Director. . . ." *Magazine of Bank Administration*, September 1977, pp. 18–21.

Comptroller of the Currency. *Duties and Liabilities of Directors of National Banks.* Rev. ed. Washington, D.C.: Comptroller of the Currency, 1987.

Chapter 5

Bank Capital and Its Management

As Chapter 4 indicates, there is considerable variation in bank organizational structure. However diverse their structures may be, however, all banks have two basic objectives: acquiring funds and utilizing them. Utilization of funds is the subject of Part IV; acquisition of funds is examined here and in Chapter 6.

A commercial bank has access to three sources of funds: capital, deposits, and borrowing. Specifically, when a bank sells stock, accepts deposits, or borrows, it is thereby provided with funds that enable it to acquire earning assets—that is, to grant loans and make investments. Interest earned on these loans and investments provides the principal source of earnings out of which the bank meets the operating expenses involved in attracting and servicing deposit accounts and in managing its loans and investments. Residual earnings accrue to the bank's owners.

The sources of bank funds constitute the right-hand side of a bank's balance sheet (the left-hand side shows the assets that a bank owns—that is, the uses to which a bank puts available funds). Unlike other businesses, however, the right-hand side of a bank's balance sheet is made up overwhelmingly of liabilities, and only to a much lesser extent of capital. Indeed, a closer look at the funds sources reveals that banks rely heavily on debt to finance the acquisition of assets, which in fact are the debts of others—the federal government, state and local governments, businesses, and individuals. This situation has earned banks the reputation of being dealers in debts.

Bank reliance upon each of the sources of funds and the extent of such reliance are neither incidental nor a matter of an attitude, such as ''the more funds, the better.'' Instead, it is a matter of policy, developed by the board of directors of each individual bank. Indeed, it is the responsibility of the board to develop policies regarding amounts and types of funds to be acquired.

The nature and characteristics of each of the sources of bank funds, as well as the extent of bank reliance upon each source, are covered here and in chapters 6 and 7. Deposits and borrowing are discussed in chapters 6 and 7, while this chapter concentrates on a bank's capital structure, describing the different types of bank capital, their cost, and their functions.

TYPES OF BANK CAPITAL

Bank capital cannot be treated as a single and homogeneous item. Such consideration might have been possible earlier in the twentieth century, but it is no longer. Management is now confronted with different forms of bank capital and even different ways of raising a given form of it. Choice of the form of capital, of the amounts needed in each form, and of the way of raising it have important implications for bank profitability. It is in this regard that the term *capital management* is often used today. It means concern with the way in which capital, like other bank funds, can best be acquired and managed.

The different types of capital available to banks are generally classified into two broad categories, equity capital and debt capital (capital notes and debentures). Capital notes and debentures, though they are instruments of indebtedness, are frequently used by banks as a permanent part of their capital structure. Many banks with continuing needs for long-term funds follow the practice of re-funding a maturing issue of such debt with the proceeds of a new issue. Such a practice makes capital notes and debentures a permanent addition to a bank's capital structure. From a regulatory perspective, too, debt instruments can qualify as part of a bank's capital base. Regulatory agencies have criteria that these instruments must meet to qualify as bank capital.

To the two sources of capital mentioned above, bankers add a third, reserves on loans and securities. These accounts represent funds earmarked from current earnings to absorb possible loan and securities losses. Thus, although explicitly reported on the asset side of the balance sheet as offsets to a bank's loan and investment portfolios (technically referred to as asset valuation reserves), in practice these accounts are viewed as another source of capital funds. Of these two accounts the more important is the loan-loss reserve account. Since loans constitute the largest single component of bank assets, proportionally more funds are set aside for loan losses than for securities losses. Moreover, because the large majority of securities holdings of banks consists of riskfree federal issues, the size of reserves for securities losses has been relatively insignificant. Thus, our discussion, in addition to equity and debt capital, will include reserves for loan losses.

The relative importance of each of these sources of bank capital for selected years, for all insured commercial banks, is shown in Table 5.1. Banks have depended overwhelmingly on equity capital, which between 1965 and 1995 increased from $28.3 billion to $344 billion. Its dominance over the other two sources is to be expected, since traditionally equity capital has been the major

Table 5.1
Capital Accounts and Reserves for Loan Losses, All Insured Commercial Banks, 1965–95 (millions of dollars)

Year	Total Capital and Reserves	Equity Capital	Capital Notes and Debentures	Reserves for Loan Loses
1965	33,916	28,252	1,653	4,011
1970	48,566	40,475	2,092	5,999
1980	123,684	107,599	6,267	9,818
1990	298,601	219,149	23,920	55,532
1991	311,807	231,699	24,962	55,146
1992	351,611	263,403	33,731	54,477
1993	386,627	296,499	37,372	52,756
1994	404,977	312,093	40,756	52,128
1995	440,684	344,085	43,724	52,875

Note: Details may not add due to rounding.
Source: Federal Deposit Insurance Corporation, *Assets and Liabilities* (Washington, D.C.: FDIC, 1965–76); *Statistics on Banking* (Washington, D.C.: FDIC, selected issues). Data for 1995 are as of September 30, and were derived from *Call Report.*

component of commercial banks' capital accounts. Following in importance, by a significant margin, were reserves for loan losses, which in 1995 amounted to $52.9 billion. Last, debt capital—in the form of capital notes and debentures—stood at $43.7 billion on September 30, 1995. This item reached this level from a mere $1.7 billion in 1965. Each of these sources of bank capital and the factors responsible for its pattern of growth are reviewed in the following sections.

Equity Capital

Equity capital identifies the value of the stockholders' investment in the business. Traditionally equity capital has been decisive in the establishment of a bank and in its functioning as a going concern. It is not a single account but a composite of the following types of accounts: common stock, surplus, undivided profits, and contingency reserves. To the extent that a bank has issued preferred stock, that account, too, would be part of its equity capital. Historically, issuance of common stock has been the dominant method of raising long-term capital. As we saw in Chapter 4, banks sell common stock when they are chartered in order to raise part of the funds needed for operation. After a bank is in operation, it can raise additional capital by issuing more shares of common stock. The total number of shares outstanding, valued at par, determines the value of the capital stock of a bank as listed on its balance sheet. This item, however, must not be interpreted as representing the total amount of capital raised by a bank through sale of its common stock. First, it may include the par value of stock distributed to stockholders in the form of stock dividends. Like other corporations, banks can declare dividends payable in stock, which adds to the total par value of the shares outstanding. Second, bank stock is customarily sold to the public—both at the time of organization and later—at a price in excess of par value, with such excess allocated to the paid-in surplus account.

The surplus account is a permanent part of a bank's equity. What this means is that a bank cannot reduce its surplus account by, for example, making dividend payments or by charging (unless in the process of liquidation) operating losses. Balances in the surplus account are derived from premiums on stock sold over par to the public and from transfers of earnings from the undivided-profits account. These transfers are made upon decision of a bank's board of directors and are intended to augment the surplus account. In fact, since 1935 national banks have been required by federal law to make such transfers until their surplus account is at least equal to the value of the bank's capital stock. This requirement came to replace the double-liability clause carried by all national-bank stock. Prior to 1935, if the capital of a national bank was depleted by losses, each stockholder was personally liable for an amount equal to the par value of the stock he or she held in that bank. Shareholder assessments were thus relied upon to restore the capital of a bank. The purpose of this double-liability clause was to ensure a double margin of safety for depositors. During the depression years this provision proved unworkable, and was therefore abandoned. The requirement that national banks maintain a surplus account that is at least equal to their common-stock capital was then substituted.

"Undivided profits" is the equivalent of the retained-earnings account of nonbank businesses. This is an operating account that includes current as well as accumulated earnings that have not been paid out as dividends, transferred to surplus, or placed in any of the reserve accounts that banks keep for specific purposes. Management has much greater flexibility with the undivided-profits account than with the surplus account. When a national bank is established, it can charge its organizational costs and other expenses approved by the Regional Administrator to undivided profits (see Table 4.1). Since profits do not yet exist, this technically results in a negative undivided-profits account balance, which will be adjusted as earnings develop. Also, management has the freedom to charge losses against the undivided-profits account when the balances of loss-reserve accounts are insufficient to absorb them.

Subject to regulatory guidelines, management can allocate funds from undivided profits to one or more reserve accounts to take care of some contingency or expected event. Amounts so allocated are reported in equity capital either as "reserves for contingencies" or as "other capital reserves." Funds set aside because of a pending lawsuit are an example of a contingency reserve; funds set aside for dividend payments or for the anticipated retirement of preferred stock are examples of capital reserves. The amounts allocated to these and other capital-reserve accounts are not deductible from income taxes.

Some banks raise capital funds through the sale of preferred stock. These stocks are called preferred because they give investors contractual rights that precede those of common stock. A preferred stock gives a prior claim—relative to a common stock—to a bank's earnings and, in the event of liquidation, to its assets. However, since preferred stock is part of equity capital, its claims with regard to earnings and assets are subordinate to deposits and all other indebtedness of the bank. Except on matters involving their own rights and privileges, preferred stockholders have no voting rights. This feature of preferred stock has rendered it especially appealing to banks that are closely held. When ownership of a bank is concentrated in a relatively small group of common stockholders, issuance of preferred stock permits this group to raise the necessary capital while maintaining close control of the bank.

Preferred-stock dividends are generally stated as a percentage of par; for instance, a dividend of 9 percent of par on a preferred stock with a par of $50 would be $4.50 ($50 $\times$ .09). A bank need not pay dividends on preferred stock if it so chooses, so long as it does not pay common-stock dividends. Therefore, nonpayment of the preferred dividend does not increase the probability of default, as is the case if interest on debt is not paid. Preferred stocks may be issued with no maturity (perpetual preferred), and hence they never need to be paid off. However, such issues often contain call provisions that permit a bank to reduce the amount of preferred stock outstanding by purchasing it at a predetermined price.

Until quite recently commercial banks have been reluctant to issue preferred stock because during the depression, distressed banks used this method of raising capital to such an extent that issuance of preferred stock came to be associated with banks in trouble. In the 1930s the Reconstruction Finance Corporation made many purchases of preferred stock in order to bail out banks experiencing financial difficulties. Following economic recovery, much of the preferred stock issued by banks in the 1930s was retired through call or open-market purchase. During the growth period of the 1950s and 1960s, when many banks increased their range of activities to national or international dimensions, they needed to raise additional outside capital to carry out these expansions. Thus there was growing pressure from the banking industry for permission to issue senior capital (debt instruments and preferred stocks). The breakthrough came in the form of a December 1962 ruling from the Office of the Comptroller of the Currency that gave national banks more flexibility in the management of their capital accounts. National banks were allowed to issue preferred stock as part of their capital structure.

Each of the equity capital accounts discussed above and its dollar balances for the period 1965–95 is shown in Table 5.2. The largest single account is undivided profits, which on September 30, 1995, amounted to $164 billion. This amount is net of dividend payments and all transfers of funds to the surplus account. In this respect, that amount is an understatement of the true magnitude and importance of undivided profits as a source of equity capital. Even so, however, a close look at the evolution of undivided profits vis-à-vis that of total equity capital during 1965–95 reveals that the former has been responsible for

Table 5.2
Equity Capital Accounts, All Insured Commercial Banks, 1965–95 (millions of dollars)

Year	Total Equity Capital	Preferred Stock	Common Stock	Surplus	Undivided Profits
1965	28,253	40	8,508	13,465	6,240
1970	39,863	107	11,138	17,461	11,157
1980	107,599	135	21,677	37,776	48,011
1990	219,148	1,673	30,858	92,382	94,235
1991	231,699	1,524	31,259	101,523	98,077
1992	263,403	1,610	32,130	117,352	113,250
1993	296,499	1,523	32,869	126,508	136,727
1994	312,093	1,505	34,617	136,056	140,931
1995	344,085	1,734	35,333	144,014	163,964

Note: Details may not add to totals due to rounding and foreign-currency translation adjustments.
Source: Federal Deposit Insurance Corporation, *Assets and Liabilities* (Washington, D.C.: FDIC, 1965–76); *Statistics on Banking* (Washington, D.C.: FDIC, selected issues). Data for 1995 are as of September 30 and were derived from *Call Report*.

most of the growth of the latter. This means that the banking industry's equity growth came essentially from internally generated funds—a product of profitable bank operations and a high earnings-retention rate for the period under consideration.

Two other sources of equity capital shown in Table 5.2 are preferred and common stocks. As indicated in the table, the contribution of preferred stocks in the equity capital structures of commercial banks has been insignificant. To some extent this has been due to the continued association of preferred stocks, by both present-day bankers and investors, with distress financing. Another reason is the hybrid character of preferred stocks in relation to bonds and common stocks. Thus, unlike bond interest, preferred-stock fixed-dividend payments are not tax-deductible, which makes the cost of such funds equal to the full percentage amount of the preferred dividend. On the other hand, unlike common-stock dividends, preferred-stock dividends are most frequently of a cumulative nature—that is, all past preferred dividends must be paid before any payment of common dividends. These disadvantages may, of course, be lessened through a convertibility feature that permits conversion into common stock at a predetermined price, at the option of the preferred stockholder. Preferred stocks have been less appealing to investors because of their limited appreciation potential.

Unlike preferred stock, common stock has been the most sizable, and definitely the most traditional, source of external capital generation for commercial banks. Despite its dominance as a source of external capital, common-stock issuance has trailed in importance, by a wide margin, behind use of undivided profits. A number of reasons are likely to have been responsible for this development. For some banks it may have been the cost involved in marketing new issues of common stock; for others, the earnings dilution or control dilution of such issues.

Marketing new issues generally involves certain costs, usually referred to as flotation costs. These include commissions to those selling the new issue, printing expenses, advertising costs, and registration fees with the SEC. Flotation costs are generally higher for the issues of smaller and less-known businesses because of the greater risk involved in marketing them. Since these expenses are relatively large and fixed, the cost percentage runs higher on small issues. Clearly, then, for most small banks—and for small businesses in general—sale of common stock entails a disproportionate cost compared with the retention of earnings, which is the most convenient and least expensive way to provide additional equity capital. And if the sale of additional common stock is essential, local investors usually provide a ready outlet. This helps explain why the common shares of many U.S. banks are held by a relatively small number of stockholders, and hence the absence of an active market for these shares. Consequently, only large banks are in a position to have their stocks traded on the over-the-counter market or a national stock exchange.

Some banks avoid equity financing because of the dilution of earnings that it entails. For a small bank whose stock is closely held, issuing new shares of stock to outsiders means giving more owners the right to share income. In other words, new stockholders acquire equal rights with existing stockholders to share in the net profits of the bank.

In other instances equity financing is avoided because it would involve dilution of control, since the sale of common stock extends voting rights or control to the additional stockholders. In closely held banks, existing stockholders are unwilling to share control of the bank's operations with outsiders. Thus, the potential dilution of earnings and/or control has in many cases caused existing stockholders to veto the sale of new shares of common stock.

Debt Capital

Another important source of funds for commercial banks has been long-term debt, frequently referred to as debt capital. Debt capital includes two types of instruments: Capital notes and debentures. Whatever the original intention of the regulators may have been with respect to the specific features of each of these instruments, supervisory agencies use the terms ''capital notes'' and ''debentures'' interchangeably, with no apparent practical distinction between them. capital notes and debentures are fixed-claim, interest-bearing obligations that enable banks to raise capital. They are unsecured and are subordinate to the claims of depositors and other creditors. Subordination of capital debt is generally required by regulators, and causes notes and debentures to serve the same protective function as equity from the viewpoint of depositors. Since the early 1960s banks have been increasingly relying on capital notes and debentures to provide for the growth of bank capital funds. The extent of bank reliance on this source is shown in Table 5.1. As indicated, between 1965 and 1995 the value of capital notes and debentures outstanding increased from a mere $1.7 billion to $43.7 billion. This increase is quite impressive and creates new perspectives on the growth of bank capital.

Bank issuance of long-term debt first occurred during the Great Depression as a means of easing financial difficulties. When issuing additional common stock was not possible, banks turned to capital notes and debentures. Because this form of capital raising was thus associated with troubled banks, many banks were reluctant to use it in the 1950s and early 1960s. However, in 1961 the Commission on Money and Credit, in its comprehensive study of the U.S. banking and financial system, recommended that banks consider the issuance of subordinated debt as a means of raising capital. Soon thereafter the Advisory Committee on Banking to the Comptroller of the Currency echoed this recommendation: "There is no sound reason why national banks should be deprived of any legitimate capital-raising method that is available to corporations generally." In December 1962 the Comptroller of the Currency issued a ruling that permitted banks to issue capital notes and debentures as part of their ordinary raising of capital. The funds thus obtained were to be viewed as part of a bank's capital for the purpose of calculating lending limits on unsecured loans to any one borrower. Most states have since enacted similar legislation.

Although bank issuance of capital notes and debentures was associated with the distress financing of the early 1930s, the present-day attitudes of bankers and investors have changed significantly enough to make such debt instruments more acceptable in bank capital structures. Thus, throughout the 1960s and in the 1970s, a great many banks sold capital notes and debentures to raise additional capital. These instruments offered banks important advantages vis-à-vis long-term deposits as a source of funds. One major advantage to the issuing bank is that notes and debentures do not require reserve backing or FDIC insurance assessments, as deposits do. Moreover, the long-term maturity of these obligations minimizes a bank's need to maintain liquidity reserves against them. As a result, most of the proceeds from the sale of these instruments can be placed in longer-term, higher-yielding assets. Also, the administrative costs associated with these instruments are much less than for large time deposits attracted from national money markets.

Similarly, capital notes and debentures compare favorably with equity capital. The flotation costs of debt instruments are usually less than those for a similar dollar amount of common or preferred stock because the latter involve a higher degree of risk. Also, unlike dividends on common or preferred stock, which are paid from after-tax income, interest on capital notes and debentures is paid before taxes. This feature significantly reduces the after-tax cost of these instruments to a bank.

Common stockholders generally view favorably issuance of capital notes and debentures by their bank. Although these instruments increase a bank's leverage, their issuance is associated with important benefits for the common stockholders.

Thus, assuming that the issuing bank is in a position to service the debt, issuance of capital notes and debentures does not cause dilution of control, since the holders of these instruments have no voting rights. Also, the holders of such debt do not participate in earnings beyond the stated interest rate on these instruments. Thus, the equity position of common stockholders in the bank is not diluted, but the bank has obtained additional capital for profitable expansion of its operations.

Banks may raise, and often have raised, capital with issues of convertible subordinated debentures. These securities are like the subordinated debentures except that they give the holder the opportunity to trade the debenture for stock at some time in the future at a specified price. Because such issues offer the investor the attractive feature of interest-payment protection plus the opportunity to convert to common stock, and thus participate in all future earnings, the interest rate on such debentures is generally lower than for those without a conversion feature. That makes convertible securities issues desirable from the bank's point of view. Moreover, since they offer a bank the opportunity to obtain permanent capital with less dilution than if stock were issued immediately, convertible issues have been used extensively, and will continue to be employed. One disadvantage of convertible, compared with nonconvertible, debt instruments is that the underwriting fees are generally higher because of the risk that the price of the stock might drop before the convertible securities are issued.

Reserves for Loan Losses

As indicated earlier, loan-loss reserves represent earnings earmarked to cover possible loan losses. As these earnings add to the difference between a bank's assets and liabilities, they increase capital, and consequently are counted as a component of the capital base. Actual loan losses (charge-offs) are deducted from this reserve, and recoveries are credited to the reserve. In 1995, reserves for losses on loans, for all insured commercial banks, had risen to $52.9 billion (see Table 5.1).

In their practice of maintaining loan-loss reserves, banks have been encouraged by both supervisory authorities and the Internal Revenue Service. Until 1969 banks were allowed to make additions to the reserve for loan losses out of pretax earnings until these reserves reached a maximum of 2.4 percent of the eligible loans. As a result of this stipulation, taxfree loan-loss reserves grew significantly and were far in excess of actual losses (between 1950 and 1968, out of $8.8 billion placed in reserves, net loan charge-offs amounted to only $3.2 billion). This development led the Tax Reform Act of 1969 to provide for the gradual phaseout of this "percentage method" by 1986 and its replacement by the "experience method." That is, banks were allowed to establish reserves only up to the average of actual losses sustained over the most recent six-year period. This method was limited by the Tax Reform Act of 1986 to banks with total assets up to $500 million. Banks with assets in excess of this amount may report only actual losses on loans as tax deductions on their income statements. These revisions took effect on January 1, 1987.[1]

The limitations on loan-loss reserves introduced by the aforementioned legislative measures have minimized the importance of this item as a source of bank capital.

COST OF CAPITAL

As indicated in the preceding section, a bank can raise capital funds in a variety of ways. Debt can be issued in the form of subordinated notes and debentures. Earnings can be retained rather than paid as dividends. Preferred stock may be issued or additional common stock may be sold. Capital funds, however, are only one of the sources of funds available to a bank. A more sizable source, and one that banks use on a regular basis to finance asset growth, is deposits. Larger banks also make use of such nondeposit sources of funds as Eurodollars and federal funds. Management needs to know the cost of bank funds in order to make profitable decisions.

A simple, often-used approach to calculating a bank's cost of funds is based on the interest rate of negotiable 90-day CDs, on the premise that the CD rate is a reliable indicator of the "free-market cost of money," as long as an active secondary market exists. This cost proxy is the basis for deciding interest rates to charge borrowers and yields to seek in making investments. Although this method does not consider the cost of all available bank funds, the importance of CDs as a source of bank funds makes this approximation useful. For example, many large banks base their loan-pricing formula for credits to large corporations on the 90-day CDs rate as follows:

$$R = \bar{R}_{cd} + M,$$

where $\bar{R}_{cd}$ stands for the 3-week average rate on 90-day CDs in the secondary market and M is the percent markup to cover risk exposure (premium to cover default risk), operating costs, and a return on equity. Assuming a three-week average CD yield of 5.0 percent and a markup of 1.25 percent, the lending rate would be 6.25 percent. Aggressive foreign banks in the United States extended corporate loans in the 1980s at rates very close to their fund-raising costs (i.e., federal funds rates plus a small margin, perhaps $\frac{1}{4}$ to $\frac{3}{4}$ of a percentage point). If the clients are very large corporations with access to the commercial paper market, banks may even price loans on the basis of cost of funds only.

A more thorough method of computing the cost of capital, and one more suitable for planning purposes, involves computing the cost of each separate type of funds as well as the overall cost of the bank's aggregate pool of funds. This concept is known in banking as the *weighted-average cost of funds*, or sometimes simply as the *pooled-funds approach*. To determine this cost, one must take into account the different dollar amounts of funds from different sources, their proportion of total funds, and the respective cost of each type of funds. The resulting figure can be used as a standard in evaluating alternative uses of funds. In other words, this cost functions as the baseline for determining allocation of funds among alternative earning assets. Thus, earning assets will not be acquired unless their projected return exceeds the weighted-average cost of funds.

An example of the computations involved in developing a bank's weighted-average cost of funds is shown in Table 5.3. This table summarizes the different sources of funds of a hypothetical community bank, the First Hellenic Bank of Tarpon Springs. The financial structure of First Hellenic is made up of deposit funds (demand, time, and savings) and funds obtained through subordinated debt and equity capital. Also shown is the proportion, or weight, of total funds represented by each source, and the individual cost per type of funds. The product of these two items represents the weighted cost of each individual type of funds (WACF). As indicated in Table 5.3, the WACF for First Hellenic is 5.2 percent. Since cost data were computed on an after-tax basis, the bank's cost of funding loans and investments (net of service costs) on a pretax basis is $.052 \div (1 - .34) = .079$ or 7.9 percent.

As implied by the data of Table 5.3, the cost of each type of funds has an important bearing upon a bank's WACF. For example, funds obtained from deposit sources and subordinated debt have a lower cost than equity capital because of the tax deductibility of interest. Computing the cost of each individual type of funds exhibits important variation. Although this material is traditionally covered in financial management textbooks, the effort will be made here to summarize, and where necessary adapt, the relevant concepts as they apply to bank funds. The following sections deal with the methods of determining the costs of individual sources of funds.

Cost of Deposits

The principal source for bank funds is deposits. Traditionally deposits have been classified into demand, time, and savings. Demand deposits were noninterest-bearing deposits, while time and savings paid interest in accordance with the provisions of Regulation Q. In recent years, as interest-rate restrictions began to break down, banks started to offer new types of accounts—NOW accounts, automatic transfer services (ATS), and money-market deposit accounts—that blur traditional differences between demand and time and savings deposits. For the purpose of our analysis, we will group deposits into two categories: interest-bearing and noninterest-bearing. In the former category belong the time and savings deposits and those demand deposits that earn interest, while in the latter category are the noninterest-bearing demand deposits.

Interest-bearing deposits entail both direct and indirect costs for a bank. Direct cost is the amount of interest that banks pay depositors for use of their funds. The indirect cost is a composite of the following items: cost of attracting deposits, cost of servicing deposits, and deposit-insurance premiums. Both direct and indirect costs must be considered in determining the effective cost of inter-

Table 5.3
Weighted-Average Cost of Funds, First Hellenic Bank

Source of Funds	Amount (in millions)	Percent of Total	Cost Rate	Pct. x Cost
Noninterest-bearing demand deposits	14.0[a]	.32	.026[c]	.008
Interest-bearing demand deposits, time and savings deposits	18.0[a]	.41	.048	.020
Debentures	3.5[b]	.08	.072[c]	.006
Preferred stock	1.5[b]	.03	.090	.003
Common stock	2.0[b]	.05	.091	.005
Paid-in surplus	1.0	.02	.091	.002
Undivided profits	4.0	.09	.090	.008
Total	$44.0	1.00		.052

Weighted-average cost of funds = 5.2%

[a]Net of legal reserves.
[b]It is a more realistic approach to report the amounts of these instruments on the basis of their current value in the marketplace. Historical values are not relevant to current decisions.
[c]Adjusted for tax purposes on the basis of the bank's marginal tax rate of 34%. That is, initial costs were multiplied in each case by (1-t) to obtain the after-tax cost. This adjustment is necessary because the other cost items of this column are by definition on an after-tax basis.
Source: Prepared by author.

est-bearing deposits. Any charges or fees earned by the bank in the servicing of deposits are treated as offsets to these costs. Cost computations should be based on the average interest-bearing deposits for any given period of time. These deposits should be adjusted for the amount of funds set aside for legal reserves. The rationale for this adjustment is that since reserve requirements limit the amount of deposit funds available for loans and investments, they must be deducted from available deposits in determining the cost of these funds. Take, for example, the First Hellenic Bank. Assume that its average time and savings deposits for the year were $18.2 million and required reserves were $200,000. If the total annual interest paid to depositors was $1.115 million, the cost of attracting and servicing these deposits was $170,000, and deposit-insurance premiums were $18,200, the effective cost of these funds would be

$$K_{ids} = \frac{1.115 + .170 + .018}{18.2 - .2} = .072 \ (7.2 \text{ percent}).$$

On an after-tax basis this would be equal to

$$K_{ids} = .072(1 - .34) = .048 \ (4.8 \text{ percent}).$$

The same process would be followed in computing the cost of First Hellenic's interest-bearing demand deposits. Differences in the reserve requirements and/ or the cost of acquiring and servicing these deposits may warrant separate cost computations for this group of deposits. The next step would be to develop an average-cost figure for the combined amount of interest-bearing deposits, using the weighting process shown in Table 5.3.

The formula for determining the after-tax cost of interest-bearing deposits can therefore be expressed as follows:

$$K_{ids} = \frac{IE + ASE + DI}{AD - R} (1 - t),$$

where:

K_{ids} = after-tax cost of interest-bearing deposits
IE = interest expense for the period under consideration
ASE = expenses of attracting and servicing deposits for this period
DI = deposit-insurance premiums for this period
AD = average value of interest-bearing deposits for this period
R = dollar amount of legally required reserves for these deposits
t = the bank's marginal tax rate.

The above formula can also be used to determine the cost of noninterest-bearing deposits. The only adjustment needed regards interest cost; since these deposits bear no interest, the bank's direct interest cost would be zero. Using this formula, we can therefore develop the cost of noninterest-bearing demand deposits for the period under consideration. Assume that First Hellenic's non-interest-bearing demand deposits for the year were $14.4 million and required reserves were $400,000. Also assume that its costs of attracting and servicing these deposits were $532,000 and its deposit-insurance premiums were $14,400. In that case, the after-tax cost of these funds would be

$$K_{ds} = \frac{.532 + .014}{14.4 - .4} (1 - .34) = .026 \text{ (2.6 percent)}.$$

Cost of Capital Notes and Debentures

The cost of debt capital to a bank is equal to the rate of return earned by investors in the bank's outstanding debt instruments or the interest rate that the bank must pay to sell new securities of this kind. The best measure of the rate of return on fixed-income instruments is the yield to maturity. This is defined as the rate of return that is expected if a debt instrument is held to its maturity (for the yield-to-maturity formula, see Chapter 9). Thus, the yield to maturity of an outstanding debt issue is ordinarily used as the cost of a bank's debt capital. However, since the interest payments on debt instruments are tax-deductible, the yield-to-maturity figure must be converted to an after-tax basis by multiplying it by a tax factor. The equation for computing the after-tax cost of debt financing is

$$K_d = (1 - t)YTM,$$

where K_d is the after-tax cost of debt capital, t is the bank's marginal tax rate, and YTM is the yield to maturity of the outstanding debt instruments or the rate of interest that would be acceptable to investors in new issues of this type. If we were to replace the elements of this equation with the corresponding data of First Hellenic Bank, we would obtain an after-tax cost of 7.2 percent. Assuming that the market value of the outstanding debentures of First Hellenic is $3.5 million and their yield to maturity is 10.9 percent, the bank's after-tax cost is

$$K_d = (1 - .34)(.109) = .072 \text{ (7.2 percent)}.$$

If First Hellenic were a larger institution, it is likely that it would have made use of some borrowed funds. In other words, its liabilities would have included such items as federal funds purchased and securities sold under repurchase agreements (RPs). Since the maturity of these transactions varies from overnight to very short periods of time, and the rate charged fluctuates according to market conditions, the before-tax cost of these liabilities (K_{bf}) for the period under consideration would be equal to the geometric average of the short-term rates paid during this period. This is expressed by the equation

$$K_{bf} = [(1 + k_{1bf}) (1 + k_{2bf}) \cdots (1 + k_{mbf})]^{1/m} - 1,$$

where k_{tbf} is the cost of the borrowed funds in period $t = 1, 2, \ldots m$. For example, the cost of successive overnight borrowings of federal funds over a 20-day period, at going market rates (7 percent, 10 percent, 12 percent), would be

$$K_{bf} = \left[\left(1 + \frac{.07}{360} \right) \left(1 + \frac{.10}{360} \right) \cdots \left(1 + \frac{.12}{360} \right) \right]^{1/20} - 1.$$

Cost of Preferred Stock

As with capital notes and debentures, the cost of preferred stock to a bank is equal to the rate of return earned by investors in the bank's outstanding preferred issue. Unlike capital notes and debentures, however, most preferred issues have no maturity—that is, they are of a perpetual nature. The holders of preferred stock thus expect to receive a fixed (stipulated) amount of dividends indefinitely. This fact, plus the absence of tax deductibility (since dividends are paid out of profits), means that the cost of a preferred issue is in essence the effective yield of the stock. This can be found by dividing the annual preferred dividend (D_p) by the price of the stock (P_p). In equation form, the cost of preferred stock is

$$K_p = \frac{D_p}{P_p}.$$

If the preferred stock is newly issued, this formula can be adjusted to reflect the net price received by the bank because of flotation costs (f). These costs, expressed as a percentage of the selling price, will be incorporated in the preceding formula as follows:

$$K_p = \frac{D_p}{P_p(1 - f)}.$$

For example, if buyers of the preferred stock of First Hellenic Bank paid $50 a share and brokers charged a commission of $5 a share, the cost of the preferred stock to the bank—assuming an annual dividend of $4—would be

$$K_p = \frac{4}{50(1 - .10)} = .09 \ (9 \text{ percent}).$$

Cost of Equity

Unlike debt issues and preferred stock, which call for fixed contractual payments, common stock has no explicit interest cost. To determine the cost of common stock, we need to compute the rate of return required by stockholders. This rate is a function of investors' perception of risk associated with the bank in question as well as the returns on alternative investment opportunities.

Issuance of common stock is but one source of equity capital. Another source is the retention of earnings. Retaining earnings has a cost that is equal to the rate of return stockholders require on the bank's common stock. The reasoning behind this is that if earnings were not retained but were paid out to stockholders, one investment option they would have would be to buy more of the bank's common stock. It is assumed that they would require a return equal to what they are earning on their present equity position. Thus the cost of retained earnings, though an opportunity cost, must equal the cost of existing common stock.

Several approaches have been put forward in the financial literature to compute the cost of equity. The three standard ways to estimate it are summarized below.

Dividend Growth Model

According to this model, the cost of common equity, K_s, is given by the equation

$$K_s = \frac{D_1}{P_o} + g_s, \tag{5.1}$$

where D_1 is the dividend expected to be received in the next period, P_o is the current market price of common stock, and g_s is the growth rate of earnings or dividends. As a practical matter g_s is estimated from the past earnings, because dividends do not usually increase (or decrease) in proportion to the earnings, even though the model assumes that they do. This model has many assumptions that must be satisfied. Two of the most important are that K_s is always greater than g_s, and that there is no debt in the capital structure and none will be added in the future. This last assumption restricts the application of the model, yet the model is simple to understand and compute, and as a result it is widely used.

If no new common stock is issued, this model provides the cost of equity as well as the cost of retained earnings. If new stock is issued, the formula can be adjusted to reflect flotation costs (f). Thus, adjusting equation 5.1 for flotation costs, we have

$$K_s = \frac{D_1}{P_o(1 - f)} + g_s. \tag{5.2}$$

Furthermore, every bank experiences a period of abnormal growth—that is, when $K_s < g_s$. If this happens for a time period (t) and then the bank's growth rate reverts back to $K_s > g_s$, the cost of equity can be computed indirectly from the following formula:

$$P_o = D_1 \left[\frac{\frac{(1 + g_n)^t}{(1 + K_s)^t} - 1}{g^n - K_s} \right] + \frac{D_1(1 + g_n)^{t-1}(1 + g_s)}{K_s - g_s} \frac{1}{(1 + K_s)^t}, \qquad (5.3)$$

where g_n is the abnormal growth ($g_n > K_s$) up to time period t. It should be noted that K_s cannot be explicitly represented in terms of D_1, g_n, g_s, and t. Thus it can be obtained only implicitly. The examples below illustrate the application of this and the preceding two formulas.

Let us consider the case of First Hellenic Bank, whose structure of equity capital, as depicted in Table 5.3, includes the following items:

Common stock	$2 million
Paid-in surplus	$1 million
Undivided profits	$4 million

The bank is expected to pay a dividend of $0.50 next year. The current market price of its common stock is $50, and the growth rate of dividends has been estimated to be 8 percent. In this particular case, no matter what the composition of the bank's equity-capital structure, the cost of equity will not be affected. The cost will depend only on the growth rate of dividends, the expected dividend payment, and the common stock's current market price. The cost of equity (per equation 5.1) would be

$$K_s = \frac{0.50}{50} + .08 = .09 \text{ (9 percent).} \qquad (5.4)$$

Assume that the First Hellenic Bank sustained flotation costs for issuing its stock. If it received only $45 instead of $50 for each share of common stock it issued, its flotation cost (f) is $5 (50–45) per share, 10 percent of the selling price. Thus, the cost of its common stock (according to equation 5.2) would be

$$K_s = \frac{0.50}{50(1 - .10)} + .08 = .091 \text{ (9.1 percent).} \qquad (5.5)$$

As is apparent, flotation charges push the cost of the common stock above the cost of retained earnings.

In the preceding examples we assumed a constant annual growth rate (g_s) smaller than the required rate on (cost of) equity (K_s). Let us assume instead an abnormal growth pattern in determining the cost of equity. Thus, assume that the current selling price (P_o) of the stock of First Hellenic is \$20.25. Moreover, the bank is expected to grow at the astronomical rate (g_n) of 15 percent for ten years, its rate of growth leveling off after that (g_s) at 8 percent. If the expected dividend for the next year (D_1) is \$0.50, what is the cost of equity?

Using equation 5.3, K_s will be the amount that satisfies

$$20.25 = 0.50 \left[\frac{\frac{(1 + .15)^{10}}{(1 + K_s)} - 1}{.15 - K_s} \right] + \frac{(.50)(1 + .15)^9(1 + .08)}{K_s - .08} \frac{1}{(1 + K_s)^{10}}. \quad (5.6)$$

By trial and error we find

$$K_s = .12 \text{ (12 percent)}.$$

CAPM Method

With the advent of the capital-asset pricing model (CAPM), an alternative approach to estimating the cost of equity was introduced. It is based upon the risk-return trade-off concept. The cost of equity capital (K_s) formulation is

$$K_s = R_f + [R_m - R_f] \beta, \quad (5.7)$$

where R_f is the riskfree rate of return estimated by the return on U.S. Treasury securities (such as Treasury bills), R_m is the expected return on the market portfolio, and β (beta) is the index of the sensitivity of the rate of return on equity to the market rate of return, popularly known as systematic risk.* This model provides the risk-adjusted cost of equity capital of a bank. The value of R_f can be obtained from the *Wall Street Journal* or similar sources on any weekday. The value of β is published by *The Value Line Investment Survey* or Moody's, and usually does not change very often. The value of R_m can be obtained from the Center for Research in Security Prices (CRSP) of the University of Chicago.

Markup-on-Debt Approach

This method is ad hoc. The presumption is that owners (the holders of common stock) will require an appreciably higher rate of return than that earned by the institution's debt holders. Thus, the cost of equity capital is

---

*The concept of systematic risk as used in the portfolio theory is that part of a security's risk cannot be diversified away. Examples of systematic risk are inflation, recession, political unrest, and general conditions that affect all stocks in the same manner. Systematic risk is distinguished in portfolio theory from unsystematic risk, which refers to conditions unique to a company (such as a strike or a lawsuit) and their effect on an individual stock. Unsystematic risk can be eliminated by diversification.

$$K_s = \text{ROR to bondholders} + \text{markup}. \tag{5.8}$$

The rate of return to bondholders is usually taken as the average return on bonds of similar risk. For example, if a bank's bonds have been classified as AAA by Moody's and the average rate of return on AAA bonds is 11 percent, this will be taken as the rate of return to bondholders. The amount of markup is determined by management. For example, if management, on the basis of historical patterns, decides that the rate of return on the bank's common stock should run four percentage points over the yield on debt, this would imply a cost of equity (K_s) of 15 percent.

FUNCTIONS OF BANK CAPITAL

Equity capital performs a variety of functions. These may be classified into the following four categories: to provide for the necessary physical facilities through which the bank will become operational, to protect the creditors, to generate a competitive rate of return to bank shareholders, and to comply with the requirements of supervisory agencies.

Providing Start-up Funds

As we saw in Chapter 4, before a bank begins operations, its organizers sell stock to raise the capital to finance (provide funds for) fixed investments, such as land, building, furniture, machinery, equipment, and supplies necessary to establish the bank as a going concern. This function of capital is typical of any new business. As the bank grows, additional capital funds are used to build and equip branches, introduce improved technology, and finance other fixed assets needed to sustain growth momentum. The high rates of interest experienced in the late 1970s have affected traditional practices in the financing of fixed assets. Since market returns have generally exceeded the relatively modest yields of fixed assets, many banks have sold their buildings and equipment to insurance companies or specially formed subsidiaries, which lease these assets back to the bank. This practice has released frozen funds to be invested or loaned more profitably.

Protecting Creditors

On September 30, 1995, 69 percent of the total assets of all insured commercial banks were financed by deposits. If one adds the portion of assets financed by nondeposit liabilities (both short-term and long-term), then 92 percent of bank assets were financed by debt. By contrast, 8 percent of bank assets were financed by equity capital. What this means is that banks utilize a high degree of leverage (a high debt/assets ratio) in the financing of their assets. This degree of leverage is uncommon among nonfinancial businesses, whose margins of leverage are generally more conservative.

This high ratio of debt to assets, so typical of the banking industry, places great importance on the function of capital to protect the interests of the bank's creditors. From the depositors' and other creditors' point of view, capital's function is to provide a margin of protection for their claims in the event of liquidation. Capital plays an even more important role in the daily operations of a bank. Its capacity to generate earnings is important in absorbing losses as they occur and in spreading their impact over time. Thus, in the broadest sense, it protects the depositors and any other creditors by providing the security with which to take sensible business risks and maintain the institution as a going concern. In other words, capital performs the function of a guarantee or safety fund against any losses arising from the lending, investing, and all other activities incidental to commercial banking.

Since the advent of the FDIC, depositors with accounts of up to $100,000 have not had to be concerned with losses in the event of bank failure; their deposits are fully insured. Those with larger deposits assume a greater risk. If a bank fails, the FDIC reimburses them up to the legal limit. Beyond this they face a loss if the failing bank liquidates. This risk to large depositors was highlighted by the liquidation of the Penn Square Bank in Oklahoma in mid-1982. The FDIC paid depositors up to the insured limits causing large depositors (with balances in excess of $100,000) to suffer sizable losses. However, if the failing bank is acquired by another bank, they usually suffer no loss. Banks also acquire funds from short-term lenders in such forms as federal funds and commercial paper. Holders of these liabilities are noninsured creditors of the bank. Because of the risk they assume, they have the greatest interest in carefully evaluating the bank's capital adequacy. A primary consideration for these creditors will be the existence of debt capital, which, as was stated earlier, is contractually subordinate to all bank liabilities. The existence of subordinated notes and debentures provides these creditors an extra margin of safety, since debt capital is second in line after equity capital to absorb losses if the bank has to be closed and liquidated. As for the holders of subordinated notes and debentures (though they, too, are liability holders of the bank), their only margin of safety if the bank fails is equity capital. Indeed, since their claims precede the residual claims of stockholders, capital note and debenture holders must rely solely on equity capital to protect against losses.

Generating a Return to Shareholders

Profits in banking, just as in other businesses, have been an important determinant of investors' interest in bank stock. Thus, from the stockholders' point of view, the function of bank capital is to achieve a sufficient yield to meet operating costs and net a fair return to its owners. With possible rare exceptions, the suppliers of bank capital are motivated solely by the desire to own a good investment. They realize, of course, that the nature of the business entails special obligations essential to the public welfare, and are in sympathy with the conduct of the business in a manner compatible with the bank's obligations to its customers, the community, and the nation. They are, nevertheless, properly insistent upon the protection of their investment (through sound planning and administration) and upon a rate of return that is as great as that which they could obtain from comparable investment elsewhere. They invest in the stock of a bank for the same reasons that they invest in the shares of any other business enterprise: to obtain a competitive return on their funds, with the hope of appreciation in the value of their stock. Unless this return is obtained, they have no reason for wishing to continue to supply capital to the bank. An unprofitable bank is, after all, an unhealthy bank, and cannot survive. The profit motive of bank shareholders is, therefore, both proper and unavoidable so long as banking is supported by private means.

Complying with Laws and Regulations

The myriad regulations that govern bank activity include stipulations regarding capital that are designed to ensure the safety and soundness of bank operations. These requirements extend from the chartering of a bank through its operations and growth. As was stated in Chapter 4, the Comptroller of the Currency prescribes minimum capital requirements for the establishment of national banks; state chartering agencies have similar requirements. States, moreover, set minimum capital requirements for the opening of branches. Acquisitions by banks or bank holding companies are also subject to capital requirements.

Of special importance to banks are lending limits, inasmuch as they are determined by a bank's capital base. State laws on lending limits may differ from the federal law. Since enactment of the Garn-St. Germain Act, national banks are permitted to loan to any single borrower, on an unsecured basis, amounts up to 15 percent of their capital and surplus, and an additional 10 percent for loans fully secured by a readily marketable collateral. Since 1982, however, when the Garn–St. Germain law was enacted, the definition of bank capital has changed and now refers to "Tier 1" equity capital, which is discussed in the next section. With the lending limit for secured loans set at 25 percent,* banks wishing to attract large borrowers must ensure that their capital base is adequate to accommodate their loan requests. The size of a bank's capital thus affects the type of clientele it can ordinarily serve.

CAPITAL ADEQUACY

Although equity capital is a prerequisite for the establishment of a bank, its most important function is to protect depositors and other creditors. If a bank

---

*There are some exceptions to the 25 percent capital lending limit imposed by the Garn-St. Germain Act. These include loans secured by bonds, notes, CDs, U.S. Treasury securities, or securities guaranteed by the United States; loans backed by deposits in the lending bank, by commercial paper, bankers' acceptances, and bills of lading; and loans to special-interest groups, such as the Student Loan Marketing Association and livestock ranchers.

is to continue as a going concern, its capital must inspire sufficient confidence among depositors and other creditors. For unless such confidence exists, a bank will not be able to retain existing deposit and nondeposit liabilities and to attract new ones.

Such has traditionally been the role of bank capital. Throughout banking history, bank capital has had almost no other purpose than the protection of depositors. Since 1962 this function of equity capital has been shared by debt capital. With debt securities subordinated to the claims of depositors, debt capital actually serves the same protective function as equity capital.

The adequacy of bank capital, and hence the safety of commercial banks, has been the concern of state and federal regulatory authorities throughout U.S. banking history. U.S. financial history is characterized by a number of periods of unrestrained bank expansion and individual bank abuses, which led to bank failures, with resulting losses to depositors and holders of banknotes. In order to avoid the destabilizing effects of bank failures, the need became apparent for regulatory intervention to supplant the judgment of the individual bank in matters relating to capital adequacy. This intervention has taken the form of laws and regulations, at both the federal and the state levels, that prescribe minimum capital requirements for the organization of a new bank and set norms to ensure the adequacy of bank capital thereafter.

With the general public basically unversed in this field, supervisory judgment has become especially decisive for a bank's continued existence over the years. Thus, today it is among supervisory authorities that a bank must inspire sufficient confidence as to its adequacy to withstand whatever strains may be placed upon it. In a closely supervised private banking system, it is the supervisory appraisal of capital adequacy that determines whether and under what conditions a bank may continue to exist. If capital is considered adequate by the examining supervisory authorities, it will be satisfactory for the general public.

Measures of Capital Adequacy

Over the years several standards or ratios have been developed for the amount of capital considered necessary for the safe and efficient operation of a bank. They related capital to a key magnitude in the balance sheet of commercial banks. Each of these ratios, introduced at a different phase of U.S. banking history, was projected as the best index for measuring a bank's capital adequacy.

The first measure of capital adequacy to be introduced by U.S. banking authorities was the ratio of capital to total deposits—a ratio that seemed quite natural, since it readily identified the extent of capital protection enjoyed by depositors. Introduced in 1909 by a California banking law, this measure appeared in the Comptroller of the Currency's annual report of 1914. The report strongly recommended use of this ratio for national banks, stipulating a minimum relationship of capital funds to total deposits of 1:10—that is, capital should be equal to at least 10 percent of total deposits. Until World War II this ratio was considered satisfactory for the safety of depositors. During the war years, however, supervisory authorities realized that the 10 percent ratio was seriously hampering bank financing of the war. Bank purchases of government securities, through deposit creation, had led to a rapid increase in bank deposits, which threatened significant narrowing of safety margins. This led supervisory authorities to abandon this traditional rule.

In 1947 the FDIC was joined by the Federal Reserve System in using the ratio of capital to total assets. This ratio identifies the extent to which a bank's assets are financed by its capital. A minimum capital:total assets ratio of 7 percent was suggested by the Federal Reserve as indication of adequate capitalization.

A refined approach to the measurement of capital adequacy was introduced in 1948 by the Comptroller of the Currency and came to be known as the risk-asset ratio. This ratio sought to measure capital adequacy by relating capital only to those assets in a bank's balance sheet that are subject to losses. The basic premise of this approach was that not all bank assets are of the same quality—some are risky and others are not. Thus, for any measure of capital adequacy to be valid, it had to relate capital to the risk factors involved in a bank's assets. The risk-asset ratio was conceived as the ratio of capital funds to risk assets, the latter being defined as all bank assets minus cash and U.S. government securities. A 20 percent risk-asset ratio was originally considered satisfactory by the Office of the Comptroller of the Currency.

In the years that followed, several variants of the risk-asset ratio were put forward. Some students of the subject, for example, defined risk assets as all assets less cash and U.S. government securities due in five years or less. The obvious reason for this definition was that although government securities are free of the risk of default (the risk that interest and/or principal will be defaulted as they come due), their prices are nevertheless subject to fluctuations as a result of changes in the market rate of interest. In other words, these assets are not free of the interest-rate risk (the risk that interest rates will change, causing the market values of securities to change). However, issues maturing in five years or less are considered to be relatively short-term and, therefore, as being close to riskless.

Another variant of the risk-asset ratio was total assets less cash, U.S. government securities, and loans insured and guaranteed by the federal government and its agencies. This approach, known as the adjusted-risk-asset ratio, included in the riskless asset category all loans insured and guaranteed by government agencies, since these are virtually free of risk.

In the 1950s efforts were directed to developing refined methods of measuring capital adequacy. Of these methods, two deserve consideration and comment because of their contribution to the problem of measuring capital adequacy. These techniques were that of the Federal Reserve Bank of New York (1952) and that of the Board of Governors of the Federal Reserve System (1956). Unlike the previous approaches, which considered all risk assets as possessing the same degree of risk, these new formulas assumed that the exposure of bank assets to risk shades all the way from a considerable loss potential to virtually no risk. To develop a realistic appraisal of an individual bank's capital adequacy, these formulas therefore allowed for varying capital requirements against a bank's different assets.

In regard to the various standards of capital adequacy described, no uniformity existed among federal banking supervisory authorities. In fact, national bank examiners, on the basis of guidelines issued by the Office of the Comptroller of the Currency in 1971, moved away from formal analysis and reliance on capital ratios, and toward qualitative factors. In other words, the capital adequacy of a national bank was determined by analyzing and appraising its capital position in relation to such factors as character of its management, quality and character of its ownership, quality of operating procedures, and capacity to provide the broadest service to the public.

Current Trends in the Regulation of Bank Capital

On July 11, 1988, in Basel, Switzerland, 12 major industrialized nations* signed the Capital Accord, which provided for a uniform 8 percent risk-based capital requirement for banks to be fully implemented in 1993. This accord was the outcome of several years of work by a committee of representatives of the central banks and supervisory authorities of the signatory nations that sought to secure the international convergence of regulations governing capital adequacy. Two fundamental objectives lay at the heart of the committee's work on regulatory convergence. These were, first, that the new framework should serve to strengthen the soundness and stability of the international financial system and, second, that this framework should be fair and have a degree of consistency in its application to banks in different countries, with a view to diminishing an existing source of competitive inequality among international banks.

The Capital Accord offered signatory nations significant flexibility in the scope of application of the new capital standards. For example, signatory nations could extend these standards to all their banks or limit them to their internationally active banks. Moreover, these standards were viewed as minimum, thus leaving it to each signatory nation to decide whether it opts for stricter rules. Finally, because of the wide variety of existing supervisory systems, and to enable banks to build up their capital toward the ultimate target standard, the Capital Accord provided

---

*These are the United States, Japan, West Germany, Britain, France, Canada, Italy, Sweden, the Netherlands, Belgium, Switzerland, and Luxembourg. With the exception of Luxembourg, the remaining signatory nations constitute what is formally known as the Group of Ten (G-10) countries. As early as 1974, the governors of the central banks of this group had created the Committee on Banking Regulation and Supervisory Practices to improve the coordination of bank supervision among its members. The capital standards were developed by this committee, which is also known as the Basel Committee because it meets in Basel, at the Bank for International Settlements—an international clearing bank for central banks.

for a transitional period (with interim and final standards) to facilitate the phasing in of the new guidelines. The transitional period expired at the end of 1992, at which date all banks had to meet the new guidelines in full.

In the United States, regulatory agencies moved to impose the Basel requirements on all of the nation's banking organizations with an exception for certain bank holding companies. Importantly, savings and loans were subjected to the same capital requirements. The new guidelines measure and assess capital adequacy by relating capital to the risk factors involved in assets. Because of the different gradations of risk in bank assets, a weighted risk ratio is used for gauging capital adequacy. This approach is viewed as more advantageous than other methods of capital measurement on the following grounds:

1. It makes regulatory capital more risk-sensitive, so that conservative institutions and those willing to take greater risks are not measured by the same yardstick.
2. It allows off-balance-sheet exposures to be incorporated more easily into the measure.
3. It does not deter banks from holding liquid or other low-risk assets.
4. It provides a fairer basis for making international comparisons between banking systems whose structures may differ.

A key feature of the Basel guidelines is their definition of capital. Capital is distinguished into *Tier 1*, or "core" capital, and *Tier 2*, or "supplementary" capital. Core capital includes common stockholders' equity (common stock, surplus, undivided profits, and capital reserves); noncumulative perpetual preferred stock;* and minority interests in consolidated subsidiaries. Intangible assets, such as goodwill, may not be counted as part of the core capital. Core capital must account for at least 50 percent of a bank's capital base. Supplementary capital includes hybrid (debt/equity) capital instruments, such as perpetual debt, cumulative perpetual preferred stock, and mandatory convertible debt; subordinated term debt issues, such as subordinated debt instruments with a minimum original maturity of over five years, and limited-life preferred stock; and general reserves for loan and lease losses. Supplementary capital is limited to a maximum of 100 percent of core capital, and term subordinated debt—within supplementary capital—to a maximum of 50 percent of core capital. In addition, general loan-loss reserves are limited to 1.25 percentage points of risk-weighted assets. Table 5.4 provides further detail on the capital components.

Due to "national discretion" provisions, there are differences in the composition of tier 2 capital across signatory nations. For example, tier 2 capital for Japanese banks includes revaluation reserves under which they may report 45 percent of the unrealized capital gains from their stock portfolios. Revaluation reserves made a significant contribution to tier 2 capital during the 1980s as a result of rising stock-market prices. With the drastic drop in stock-market activ-

---

*The noncumulative feature makes this type of preferred stock a closer substitute for common stock than cumulative preferred stock, since any dividend payments that have been waived do not represent a contingent claim on the issuer.

Table 5.4
Definitions of Qualifying Capital

	Minimum Requirements and Limitations
Core Capital (Tier 1)	Must equal or exceed 4% of risk-weighted assets
Common stockholders' equity	No limit
Qualifying noncumulative perpetual preferred stock	No limit
Minority interest in equity accounts of consolidated subsidiaries	No limit
Less: goodwill and other disallowed intangibles	
Supplementary Capital (Tier 2)	Limited to 100% of Tier 1
Allowance for loan and lease losses	Limited to 1.25% of risk-weighted assets
Perpetual preferred stock	No limit within Tier 2
Hybrid capital instruments (including perpetual debt and mandatory convertible securities)	No limit within Tier 2
Subordinated debt and intermediate-term preferred stock (original maturity of 5 years or more)	Limited to 50% of Tier 1; amortized for capital purposes as they approach maturity
Revaluation reserves (equity and building)	Not included
Deductions (from sum of Tier 1 and Tier 2)	
Investments in unconsolidated banking subsidiaries	
Reciprocal holdings of banking organizations' capital securities	
Other deductions as determined by supervisory authority	
Total Capital (Tier 1 + Tier 2 - Deductions)	Must equal or exceed 8% of risk-weighted assets

Source: Board of Governors of the Federal Reserve System, *Capital Adequacy Guidelines*, May 1994.

ity in the early 1990s, however, the contribution of these shareholdings to tier 2 capital suffered accordingly.

Because of variations in the risk exposure of bank assets, the new guidelines divide all assets into four broad categories weighted according to risk (see Table 5.5). Each asset is assigned a category depending on its credit risk, which is based mainly on the type of borrower. The first asset category includes riskless assets, such as cash, Federal Reserve deposits, and U.S. government securities against which, clearly, no capital is required. General obligations of state and local governments are considered somewhat more risky and are classified into the second category, against which there is a weight of 20 percent. Revenue bonds and residential mortgage loans are examples of assets in the third category, weighted at 50 percent. Assets in the fourth and highest-risk category receive a 100 percent weight, meaning they count fully as assets when calculating the risk-adjusted capital ratio. Many of the usual bank assets fall within this group, including business, consumer, and foreign loans; corporate securities; and fixed assets. An example of the process followed in determining the capital adequacy of a bank is provided at

Table 5.5
Risk Categories and Weights for Balance-Sheet Items

Category 1: 0%
1. Cash
2. Balances due from, and claims on, Federal Reserve banks and central banks in other OECD countries
3. Securities issued by the U.S. government or its agencies and the central governments of other OECD countries
4. Federal Reserve bank stock

Category 2: 20%
1. All claims on domestic depository institutions
2. Claims on foreign banks with an original maturity of one year or less
3. Claims guaranteed by, or backed by the full faith and credit of, domestic depository institutions
4. Local-currency claims on foreign central governments to the extent the bank has local-currency liabilities in the foreign country
5. Cash items in the process of collection
6. Securities and other claims on, or guaranteed by, U.S. government-sponsored agencies
7. Portions of loans and other assets collateralized by securities issued by, or guaranteed by, U.S. government-sponsored agencies
8. General-obligation claims on, and claims guaranteed by, U.S., state, and local governments that are secured by the full faith and credit of the state or local taxing authority
9. Claims on official multilateral lending institutions or regional development institutions in which the U.S. government is a shareholder or contributing member
10. Securities and other claims guaranteed by the U.S. government, or its agencies, and OECD governments
11. Portions of loans and other assets collateralized by securities issued by, or guaranteed by, the U.S. government and its agencies or by cash on deposit at the lending institution

Category 3: 50%
1. Loans fully secured by first liens on 1–4 and multifamily properties
2. Mortgage-backed securities backed by home mortgage loans with at least 80% loan-to-value ratios
3. U.S. state and local government revenue bonds
4. Credit-equivalent amounts of derivative contracts, except for those assigned to a lower risk category

Category 4: 100%
1. All other claims on private obligors
2. Claims on foreign banks with an original maturity exceeding one year
3. Claims on foreign central governments that are not included in item 4 of Category 2
4. Obligations issued by state or local governments repayable solely by a private party or enterprise
5. Premises, plant, and equipment, other fixed assets, and other real estate owned
6. Investments in any unconsolidated subsidiaries, joint ventures, or associated companies–if not deducted from capital
7. Instruments issued by other banking organizations that qualify as capital
8. All other assets, including intangible assets not deducted from capital

---

Source: Board of Governors of the Federal Reserve System, *Capital Adequacy Guidelines*, May 1994.

the top of page 124 and assumes an 8 percent capital requirement, the internationally agreed standard ratio of capital to weighted-risk assets.

If the bank has off-balance-sheet items, conversion factors would translate them into on-balance-sheet equivalents that would then be weighted according to the risk factor applicable to the category of the counterparty. For example, the Basel guidelines apply a 100 percent conversion factor to loan commitments to private corporations with an original maturity in excess of one year. Perfor-

Risk Asset Categories	(1) Amounts (in millions of dollars)	(2) Risk Weight (in percent)	(3)=(1)x(2) Risk-Weighted Assets (in millions of dollars)
1. Cash, balances at Federal Reserve Bank, and U.S. government securities	$ 75	0 %	$ 0
2. Cash items in process of collection, balances at domestic banks, and general-obligation bonds of state and local governments	220	20	44
3. Revenue bonds of state and local governments and residential mortgage loans	90	50	45
4. Loans, corporate securities, and fixed assets	350	100	350
Total	$ 735		$ 439

Requirement
Tier 1 capital: 0.04($439,000,000) = $17,560,000
Total capital: 0.08($439,000,000) = $35,120,000

mance standby letters of credit are subject to a 50 percent conversion factor, and commercial letters of credit to a 20 percent conversion factor. If these were a bank's off-balance-sheet items, then its risk-weighted assets and the combined capital requirement would be determined as shown below.

Items	Amounts (in thousands of dollars)	Conversion Factor (in percent)	Risk Weight (in percent)	Weighted Assets (in thousands of dollars)
Long-term loan commitments	$ 500	50 %	100 %	$ 250
Performance letters of credit	400	50	20	40
Commercial letters of credit	600	20	100	120
	$1,500			$ 410

Combined Requirement
Tier 1 capital: 0.04($439,000,000 + 410,000) = $17,576,400
Total capital : 0.08($439,000,000 + 410,000) = $35,152,800

Table 5.6
Credit Conversion Factors for Off-Balance-Sheet Items

100% Conversion Factor
1. Direct credit substitutes (general guarantees of indebtedness and guarantee-type instruments, including standby letters of credit serving as financial guarantees for, or supporting, loans and securities)
2. Risk participations in bankers' acceptances and direct credit substitutes, such as standby letters of credit
3. Sale and repurchase agreements and asset sales with recourse, if not already included on the balance sheet
4. Forward agreements to purchase assets, including financing facilities with certain drawdowns
5. Securities lent for which the bank is at risk

50% Conversion Factor
1. Transaction-related contingencies (such as bid bonds, performance bonds, warranties, and standby letters of credit backing the nonfinancial performance of other parties)
2. Unused commitments with an original maturity exceeding one year, including underwriting commitments and commercial credit lines
3. Revolving underwriting facilities (RUFs), note issuance facilities (NIFs), and other similar arrangements

20% Conversion Factor
1. Short-term, self-liquidating trade-related contingencies, including commercial letters of credit

0% Conversion Factor
1. Unused commitments with an original maturity of one year or less or that are unconditionally cancelable at any time

Credit Conversion for Derivative Contracts

The credit-equivalent amount of a derivative contract is the sum of the current credit exposure of the contract and an estimate of potential future increases in credit exposure. The current exposure is the positive mark-to-market value of the contract (or zero if the mark-to-market value is zero or negative). For derivative contracts that are subject to a qualifying bilateral netting contract, the current exposure is, generally, the net sum of the positive and negative mark-to-market values of the contracts included in the netting contract (or zero if the net sum of the mark-to-market values is zero or negative). The potential future exposure is calculated by multiplying the effective notional amount of a contract by one of the following credit conversion factors, as appropriate:

Remaining Maturity	Interest Rate	Exchange Rate and Gold	Equity	Commodity, Excluding Precious Metals	Precious Metals, Except Gold
One year or less	0.0%	1.0%	6.0%	10.0%	7.0%
Over one to five years	0.5%	5.0%	8.0%	12.0%	7.0%
Over five years	1.5%	7.5%	10.0%	15.0%	8.0%

No potential future exposure is calculated for single-currency interest-rate swaps in which payments are made based upon two floating indices, that is, so-called floating/floating or basis swaps. The credit exposure on these contracts is evaluated solely on the basis of their mark-to-market value. Exchange-rate contracts with an original maturity of 14 days or less are excluded. Instruments traded on exchanges that require daily receipt and payment of cash-variation margin are also excluded.

Source: Board of Governors of the Federal Reserve System, *Capital Adequacy Guidelines*, May 1994; *Federal Reserve Bulletin*, October 1995, p. 959.

Derivative contracts entail a more complex conversion process to determine on-balance-sheet equivalents. Table 5.6 identifies the various conversion factors applying to different off-balance-sheet items.

To emphasize the importance of bank capital and authorize early regulatory intervention, the FDICIA of 1991 introduced the *prompt corrective action* framework. Specifically, the act establishes five capital-adequacy categories or zones and mandates certain actions if capital minimums are not met. Table 5.7 identifies the capital-adequacy ratios that define each zone. The first two categories represent well-capitalized and adequately capitalized institutions, and as such they are not subject to any regulatory action, except that banks in the second zone cannot accept brokered deposits (funds received through third-party intermediaries) without FDIC approval.

The next three categories refer to undercapitalized institutions against which the act prescribes a specific course of action for regulators to follow. FDICIA's intention is to curtail risk-taking and prevent management from depleting an undercapitalized institution's equity capital. Once an institution becomes undercapitalized (that is, fails to meet at least one of the three minimum capital standards), it is subject to a variety of regulatory restrictions, such as the requirement to submit a capital restoration plan within 45 days, suspend dividends, limit asset growth, and obtain approval before acquiring other entities, opening new branches, or developing new lines of business. Regulatory agencies retain some discretion in imposing additional penalties.

Significantly undercapitalized institutions are subject to all the restrictions faced by undercapitalized banks, plus they are expected to merge with or be bought by another institution, and limit the pay of bank officers, the interest rates paid on deposits, and their transactions with sister banks. Here, too, regulatory agencies retain some discretion in imposing other penalties.

Critically undercapitalized depositories face all the restrictions applying to undercapitalized banks, including regulatory approval to engage in such transactions as opening new lines of business, extending credit to highly leveraged borrowers, paying excessive compensation or bonuses, paying above-market rates on new or renewed liabilities, altering accounting methods, or amending bylaws and charters. Once a bank reaches this lowest capital zone, the appropriate regulator may appoint a receiver or conservator within 90 days. A bank's tangible equity capital may equal 2 percent or less of total assets and it may still be closed by regulators. Closure of banks limits losses to the insurance fund and concentrates more of the risk of failure on equity holders. Moreover, it prevents regulatory forbearance, which proved costly in the past.*

Capital Requirements Against Market Risks

Since risk-based capital requirements address only credit risk, FDICIA sought to remedy this weakness by requiring regulators to allow in the existing framework for banks' exposure to interest-rate risk. This was also the intention of the

*Between 1980 and 1989 the average length of time an insolvent bank had been on the regulator's problem list increased from 15 months to 28 months. This development accounted for an increase in the FDIC's resolution costs from 12 percent to 22 percent of failed banks' assets.[2]

Basel Committee, so an amendment to the Capital Accord of 1988 was introduced in early 1996 that incorporated market risk—a further step in strengthening the soundness and stability of the international banking system and of financial markets in general. The amendment provided for the implementation of capital standards for market risk by year-end 1997, or earlier at the discretion of supervisory authorities. Market risk is defined as the risk of losses in on- and off-balance-sheet positions arising from movement in market prices. In this context, the amendment addresses the risks pertaining to interest-rate-related instruments (e.g., debt securities, future and forward contracts, and swaps); equities (e.g., long and short positions in equity securities, derivatives products, stock indices, and index arbitrage) in the trading book; and foreign-exchange and commodities risks throughout the bank (total currency and commodity positions).

In measuring market risk, banks have a choice between two broad methodologies. One alternative is to measure risk in a standardized manner, using the measurement framework as provided in the amendment for each individual case (i.e., interest rate, equity position, foreign-exchange and commodities risk while a number of possible methods are suggested for measuring the price risk in options of all kinds). The alternative methodology—a significant innovation in supervisory practices—allows banks to use risk measures derived from their own internal risk-management models. However, to ensure a minimum degree of prudence, transparency, and consistency of capital requirements across banks, proprietary models must meet several sets of criteria (both qualitative and quantitative) and must receive prior approval from the bank's supervisory authority.

The principal form of eligible capital to cover market risk consists of core and supplementary capital. However, banks may also, at the discretion of their national authority, employ a third tier of capital (tier 3) subject to certain conditions. Qualified tier 3 consists of short-term subordinated debt that may be used to meet part of the capital requirements for market risk. The 1988 Capital Accord provided that tier 1 capital should represent at least half of the total eligible capital. The decision whether to extend this requirement to the new definition of eligible capital (i.e., for tier 1 capital to equal or exceed the sums of tier 2 and tier 3 capital) is a matter of national discretion.

In the same way as for credit risk, the capital requirements for market risk are to apply on a worldwide consolidated basis. To determine capital requirements against market risk, the amendment introduces a capital ratio of 12.5 percent (i.e., the reciprocal of the minimum capital ratio of 8 percent). By multiplying the measure of market risk by 12.5 percent and adding the resulting figure to the sum of risk-weighted assets compiled for credit risk purposes, the bank's overall capital requirement is determined. Eligible capital will be the sum of the bank's tier 1 capital, qualifying tier 2 capital, and (at national discretion) those tier 3 capital elements which can be used to support market risk (unused but eligible tier 3 capital may be reported separately). Eligible capital (excluding unused tier 3) divided by the total (notional) risk-weighted assets would deter-

Table 5.7
Capital Zones and Prompt Corrective Action

I. Capital Zones

Category	Total Risk-Based Ratio[1]		Tier 1 Risk-Based Ratio[2]		Leverage Ratio[3]
Well capitalized	10 or above	and	6 or above	and	5 or above
Adequately capitalized	8 or above	and	4 or above	and	4 or above[4]
Undercapitalized	Under 8	or	Under 4	or	Under 4[5]
Significantly undercapitalized	Under 6	or	Under 3	or	Under 3
Critically undercapitalized[6]					

II. Supervisory Actions

Category	Mandatory Provisions	Discretionary Provisions
1. Well capitalized	None	None
2. Adequately capitalized	1. No brokered deposits, except with FDIC approval	None

	Mandatory provisions	Discretionary provisions
3. Undercapitalized	1. Suspend dividends and management fees 2. Require capital restoration plan 3. Restrict asset growth 4. Approval required for acquisitions, branching, and new activities 5. No brokered deposits	1. Order recapitalization 2. Restrict interaffiliate transactions 3. Restrict deposit interest rates 4. Restrict certain other activities 5. Any other action that would better carry out prompt corrective action
4. Significantly undercapitalized	1. Same as for Zone 3 2. Order recapitalization[7] 3. Restrict interaffiliate transactions[7] 4. Restrict deposit interest rates[7] 5. Pay of officers restricted	1. Any Zone 3 discretionary actions 2. Conservatorship or receivership if fails to submit or implement plan or recapitalize pursuant to order 3. Any other Zone 5 provision, if such action is necessary to carry out prompt corrective action
5. Critically undercapitalized	1. Same as for Zone 4 2. Receiver/conservator within 90 days[7] 3. Receiver if still in Zone 5 four quarters after becoming critically undercapitalized 4. Suspend payments on subordinated debt[7] 5. Restrict certain other activities	

[1]Ratio of qualifying total capital to weighted-risk assets.

[2]Ratio of Tier 1 capital to weighted-risk assets.

[3]Ratio of Tier 1 capital to average total consolidated assets.

[4]The standard is 3 percent or above for a bank with a composite CAMEL rating of 1 in its most recent report of examination.

[5]The standard is under 3 percent for a bank with a composite CAMEL rating of 1 in its most recent report of examination.

[6]The only criterion is a tangible equity-to-assets ratio that is equal to or less than 2 percent. Tangible equity includes core capital, plus cumulative perpetual preferred stock, minus all intangible assets except purchased mortgage servicing rights (up to a specified limitation). The denominator is quarterly average total assets minus the deductions made in the numerator.

[7]Not required if primary supervisor determines action would not serve purpose of prompt corrective action or if certain other conditions are met.

Sources: Federal Reserve Board of Governors, September 10, 1993; Catherine Lemieux, "FDICIA: Where Did It Come from and Where Will It Take Us?"; Federal Reserve Bank of Kansas City, *Financial Industry Perspectives*, November 1993, p. 3.

mine the bank's overall capital ratio—the capital that is available to meet both credit risk and market risk.

The capital guidelines for market risk reinforce the continued efforts within the supervisory community to achieve improvements in risk-management techniques across the full range of financial-market participants. Implementation of these guidelines, and especially the internal models alternative in the market-risk package, will provide a valuable starting point. It will take some time until the experience acquired is fully evaluated. As more experience is gained, further adjustments will be made in regulatory standards on capital policy.

Meeting Capital Requirements

How did the Basel capital requirements and FDICIA's prompt corrective action provisions affect U.S. banks? Banks not sufficiently capitalized opted for one or more of the following actions:

1. Restructure assets
2. Shrink the bank
3. Leasing arrangements
4. Pricing policies
5. Raise capital (internally, externally)
6. Merger with another bank.

The capital requirements induced U.S. banks to rethink their asset-management strategies. Differences in the risk weighting of the various asset categories renders *restructuring* an important option in meeting capital requirements. The larger allocation of capital against higher-risk assets (e.g., loans) favors redistribution of resources toward lower- or no-risk assets (e.g., U.S. government securities). Restructuring has the desired effect of reducing the required risk-based capital, but it also affects the potential profitability of the bank.

Shrinking the bank entails downsizing the balance sheet (e.g., curbing lending activity, selling assets). A reduction in risk-weighted assets would make the existing capital a higher percentage of the equity ratio. This approach is not very appealing to banks because it deprives them of economies of scale and harms profitability.

Leasing is a related alternative to shrinking. Banks may sell their head office building and other real estate and simultaneously lease them back from the buyer. A sale-and-leaseback transaction removes a high-risk asset from the balance sheet and lowers capital requirements. It also enables the bank to convert into cash the appreciated value of the properties listed in its books at cost. The gain is subject to normal income-tax rates, and the funds many be invested to yield the bank a competitive rate of return.

Pricing enables a bank to pass on to its customers the effect of the higher capital requirements on its assets and off-balance-sheet items. Thus, whether it makes a loan or issues a letter of credit, a bank may charge higher fees to compensate itself for the larger amount of capital required to support them.

The need to meet the Basel requirements prompted many banks to *raise capital*. Internally generated capital offers some latitude for a bank to expand its assets and still meet capital requirements. The extent of asset growth that can be sustained by retained earnings may be determined by the *internal capital generation rate* (ICGR), which can be calculated as follows:

$$ICGR = \frac{1}{EC/TA} \times ROA \times (1-DPR),$$

where EC/TA is the bank's ratio of equity capital to total assets, ROA is the rate of return on assets, and DPR is the dividend payout rate, which in the equation format of (1–DPR) determines the bank's earnings-retention rate. Thus, a bank that targets a 4 percent equity/assets ratio, a 1 percent ROA, and a 40 percent dividend payout rate can increase its assets by ICGR = (1/.04) ×. 01 × (1 − .40) = .15 or 15 percent. The equation is important in management planning because it highlights the interrelationship between capital constraints and profit rates, asset growth rates, and dividend policy.

The need to restore and even increase capital ratios prompted many large banks to raise capital through public offerings of securities. Thus, from the early 1990s on, many banks tapped capital markets to raise different forms of capital, such as long-term debt, perpetual preferred stock, and common stock. Smaller banks whose stocks are traded over the counter have often issued new shares to existing stockholders or current customers within their local communities.

For banks in financially weak condition, a new issue is likely to be costly. An alternative is *merger* with a stronger bank. There has been a wave of such mergers over the years that have resulted in stronger equity positions. Money-center banks were no exception to this trend. Some of the most notable mergers took place in 1992: between BankAmerica and Security Pacific, with the new bank called BankAmerica; Chemical Bank and Manufacturers Hanover, with the new bank called Chemical Bank; and NCNB and C&S Sovran, which became Nationsbank.

NOTES

1. *Standard Federal Tax Reporter*, 9 vols. (Chicago: Commerce Clearing House, 1967), vol. 4, para. 3458.01. For the relevant provisions of the 1986 Tax Reform Act, see the 1988 edition of the same work, vol. 1, sec. 585.

2. Catherine Lemieux, "FDICIA: Where Did It Come from and Where Will It Take Us?" Federal Reserve Bank of Kansas City, *Financial Industry Perspectives*, November 1993, pp. 1–2.

SUGGESTED REFERENCES

Borowsky, Mark. "Stock Doldrums Won't Hold Back Mergers." *Bank Management*, September 1993, pp. 38–43.

Eubanks, Walter W. "Risk Based Capital and Regulatory Enforcement." *CRS Review*, May/June 1991, pp. 16–18.

Harvey, James. "Commercial Bank Performance, 1992." Federal Reserve Bank of Kansas City, *Financial Industry Trends*, 1993, pp. 3–10

Lemieux, Catherine. "FDICIA Mandated Capital Zones and the Banking Industry." Federal Reserve Bank of Kansas City, *Financial Industry Trends*, 1993, pp. 11–14.

Levonian, Mark E. "Market Risk and Bank Capital: Part I." Federal Reserve Bank of San Francisco, *FRBSF Weekly Letter*, January 7, 1994, pp. 1–3.

———. "Market Risk and Bank Capital: Part II." Federal Reserve Bank of San Francisco, *FRBSF Weekly Letter*, January 14, 1994, pp. 1–3.

Chapter 6

Deposits

In every study on money and banking, it is expounded that in the commercial banking system as a whole, the volume of deposits depends essentially upon the amount of credit extended by banks. When banks extend loans or make investments, they do so by granting their customers deposit credits against which they can, and usually do, write checks. Through its lending and investing activities the banking system thus affects the volume of demand deposits in the economy and, consequently, the total stock of money. The deposit-creating powers of commercial banks are subject to one important limitation: the legal requirement of maintaining reserves equal, at the minimum, to a certain percentage of their deposit liabilities. Thus, depending upon what the legal reserve ratio may be, the banking system as a whole can lend and create demand deposits equal to a multiple of its excess reserves.

What follows from the deposit-expansion process of the banking system is that the line of causation runs from the assets side to the liabilities side of the balance sheet. In other words, assets give rise to liabilities. For the individual bank, however, the line of causation is reversed. That is, liabilities give rise to assets. An individual bank first must attract deposits, and then put them to work. Since Part II is examining the sources of funds available to an individual bank, in this chapter deposits will be studied from that perspective.

As we saw in Chapter 5, in connection with capital adequacy, banks have been relying extensively on deposits in the financing of their assets. On September 30, 1995, deposits accounted for 69 percent of the total assets of all insured commercial banks; nondeposit liabilities and capital accounted, respectively, for 23 and 8 percent of bank assets. Deposits have always been the principal source of bank funds. Recognizing their importance in the financing of assets, banks have always been pleased to receive deposits, and most banks have made a continuing effort to solicit them from various sources.

Traditionally the deposit structure of a commercial bank was thought to be determined primarily by the depositors, and not by bank management. This view has been undergoing important changes. With the introduction of negotiable CDs in the early 1960s and the subsequent liberalization of regulatory controls, banks have become increasingly effective in influencing the volume and types of deposits they receive and, hence, in bringing about desired shifts in their deposit structure. Thus banks have evolved from relatively passive acceptors of deposits to active bidders for funds. Deposits, however, are but one aspect of the bank liabilities that management has been influencing through deliberate policy actions. The other aspect is nondeposit liabilities, the diverse channels through which banks borrow funds to relend to their customers or to meet unexpected deposit outflows. Most of these borrowing channels, developed first by large money-center banks, have evolved into important devices for attracting interest-sensitive funds. Eurodollar borrowings, RPs, and federal funds are only a few of the nondeposit sources of funds developed by commercial banks.

This new approach of influencing liabilities through management policy actions, generally called *liability management*, is an important aspect of the funds management of a commercial bank. As such, it is complementary to capital management. Liability management involves obtaining funds from depositors and other creditors (that is, choosing among alternative deposit and nondeposit sources) and determining the appropriate mix of funds. In a stricter sense, however, liability management implies obtaining interest-sensitive funds when they are needed to supplement a bank's liquidity requirements.

This chapter describes the main deposit classifications, addresses deposit policy, and reviews the changing nature of the payments mechanism.

NATURE AND CLASSES OF BANK DEPOSITS

Bank deposits are subject to various forms of classification. The most common are according to ownership, to security, and to availability of funds. On the basis of these criteria, deposits may be distinguished into public, private, and interbank; secured and unsecured; and demand and time. Each of these types is examined below.

Public, Private, and Interbank Deposits

Public deposits are those owned by all levels of government: federal, state, and subdivisions of states. The deposits of the federal government at commercial banks have been known as tax-and-loan (T&L) accounts. First established in 1917 in banks throughout the country, these accounts are maintained for the deposit of income-tax receipts, Social Security taxes, proceeds from the sale of securities, and other types of government receipts. The Treasury's T&L accounts have generally been used as feeder accounts for its "general accounts" at Federal Reserve banks, against which all payments are made. Transfers made several times each week out of T&L accounts enable the Treasury to draw on its general accounts to make payments to the public.

Banks formerly paid no interest on government balances in T&L accounts but provided various services for the U.S. Treasury at little or no cost. The high rates of interest experienced since the 1960s led the Treasury to sponsor legislation in 1977 that allowed it to earn interest on its cash balances. As a result, a depository bank no longer has free use of balances in T&L accounts. Generally such a bank has a twofold option in processing T&L receipts. It may transfer them, within one day, to the Treasury's general account at the Federal Reserve bank or to an interest-bearing demand note issued by the bank. The funds invested in these notes are made available to the Treasury upon request. Since these notes do not constitute a deposit account, no reserve requirements are held against them. The rate of interest paid by banks is determined by the federal government. It has been set at 25 basis points below the going federal funds rate. Banks are compensated for the services they perform for the Treasury by payment of set fees.

For a bank to become a qualified depository for U.S. government funds, it must pledge qualified securities for the uninsured portion of those funds. Requirements for becoming a state or municipal depository vary from locale to locale, but they frequently require bidding on the interest rate the bank is to offer. An additional consideration may be the bank's willingness to underwrite or purchase the state's or municipality's securities. Competition for these deposits is often intense.

Interbank deposits are owned by other commercial banks—domestic and foreign—as well as mutual savings banks. The bulk of deposits in this category is correspondent bank balances.

Private deposits are those owned by individuals, partnerships, corporations, and other private institutions. As might be expected, most of the deposits in the United States are owned by individuals and businesses. On September 30, 1995, business and personal deposits at insured commercial banks accounted for 88.4 percent of total deposits; interbank deposits accounted for 5.5 percent; and public and other deposits for 6.1 percent.

Secured and Unsecured Deposits

Secured deposits are those that require the pledging of security. Public funds—those of federal, state, city, county, and other state subdivision governments—are the most common type of secured deposits. The bank has to guarantee the safety of these deposits by pledging securities as collateral. For example, commercial banks that accept federal government deposits greater than the amount insured by the FDIC must pledge U.S. government securities or

Table 6.1

Size and Importance of Domestic Deposits of Insured Commercial Banks, 1965–95 (in billions of dollars)

Year	Transaction Accounts	Nontransaction Accounts			Total Deposits
		Savings	Time	Total	
1965	183.8	92.6	55.1	147.7	331.5
1970	246.2	98.2	134.8	233.0	479.2
1980	432.3	201.2	558.7	759.9	1,192.2
1990	684.5	577.5	1,094.7	1,672.2	2,356.7
1991	706.8	660.5	1,015.7	1,676.2	2,383.0
1992	810.3	747.2	854.4	1,601.6	2,411.9
1993	854.7	774.5	795.2	1,569.7	2,424.4
1994	852.8	740.6	849.1	1,589.7	2,442.5
1995	826.6	780.1	966.8	1,746.9	2,573.5

Note: Details may not add to totals due to rounding.

Source: Federal Deposit Insurance Corporation, *Annual Report* (various issues); *Statistics on Banking* (Washington, D.C.: FDIC, selected issues). Data for 1995 year-end were derived from *Call Report*.

other form of collateral approved by the Secretary of the Treasury to cover the uninsured excess.

Most private deposits are unsecured, in that the bank pledges no specific assets to guarantee their safety. However, all accounts in banks insured by the FDIC are automatically covered up to a maximum of $100,000. Depositors with balances exceeding this amount stand to lose if a bank liquidates.

Transaction and Nontransaction Accounts

Transaction accounts—also known as checkable or checking accounts—are deposit arrangements permitting funds to be withdrawn or transferred to third parties, usually by check, although telephone transfers and transactions via ATMs are common. Transaction accounts ensure the availability of funds when needed. Nontransaction accounts include time and savings deposits. Time deposits permit withdrawal of funds after the elapse of a stated period of time, such as 30, 60, 90, or 180 days. Savings deposits do not have specified maturity dates or size limits; they may be closed at any time, and additions or withdrawals may be effected at the holder's will. Checking accounts are of special importance because they are the dominant medium of exchange in the economy. Time and savings accounts, on the other hand, have grown to become the principal source of deposit funds for commercial banks. At year-end 1995, time and savings accounts represented about 68 percent of the total deposits at domestic offices of all insured commercial banks. The size and importance of each type of deposit is shown in Table 6.1

Transaction Accounts

Checking accounts are highly liquid; they provide a mechanism for the safe transfer of funds; they are relatively immune to financial loss due to robbery or forgery (the bank is at fault if a forged check is paid); and checks serve as receipts for payments made. One category of checking accounts, demand deposits, earns no explicit interest payment, while the other—negotiable order of withdrawal *(NOW)* accounts—does. Prior to 1933 banks typically paid interest on demand deposits, but in subsequent decades that practice was rendered illegal by the Glass-Steagall Act of 1933. Because they can be withdrawn without prior notice to the bank, demand deposits are among the most volatile sources of funds, with the shortest potential maturity. Most demand deposits are held by businesses and are largely compensating balances that are required by banks in return for various commercial services (e.g., credit services and check-clearing services).

Interest-bearing demand deposits—known as NOW accounts—were first introduced by thrifts in the New England region in 1972. The NOW accounts broke with tradition in two ways. They not only permitted interest to be paid on demand deposits but also broke the monopoly on demand deposits that commercial banks had enjoyed. In 1980 enactment of DIDMCA extended authority to depository institutions nationwide to offer NOW accounts. Only natural persons, government bodies, and nonprofit organizations are eligible for a NOW account.

In the fall of 1982, the Garn-St. Germain Act, in an attempt to enhance the competitiveness of banks and thrifts vis-à-vis mutual funds, authorized regulators to offer a deposit instrument that would be directly equivalent to and competitive with private funds. In response to this mandate, the Depository Institutions Deregulation Committee (DIDC)—which was established by the DIDMCA to handle the gradual phaseout through 1986 of Regulation Q ceiling rates on deposits in all depository institutions—created the money-market deposit account. Through this account banks and thrifts were freed to pay their customers ceiling-free interest rates and to offer them limited checking privileges. Since this account is a saving instrument, the DIDC authorized banks and thrifts to offer another high-interest-paying account, this one for checking. Dubbed "Super NOW" account, the new deposit instrument allowed customers to write an unlimited number of checks, just like regular checking accounts, yet offered them a rate of interest higher than that paid by regular NOW accounts. The Super NOW was first offered to the public in early January 1983. A key regulatory requirement was a minimum balance of $2,500; if balances fell below this minimum amount, deposits earned only the rate paid on regular NOW accounts. With the phaseout of Regulation Q in 1986, the minimum-balance requirement for Super NOW accounts was eliminated. This prompted many banks to collapse their NOW and Super NOW accounts into one two-tier NOW account whereby balances in excess of a certain amount earn a higher rate of interest.

NOW accounts are generally a costlier source of funds than money-market deposits. By being considered a transaction account, the NOW is subject to reserve requirements from which personal money-market accounts are exempted because of their savings-deposit character. In addition, the unlimited checking and transfer privileges offered by this account make its cost to a bank quite high. For this reason banks are paying somewhat lower rates of interest on NOWs than they do on money-market accounts. Moreover, they have imposed stiff requirements on these accounts. Many institutions require minimum balances, with monthly service charges and/or check fees for accounts that fall below certain levels. The high employee and equipment costs associated with the processing of checks and recording of deposits have prompted many banks to pass on to depositors a bigger share of the activity expenses associated with their accounts.

Automatic transfer services (ATS), which were introduced in 1978, provide a function similar to that of the NOW account. Although they usually involve service charges, often in the form of monthly maintenance fees, ATS accounts automatically transfer funds from a savings account to a checking account in order to cover overdrafts and to maintain a minimum balance in the checking account. They thereby allow the customer to keep in an interest-earning savings account funds that otherwise would be tied up in a checking account that pays no interest. The DIDMCA classified ATS accounts, NOW accounts, and telephone and preauthorized transfers as transaction accounts and subjected them to the reserve requirements for these accounts.

Savings Deposits

Unlike demand deposits, which can be withdrawn or transferred without prior notice, a bank reserves the right to require advance notice before funds can be withdrawn from savings deposits. Since banks rarely exercise this authority, depositors can withdraw their funds immediately. Savings deposits earn interest and have indefinite maturity. Until 1975 only individuals and certain nonprofit organizations could hold savings deposits, but now partnerships and corporations can have savings deposits of up to $150,000.

The *passbook savings account*, so named because at each transaction the customer must present a passbook that records the transaction and contains the rules and regulations governing the account, has been the traditional form of savings deposit. Recently, though, banks have been offering ''statement savings'' instead of passbook accounts. With statement savings the depositor maintains the transaction records, which are confirmed by a bank statement mailed quarterly or more frequently. The statements include the amount of interest earned. With the advent of computerization, banks can credit interest from date of deposit to date of withdrawal, and they can compound interest daily, a practice that costs little but is a good advertisement.

Until the enactment in 1980 of the DIDMCA, which provided for the six-year phaseout of ceiling interest rates on savings and time deposits, the passbook and statement savings market was not a major source of bank funds. In the fall of 1982, Congress, through the DIDC, authorized banks and thrifts to offer *money-market deposit accounts* in order to recover part of the $232 billion that had been diverted over the years to mutual funds. Although—as anticipated—some funds were shifted into money-market deposits from lower-interest-paying savings accounts, significant amounts of new money came to banks and thrifts from outside sources. A week after their introduction, the new accounts took their toll on money-market funds, whose assets plunged by $6.5 billion.

A minimum balance of $2,500 was required when the account was first offered to the public in December 1982. However, with the phaseout of Regulation Q in 1986, this requirement was eliminated. The principal characteristics of the money-market deposit account (MMDA) are as follows. Though a savings and not a transaction account, it offers depositors a limited checking privilege; that is, savers may write a limited number of checks per month against their balances. Deposits of as much as $100,000 are insured by the FDIC (the shares of money-market funds enjoy no such coverage). Additional deposits need not be in any minimum amount and need not be made at any specific time. The yield on money-market deposit accounts exceeds that on NOWs because the depositor gives up the unlimited transactions feature. The interest rate is variable and may be adjusted once a month or even more often.

No minimum amount requirements are imposed on withdrawals or transfers from a money-market deposit account. However, if the account's average monthly balance falls below a minimum amount, a lower rate of interest is paid. In addition, monthly service charges may be applied. The institution reserves the right to require at least seven days' notice before funds are withdrawn from the money-market account, though it may seldom insist on such a notice. The depositor receives a monthly record of the interest earned and of the amounts deposited, withdrawn, or transferred.

Time Deposits

Time deposits may take any one of three forms: certificates of deposit, individual retirement accounts, and time-deposit open accounts. Certificates of deposit constitute the dominant type of time deposits. The certificate of deposit (CD) is an interest-earning deposit of funds left with the bank for a fixed, stated time period. The bank knows exactly how long it will have these funds available for lending or investing, and so it rewards the customer for providing it a greater level of certainty by offering higher interest rates than those paid to savings accounts. CDs are the major form of time deposit. They may be purchased at any time and begin earning interest on the date of purchase. Introduced in February 1961 by First National City Bank of New York (Citibank), CDs were conceived as a means to retain and attract interest-sensitive deposit funds. Prior to 1961, a few large CDs had been issued, but the total dollar value was unimportant because they were not negotiable; thus they did not offer corporate treasurers the same options as other money-market instruments. When First National City Bank announced the acceptance of term deposits in the form of large CDs, it provided for the full negotiability of these instruments. A government securities dealer had agreed to make a secondary market for these new instruments by matching buyers and sellers.

Since their inception negotiable CDs have become a convenient source of deposit funds, and many banks issue them. In 1995, the volume of outstanding CDs issued by insured commercial banks amounted to $241.5 billion, compared with about $1 billion in 1961. Because CDs are negotiable, a significant number of securities houses provide an active secondary market in these instruments. This fact has enabled banks to attract funds from large investors who otherwise might place their funds in Treasury bills or other money-market instruments. Negotiable CDs are generally short-term, with maturities of one year or less, and are most commonly sold to corporations, pension funds, and government bodies in denominations of $100,000 to $1 million or larger.

In recent years bankers have sought to increase the appeal of negotiable CDs to investors by introducing variations in the terms under which CDs are offered. One such variant is the *variable-rate CD*, also known as variable-coupon CD or floating-rate CD. It draws its name from the periodic adjustment of its rate. The maturity of the CD is divided into equal rollover periods—also known as legs or roll periods—in each of which the interest rate is set anew at some fixed spread to a reference rate or index. Examples of such an index are the secondary market rate for domestic CDs (published by the Federal Reserve Bank of New York) or the London Interbank Offered Rate (LIBOR).

Another CD innovation has been the *index CD*, which ties the deposit yield to the performance of an index. The first to announce a CD of this nature was Chase Manhattan Bank, which introduced the "bull CD" in early 1987. This CD was linked to the Standard and Poor's (S&P) 500 Stock Index. Investors received no set interest but, depending on the CD's term, they earned a set percentage of any increase in the S&P Stock Index. Later that year, Chase unveiled a "bear CD" that offered investors a multiple of any decline in the S&P Stock Index. At about the same time, the First National Bank of Chicago introduced a similar product that offered investors a choice of indexes: the Commodity Exchange gold price (Comex price of gold) or the New York Stock Exchange Composite Index.

Negotiable CDs issued by the branches of foreign banks in this country have customarily been referred to as *Yankee CDs*. Introduced in the early 1970s, Yankee CDs enable these banks to finance their loans to U.S. corporations and foreign businesses operating in this country. Most of the banks issuing Yankee CDs are located in New York and represent reputable international banking organizations headquartered in Japan, Canada, and Western Europe.

Just as foreign banks issue CDs in the United States, so U.S. banks purchase funds offshore by offering *Eurodollar CDs*. These are negotiable, dollar-denominated deposits that, by virtue of being issued abroad, are exempt from reserve requirements and FDIC insurance assessments. First offered by Citibank in 1966, Eurodollar CDs are now offered by foreign branches of many U.S. banks and by some foreign-owned banks.

Prompted by the success of the large CDs, banks began to offer *consumer* or *retail CDs* in smaller denominations. Consumer CDs pay a higher interest rate than savings deposits and have a minimum maturity of at least seven days. The rate of interest tends to increase with the duration of the certificate. Consumer CDs are usually not negotiable, though depositors can recover their funds prior to the certificate's maturity by paying a penalty.

Deregulation of retail CD rates in the early 1980s prompted depositors to look around for the best available rates. With a large number of institutions and with deposit rates constantly changing, the demand for rate information became very important. This situation led securities brokers to enter the deposit market as middlemen; they pooled the funds of customers and placed them at institutions offering the highest interest rate. To insure against the risk of loss, they broke up the funds into packages of no more than $100,000 and placed them into insured accounts with different banks. Because large CDs paid higher rates than smaller CDs, brokers offered smaller depositors better yields.

This practice gave rise to *brokered deposits*, which proved a boon especially to small banks and thrifts. Lacking the credit standing to borrow in money markets, these institutions could obtain brokered funds by quoting a high enough rate. Concerned that brokered deposits may compromise institutional safety and soundness, the FDIC took the stand in 1982 that in the event of bank failure, it would treat all deposits placed by the same broker in that bank as belonging to a single depositor, and hence would subject them to the $100,000 insurance limit. A court decision in 1984, however, found this rule illegal, and the FDIC was forced to back down. The FDICIA of 1991 prohibits undercapitalized banks from accepting brokered deposits and allows adequately capitalized banks to accept such deposits only after obtaining a waiver from the FDIC; well-capitalized banks can accept brokered deposits without regulatory approval. The Federal Reserve monitors—through financial reports—the institutional use of brokered funds, and where it is excessive (i.e., more than 5 percent of total deposits) a formal examination may follow.

Time deposits may also take the form of *individual retirement accounts*. Enactment of the Economic Recovery Tax Act of 1981 authorized financial institutions (banks, thrifts, brokerage firms, insurance companies, and mutual funds) and employers with qualified pension or profit-sharing plans to offer individual retirement account (IRA) plans to all wage earners and salaried individuals. IRA plans had a precedent; in 1962 Congress had enacted the Keogh Act, which permitted self-employed individuals to establish voluntary retirement plans for themselves. IRAs and Keogh plans have thus grown over the years to become an important source of funds. In spite of the intensity of market competition, attractive interest rates and good service have enabled banks to attract a sizable amount of deposit funds. Eligible depositors may make tax-deferred additions to these accounts up to an allowable maximum per year. Earnings on all contributions are also tax-deferred, regardless of depositor income. Funds may be withdrawn at age 59.5 or later, at which time the depositor will probably be in a lower tax bracket. The tax-sheltered nature of these deposits has contributed to their development into a long-term, stable source of funds for banks.

Compared with the other types of time deposits, *open-account time deposits* are generally a minor source of bank funds. These are short-term deposit plans offered by banks to induce savers to make regular deposits of a stated amount of money. The understanding is that within a specified period of time, there will be a large enough balance to enable the depositor to meet bills (for instance, at Christmas or for a vacation). In accordance with the nature of the anticipated expenditure, these plans have been known as Christmas Club, Vacation Club, Tax Club, and so on. They are covered by written contracts that do not permit their owners to withdraw all or any part of the funds deposited prior to maturity of the accounts or without giving written notice not less than 14 days in advance of withdrawal. If funds are withdrawn prior to maturity, the depositor incurs an interest penalty. The maximum rate payable on these deposits depends upon the maturity of the account and the amount involved. Small banks find these plans beneficial because they help increase their deposit holdings and induce customers to save money.

DEPOSIT POLICY

Growth of a bank depends primarily upon the growth of its deposits. Although individual banks do not have absolute control over the level of their deposits, they can nevertheless influence the amounts they hold. Because deposits are so important to the profitability of bank operations, most banks tend to compete aggressively for them. Some of the factors that determine the level of deposits in a bank are exogenous, and hence beyond its control (e.g., monetary and fiscal policy, and the level of general economic activity). An intermediate group of factors may be controlled up to a certain extent, such as size and physical location of the bank and its offices. However, the bank is in a position to control a number of other factors, such as promotional activities (e.g., advertising and call programs), physical facilities and personnel, participation in civic activities, services offered to depositors, and the rates of interest paid—or fees charged—to depositors (pricing). The major factors contributing to the attraction of deposits are taken into account in the formulation of a bank's deposit policy. Of course, pricing of deposit services is a dominant consideration because it determines the volume of deposits that management will use for creating income through loans and investments. The sections that follow address pricing strategy in the context of current trends compared with the Regulation Q era, and describe the effects of the changing composition of bank deposits.

Pricing Strategy

Competition for deposit funds has prompted banks to introduce a wide variety of deposit products and related services. This diversity has led many banks to pursue product differentiation in order to distinguish themselves from competing institutions. Product differentiation, in turn, has rendered the pricing of deposit services a challenging task. In the pricing of their products and services, banks make use of both explicit pricing (interest expenses) and implicit pricing (non-interest expenses). Since the dismantling of Regulation Q, banks have made greater use of explicit pricing to reflect unbundled costs (true costs of producing specific products and services). As a result, deposits have been priced independently from the pricing of loans and other bank services. An explicit pricing strategy for deposits must combine such features as convenience (e.g., ATM availability), transaction fees, minimum balances required to earn interest, and benefits offered by the particular account. These pricing features are traded off against one another in the framework of the desired deposit volume mix.

In pricing deposit services, banks may pursue a number of alternative approaches. *Cost-plus-profit pricing* is based on the notion that the pricing of a deposit service must be high enough to enable the bank to recover the cost of providing that service plus an adequate profit margin. The cost component should take into account both the operating expense per unit of deposit service plus the estimated overhead expense allocated to the deposit function. Pricing will thus reflect a bank's true cost in the extension of deposit services. *Penetration pricing* entails setting deposit interest rates as high as possible—or, conversely, reducing deposit fees as low as possible—to capture the greatest share of the deposit market. The expectation is that the resulting higher volume of deposits and the additional loan business generated will offset the reduction in profit margins. This approach may be used to introduce new products or support existing ones, with the exception of checking accounts, where considerations other than price (e.g., convenience, service availability) dominate the decisions of businesses and households as to the bank of choice. *Scheduled, or conditional, pricing* calls for assessing deposit services based upon the extent of their usage over a designated period. For example, a fee schedule identifies the minimum average balances required and the charges involved for transactions passing through the account (e.g., number of checks written, stop-payment orders, and notices).

Upscale target pricing customizes the terms of a standardized product for certain sectors of the market. Thus, the high-balance, low-activity deposits of professionals will be priced differently from the low-balance, high-activity accounts of students. *Relationship pricing* recognizes the importance of "total customer relationship" or "relationship banking," whereby customers rely on the bank to meet all their financial needs. Thus, to clients who maintain a strong and multiple-service relationship, the bank extends favorable terms in the form of lower fees or better deposit yields.

Whatever the pricing strategy, the Truth-in-Savings Act (TISA) of 1991 requires depository institutions in the United States (both domestic and foreign-owned) to disclose their fees, interest rates, and all the terms and conditions associated with the deposit services they sell to the public. Taking advantage of deregulation, some banks were paying interest on only 88 to 90 percent of account balances because they had to set aside 10 to 12 percent of their funds in reserve and could not earn any income on them. Other banks based their interest payments on the lowest, rather than the average, deposit balance. TISA not only outlawed these practices but also required all banks to calculate interest payments the same way, by compounding the entire account balance daily to produce an annual percentage yield (APY). By standardizing the method of calculating the APY, TISA sought to enhance consumers' comparison shopping. The formula used to determine the APY is

$$APY = 100 \; [(1 + \text{Interest earned/Average daily balance})^{(365/\text{days in period})} - 1].$$

TISA calls on depository institutions to send depositors a 30–day advance notice concerning any planned change in deposit terms (e.g., fees or interest rate) that could result in reduced deposit yields. To safeguard against any institutional violation, TISA provides for civil liability and administrative enforcement mechanisms. Enactment of the Riegle Community Development and Regulatory Improvement Act of 1994 limited the disclosure requirements of TISA to deposit accounts held by individuals for a personal, family, or household purpose. Regulation DD of the Federal Reserve encompasses the rules that implement the provisions of TISA.

Deposit Competition Under Regulation Q

Regulation Q had its origin in the Banking Act of 1933, which prohibited the payment of interest on demand deposits and authorized the Federal Reserve to set maximum rates on time deposits. Regulation Q reflected much of the determination so characteristic of the Great Depression to establish a sound banking structure. The wave of bank failures that occurred in the early 1930s led many to believe that it was essentially a product of deposit competition among banks and the payment of excessive rates, which in turn encouraged unsafe lending and investing practices in the effort to earn enough to cover the cost of higher rates. Hence the reasoning that by regulating interest payments on deposits, price competition among banks would be eliminated, thereby producing a safer banking system. Another argument in favor of interest regulation was the concern that the payment of higher interest rates by larger banks would attract funds from rural areas and lessen the availability of credit in those areas. However plausible these arguments may have appeared at the time, regulation Q had important implications not only for banks but also for the entire financial system.

By prohibiting banks from paying interest on demand deposits and by imposing ceiling rates on time and savings accounts, Regulation Q was instrumental in controlling the lending ability of banks and, consequently, their role in the process of allocating credit among the various sectors of the economy. Regulation Q thus evolved into an active tool of monetary policy.

Demand Deposits

The immediate effect of the prohibition of interest payments on demand deposits was to limit the importance of these deposits as a source of loanable funds. This led banks to make use of implicit pricing as a means of attracting demand deposits. In other words, they engaged in nonprice competition that took many forms. It was a common practice, for example, to charge lower loan rates to corporate borrowers maintaining large balances in their checking account. In other instances reduced service charges were applied to accounts with large balances, and some banks went so far as to waive service charges entirely to attract demand deposits. Still others introduced premiums in an effort to boost their new accounts. A few large banks made it a practice to assist corporate treasurers in investing corporate funds in the money market.

Higher interest rates over the years made demand depositors more conscious of the advantages of careful cash management. With many large depositors, especially business firms, increasingly concerned with conserving their use of demand deposits, some large banks stressed prompt collection and payment services to lure them. Such services were made possible in a number of ways: through direct arrangements with the Federal Reserve banks in other districts or with major-city correspondent banks, altogether bypassing the Federal Reserve System; through use of special carrier services to major cities to ensure faster collection than could be afforded by mail; through wire transfer of funds; and through locked-box arrangements.* Through these and other cash-management techniques, banks sought to lure corporate demand deposits. The more economical use of demand deposits made possible by these banks, however, affected the velocity or turnover of demand deposits. With demand deposits used more actively, the level of such deposits fluctuated more rapidly and widely. As a result, banks found it difficult to use these funds for short-term loans or investments.

Savings and Time Deposits

In the years that followed its introduction, Regulation Q had little impact on bank time deposits because market rates of interest were much lower than established ceiling rates. By the mid-1950s, however, this situation had changed

---

*Under a locked-box plan, local and regional payments on company billings are sent directly to a post office box under the control of the collection bank, thereby saving time in the collection and clearing of these items. If the billing company is located in another city, once the checks are cleared, the local bank remits the funds by wire to the company's bank of deposit. Through such a method, collection time can be reduced by one to five days. Examples of freeing funds in the amount of $5 billion or more by this method have been cited by firms.

significantly. Much of the change was brought about by many new savings and loan associations, which, established in the immediate postwar years in response to the rising demand for mortgage credit, began to bid actively for household savings by offering rates that exceeded those commercial banks were willing or able to pay. Requests for larger commercial loans by corporate borrowers made apparent to banks the need to actively seek time and savings accounts. Since the rates paid for such funds by competing deposit institutions were free from regulation, banks soon found themselves at a competitive disadvantage in attracting time and savings deposits. In this and in other instances, the symptoms were the same: during periods of high business activity and interest rates, the banking industry was experiencing shortages of funds as a result of the "price control" imposed by Regulation Q.

Although the Board of Governors of the Federal Reserve System made frequent adjustments of Regulation Q ceilings to improve the competitive position of commercial banks, there were times (for instance, in 1966, 1969, and 1973) when its action came after significant delay. This delay led depositors to withdraw their funds from (or deposit less funds in) commercial banks and place them instead in higher-yielding marketable securities. These massive withdrawals of funds—known as *disintermediation*—forced banks to reduce their loan commitments and generally to slow their lending activity. The Federal Reserve appeared to view Regulation Q as a monetary instrument, and welcomed the limitation that it indirectly imposed on the expansion of bank loans.

June 1970 was a turning point in the development of time deposits, and particularly large CDs, as a major source of bank funds. In that month the Penn Central Railroad, the sixth largest corporation in the country, defaulted on $82 million of maturing commercial paper. This default undermined investor confidence in commercial paper and threatened corporations facing cash-flow problems with a severe shortage of funds. To prevent a liquidity crisis, the Federal Reserve encouraged banks to suspend Regulation Q ceilings on large CDs with maturities of less than 90 days. Because this measure was thought to be a temporary one, the suspension of ceiling rates for large CDs did not apply to maturities longer than 90 days. In mid-1973, as the business cycle was reaching the peak of its expansion, the Federal Reserve chose to extend the suspension of Regulation Q ceilings to all maturities of large CDs. The ability of large banks to innovate by developing new nondeposit sources of funds convinced the Federal Reserve of the need to reduce its reliance on Regulation Q in favor of additional reserve requirements, which affected the cost rather than the availability of additional liabilities. The 1973 suspension of Regulation Q ceilings on all maturities of large CDs was accompanied by the imposition of an 8 percent reserve requirement on any further increases in large CDs.

Removal of interest-rate ceilings on large CDs left banks free to compete for funds in the money markets in order to supply the credit needs of their corporate clients. Thus, though market rates of interest reached record levels in 1974, banks were in a position to compete effectively for funds. In the years that followed, reliance on large CDs increased further as banks sought to meet the enormous credit demands of the late 1970s and early 1980s. At the same time the Federal Reserve began to shift away from Regulation Q, relying instead upon reserve requirements and the market rates of interest for the allocation of funds among borrowers.

Since removal of Regulation Q ceilings on large CDs, banks have made increasingly frequent use of CDs in financing their activities. The funds tapped through large CDs are so interest-sensitive that some prefer to call them "purchased monies." Large certificates of deposit—especially of money-center banks—are purchased and sold in active, well-developed, and impersonal financial markets largely on the basis of interest rate. Sizable investors (businesses, pension funds, and mutual funds) interested in purchasing large CDs ordinarily call various recognized banks to inquire about their issuing rates and buy the CD of the bank paying the highest rate. If rates are comparable, they are likely to acquire the certificate of the bank with which they maintain an account.

Banks typically post the rates they are offering for negotiable CDs of various maturities, and may adjust these rates daily or even hourly. Whenever a bank needs or desires funds with a particular maturity, it raises the rate to make it competitive with rates of comparable money-market instruments, including the CDs of other large banks. When the bank has obtained sufficient funds, it lowers the rate and keeps it noncompetitive until it desires to obtain additional funds. The negotiable CD is thus an excellent example of the liability management referred to earlier. By varying the interest rates offered on CDs, a bank is in a position to purchase interest-sensitive funds every time loan demand outstrips the size of its regular deposit base. CD issuance therefore offers a significant degree of liquidity for a commercial bank. Instead of liquidating assets to obtain funds, a bank now has an alternative; it can elect to use CD financing.

Just as the debt issues of nonfinancial corporations are rated as to their investment quality, so are the large CDs of various banks. This information is becoming increasingly important to potential investors and depositors, especially to those with accounts in excess of the FDIC-insured maximum. Large CDs are rated by such agencies as Standard and Poor's; Moody's Investors Service; Keefe, Bruyette and Woods; and Duff and Phelps. Unlike Duff and Phelps, which ranks only domestic CDs, Standard, Moody's, and Keefe rate both domestic and foreign banks' CDs. Moody's and Phelps make their ratings public, while the other two provide them only on a subscription basis. Just as with all rated instruments, CDs of high quality (low default risk) enjoy high ratings, and vice versa.

The increased vigilance necessitated by the phaseout of Regulation Q ceilings brought an end to the day when bankers relied on the simple 3–6–3 management concept. Pay 3 percent interest on time deposits, lend them out at 6 percent, and adjourn to the golf course at 3:00 P.M.[1]

Changing Composition of Deposits

Within almost a decade and a half, the large CD emerged as a dominant source of bank funds. From 1961, when it was first introduced to retain interest-sensitive funds, to 1973, when ceiling rates were suspended for all large CD maturities, this instrument grew into the largest single source of funds for banks. The high rates of interest experienced during this period made depositors, both small and large, increasingly sophisticated in their approach to cash management. The forgone income inherent in demand deposits when interest rates were high led depositors to shift more and more of their demand-deposit balances into time and savings deposits. Thus in retail banks, the real growth in deposits came from consumer time and savings deposits, while in wholesale banks it came from large negotiable CDs. From the late 1960s on, the dominant role as a source of funds that demand deposits had enjoyed was assumed by the faster-growing (consumer) time and savings deposits.

The change in the banks' deposit mix led to their evolution from demand-deposit-oriented to time-deposit-oriented institutions. One result of this development was the introduction of a new pricing policy by large banks. They started charging fees for services with which they used to compensate demand depositors for their inability to pay interest on their accounts. Thus, depositors earn explicit interest rates and customers are charged explicit fees for various services. However, a more important effect of the change in banks' deposit mix has been a shift in the management of bank funds. As long as demand deposits dominated their sources of funds, banks sought to match the very-short-term nature of these liabilities with corresponding assets: highly liquid investments and loans. With lengthening of their deposit maturity, however, banks have extended the maturities of their earning assets. Many banks have expanded their holdings of higher-yielding intermediate- and longer-term government securities, and have increased their mortgage loans to individuals and term loans to businesses. Whether because of the longer-term nature of their liabilities or because of the need to cover the higher rate of interest paid on time deposits, the increase in the maturity of their assets portfolios is transforming commercial banks into more effective competitors of life insurance companies and other institutions engaged in long-term financing.

THE PAYMENTS MECHANISM

The writing of checks represents the chief means of exchange of funds in the United States. The routing of these checks to the banks on which they are drawn and the return flow of funds to the depositor's account is referred to as check clearing. Millions of checks are written every day, many of them originating at points a great distance from the banks on which they are drawn. Since the convenience of being able to pay for things with checks is a major reason people

Table 6.2
Clearinghouse Transactions

Checks Drawn on	Checks Received by			Total Debits	Net Debits
	Bank A	Bank B	Bank C		
Bank A	–	300	100	400	
Bank B	$400	–	700	1,100	300
Bank C	200	500	–	700	
Total credits	600	800	800	2,200	
Net credits	200		100		

Source: Prepared by author.

put money in banks as demand deposits, it is in the interest of banks to accomplish check clearing as smoothly and expeditiously as possible.

Check-clearing methods vary, depending primarily on the geographical proximity of the banks involved. In small towns or rural areas where communities are served by only a few banks, bilateral transfers of funds between banks may be arranged by messenger every day. The amounts drawn on each bank by the other are compared and the difference is credited appropriately, usually by adjusting each bank's balance at the regional Federal Reserve bank. In larger towns and cities, representatives of all banks in the community meet daily at a designated location, called a clearinghouse, to clear checks. The clearinghouse location may be permanent or rotating (such as the back room of a different bank each week). Each bank sends its clerk to the clearinghouse at a specified time each day with bundles of checks. Each bundle contains checks of one of the other banks and includes a list of the amounts due the clerk's bank from the other bank. At the clearinghouse the clerks hand over the checks drawn on the other banks, receive the checks drawn on their banks, and settle net differences among themselves.

A hypothetical record of a net settlement among participating banks is reproduced in Table 6.2. Total credits equal total debits. The difference between the total credits and total debits for any bank determines the net position of the bank. Net settlement is effected by notifying the Federal Reserve bank which bank accounts are to be credited and which are to be debited. In Table 6.2 the accounts of Banks A and C at the Federal Reserve are credited $200 and $100, respectively, while the account of Bank B is debited $300. The reserve accounts of banks are then adjusted according to the net result of the day's check-clearing process.

When the banks involved are located at some distance, collection may be effected through the correspondent banking system or through the Federal Reserve System. In cases where banks choose to collect items through their correspondents, they will send these items to their correspondent banks, without having to sort them (as they must if they clear through the Federal Reserve). For banks located in the same Federal Reserve district, collection through the Federal Reserve is quite simple. The reporting bank receives credit to its account at the Federal Reserve bank, while the bank on which the check is drawn will have its account debited a like amount. If the banks are located in different districts, the bank receiving the check sends it to its district Federal Reserve bank, which in turn sends it for collection to its counterpart in the district in which the drawee's bank is located. Settlement between the two Federal Reserve banks is effected through the Interdistrict Settlement Fund, which is a sort of clearinghouse for the Federal Reserve banks. The fund, in which each Federal Reserve bank maintains a balance, settles net amounts due between Federal Reserve banks daily.

To make the payments system more efficient, the Federal Reserve operates regional check-processing centers throughout the nation, thus cutting both cost and time to process checks. Other checks are collected by correspondent banks, local clearinghouses, or directly between banks. Projections for the 1990s estimate that well over 40 billion checks will flow through the commercial banking system.

Growing concern over the rising volume of checks and its effects upon the check-clearing and collection mechanism has led some banks to adopt a policy of retaining the checks drawn on their customers' accounts rather than returning them with the monthly statement. This process, known as truncation, reduces both postage costs and the costs of sorting the checks by customer account at the bank. Should a customer require a particular canceled check—to verify, for example, payment of a bill—it can be obtained from the bank. The vast majority of U.S. banks, however, have responded to the rising volume of checks by embarking upon the increased mechanization of funds transfers. The actual transfer of paper is being replaced by the transmission of electronic impulses in systems known generically as electronic funds transfer systems (EFTS). Several types of EFTS are currently in various stages of experimentation and implementation.

The Fedwire, as the Federal Reserve Communications System is known, represents the first U.S. experience with electronic funds transfer. Although established in the 1910s, it has become a significant means of funds transfer only with the advent, in the 1970s, of high-speed computers and sophisticated corporate cash-management techniques. The Fedwire connects all of the Federal Reserve banks and their branches, the Treasury and other government agencies, and member banks. By this means funds can be transferred from one bank's reserve account to another; transactions can be conducted in the Federal funds market; funds can be transferred for bank customers; and transfer book entries representing U.S. government and federal agency securities can be made. In 1950 a group of 14 banks established a similar communication system among themselves, and since that time Bankwire has grown to link hundreds of banks across the country.

Another way the Federal Reserve contributes to the payments mechanism is through its automated clearinghouse (ACH), a system that offers users national clearinghouse services. The ACH system is all electronic: banks use computers linked to a computer at the processing center and relay payment information over telephone lines. As a result, funds can be transferred between accounts in different banks. The ACH is used primarily to process repetitious payments, such as insurance premiums, mortgage notes, payrolls, welfare payments, and federal government transactions. For instance, Social Security payments are routed into the accounts of recipients who have authorized direct deposit of their benefits. Similarly, many businesses make payroll disbursements via the ACH, which effects the transfer of funds from the employer's account directly to the accounts of individual employees. This method of transferring funds realizes substantial savings through reduced paperwork, and for this reason ACH activity has expanded and proliferated. A recent survey indicated that the total bank processing cost of an ACH item averaged 5.7 cents, while the corresponding processing cost of a check averaged 10.5 cents.[2] These differences in processing costs are reflected in the fees that banks charge their customers for each type of transaction. However, a payer who wishes to benefit from float may still prefer the check even though the cost of its processing is higher than the cost of processing an ACH transaction. In 1994, private-sector ACH operators—recognizing the need to offer national ACH processing to compete with the system of the Federal Reserve—established the private-sector ACH exchange (PAXS), which offers its members national clearinghouse services.

Increasing deployment of EFTS at the consumer level, such as automatic teller machines (ATMs), is also affecting the nature of the payments mechanism, reducing both payroll and paperwork costs for banks. With the rise in technology, the "brick and mortar" system of providing banking services is giving way to one that is completely automated. ATMs allow a bank to offer retail banking services without constructing and staffing a branch. For a banking public that values personal comfort, ATMs provide 24-hour service at minimal cost in many convenient locations.

Point-of-sale (POS) banking suggests the possibility of even greater savings in transaction costs as well as increased customer convenience. Introduced in the mid-1970s, POS services are expected to experience significant growth in the 1990s. A POS system provides for the electronic payment for purchased goods or services at the point of sale by means of a direct transfer of funds from the customer's account to that of the commercial establishment. Customer use of POS terminals requires an encoded plastic card—the debit card—to prevent unauthorized access to the account. POS systems provide several advantages. The principal advantage for the merchant is that this method verifies the transfer of funds from the customer's account as payment for the goods purchased, thereby eliminating the possibility of losses from bad checks. The advantage for the bank is that it realizes savings because less paperwork is needed to document the various funds transfers. A bulky bundle of checks no longer needs to be processed and mailed. The principal benefit to consumers is convenience and ease of use. Also, record keeping might be easier because at the time of the transaction, the consumer obtains a receipt from the merchant and, each month, a bank statement listing all transactions in and out of the account. Beyond this basic function of the debit card, a cardholder can use POS terminals to withdraw cash from the account.

POS systems may be on-line or off-line. In the former system, each individual transaction is deducted from the customer's account at the time it is made. In the latter system, all transactions accumulate until the end of the day, when they are aggregated and subtracted from the customer's account. While on-line may reduce the frequency of customer overdrafts, off-line offers banks cost savings in the processing of transactions.

In spite of an initial slow start in the adoption of this technology, POS networks have increased rapidly in recent years, both in this country and abroad. By 1995 there were over 90,000 POS terminals in the United States, many of them owned by MasterCard and Visa under the trade names of Maestro and Interlink, respectively. With checking fees on the rise, consumer usage of POS terminals is likely to increase further in the years ahead.

The spreading of the above-described forms of EFTS is triggering the development of in-home banking. This system can effect transfers of payments as the customer's instructions to debit his or her account and to credit another's are routed among the banks involved. Other financial services currently considered include applying for a loan and—upon approval—drawing on it, seeking extension of an old loan, inquiring about rates on different forms of investments, and—last but not least—seeking investment advice. The desired investment transactions could also be conducted via the home computer. Eventually, individuals will have minimal need for personal contact with the banks that hold their accounts. They will be able to conduct virtually all their banking transactions without having to leave home!

Individuals may shop not only for banking services through a home TV but for other things as well. Linkage of POS systems with home terminals will allow individuals to make retail purchases from their homes. Future data networks delivering home information will operate much like today's networks that deliver entertainment to the home. A network company will be responsible for providing both the massive information of various databases and the conduits that link homes to these bases. Individual banks—in contrast with their present-day direct connection to customers—will be an integral part of a financial service supplier that, along with other database suppliers, will be delivering information to a home. A user will subscribe to a network for services and will pay a monthly fee accordingly.

As implied by the preceding, in-home banking is still in the early developmental phase. Mass introduction of home information is not expected until the late 1990s, when data networks will be fully operative and low-cost home terminals widely available. By then, society will be more ripe to ensure the growth

Figure 6.1
Delivery System Life Cycle

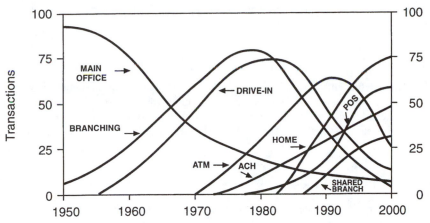

Source: John F. Fisher, "In-Home Banking Today and Tomorrow," reprinted from *Journal of Retail Banking* 4, no. 2 (June 1982): 25. Copyright © 1982, Lafferty Publications. By permission.

of the home information industry. Indeed, as the "video" youth of the 1980s arrive in full force in the marketplace, they will affect individual attitudes and increase public acceptance of this technology.

The importance of the various forms of EFTS in the delivery of banking services, and their relationship to past trends and future prospects, are depicted in Figure 6.1. This figure traces the delivery system of banking services over time by means of life-cycle curves.* As seen in this figure, the principal delivery system of banking services until the early 1950s was the main office, because of the dominance of the unit-banking form of organization. Structural changes in the banking industry during the postwar decades led to the emergence of two other delivery systems, branching and drive-in banking, which peaked in importance in the early 1980s and have since been on the decline. The place of these "brick and mortar" systems in the delivery of banking services is gradually being taken by the electronic technology currently sweeping the country. The various forms of EFTS are transforming the nation's payment mechanism and signal the beginning of the process toward a checkless society. Shared branching will also play a role in the bank delivery system. As stated in Chapter 3, integration of financial markets across institutions and space will lead to the emergence of financial supermarkets offering a full array of financial services. A shared branch would be a facility shared by the affiliated institutions owned by the same bank holding company. This delivery system will entail significant

---

*The concept of life cycle can be applied to a system, a product, a firm, or an industry. Whatever the application, a life cycle covers four phases: pioneering, expansion, stabilization, and decline. Each of these phases is associated with different risks and rewards, and calls for different strategies. Life-cycle analysis is thus of special importance in financial management and strategic planning.

economies of scale that, in a competitive environment, should benefit the banking public. As implied by Figure 6.1, shared branching is expected to develop during the balance of this century and become a major delivery system in later decades.

NOTES

1. John Helyar and Julie Salamon, "Big Banks Set Agenda for the Entire Industry as Regulation Loosens," *Wall Street Journal*, November 18, 1982, p. 1.

2. James McAndrews, "The Automated Clearinghouse System: Moving Toward Electronic Payment," Federal Reserve Bank of Philadelphia, *Business Review*, July/August 1994, p. 17.

SUGGESTED REFERENCES

Conner, Glenn B., and Ellen Maland. "Basic Banking." *Federal Reserve Bulletin*, April 1987, pp. 255–69.

Davis, Richard G., Leo Korobrow, and John Wenninger. "Bankers on Pricing Consumer Deposits." Federal Reserve Bank of New York, *Quarterly Review*, Winter 1987, pp. 6–13.

Fox, R. Gerald. "Future Direction of Branch Banking." *World of Banking* 11, no. 3 (May/June 1992): 4–7.

Hannan, Timothy H. "Recent Trends in Retail Fees and Services of Depository Institutions." *Federal Reserve Bulletin*, September 1994, pp. 771–81.

McAndrews, James. "The Automated Clearinghouse System: Moving Toward Electronic Payment." Federal Reserve Bank of Philadelphia, *Business Review*, July/August 1994, pp. 15–23.

Phillips, Susan M. *Testimony Before the Subcommittee on Consumer Credit and Insurance of the Committee on Banking, Finance, and Urban Affairs*, U.S. House of Representatives, June 22, 1994.

Chapter 7

Nondeposit Liabilities

Nondeposit liabilities, the second largest source of bank funds, are not a homogeneous category of accounts. Instead, they represent a broad concept encompassing a variety of items, such as liabilities for borrowed money, capitalized leases, expenses accrued and unpaid, deferred income taxes, mortgage indebtedness, subordinated notes and debentures, and minority interests in subsidiaries. Dominant are liabilities for borrowed money as well as subordinated notes and debentures, both of which represent purchased funds. Because of their importance in liability management, they are often referred to as managed liabilities. Because subordinated notes and debentures have been previously discussed (Chapter 5), we shall focus our attention in this chapter on borrowed liabilities and their development as sources of bank liquidity in satisfying loan demands. Moreover, we will discuss the considerations that determine bank reliance on one or more sources of borrowed funds at any particular time, and review trends in interest rates in the money market.

BORROWING

The increasing importance of borrowed funds for commercial banks in recent years is depicted in Table 7.1. Total borrowings increased from $163 million in 1960 to $19.4 billion in 1970, more than a hundredfold increase in a decade. By 1995 aggregate bank borrowings had risen to $660 billion. As follows from these data, the 1960s were benchmark years in the growth of bank borrowings. This decade saw an unprecedented expansion in economic activity and a concomitant growth in the financing needs of corporations and the private sector in general.

Much of this demand for credit was directed to money-center banks in the

Table 7.1
Borrowings of Domestically Chartered Commercial Banks, Selected Years

Year	Amount (billions of dollars)	Year	Amount (billions of dollars)
1970	$ 19.4	1991	$ 397.7
1975	60.2	1992	436.3
1980	156.8	1993	518.3
1985	295.7	1994	550.4
1990	433.8	1995	659.7

Source: Federal Reserve Bulletin, selected issues. Data for 1995 are as of October 31.

form of requests for short-term loans. During the early phases of the 1966 and 1969 expansions, banks responded to the rising loan demand by increasing their reliance upon negotiable CDs to raise the necessary funds. However, as the loan demand intensified and inflation began to increase, rates on competitive money-market instruments rose above Regulation Q ceilings, undermining the ability of banks to compete for interest-sensitive funds. When the Federal Reserve— in its effort to control the pace of economic activity—did not adjust, or delayed adjusting, bank interest-rate ceilings upward, maturing CDs were not renewed by depositors. In addition, banks began experiencing large outflows of funds, which placed them in an awkward and precarious situation. Disintermediation was making it difficult for commercial banks to honor their loan commitments to traditional customers and to maintain adequate liquidity levels. It was under these pressures that banks began to develop new sources of loanable funds by incurring, at their own initiative, liabilities for borrowed money. To offset their shortages of loanable funds and reduced liquidity, they started bidding for interest-sensitive funds in such markets as the commercial-paper market and the overseas dollar-denominated markets (Eurodollar markets).

Bank reliance on interest-sensitive deposits and borrowed funds during the credit crunches of 1966 and 1969 gave prominence to liability management. Bank reliance on liability management as a liquidity-management technique represented an important departure from earlier practices. In preceding tight-money periods, when demands for credit outstripped deposit growth, banks usually sold off large amounts of U.S. Treasury bills or other marketable securities accumulated during the war years to accommodate their customers' credit needs. Banks thus relied heavily on asset management and paid little attention to the management of liabilities. However, during the tight-money period of 1966, though banks again liquidated significant amounts of securities from their investment portfolios, reliance on borrowed funds became increasingly important in cushioning the effects of a contracting deposit volume. Especially aggressive in their bidding for such funds, and hence effective in the development of these sources, were the larger banks, which, despite the prevailing tightness, were able to provide for the short-term finance needs of their corporate clients. From then on, liability management took on—for a great many banks—an importance comparable with that of asset management.

Liabilities for borrowed money include a variety of interest-sensitive sources of loanable funds. One such source—interest-bearing demand notes issued to the U.S. Treasury—was discussed in Chapter 6 in connection with public deposits. Our discussion here will therefore concentrate on the other sources of loanable funds that constitute the thrust of bank borrowing.

Depending upon prevailing financial and economic circumstances, banks may acquire funds through one or more of the following arrangements: purchase of federal funds, sale of securities and loans under agreement to repurchase, sale of bankers' acceptances, sale of commercial paper, borrowing of Eurodollars, and borrowing from the Federal Reserve bank. Liabilities of this type, with one exception (Federal Reserve credit), are known as money-market liabilities because they are generally purchased or acquired by paying a competitive price for them in the money market. Each of these liabilities is discussed below.

Federal Funds

"Federal funds" refers to banks' deposit balances at Federal Reserve banks. Since enactment of the DIDMCA in 1980, all banks have been required to maintain reserves against their deposit liabilities in the form of vault cash and balances with their district Federal Reserve bank. Because these reserves yield no income, and any deficiency is penalized by the Federal Reserve, well-managed banks try to avoid more of them than is necessary. The federal-funds market thus provides the vehicle for the efficient management of a bank's reserve position.

If a bank has excess reserves on deposit with a Federal Reserve bank on a particular day, it can sell them to a bank with a shortage in its legal reserve position. If the banks involved are located in the same area, the transaction is effected through a telephone call. The lending institution authorizes the Federal Reserve bank to transfer the agreed amount of reserve funds from its reserve account to that of the borrowing bank. Accordingly, the Federal Reserve bank debits the reserve account of the lending institution and credits the reserve account of the borrowing institution. Since these transactions are usually for overnight, the bookkeeping entry will be reversed the following day. If the banks are located in different parts of the country, the transfer of funds will be accomplished through the Fedwire and will involve a series of instantaneous accounting entries to reflect the interdistrict nature of the transaction.

In terms of maturity, more than 90 percent of the transactions in this market are overnight (one-day) or continuing contracts. Continuing-contract federal funds consist of a series of overnight transactions that are automatically renewed each day unless terminated by either party. A typical example of such a contract is the purchase by a correspondent bank of the federal funds that a respondent bank has available for sale. The automatic rollover of overnight funds represents, in essence, an arrangement of open maturity. The interest payment, though it varies from contract to contract, is computed on the basis of the daily rate quotation.

A limited number of transactions take the form of term federal funds. Banks anticipating a need for borrowed funds over a period of time or a trend of a higher federal-funds rate in the months ahead, may contract for term federal funds (for 30 days, 90 days, or occasionally 180 days). Since federal-funds transactions are exempt from reserve requirements, this alternative would be preferred, for example, to the issuance of comparable maturity CDs as a means of securing funds for loan commitments. Many large banks use this market to fund their entire reserve requirements on a rather permanent basis.

Federal-funds transactions are not subject to reserve requirements. However, from October 1979 to July 1980, the Federal Reserve imposed a marginal reserve requirement of 8 percent (later during this period it was raised to 10 percent) on member banks' federal-funds purchases, security repurchase agreements, and other managed liabilities (large negotiable CDs and borrowings of Eurodollars). The requirement applied only to borrowings that were over $100 million or in excess of a certain amount in a base period. By raising the effective cost of federal funds and security repurchase agreements, the Federal Reserve sought to slow bank borrowing and, hence, continuation of inflationary pressures in the economy. The practical implication of this move is that the Federal Reserve will not hesitate to impose reserve requirements on banks' managed liabilities in order to prevent excessive and reckless borrowing by individual institutions.

Federal-Funds Rate

The rate charged on federal-funds transactions is called the federal-funds rate. Although expressed on an annual basis, the federal-funds rate is computed to reflect the daily nature of the transaction. For example, assuming a federal-funds transaction for $2 million at a going rate of 6 percent, the bank selling federal funds would earn for one day $333.33 ($2,000,000 $\times$ .06 $\times$ 1/360). If the transaction was effected on a Friday, the selling bank would earn $1,000, since it would take three days (until the next clearing on Monday) to get its funds back. The purchasing bank's reserve balances would be adjusted to reflect access to these funds over the weekend. The amount of interest earned would be added to the value of the loan at the time of its repayment. However, it may also be paid by separate check or by adjusting correspondent bank balances through bookkeeping entries.

The rate of interest paid on federal funds on any particular day or at a specific time of day is a function of demand and supply conditions in the marketplace. Since the purchase of federal funds is primarily induced by the need to offset a reserve deficiency, heavy trading is frequently encountered on the last day of

Table 7.2
Effective Federal-Funds Rate, Selected Years (percent per annum)

Year	Average Daily Rate	Year	Average Daily Rate
1970	7.17	1991	5.69
1975	5.82	1992	3.10
1980	13.36	1993	3.02
1985	8.10	1994	4.21
1990	8.10	1995	5.76

Source: Federal Reserve Bulletin, selected issues. Data for 1995 are as of October 31.

the reserve settlement period (Wednesday). This fact, along with time differences across the nation, has been responsible for significant volatility in the federal-funds rate during a single trading day. Similar volatility is frequently encountered on the last day of the year, which constitutes the closing date for banks' financial statements. The need for "window dressing" by certain banks helps, for example, to explain why on December 31, 1982, the federal-funds rate fluctuated between 3 and 20 percent.

Apart from demand and supply conditions, the rate is affected by monetary policy. When monetary policy is restrictive and money-market conditions are tight, the federal-funds rate will remain high. In the summer of 1981, for example, the rate fluctuated around the 20 percent mark. When conditions eased in the spring of 1983, the rate hovered around 8 percent.

The rate on federal funds is an indicator of major significance. By representing a key marginal cost of bank funds, it affects the market rates of interest, including the prime rate. The federal-funds rate is so sensitive that the Federal Reserve looks to it to identify the degree of tightness or ease of the money market. Moreover, it uses this rate as a target of monetary policy—that is, it buys or sells securities in the open market to affect the rate and bring it to the desired level. Table 7.2 shows the effective federal-funds rates for selected years. Since these rates are averages of daily effective rates for each week during the indicated year, the magnitude of the rate's day-to-day or week-to-week volatility is not identified.

Development of the Federal-Funds Market

Trading federal funds is not a recent development. Although the federal-funds market has been in existence since the 1920s, it was not until the 1960s that its growth and development began in earnest. Before the early 1960s federal funds were viewed as an alternative mode of reserve adjustment to borrowing from the Federal Reserve discount window. In other words, banks needing reserves borrowed federal funds only if their cost was lower than the discount rate. By late 1964, however, the character of this market started to change as the practice of liability management gained momentum. Confronted with a growing demand for loans and a tight monetary policy, major money-center banks—located principally in New York City—began to bid for federal funds at rates above the discount rate. To them, paying a premium rate for federal funds was justified in the light of the higher rates at which they could profitably lend these funds. As more and more banks realized the potential of the federal-funds market as a source of purchased liabilities, their participation in this market and the volume of trading expanded rapidly. The phenomenal growth experienced by the federal-funds market during this period can be sensed from the trading activity of 46 large money-center banks, whose daily average purchases of federal funds between 1960 and 1970 jumped from $1.1 billion to $8.3 billion.

In recent years the federal-funds market has expanded even further with the entry of other participants as sellers of funds. The U.S. offices of foreign banks, thrift institutions, businesses, and even the International Bank for Reconstruction and Development (IBRD or World Bank) have been feeding the market with their temporarily surplus funds. For the former two types of institutions, their participation in the federal-funds market does not change the process of transferring funds, since the DIDMCA, enacted in 1980, requires them to maintain reserve accounts at Federal Reserve banks. However, even if the participants maintain no reserve account, the transfer of funds is, in the final analysis, effected through a bank or other depository institution that maintains balances with a Federal Reserve bank.

The developments described above were instrumental in transforming the federal-funds market from a negotiated market into an impersonal open market with a standardized commodity and rates that respond rapidly to changing market conditions. Many banks prefer to borrow in this market rather than subject themselves to the scrutiny of the Federal Reserve bank when requesting a loan. Commercial banks purchase billions of dollars of federal funds each business day. Table 7.3 shows the year-end volume of federal funds sold and purchased (including security resale agreements) by all insured commercial banks from 1989 through 1995. The excess of the funds purchased over those sold reflects the increased participation in this market of foreign banks, thrifts, and other suppliers of temporarily available funds.

Correspondent Banks and the Integration of the Federal-Funds Market

A bank wishing to purchase or sell federal funds has three options: it may approach and deal directly with another bank, go through a federal-funds broker, or contact its correspondent bank. Stockbrokerage firms in New York City may function as federal-funds brokers by bringing together, at a commission, institutions buying and selling federal funds. Correspondent banks often make a market for federal funds to accommodate respondent banks— because they realize that if they do not do so, competing institutions will. The process is initiated when the respondent bank, through a telephone call, informs the correspondent bank of its intention to sell funds. This call solicits

Table 7.3
Federal Funds Sold and Purchased by All Insured Commercial Banks, 1989–95 (billions of dollars)

Item	1989	1990	1991	1992	1993	1994	1995
Federal funds sold and securities purchased under agreements to resell	146.4	146.6	149.2	158.4	150.7	149.1	155.7
Federal funds purchased and securities sold under agreements to repurchase	275.6	245.3	230.9	252.3	274.6	312.5	330.9

Note: Since separate reporting of federal-funds transactions has been discontinued, the above data include security resale agreements.
Source: Federal Deposit Insurance Corporation, *Statistics* on Banking (Washington, D.C.: FDIC, 1994). Data for 1995 are as of September 30, and were derived from *Call Report.*

the purchase of funds by the correspondent bank. If the latter has more funds than it needs, it will sell some of its excess federal funds to other banks. Thus, many money-center banks and regional banks are both purchasers and sellers of federal funds.

This activity of correspondent banks opened the federal-funds market to banks of all sizes, a development that has had a number of effects. First, transactions of less than $1 million have become more common than in the past. Second, small banks, because of limited loan opportunities in their markets, have become—through their correspondent banks—net suppliers of federal funds while large banks have become net borrowers of these funds. In essence, the federal-funds market has been functioning as a conduit for the excess funds of smaller banks to support the lending activity of larger banks. A third effect, and a direct result of the preceding development, is that by converting excess funds into loanable, and hence profitable, funds, the federal-funds market has enabled the banking system to make more efficient use of its reserves. A fourth and more important effect is that the federal-funds market has joined banks of disparate size and thrift institutions into an integrated banking system. This integration process has enhanced the effectiveness of Federal Reserve action in pursuit of tight monetary policy. The federal-funds market transmits the effects of Federal Reserve action nationwide and, in turn, makes the commercial banking system more responsive to the tightening actions of the Federal Reserve.

The growing presence of foreign banks in the United States and their participation in the federal-funds market are linking the domestic interbank market with foreign financial markets. As a direct consequence, trends in the domestic interbank market are transmitted to the international financial markets and vice versa, thus integrating financial markets across national boundaries.

Repurchase Agreements

In recent years repurchase agreements (RPs) have become a major source of money-market funds, rivaling more familiar financial instruments such as negotiable CDs or commercial paper. Under a repurchase agreement a bank can obtain supplementary funds by selling securities from its portfolio with a simultaneous agreement to repurchase at a later date. In essence, RPs are a secured and liquid means of borrowing and lending funds for short periods; the securities involved in the transaction are usually obligations of the federal government or its agencies, and most transactions take place between large, prime-credit institutions. In addition, the securities serve as collateral against the loan, and the lender (buyer) is assured a repurchase price that equals the original sale price plus earned interest. As a further protection to the lender against adverse conditions in the marketplace, the securities pledged are valued at a discount from their current market prices.* The Bankruptcy Amendments Act of 1984 permits lenders to liquidate the underlying securities if the seller is unable to fulfill the terms of the agreement at settlement.

From the lender's perspective, the RP transaction is termed a reverse repurchase agreement; the lender buys a security and resells it upon maturity. Reverse RPs are often arranged by large commercial banks and government securities dealers to cover short positions or to meet specific customer needs. Using a reverse repurchase to cover a short position is similar to making a security borrowing arrangement whereby the dealer obtains securities in exchange for funds. However, a reverse repurchase is typically cheaper than outright borrowing, and it also gives the dealer greater flexibility in the use of the repurchased securities.

In order to engage in an RP transaction, the lender must have the necessary funds readily available the same business day the transaction takes place. Whether in the form of deposit balances with the district Federal Reserve bank or with a local commercial bank, these funds can be made immediately available to the borrowing bank through the Fedwire. RP negotiations are handled directly between the borrower and lender, or through a small group of U.S. government securities dealers who are market specialists. Large banks and businesses usually employ traders who negotiate interest rates with potential participants. Since there is no central marketplace for arranging RPs, all transactions are negotiated on the telephone. Interest rates are usually comparable with the federal-funds rate, but are often slightly lower because RPs are collateralized and federal funds are not.

Most RPs are in sums of $1 million or more, although they can be for less. The time of maturity is either fixed (from overnight to several days) or negotiated under a continuing contract agreement, which automatically renews the RP daily until terminated by either party.

Market Participants

Some of the more important participants in the RP market are commercial banks, government securities dealers, insurance companies, businesses, foreign financial institutions, state and local governments, and the Federal Reserve System. RPs offer holders of sizable cash balances a means of converting their demand-deposit accounts into interest-earning assets, with funds committed for very short periods and thus readily available. Larger commercial banks are usually borrowers in the RP market. Funds so obtained are not subject to reserve requirements. Effective October 11, 1979, managed liabilities of member banks (including RPs issued against U.S. government and federal agency securities)

---

*The failures of Drysdale Government Securities and Lombard-Wall in 1982 had an important effect on RP pricing practices. While in the past accrued interest was ignored in computing the value of repurchased securities, these failures led to the adoption of full accrual pricing. That is, since October 1982, RP transactions have been valued to include accrued interest (on coupon-bearing securities) calculated to the maturity date of the agreement.

were subject to an 8 percent marginal reserve requirement. On April 3, 1980, Regulation D was amended to increase marginal reserve requirements to 10 percent, then reduced to 5 percent in June 1980, and finally to zero beginning July 24, 1980.

The use of RPs as a source of funds for commercial banks increased significantly in the early 1980s, in response to rising short-term interest rates. During 1981 bankers used RPs as a means of attracting consumer funds in retaliation against money-market mutual funds. In an effort to tap small investors as a source of financing, the parent companies of large banks offered small-denomination ''repurchase agreement certificates'' that could be cashed in prematurely without penalty. As implied by their name, these certificates were issued against securities that were sold by the institutions to savers' pools under agreements to repurchase.

Other important participants in the RP market are government securities dealers, who borrow RP funds to finance their inventories of government securities. They have also become lenders in this market, through reverse RPs. As a result, dealers have emerged as important intermediaries in the RP market for borrowers and lenders of funds. Large, well-known dealers obtain more competitive rates than smaller dealers and corporations, thus generating their profits through arbitrage (matching an RP transaction with a reverse RP at a higher rate but of equal maturity).

The RP market has grown considerably over the years for several reasons. The prohibition of interest payments on demand deposits and rising market interest rates in the late 1960s induced many state and local governments, as well as businesses, to enter the RP market to lend their temporarily idle funds. In the case of businesses, the increasing use of computers and more sophisticated cash-management techniques have played an important role in the extent of their participation in this market. The end result has been that both businesses and municipalities have come to view RPs as an income-earning substitute for their demand-deposit balances. RPs are also a more attractive alternative to commercial paper and newly issued negotiable CDs. It is very rare for commercial paper to be issued for a period as short as a day or two, and the shortest maturity of large CDs commonly issued is 14 days. For these reasons substantial funds have been channeled daily into the RP market, contributing to its further development. The growth of RP transactions has also improved the liquidity of the securities used as collateral, since they may generate funds on short notice, without incurring the possible losses resulting from an outright sale. In effect, RPs offer investors and borrowers an instrument with flexibility, liquidity, short-term maturity, and low-risk factors unsurpassed by other money-market instruments.

Role of the Federal Reserve in the RP Market

Large banks have traditionally sold loans to smaller correspondents as a way of increasing their own loanable funds while providing the smaller bank with a return exceeding security investments. To maintain satisfactory correspondent relations, these loans were usually sold with the understanding that the selling bank would buy back any of the loans that experienced difficulty in repayment. Since the selling bank generally continued servicing the loan, the original borrower would probably never become aware of the sale of the loan.

A technique was developed early in 1969 by which money-center banks needing to improve the liquidity of their portfolios could do so by selling loans, or participation in pools of loans, to nonbank customers under agreement to repurchase. As banks realized the potential for acquiring loanable funds through use of this type of agreement, RPs became increasingly widespread. In the early months of 1969, banks began to extend this practice to customers holding maturing CDs at interest rates comparable with the money-market rates. It is estimated that during the summer of 1969, RPs involving loans or participations in pools of loans doubled, with most of these transactions directed to unaffiliated bank customers.

The Board of Governors finally interceded, concluding that banks were using RPs in much the same way as deposit transactions, but not conforming to the purposes and policies of regulations D and Q. Consequently, these regulations were amended to state that after July 25, 1969, any RPs entered into with a nonbank institution or customer, using any asset other than U.S. government or agency obligations, would be subject to reserve requirements. This made the sale of loans under RPs too costly for banks and contributed to its gradual loss of appeal.

The Federal Reserve System plays a dual role in the RP market. It regulates the market by limiting the types of transactions undertaken by member banks, and largely affects interest rates available daily on the RP market by influencing the federal-funds rate. The Federal Reserve is also a significant direct participant in the RP market, temporarily absorbing or supplying reserves to commercial banks through RPs or reverse RPs.

Bankers' Acceptances

A banker's acceptance is a short-term time draft drawn by an individual or business concern upon a bank ordering it to pay a stipulated amount of money at a specified date in the future. When the bank accepts the draft, it guarantees its redemption at maturity. This guarantee raises the credit quality of the draft and makes it negotiable. In return for this guarantee, the party on whose behalf the bank accepts the draft agrees to provide the bank with the necessary funds prior to maturity and pays a nominal charge. The customer's outstanding debt to the bank is noted on the bank's books as an asset, while the bank's guarantee to the customer is shown as a liability.

Although bankers' acceptances have for centuries been an important instrument in international commerce, this market grew only recently in the United States. The amount of bankers' acceptances outstanding rose from less than $400 million in 1950 to $64 billion by mid-1988, declining thereafter to $29 billion by September 1995. Most of the growth in bankers' acceptances took place in the 1970s and 1980s, and reflected the spectacular increase in foreign trade. While the volume of acceptances created to finance U.S. foreign trade rose significantly, most of the growth in acceptances came from the expansion in the foreign-trade transactions between foreign countries. The latter type of acceptances is generally referred to as "third-country bills." The recession of the early 1990s and the slow recovery of Japan adversely affected the growth of third-country bills, which represented, at year-end 1994, 45 percent of the total value of acceptances outstanding.

Despite the sizable development of this market, bankers' acceptances continue to be one of the least familiar of all money-market instruments. A banker's acceptance may arise out of import or export transactions, commodity warehousing, or domestic shipping. The banker's acceptance market consists of three major participants: the accepting banks, the dealers, and the investors. Since an accepting bank simply guarantees payment upon maturity, bankers' acceptances offer banks the advantage of financing their customers' credit demands without reducing their own loanable funds. Thus, during periods of restrictive credit, when liquidating or rediscounting conventional loans can be inconvenient and costly or poor customer relations, bankers' acceptances become an attractive option in funding customer needs, since they can easily be sold in the money market to generate the necessary funds.

The great majority of bankers' acceptances are issued by large banks with specialized staffs, good foreign connections, and an established name. Increasingly in recent years smaller regional banks have become important issuers of bankers' acceptances. In order to sell their paper, however, they must locate dealers interested in making a market in their acceptances.

The trading activity of about a dozen dealers determines the marketability of bankers' acceptances. These dealers are also primary dealers in government securities. Dealers in acceptances function as dealers in other money-market instruments do; they post their bid and asked prices, buying and selling acceptances and profiting from the spread.

Table 7.4 shows the volume of acceptances outstanding between 1990 and September 30, 1995, and the different holders. Volumewise, Table 7.4 indicates a decreasing trend in acceptances outstanding. This decrease is partly attributable to declines in commodity prices that affected the dollar volume of world trade accordingly, and to a number of developments that have diminished the appeal of bankers' acceptances to both banks and borrowers. These include the growing importance of Euro commercial paper in international financial markets, and the fall in the spreads between rates on Eurodollar deposits and rates on acceptances. As these developments persist, the acceptance market will suffer accordingly.

Money-market investors buy bankers' acceptances because they recognize the safe and liquid nature of this type of investment. Banks themselves had holdings on September 30, 1995, that amounted to $11.8 billion. As indicated by Table 7.4, most banks held their own acceptances. Holdings of the Federal Reserve

Table 7.4
Bankers' Acceptances Outstanding, 1990–95 (millions of dollars)

Holders	1990	1991	1992	1993	1994	1995
Accepting banks	$9,017	$11,017	$10,555	$12,421	$11,783	$11,765.2
Own bills	7,930	9,347	9,097	10,707	10,462	10,516.5
Bills bought	1,087	1,670	1,458	1,714	1,312	1,248.7
Federal Reserve Banks						
Foreign correspondents	918	1,739	1,276	725	410	n.a.
Other	44,836	31,014	26,364	19,202	17,642	n.a.
Total	$54,771	$43,770	$38,194	$32,348	$29,835	$29,241.8

Note: Details may not add to totals due to rounding.
Source: Federal Reserve Bulletin, selected issues. Data for 1995 are as of September 30.

were for the accounts of foreign central banks, while the dominant share of the total market (59.1 percent in 1994) was held by other financial and nonfinancial corporations.

Since the late 1970s, the Federal Reserve has reduced its own market participation. In March 1977 the Federal Open Market Committee decided that the Federal Reserve would no longer buy acceptances in the open market, except under two specific circumstances: at the request of its foreign correspondents (such as foreign central banks) and under repurchase agreements in order to increase bank reserves. This decision of the Federal Reserve did not extend to its accepting them as collateral from member banks borrowing from the discount window.

Even though the Federal Reserve no longer buys acceptances for its own account, it still specifies the conditions that make acceptances eligible for discount and purchase. The implication of this regulation is that bank proceeds from the sale of eligible acceptances are not subject to reserve requirements. By contrast, the proceeds from the sale of ineligible acceptances were, until recently, subject to reserve requirements, which raised the cost of acceptance financing.

During 1969 several large banks sought to obtain market funds to meet their customers' credit needs through the creation and sale of acceptances that were not eligible for discount at the Federal Reserve bank because they did not arise from foreign-trade-related transactions or the storage or shipment of readily marketable staples. Reflecting the original purpose of these acceptances, they were often referred to as ''working-capital acceptances'' or ''finance bills.''

During the credit crunch of 1969, and more significantly during that of 1973–74, the creation of ineligible acceptances reached such proportions as to warrant the intervention of the Federal Reserve. On June 18, 1973, the Board of Governors extended reserve requirements to funds raised by member banks through the sale of finance bills. The requirements remained in force until the end of 1990, when the Board of Governors removed them for nonpersonal time deposits, which include ineligible acceptances in addition to large CDs. This move did not prompt revival in ineligible working-capital acceptances.

Commercial Paper

Commercial paper is an unsecured promissory note that provides creditworthy corporations with short-term funds without the intermediary services of commercial banks. It is sold to money-market investors as unsecured obligations bearing only the name of the issuer. For that reason companies successfully issuing commercial paper are nationally known, prime-credit corporations that inspire investor confidence and have minimum risk of default. Denominations of commercial paper are usually in multiples of $100,000, with an average purchase of $2 million. The exact time of maturity is determined by individual requirements and investor preference; it usually averages 20–45 days and has a mandatory 270-day ceiling.

A company issuing commercial paper may choose to sell directly to money-market investors through its own sales force, or contract one of the ten or so investment banking or brokerage houses specializing in the marketing of commercial paper. Dealer-placed issuers usually have limited, very specific borrowing needs, whereas large companies with continuous, sizable funding requirements will place paper directly through their permanent, in-house sales staff. On September 30, 1995, the volume of commercial paper outstanding amounted to about $670 billion, with bank-related commercial paper accounting for approximately 5 percent of the total market. Bank holding companies issue commercial paper to finance operating expenses and other nonbank activities. Most of these companies opt for direct placement of their paper. Although there is no secondary market for commercial paper, investors facing an urgent need for cash prior to the maturity date may redeem their notes from the issuer on a rate-adjusted basis or arrange a resale through the dealer originally contracted, who often maintains a limited secondary market for such resale transactions.

The Federal Reserve and the Commercial-Paper Market

One of the provisions of the 1962 ruling by the Comptroller of the Currency with respect to bank debt capital provided that it was within the corporate powers of a national bank to borrow for general banking purposes by issuing commercial paper. Immediately after this ruling was made, several large-city banks began to offer such notes to tap short-term funds. Bank interest in the issuance of these notes stemmed basically from the fact that they were looked upon as nondeposit obligations. As such, they were exempt from a number of supervisory regulations: they were not subject to interest-rate ceilings (Regulation Q); no reserves were required against them; and they were not part of the deposit base upon which FDIC assessments were calculated for deposit-insurance premium payments.

Commercial paper, however, was rendered uneconomical for banks in 1966. During that year Federal Reserve authorities ruled that these note issues constituted time deposits and therefore were subject to all the provisions applicable to such deposits.

Banks were then able to circumvent existing regulations and obtain the necessary funds from the open market through bank holding companies. In other words, a bank could tap market funds by having its holding company issue its own commercial paper. Typically the funds acquired through the issuance of commercial paper to the public by the holding company were used to acquire loans and investments from the subsidiary bank. So far as the banking organization as a whole (holding company plus bank subsidiary) was concerned, the result of commercial paper issuance was the same as in the case of direct bank-issued obligations. As far as the investors were concerned, the holding company's paper was of a quality at least equal to that of issues of promissory notes by the bank itself. The holding company's physical assets may be virtually nil, but it owns the stock of the commercial bank.

In other cases, banks formed independent companies, not holding companies, that sold paper in the market, then bought loans and investments from the commercial bank. The two techniques were analogous, although the legal aspects differed.

The Board of Governors finally concluded that restrictions applying to interest payments on deposits were being circumvented through these practices; effective September 17, 1970, commercial-paper sales by bank holding companies or their nonbank affiliates were subject to marginal reserve requirements and Regulation Q, if the proceeds of the issue were being channeled to the bank's funds. As a result, the sale of commercial paper by bank holding companies or their affiliates declined sharply. From the mid-1970s on, however, holding companies acquired a record number of nonbanking firms, and growth in bank-related commercial paper resumed. The primary activities of these nonbank firms include commercial finance, factoring, and leasing.

Recent Developments in the Commercial-Paper Market

Besides bank holding companies, finance companies have been important participants in the commercial-paper market. These companies rely heavily on the sale of their paper to finance consumer purchases and to extend credit to businesses in the form of receivables financing, inventory financing, and leasing financing. Since the mid-1960s nonfinancial corporations have also increased their reliance on the commercial-paper market, in order to offset seasonal variations or meet short-term operating needs. The high credit rating of these corporations has enabled them to tap this market directly and enjoy significant savings compared with the cost of bank credit. This differential is understandable, since CDs—banks' primary source of financing loans—are subject to reserve requirements. In addition, since bank loans are negotiated on a personal basis and banks often extend concessions that are unobtainable in the open market, there is a significant spread between the prime rate and the commercial-paper rate. Consequently, the number of businesses issuing commercial paper as a means of acquiring operating funds increased considerably in the 1970s. Although the Penn Central Railroad defaulted on $82 million worth of commercial paper in 1970, the market did not suffer any serious long-term difficulties. The practice of issuers to back their paper with lines of credit from banks (backup liquidity) and to secure quality ratings from rating agencies proved instrumental in restoring investor confidence in the commercial-paper market. As a result, this market grew rapidly in the 1970s and 1980s. However another setback occurred with defaults on lower quality paper in 1989 and 1990. This development made it difficult for companies with less-than-top credit ratings to sell their paper in the money market.

Over the years banks have responded to their loss of market share through a more aggressive lending policy. Many large banks sought to lure back large corporations by extending them loans of maturity comparable with the average maturity for commercial paper and pricing such loans below prime, at market-related rates. In addition, banks introduced more flexible borrowing arrangements to accommodate issuers of commercial paper. An example of such service is Morgan Guaranty Trust Company's "commercial paper adjustment facility," an open line of credit that is priced below the prime rate and allows commercial-paper issuers flexibility in the timing of their paper sales. Both of the arrangements discussed above have been provided by banks in addition to the availability of backup lines of credit and banks' functioning as issuing and paying agents for the commercial-paper issuers.

Still another service extended by banks is credit enhancement—that is, guaranteeing customers' paper issued in the money market. Smaller firms can now enter the commercial-paper market by obtaining a letter of credit from a commercial bank, thereby substituting the credit of a strong institution for theirs and reducing issuance costs. This arrangement is often referred to as a "documented discount note," since the letter of credit is appended to the commercial paper. In order to have a commercial bank support the issue of a firm's paper, the firm must pay a fee to the bank. The issuers of commercial paper supported by a letter of credit are usually subsidiaries of larger corporations, including firms involved in auto leasing, power plant construction, and nuclear fuel supply. Credit enhancement may also be obtained by purchasing indemnity bonds from insurance companies.

Two recent participants in the commercial-paper market have been small firms and foreign banks. Small, risky firms can access the commercial-paper market by backing their issues with specific financial assets (e.g., trade or credit card receivables). Asset-backed commercial papers have grown rapidly since their introduction in 1983, and currently many large, lower-risk firms, too, participate in this market through similar issues.

In recent years an increasing number of foreign banks have become participants in the U.S. commercial-paper market. This participation has been in a dual capacity—funding their own activities and guaranteeing, through a letter of credit, their clients' commercial paper. In the former instance foreign banks were able occasionally to acquire operating funds below the London Interbank Offered Rate (LIBOR). On these occasions the U.S. market was a more economical source of dollar borrowing than the Eurodollar market. As guarantors of commercial paper, foreign banks have been extending their clients the same kind of support arrangement offered by their U.S. counterparts. As a result, foreign firms have access to one of the cheapest dollar sources currently available. In either case the selling of paper within the commercial-paper market serves to expand the foreign issuers' investor base and to facilitate their entry into, and acceptance by, the U.S. capital markets. The reverse trend has also been true. U.S. companies have issued commercial paper offshore, in the Euromarket. This paper is known as Euro commercial paper and is denominated in dollars (75 percent) and other major currencies (25 percent). Unlike its U.S. counterpart, the Euro commercial paper has a longer maturity and enjoys an active secondary market. At year-end 1994, outstanding Euro commercial paper totaled $114 billion.

Borrowing of Eurodollars

The vast need for funds denominated in dollars, pounds, marks, yen, and other fairly stable currencies after World War II gave rise to the emergence of a worldwide network of international financial centers trading in the world's most convertible currencies. These centers make up the Eurocurrency market. A Eurocurrency is simply a deposit account in a bank denominated in a currency other than that of the host country. A deposit account denominated in dollars, marks, or yen in a London-based bank is a Eurocurrency. Since the dollar is the main international currency in use today, Eurodollars occupy a dominant position in the Eurocurrency market.

Eurodollars are dollar-denominated deposits offered by banks located outside the United States or within the United States itself but via international banking facilities (IBFs).* As implied, Eurodollar deposits are held by banks located outside the United States, including overseas branches of U.S. banks. However, since December 1981, banks in the United States—with Federal Reserve Board approval—can establish IBFs and accept in their domestic offices nonresident time deposits, free of U.S. banking regulations. These funds cannot be used domestically but may be used to make foreign loans. IBF-related deposits are limited to non-U.S. residents; offshore Eurodollar deposits may be owned by any party from anywhere in the world.

Development of the Eurodollar Market

The term "Eurodollars" originated during a time when the market was almost exclusively located in principal European financial centers. Although the major portion of Eurodollar deposits is still held in Western Europe, they are also held in such places as Hong Kong, the Cayman Islands, the Bahamas, Panama, Singapore, and Bahrain. These geographic locations, known as offshore banking centers, have succeeded in attracting Eurodollar business by offering low taxes, few regulations, and other incentives.

The Eurodollar market owes its origin to the cold war shortly after World War II.[†] However, it was not until the late 1950s that this market began to

---

*IBFs operate as a record-keeping entity identifying and segregating nonresident assets and liabilities that qualify under the Federal Reserve regulation applicable to IBFs. IBFs were permitted in an effort to encourage U.S. banks to bring into the United States some of the Eurodollar business they conduct through other financial centers.

[†]The beginnings of the Eurodollar market are usually traced to two Russian-owned banks in Western Europe, the Banque Commerciale pour l'Europe du Nord in Paris and the Moscow Narodny Bank in London. These banks actively solicited dollars and other foreign-currency deposits for use as working balances and to supply funds for investment. As the cold war heightened, however, fear of expropriation of their dollar deposits at U.S. banks led these institutions to disguise their dollar balances by placing them with Western European banks in exchange for dollar claims on these banks—hence the reference to these dollars as Eurodollars.

Mendelsohn indicates that it was actually the Chinese Communist government that initiated this practice in 1949, a year before the outbreak of the Korean war and the blocking of Beijing's identifiable dollar balances in the United States under legislation forbidding trade with the enemy.[1]

develop. The main thrust came from the innovation of lending or investing dollar deposits in Europe. Although the efficient functioning of this market was the basic cause of its growth, a number of forces combined to bring about an environment conducive to the development of this institution. These forces were the emergence of the dollar as a medium exchange for international transactions, the free convertibility of the currencies of major European nations after the formation of the Common Market (1958), and the sterling crisis (1957) that led to the imposition of foreign-exchange controls on U.K. banks to curb third-country financing in sterling. In the latter case, U.K. banks responded to these controls by turning to dollar financing to maintain their leading position in international markets.

In the 1960s, additional support for a European-based dollar market came from U.S. balance-of-payments difficulties. These difficulties led to capital controls that effectively segmented the U.S. domestic capital market from that of the rest of the world. U.S. capital controls consisted of the Interest Equalization Tax (IET) of 1963, the Foreign Direct Investment Program (FDIP) of 1964, and the Voluntary Foreign Credit Restraint (VFCR) Program of 1965. The direct effect of these controls was to keep foreign borrowers (including U.S. multinational firms and their foreign affiliates) from sourcing their credit needs in the United States through the domestic capital market and banking system. The indirect effect was to reinforce the need for developing intermediate- and long-term sources of funds in the Eurocurrency and Eurobond markets and for creating banking alternatives based in Europe. The latter prospects led many U.S. banks to leap into the more profitable offshore markets and become key sources of short- and medium-term funds. Although the capital controls were dismantled in 1974, the market continued to grow because it had become highly efficient at attracting both depositors and borrowers away from purely domestic financial intermediaries, an ability fostered by the accumulated experience in international money matters available in London.

The 1970s and 1980s experienced the development and growth of offshore banking centers and the decentralization of the Eurocurrency market. These centers have competed aggressively for Eurodollar business by creating a favorable regulatory and tax environment to attract a portion of the Eurodollar banking industry. As a result, these centers have experienced significant growth over the years. Thus, the share of the Eurodollar market in the world dollar financial intermediation has continued to grow.

Banks can avoid many U.S. banking regulations by accepting dollar deposits and making loans outside the United States or through IBF facilities. They are not required to maintain reserves against their Eurodollar deposits. In addition, there is no FDIC insurance associated with Eurodollar deposits; virtually no restrictions are in effect concerning maximum interest rates charged on Eurodollar loans (usury laws); few restrictions govern the types of assets allowed in portfolio; and banks can effect Eurodollar transactions anywhere that tax rates are low, such as Nassau or the Cayman Islands.

Foreign monetary authorities do not impose limiting regulations on the Eurodollar market for two reasons: a host country would lose income-tax revenue and jobs; and it would be virtually impossible to enforce regulations unless every country would agree not to host unregulated Eurodollar business—an unlikely consensus in a business with fierce competition.

Since the Eurodollar market is relatively free of regulation, banks can operate on narrower margins or spreads between deposit rates and lending rates than can banks in the United States. The size of the spread (often less than 1 percent) has been a key factor in attracting both depositors and borrowers to the Eurodollar market. Lending rates are normally quoted as premiums above the LIBOR, which is the rate paid for deposits in the interbank market.

Since the Eurodollar market thrives in areas having minimal or no controls (no disclosure requirements exist for international banks), estimates on the size of the Eurodollar market are derived from aggregate Eurocurrency data. Figures compiled by the Bank for International Settlements identify the gross size of the Eurocurrency market—as measured by the amount of credit outstanding—at the end of September 1995 at about $9.2 trillion. Netting out interbank transactions, the net size of this market was determined at that date as $4.6 trillion. Eurodollar liabilities accounted for 67 percent of all Eurocurrency liabilities, and the net size of the Eurodollar market was placed at $3.1 trillion.[2]

Eurodollar Instruments

The bulk of the Eurodollar market consists of fixed-rate time deposits (TDs), with maturities ranging from overnight to several years. However, most of these deposits mature in anywhere from one week to six months. An important difference between Eurodollar TDs and their domestic counterparts is that the former are to a large extent interbank liabilities. Eurodollar TDs are nonnegotiable and pay a fixed rate of return for the term of the deposit. Quoted rates for TDs are determined competitively.

Eurodollar certificates of deposit (CDs), introduced in 1966, are negotiable receipts for dollars deposited in a bank located outside the United States. Eurodollar CDs can be sold prior to their maturity through an active secondary market. Banks issue Eurodollar CDs in order to tap the market for funds. As a result these CDs are known as tap CDs; their denominations usually range from $250,000 to $5 million. Tranche CDs (from the French *tranche*) are sizable Eurodollar CD issues—in amounts of $10 million to $30 million—marketed in several smaller portions to appeal to investors with a need for smaller instruments. Tranche CDs are usually offered in $10,000 certificates, each bearing the same interest rate, issue date, interest payment dates, and maturity.

In order to minimize interest-rate risks for both the borrower and the lender, Eurodollar floating-rate CDs (FRCDs) and Eurodollar floating-rate notes (FRNs) have come into use. FRCDs serve as an alternative to short-term money-market instruments; FRNs, to straight fixed-interest bonds. Both shift the risk from the principal value of the issue to its coupon. They are negotiable bearer paper, with the interest rate reset at a marginal spread above the LIBOR approximately every

Table 7.5
Eurodollar Borrowings by Banks in the United States, 1985–95 (billions of dollars)

Item	1985	1990	1991	1992	1993	1994	1995
Net due to related foreign offices	(25.9)	34.6	41.3	71.4	119.4	221.4	93.4

Source: Federal Reserve Bulletin, selected issues. Data for 1995 are as of September 30.

three to six months. FRCDs are normally issued in maturities ranging from one and a half to five years, whereas FRNs can mature in anywhere from four to twenty years, but average five to seven years. A secondary market exists in both Eurodollar FRCDs and FRNs. FRNs were a popular instrument in the early 1980s, when world markets were characterized by fluctuating interest rates.

Role of Eurodollars in Domestic Banking Activity

During periods of rising interest rates in the United States, Eurodollar borrowing increases significantly. Between January and December 1966, liabilities of U.S. banks to foreign branches (a measure often used to indicate Eurodollar borrowings) rose sharply, from $1.7 billion to $4.0 billion. Banks with foreign branches were able to offset approximately 80 percent of their CD losses with borrowings from these branches. In 1969, when demand for credit far outdistanced the ability of banks to supply it, borrowings by U.S. banks from their foreign branches rose throughout the year from $6 billion to nearly $15 billion. This development led the Federal Reserve Board to impose, effective September 4, 1969, a 10 percent reserve requirement against any additional borrowings from overseas branches, in an effort to raise the cost and curtail the additional use of these funds. In the 1970s and 1980s, this requirement was adjusted by the Federal Reserve on several occasions, as warranted by prevailing conditions. At the end of 1990 the Board of Governors removed reserve requirements from Eurocurrency liabilities, and all time deposits as the U.S. economy entered into recession. This move eliminated the cost of net transfers from banks' overseas offices to their U.S. offices.

Past experience indicates that borrowings fluctuate significantly and are extremely sensitive to changing interest rates. For example, during the early and mid-1980s, when U.S. money-market rates plummeted from their all-time highs and domestic funds became much less costly to acquire, U.S. bank net Eurodollar borrowings turned negative, amounting in 1985 to $25.9 billion (see Table 7.5). In essence, U.S. banks were making net advances to foreign-related institutions, advances that continued through 1986. Clearly, during this period foreign markets offered greater opportunities for the placement of funds than the domestic market, which was experiencing a slackening in economic activity. As domestic money-market rates started to rise from 1987 on, the preceding trend reversed itself, and U.S. banks were tapping the Eurodollar market for short-term funds. By year-end 1994, Eurodollar borrowings amounted to an impressive $221.4 billion.

As implied in the preceding discussion, there is a great deal of substituting (arbitraging) between the CDs issued by U.S. banks domestically and the CDs issued offshore in the Eurodollar market. Clearly the extent of substitution between the two markets is a function of the effective cost of CDs in each market. For example, suppose that the 90–day rate in the secondary market for domestic CDs is 12 percent while the 90–day offer rate on Eurodollar deposits is 12.10 percent; the FDIC insurance premium (P) on assessable deposits, 0.037 percent per year; and the reserve requirements (RR) on the CDs and Eurodollars, 6 percent and 3 percent, respectively. The effective cost of each funding alternative may be determined as follows:

$$\text{Effective cost of domestic CD}_s = \frac{CD_{US} + P_{FDIC}}{1 - RR_{CD}}.$$

$$\text{Effective cost of Eurodollar CD}_s = \frac{CD_{ED}}{1 - RR_{ED}}.$$

Considering the financial data provided above,

$$\text{Effective cost of domestic CD}_s = \frac{0.12 + 0.00037}{(1 - 0.06)} = .1281 \text{ or } 12.81 \text{ percent.}$$

$$\text{Effective cost of Eurodollar CD}_s = \frac{.1210}{(1 - 0.03)} = .1247 \text{ or } 12.47 \text{ percent.}$$

The spread is $12.81 - 12.47 = .34$ percent.

Although the nominal rate paid on Eurodollars is higher than the nominal rate paid on domestic CDs, the effective cost of the Eurodollars is 34 basis points lower. Therefore, U.S. banks will borrow the funds needed offshore, and will continue to do so until upward pressure on the Eurodollar rates and downward pressure on domestic CD rates change the effective-cost relationship around.

Borrowing from the Federal Reserve's Discount Window

Commercial banks and other depository institutions have an extra source of borrowing in their regional Federal Reserve bank. This source of funds has been available to commercial banks, particularly member banks, since the inception of the Federal Reserve System. Federal Reserve loans take the form of discounts (often called rediscounts) and advances. If the borrowing institution resorts to a rediscounting transaction, it offers for discount at the Federal Reserve bank eligible paper: notes, drafts, and bills of exchange arising out of commercial transactions. In effect, the borrowing institution sells its customers' paper to the Federal Reserve bank, and by endorsing them becomes liable to the Federal Reserve bank if the original maker defaults at the maturity date of the instrument. But the institution may elect to obtain a direct advance from the Federal Reserve Bank on its own promissory note, pledging as collateral some acceptable asset, such as U.S. government securities. Both transactions have the effect of increasing the commercial bank's reserve balances at the Federal Reserve bank.

Most borrowing from the Federal Reserve banks takes the form of advances. Securing funds by means of an advance is generally believed to be a simpler and more flexible tool than discounting in correcting imbalances in the reserve position. By keeping government securities in the vaults of the district Federal Reserve bank, and having signed in advance loan authorization agreements (''continuing lending agreements'') with its discount department, it takes only a telephone call for a bank to borrow. In contrast, by discounting customer paper the bank has to provide financial statements and other information routinely required by the Federal Reserve bank about the individuals or companies liable for paying the discounted instrument on maturity. More important, banks frequently want to borrow for only a limited number of days, and eligible paper of the right amount and maturity may not be readily available.

Types of Credit

Regardless of the method of borrowing, Federal Reserve credit is generally granted as a privilege rather than a right. In other words, extension of credit by the Federal Reserve is never assured. Federal Reserve banks observe certain guiding principles in the administration of credit. Regulation A provides for Federal Reserve lending to eligible depository institutions under two programs: the adjustment credit and the extended credit. Each of these is described below.

Adjustment Credit. The primary form of Federal Reserve lending is adjustment credit. It is advanced to banks for brief periods to help them meet their short-term needs when funds are not readily available from other sources. Enactment of the DIDMCA in 1980 directed the Federal Reserve to open its discount window to all depository institutions that maintain transaction accounts or nonpersonal time deposits. In addition, the Fed may lend to the U.S. branches and agencies of foreign banks if they hold deposits against which reserves must be kept.

At the time of each request, the borrowing institution must provide information regarding liquidity needs and proposed use of funds obtained. The discount officers will monitor an institution's borrowing record by noting fluctuations in its key weekly financial statement items and federal funds transactions, as well as reviewing its past and current use of the discount window, often maintaining periodic personal and telephone contact with bank officials.

The largest institutions are expected to borrow only to the next business day, since they have access to money-market funds and their reserve positions change daily. Other large institutions, which may have somewhat more limited market access, should not borrow past the current reserve period. Medium-size and smaller institutions may extend advances beyond the current reserve period, however, and slightly longer maturities are permitted for small institutions. The borrowing institution should demonstrate in its overall performance its ability to operate within the limits of its own resources, and continuous borrowing may indicate that the borrowing bank has permanent reserve problems that require basic portfolio adjustments. Borrowing to support increases in loan or investment portfolios, to profit from interest-rate differentials, or when other short-term, interest-sensitive funds are available is deemed inappropriate by the Federal Reserve.

Extended Credit. Extended credit is provided through three programs that meet the longer-term needs of depository institutions. Like adjustment credit, extended credit has been accessible to all depository institutions since 1980. The different types of extended credit are outlined below.

Before 1970 many small banks were unable to provide full service to customers in their local communities because of inadequate access to national money-market funds. This lack of funds led small institutions to accumulate excess liquid asset positions throughout the year that would allow them to meet peak seasonal demands. In the early 1970s the Federal Reserve *seasonal credit* program was initiated, enabling these smaller banks to maintain fewer liquid assets during regular periods, thus releasing additional funds for local lending. Small institutions showing a recurrence of intrayearly need are extended advances for up to nine months. A seasonal line must be established with their Federal Reserve bank in order for them to become eligible for such credit.

Institutions experiencing difficulties arising from exceptional circumstances involving only that institution may be allotted what is called *extended credit in exceptional circumstances.* In 1974 Franklin National Bank experienced massive deposit withdrawals and deteriorating earnings, which prompted the Federal Reserve, in its capacity as a lender of last resort, to advance funds to this bank. These funds peaked at $1.75 billion before Franklin's assets and deposits were finally taken over by the European American Bank.

Lending to a large, failing bank was viewed as important in order to avert what were perceived to be more serious consequences for the banking system. This action set a precedent for loans extended later to such institutions as First Pennsylvania Bank (1980), Continental Illinois National Bank and Trust (1984), and Southeast Bank (1991). The FDICIA of 1991 reduces the Fed's discretionary authority as a lender of last resort in cases involving troubled depository institutions. Specifically, discount window lending is limited to 60 days in each 120–day period for undercapitalized institutions and to a 5–day period after

Table 7.6
Volume of Borrowings from Federal Reserve Banks, Selected Years (monthly average of daily figures)

Year	Amount (millions of dollars)	Year	Amount (millions of dollars)
1970	$ 335	1991	$ 192
1975	211	1992	124
1980	1,617	1993	82
1985	1,318	1994	209
1990	326	1995	278

Source: Federal Reserve Bulletin, selected issues. Data for 1995 are as September 30.

institutions become identified as critically undercapitalized. These limits can be exceeded only if the institution involved is certified by the appropriate federal regulator as a "viable entity." If the Federal Reserve exceeds these limits, it could be held liable for any "increased loss" to the FDIC should this institution ultimately fail. Regulation A authorizes emergency credit to nondepository institutions when other sources are not available and the failure to obtain such credit would have adverse effects on the economy. However, such credit will ordinarily be extended at interest rates above those applicable to depository institutions.

Other extended credit is still another form of credit. It was established as a result of the DIDMCA and the ensuing revision, in September 1980, of Regulation A to implement the provisions of the act. Other extended credit can be arranged for groups of institutions facing deposit outflows because of changes in the financial system, natural disasters, or other problems common to the group.

Borrowing Levels

Member bank borrowings from the Federal Reserve System have fluctuated over the years. Table 7.6 shows the aggregate amounts borrowed by banks and other depository institutions from the discount window, from 1970 to September 30, 1995. Recessionary years, or years of slow growth, are characterized by a low volume of borrowings; periods of economic expansion, by a high volume of borrowings. The extent of such borrowings during boom periods is significantly affected by the magnitude of the differential between the federal-funds rate and the discount rate (the rate charged by the Federal Reserve on loans to banks). Rapidly rising money-market rates and infrequent changes in the discount rate can significantly increase the (federal-funds–discount rate) differential and, consequently, demands on the discount window. In other words, in periods of economic expansion, lag of the discount rate behind money-market rates renders the cost of borrowing at the discount window significantly more economical. Such was the case in 1979, when increases in the discount rate lagged behind open-market rates, resulting in a general increase in banks' borrowing levels. In October 1979 bank borrowings grew quite rapidly, reaching a level of $3 billion.

In recent years the Federal Reserve has sought to refine its administration of the discount window. Instead of the infrequent and sharp changes in the discount rate of the past, current changes in the discount rate have been more frequent and of a relatively smaller magnitude. This practice, though reducing the announcement effect that a change in the discount rate traditionally had for financial markets, enables better control of the spread between money-market rates and the discount rate, and affects banks' incentive to borrow accordingly.

The spread between the discount rate and the cost of alternative reserve-adjustment media is not the sole determinant of the volume of commercial bank borrowing from the Federal Reserve. Traditional dislike for operating on borrowed funds is also an important element. As might be expected, sensitivity to indebtedness varies from bank to bank. Certain banks may consider borrowing from the Federal Reserve as a last resort, while for others it may be a matter of managerial policy to avoid such borrowing altogether. The latter attitude holds especially true among small banks, which are very sensitive about listing borrowings in their published statements.

The Discount Rate

As indicated above, the rate of interest that depository institutions are charged for borrowing reserves from the discount window is known as the discount rate. In principle, discount rates are set by each individual Federal Reserve bank, subject to the approval of the Board of Governors of the Federal Reserve System. When the Federal Reserve System was established, it was felt that discount rates should be set in the light of prevailing conditions in each Federal Reserve district. As a result, during the 1920s there was significant variation from one district to another in prevailing discount rates. Over the years, however, the emergence of a national money market has contributed to uniform discount rates.

A closer look at the discount rates reveals that in reality there is not one single rate but a variety of rates, depending upon the type of credit involved. The base rate (or discount rate proper) is the lowest one and applies to advances for short-term liquidity adjustment or seasonal credit needs, secured by eligible commercial paper, bankers' acceptances, or U.S. government securities. On loans to institutions in exceptional circumstances and on the other extended credit, the base rate is adjusted upward as the term of borrowing grows longer.

In September 1980 a revision of Regulation A authorized the Federal Reserve to add, at its discretion, a surcharge on the discount rate charged to borrowing institutions. This authorization covered both adjustment and extended credit. In March 1980 the Federal Reserve had briefly imposed—as part of its credit restraint program—a 3 percent surcharge on any adjustment to credit for large depository institutions (with deposits in excess of $500 million). This penalty rate applied when these institutions attempted to borrow from the discount window in two or more successive weeks or in more than four weeks in a calendar quarter. Its purpose was to bring the cost of Federal Reserve credit closer to open-market rates, and thus discourage frequent use of the discount window by the nation's largest depository institutions. The surcharge proved quite effective and was eliminated in May of the same year. Thereafter it was reinstated as dictated by circumstances.

The discount rate has been an important tool of monetary policy. In fact, the founders of the Federal Reserve System envisaged the discount policy as the main monetary policy tool. For many decades the discount mechanism has been used in a manner consistent with the objectives of the monetary policy—that is, to influence economic conditions in a manner conducive to economic growth, price stability, and a high level of employment. Thus, when the Federal Reserve pursued a policy of tightening credit, the discount rate was raised to discourage bank borrowing and curb inflationary pressures; when monetary authorities pursued a policy of easing credit, the discount rate was lowered. Discount-rate changes were used by the Federal Reserve to signal its intentions in monetary policy. Indeed, announcing discount-rate changes signaled to the financial markets the intention of the Federal Reserve to tighten or ease money and credit (announcement effect). Increasingly in recent years, however, use of the discount rates to signal policy changes has become incompatible with the need for more effective coordination of those rates with open-market operations.

To coordinate these two instruments effectively, the Federal Reserve must make frequent, small adjustments in the discount rate to keep it in line with money-market rates if banks' incentive to borrow is to be controlled. Although discount-rate adjustments by the Federal Reserve are discretionary, the fact remains that this rate has been trailing, rather than leading, other rates in the money markets. These and other related issues have led academicians and financial experts to propose changes in the administration of the discount window. Some of these proposals (for instance, those of the Nobel Prize winner Milton Friedman) take the extreme position of recommending the abolition of the discount mechanism. Banks would still have access to money markets to tap reserve-adjustment funds or even could maintain higher-than-necessary excess reserves. As for emergency credit, the existence of the FDIC—according to Friedman—reduces the need for the Fed to function as a lender of last resort for the banking system in the event of runs on banks.

Despite the various proposals advanced, no consensus has been reached with respect to the role of the discount mechanism. The debate continues.

MONEY-MARKET STRATEGY

The 1970s saw a growing dependence of banks upon money markets to meet their seasonal and other needs for funds. While before this period it was only the larger U.S. banks that generally relied upon liability-management strategies, recent years have seen expanded use of these strategies as medium-size banks have increased their reliance on money markets. Four basic concerns determine policy in managing money-market liabilities: outlook for interest rates, considered in conjunction with maturity dates; liquidity need; diversification of the liability portfolio; comparative interest rates of different forms of liabilities.

The overriding goal in liability management is to obtain funds at the least cost, given maturity requirements. To do this, the bank must consider not only the current level of interest rates but also project their likely changes in the period ahead. For instance, suppose that a bank faces a seasonal increase in loans that can be financed either by repurchase agreements or by large CDs. As repurchase agreements are usually for one day, the bank will have to engage in a series of one-day repurchase agreements throughout the period under consideration, as against issuing large CDs only once to raise the same amount of funds. Thus, funding through repurchase agreements exposes the bank to daily rate fluctuations, whereas funding through CDs enables the bank to lock in a fixed rate. In determining the net cost of each alternative, the repurchase agreements' rate must be adjusted for administrative costs; the CDs' rate, for reserve requirements and FDIC assessments. Figure 7.1 illustrates a hypothetical example of the net cost of each alternative over time. As seen in this figure, if the bank needs the funds for a period of less than 45 days, it is better off relying on repurchase agreements. However, if it needs the funds for a longer period, it is better off with CDs.

Liquidity constraints also come into play in managing liabilities. Short-term liabilities must be balanced against short-term assets in order to assure liquidity as maturity dates arrive. In practice, banks try to match terms and amounts of funds raised in the money market to the terms and amounts of loans made. At times, however, there may be a deliberate mismatching in maturities—that is, purchasing short-term funds for longer-term loans, in hopes of rolling them over under more advantageous terms.

The bank distributes its liabilities across several sources in order to avoid excessive reliance on any single source of purchased funds. Depending too heavily on one source of funds increases bank vulnerability to changing conditions in that segment of the market. In addition, banks wish to stay active in a variety of markets in order to keep trading channels open for each type of funds. Finally, banks maintain diversification within each type of funds so as not to become overly dependent on any single supplier. For instance, some CDs may be sold through brokers while others are issued directly to a variety of corporate buyers.

The fourth consideration, lowest comparative cost of funds, dominates the actual practice of purchasing funds. As will be seen below, trading activity occurs briskly throughout the banking day, in response to ever-fluctuating rates for different types of funds. The traders seek those funds available at least cost. Only when one of the other factors, such as market diversification, is out of kilter are the traders instructed to diverge from the practice of following lowest interest cost in making their purchases.

Figure 7.1
The Net Cost of Large CDs and Repurchase Agreements

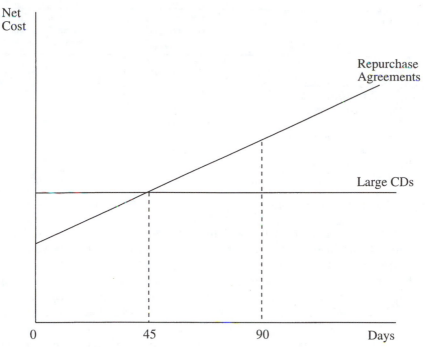

Source: Benton Gup, *Management of Financial Institutions* (Boston: Houghton, Mifflin, 1984), p. 212. Reprinted by permission of author.

Thus, the day-to-day purchase of funds is not conducted as a careful orchestration of all four of these considerations, but is based on the feel of the market at any given time. The analogy of strategy versus tactics is useful for understanding the implementation of money-market funds policy. Strategy is the overall game plan intended to achieve a goal, while tactics are the small-scale or daily decisions that constitute the real action in the field. The interest outlook for given maturities and diversification are strategic concerns, and are gauged periodically—for example, once a month or once a quarter. Liquidity and current interest rates, on the other hand, are concerns of a more tactical nature. Liquidity checks are made on a weekly basis, so that quick adjustments can be made. On a daily basis, prevailing interest rates govern trading activity.

On a typical business day the money-market team—consisting of specialists in federal funds, CDs, Eurodollars, RPs, and government securities trading—exchanges information on the market rates at the day's opening. As the day progresses, the members stay in constant touch, trading information and identifying the most advantageous rates and terms for meeting their daily needs for funds. For example, the rate for a 90–day domestic CD would be compared

Table 7.7
Money Market Rates, October 27, 1995

Instruments	Yield Rate (percent per annum)	Spreads over U.S. Treasury Bills Rate (basis points)
Federal funds rate	5.76	52
Bankers' acceptance, 3-month	5.73	49
Certificate of deposit (large), 3-month[a]	5.79	55
Eurodollar deposits, 3-month	5.82	58
U.S. Treasury bills, 3-month	5.24	—
Commercial paper, 3-month	5.82	58
Prime rate on business loans	8.75	351
Federal Reserve discount rate	5.25	1

[a]Secondary market.
Source: Federal Reserve Bulletin, January 1995, pp. A 25–A26.

with those for a Eurodollar CD and for term federal funds of corresponding maturity. Or, for overnight money, the rate of federal funds would be compared with that of one-day RPs.

Despite the growing importance of liability management for liquidity, bank reliance on this strategy should not be absolute. Reliance upon purchased funds has to be carefully controlled and managed because of its effects upon the total cost of funds and the rates of return that can be earned from the employment of these funds. These factors emphasize the close relationship between asset and liability management in determining bank profitability.

Furthermore, in periods of inflation, Federal Reserve System concern over the growth of the aggregate amount of bank credit may lead to regulatory controls limiting banks' access to these sources of funds. In other words, the ability of banks to purchase interest-sensitive funds is conditional upon the support of regulators. Past experience indicates that when they are faced with unusual financial and economic circumstances, regulators' attitudes and objectives can change quickly.

INTEREST RATES IN THE MONEY MARKET

Banks borrow huge amounts of money every day from the money market that they, in turn, use to accommodate other borrowers in that market. Through their extensive borrowing and lending activities, banks have come to dominate the money market. The rates at which they purchase funds, although they vary from time to time and from source to source, are fundamentally determined by the prevailing yield of U.S. Treasury bills. Because they are the lowest-risk instruments in the market, they carry the lowest yield. Table 7.7, which shows interest rates for different instruments on October 27, 1995, illustrates the relationship between Treasury bill yields and those of other money-market instruments.

As the table indicates, the three-month yields of the various money-market instruments were paying premium rates over the Treasury bill. One factor responsible for this spread is the perceived risk of these instruments. In other words, since Treasury bills are default-free, spreads offered by the other instruments are higher to compensate money-market investors for the higher element of risk. Another factor determining the size of the spreads is demand and supply forces in the marketplace. Since the U.S. economy was going through a process of slow expansion at this time, it is not surprising that spreads over the Treasury bill rate were of small magnitude. In the case of Eurodollar deposits, the higher yield also reflected the lower cost of these funds due to the absence of reserve requirements and deposit-insurance fees.

Table 7.7 includes the prime rate for business loans and the commercial-paper rate. Large corporations, because of their prime credit standing, can go directly into the market and issue their own commercial paper at a cost lower than the prime rate charged by commercial banks. The cost savings to corporations is greater than the differential between the prime rate and the commercial-paper rate, since banks ordinarily require corporate customers to maintain large minimum balances (compensating balances) amounting to a specified percentage of the loan amount (15 to 20 percent).

The discount rate reflects at any moment in time the Federal Reserve System's assessment of credit conditions in the market and the state of the economy. The level of this rate can either attract bank borrowing to the Federal Reserve or drive it into the open market. Of course, the discount rate is not a natural market rate, but an administered rate altered by Federal Reserve authorities to conform to prevailing money-market rates. The other rates illustrated are market-determined, and some of them are more volatile than others. This is especially true for the federal-funds rate. As stated earlier, federal-funds transactions are affected by the reserve position of individual banks. Since most banks wait to adjust their reserve positions with the Federal Reserve bank until the reserve settlement period is drawing to a close, the federal-funds rate often exhibits important volatility on the last day of this period. In other words, banks that did not adjust their reserve positions earlier in the period are actively in the market so as to avoid any deficiency in their reserves with the Federal Reserve bank (and, consequently, the penalties involved).

Although all the instruments in Table 7.7 are key magnitudes, the best single indicator of conditions in the money market is frequently regarded to be the going rate on federal funds. Since federal funds represent monies available for immediate payment in the money market, the federal-funds rate identifies the cost of the principal means of payment in this market.

NOTES

1. M. S. Mendelsohn, *Money on the Move* (New York: McGraw-Hill, 1980), pp. 18–19.

2. Bank for International Settlements, *International Banking and Financial Market Developments*, February 1996, pp. 3, 5.

SUGGESTED REFERENCES

Board of Governors of the Federal Reserve System. *The Federal Reserve Discount Window*. Washington, D.C.: Board of Governors, 1990.

Cook, Timothy. "Determinants of the Federal Funds Rate: 1979–1982." Federal Reserve Bank of Richmond, *Economic Review*, January/February 1989, pp. 3–19.

Cook, Timothy, and Robert K. LaRoche, eds. *Instruments of the Money Market*. Richmond, Va.: Federal Reserve Bank of Richmond, 1993.

Lumpkin, Stephen A. "Repurchase and Reverse Repurchase Agreements." Federal Reserve Bank of Richmond, *Economic Review*, January/February 1987, pp. 15–23.

McCauley, Robert N., and Lauren A. Hargraves. "Eurocommercial Paper and U.S. Commercial Paper: Converging Money Markets?" Federal Reserve Bank of New York, *Quarterly Review*, Autumn 1987, pp. 24–35.

Morgan Guaranty Trust Company of New York. *World Financial Markets*, various issues.

Stigum, Marcia. *The Money Market: Myth, Reality and Practice*. 3rd ed. Homewood, Ill.: Dow Jones-Irwin, 1990.

Part III

Objectives of Portfolio Management

Chapter 8

Liquidity

The nature of a bank's liabilities, together with the thin layer of equity on which it operates, renders the employment of bank funds a factor of primary significance. The process of allocating funds among the different types of assets is known as *asset management*. Available resources must be allocated in a manner that will permit the bank to attain a number of objectives. This fact leads naturally to a discussion of the basic objectives of bank portfolio management and, hence, the factors that affect the general character and composition of commercial bank assets.

First, a bank's portfolio policies should be designed to enable the bank to meet liquidity requirements without exposing itself either to embarrassment or to unusual pressure—in other words, to maintain the degree of liquidity necessary to meet deposit withdrawals and increased requests for loans.

Another consideration that must govern portfolio policies is that the greatest part of a bank's liabilities is subject to withdrawal either on demand or on very short notice. Bank portfolio policies must therefore be guided by prudence; that is, lending and investing are meaningful only when undertaken with almost complete assurance that the principal will be returned. Another way of stating this objective is that the bank has specific liabilities, and the bulk of its assets must take the form of specific claims that are reasonably protected against risk. Clearly, asset quality, and hence solvency, considerations are in the foreground of this objective.

In addition to the maintenance of liquidity and solvency, bank policies should be geared toward achieving sufficient income on the bank's portfolio so that operating costs can be met and the bank can continue profitably as a going concern.

To attain these objectives, bankers must achieve a certain pattern and distribution of bank assets. In other words, the bank's asset structure must strike a delicate balance among liquidity, solvency, and income. Here lies the difficult task of asset management. If one considers income to be complementary to quality, attaining these ends means solving the basic conflict between liquidity and income. This conflict arises from the inverse relationship of liquidity to income. The nearer an asset is to cash, the more remote is the possibility of potential loss to the bank. Such a highly liquid asset, however, would yield a relatively lower income over time than a less liquid, and riskier, asset. In other words, the rate of return on assets tends to vary inversely with their degree of liquidity. This trade-off between liquidity and profitability constitutes the core of asset management. "The are of commercial banking," wrote Roland I. Robinson, "is solving this basically conflicting requirement: that of being safe and yet profitable."[1]

As might be expected, solving this conflict rests entirely upon each bank's management. It is a matter of individual judgment based upon experience and knowledge. Hence, no two banks would solve this conflict in the same way, and the composition of their portfolios would vary accordingly. This chapter examines how banks attempt to resolve the liquidity-profitability conflict and concentrates on the liquidity issue: identifying, estimating, and providing for bank liquidity needs.

ALTERNATIVE APPROACHES TO THE LIQUIDITY-PROFITABILITY CONFLICT

Commercial bank assets may be classified into four groupings—cash assets, security investments, loans, and fixed assets. Asset management must address the allocation of funds among and within the first three groupings. Investment decisions involving fixed assets are not made on a day-to-day basis. However, when expenditures for buildings and equipment are planned, provisions must be made in advance for sufficient cash to be available at the appropriate time. In allocating funds among, and within, the first three categories, management must take into account the various requirements served by these assets (e.g., meet operating and legal provisions, supply liquidity and produce income, and address the credit needs of the market served). Recognizing the importance of these requirements, management has established an order of priorities in the allocation of bank funds. Such allocation is implicit in any attempt to provide for a rational solution to the fundamental banking problem. The "schedule of priorities" indicates that bank funds are used in four basic ways: to maintain primary reserves, to provide secondary reserves, to meet customer credit demands, and to make purchases of investment securities for income.

Of top priority in a bank's employment of its funds is the maintenance of adequate *primary reserves*. The term is an economic rather than an accounting concept, coined to designate a bank's cash assets. Hence it is not found in a bank's statement of condition, but it is a key part of the functional balance sheet that stresses the uses of the bank's resources.

The assets generally designated as primary reserves are the nonearning assets of commercial banks that are in the form of cash or are convertible into it on demand. Nothing else can provide the immediate liquidity of cash holdings, which are immediately available with no risk of loss whatsoever. But cash holdings generate no income. Primary reserves constitute a bank's source of pledgeable assets. They enable commercial banks to fulfill the requirement of the law that they maintain cash reserves against their deposits. Another function of primary reserves is to serve as the first line of defense in meeting the withdrawals of depositors. Depositors can draw against their deposit accounts either by demanding hand-to-hand money or by writing checks payable to others. If they demand hand-to-hand money, the bank must pay out of its cash holdings carried in the vault. If they write checks, the bank must use its balances with other banking institutions (the Federal Reserve bank and correspondent banks) to meet them as they come in for payment through clearing channels (providing that the clearing balance is "adverse"—that is, that the amount of incoming checks on any day exceeds the amount of checks upon which the bank obtains payment from other banks on that day). These different functions of primary reserves led to the distinction between legal reserves (the cash reserves that the law requires a bank to maintain with the Federal Reserve bank) and working reserves, which are held in the form of vault currency, cash in process of collection, and deposits at other banks, including deposits at the Federal Reserve bank over and above the amount required by law (excess reserves).

The second priority in the allocation process is to provide for *secondary reserves*. The origin of this term is traced back to the late 1920s. It was then that, for the first time, bankers and prominent students of banking began to realize the significance of the subject and to discuss it. Like primary reserves, secondary reserves represent an economic rather than an accounting concept, and hence they do not appear in commercial banks' balance sheets as a separate category. However, this item constitutes a key part of a bank's resources. Secondary reserves, or protective investments, perform precisely the role suggested by their name. They are assets that yield some income to the bank but, more important, can be converted from earning assets into cash with little or no delay or loss of principal. Secondary reserves are thus the principal source of bank liquidity. They constitute a reservoir of near-cash assets that is drawn upon to replenish the primary reserves when they become depleted.

The first two priorities serve to ensure the bank's ability to continue in business by meeting the claims presented to it for payment. After providing for these the bank is able to consider its third priority item in the funds allocation process, customers' demand for *loans*. A basic function of the commercial bank is making funds available to the local community. Traditionally banks have been primarily direct lenders to their customers. Business firms have demanded credit to finance their productive and distributive processes; consumers, to finance the acquisition of goods and services for which they will pay at a later date. Through extending credit to customers whose operations and needs are intimately known and understood, commercial banks tend to have a thorough knowledge of their market area.

The last priority in the allocation process of bank funds is the purchase of *investment securities* for income. If the first three use priorities have not exhausted bank funds, then, to maximize income, the otherwise idle funds are used in the open market for the purchase of long-term securities. The investment portfolio is thus viewed as residual in character, although this should not be taken to imply any inferiority in the quality of assets of which it is composed. As a matter of fact, the quality of these assets is thought of as being as important for the bank as that of the loan portfolio assets.

Over the years four different methods have been proposed to assist management in the process of allocating funds to the different classes of assets identified above. Although each method has its flaws, all four seek to produce the best returns possible for the risk level that management is willing to take. These methods are the pool of funds, asset allocation, management science, and liability management. The last was addressed in chapters 6 and 7; the other three are presented below.

Pool of Funds

This approach derives its name from the fact that it views the right-hand side of a bank's balance sheet as a pool of funds that a bank has available to use. Whatever the nature of these funds, they must contribute toward meeting the goals of the bank. To this end, management must first define its liquidity and profitability requirements and then proceed with the allocation of funds among the various classes of assets in a manner that best satisfies these requirements. In other words, within the liquidity/profitability parameters established by management, different proportions of available funds may be allocated to primary reserves, secondary reserves, loans, and investments for income. The pool-of-funds approach does not include investment in fixed assets such as land and buildings in these priorities. These are treated separately.

The pool-of-funds model for asset management has both advantages and disadvantages. The advantages include its simplicity, which makes it easy to learn, and its low administrative costs, which can increase profitability. The drawbacks are more numerous, although they are neither serious enough nor numerous enough to rule out use of this approach. The pool-of-funds approach to asset management is essentially a rigid model that offers a general framework as a basis for decision making. Determining a bank's liquidity and profitability requirements is left up to the judgment and intuition of management in each individual bank. Moreover, it fails to provide any explicit guidelines as to the proportion of funds to be allocated to each asset category. Furthermore, it fails to take account of future conditions or of the interaction among balance-sheet items. Its conservative stance may result in loss of potential income and, thus, diminished profitability.

Asset Allocation

One of the criticisms advanced against the pool-of-funds approach is that by failing to distinguish among the differing liquidity requirements of the various funds that are pooled, it overestimates overall liquidity needs at the expense of profitability. During the 1950s and 1960s prosperity and economic growth led to increases in time and savings deposits compared with demand deposits. Since the former require less liquidity than the latter, this development in essence reduced banks' aggregate liquidity requirements; however, the pool-of-funds method failed to account for this change and thus sacrificed potential profits by calling for higher-than-necessary liquidity reserves. To correct this situation, the asset-allocation or conversion-of-funds approach was developed. This method, recognizing the differing liquidity requirements of the various sources of funds, divides these sources into categories according to their legal reserve require-ments and velocity, or turnover, rate. Then it provides guidelines for the per-centage of each source of funds to be allocated among the different classes of assets. In other words, the funds from each source are allocated independently from the allocation of funds from the other sources, which are viewed individ-ually as separate liquidity-profitability centers. For example, for demand depos-its—which have a high legal reserve requirement and a high velocity rate—a larger share of each dollar is allocated to primary and secondary reserves and a smaller share to loans, mainly short-term commercial loans. Savings and time deposits, on the other hand, are subject to lower legal reserve requirements and exhibit a lower degree of volatility; therefore, greater proportions of these funds can be devoted to loans and investments. Capital funds require the least liquidity, and thus can be used to finance fixed assets (such as land and buildings), with any excess funds allocated to long-term loans and less liquid securities invest-ments.

This method's advantages lie in its relative simplicity and ease of mastery, which make it relatively inexpensive to implement, and in its ability to increase profits by eliminating excess liquidity provisions against the different forms of bank funds. However, it has limitations. Although velocity is a basic criterion in distinguishing among deposit categories, there may not be a strong relation-ship between the velocity of a group of accounts and the variability of the total deposits in that category. For example, while a bank's demand deposits may, in the aggregate, turn over 30 times per year, a group of accounts within this category may exhibit a significantly lower degree of volatility that would justify the allocation of these funds in longer-term, higher-yielding securities than would otherwise seem appropriate. Another limitation of the asset-allocation approach is that it assumes that sources of funds are not related to their uses. This is unrealistic, for as deposits in a particular category grow, they represent a growing group of customers who expect other forms of service from the bank, such as commercial loans. Allocations must be made to allow for these increased service demands. A more important limitation of the asset-allocation approach, however, is that it is essentially a rigid model that does not allow for any seasonal movements in deposit flows and loan demands. In other words, it ignores the ongoing changes in a bank's economic environment or any new developments that would have important bearing upon asset management. The model implicitly assumes that the future will be identical to the present.

There are other disadvantages of asset allocation that also apply to the pool-of-funds approach. First, both approaches stress the need for liquidity to provide for legal reserves and deposit withdrawal demands, but give less attention to the equally important requirement of meeting customers' loan requests. In periods of economic expansion, both deposits and loans tend to increase as the pace of business activity gains momentum. During such periods liquidity is needed mainly to meet the loan demands of businesses and individuals, which tend to outstrip deposit growth. Second, both asset-management models emphasize average, rather than marginal, liquidity requirements. Actual liquidity needs for any individual bank can be determined only through examination of its deposit structure, individual customer accounts, and the general business climate within which it operates.

Management Science

A more sophisticated approach to asset management lies in the use of elaborate mathematical models and statistical techniques to analyze—with the aid of computers—the complicated relationships among the components of the balance sheet and the income statement. These methods are basic tools of management science or operations research. Three common bank applications of these methods are the determination of the optimal number of teller lines by the use of queuing theory; the use of simulation to replicate financial statements of a bank (playing ''what if'' games) or operations (to determine the best number of computer centers or proof machines); and the use of linear programming to solve the allocation-of-funds problem in asset management and portfolio selection.

In order to use management-science techniques for asset management, there must be a statement of objectives, identification of the relationships among the elements of the problem and of the variables that are—and are not—controlled by management, an estimate of the behavioral pattern of the uncontrolled variables, and identification of (internal and external) management constraints. Once these parameters have been drawn up, the program can address specific problems, generate alternative solutions, and identify the best alternative.

Linear programming is a mathematical model that shows the relationships among decision elements. Various computational methods are used to determine the best combination of elements that can be controlled by the decision maker.

Standard computer programs have been developed to perform the complex computations. Nevertheless, in order to be able to interpret and evaluate the results of the analysis, bank management must know the kinds of problems that can be solved by linear programming and be aware of the implications of the model's assumptions regarding economic developments and banking activity.

Linear-programming models are characterized by an objective function specified by the decision maker and a set of variables subject to constraints. Since the linear program has only one optimum solution, the constraints must be specified or approximated.

Every linear-programming model is developed around an explicit objective to be optimized. This objective must be continuous (the coefficients of the decision variables must be able to assume any value), and it must be stated in linear form (each variable must contribute proportionally to the value of the objective function). Optimization may be defined as minimal costs or maximal profits. If the objective is to maximize profits, a bank's management naturally would be interested in the combination of investments and loans that generates the most profits. A simplified example may illustrate this point. If the alternatives (decision variables) available to a bank are a Treasury bill, an AAA corporate bond, a consumer loan, a commercial loan, and a term loan with net yields (after expenses of administering and servicing these assets) of 5.5, 6, 7.5, 9, and 10.5 percent, respectively, we would have a hypothetical equation of the following form:

$$P = .055x_1 + .06x_2 + .075x_3 + .09x_4 + .105x_5,$$

where P stands for profits and x for the amounts to be loaned or invested among the alternative types of assets considered. In this case, maximizing the objective function P maximizes profits. If there was no concern for risk or for liquidity, then all available funds would be placed in term loans (x_5), which offer the highest yield (10.5 percent). Obviously this is impossible, since bank customers demand diverse services, and both common sense and government regulations forbid such a concentration of funds.

Constraints are another characteristic of linear-programming models. They are based on both law and common sense; some are matters of management judgment, while others, such as reserve requirements, are stated specifically. In addition, some, such as reserves, are easily computed as the sums of percentages applied to various deposit categories, while others, such as commitments to mortgages and other loans, cannot be predicted or estimated with great certainty. One can sometimes estimate the demand for loans of various types. If, for instance, the demand for auto loans with a net yield of 7.5 percent is estimated at $3.5 million, then the maximum value of x_3 in the objective function above would be $3.5 million. The principle of formulation is the same, regardless of the complexity of the constraints.

Additional constraints that may be part of a linear program are liquidity, risk, and legal limitations. The liquidity constraint might include a requirement that specific types of investments be related to total deposits, with minimums and maximums specified. Such a stipulation must be based upon predicted withdrawals, loan requests, and consumer perceptions of the bank's position. The risk constraint might include a requirement that the total volume of risk assets must be a set percentage of the value of capital funds. Management may also incorporate into the model those legal restrictions that it deems appropriate.

Restrictions play an important role in multiperiod models, which link one period to the next. For instance, they can limit the available funds in a given period to sums generated in the preceding period: loan repayments, securities matured or sold off, new deposits, and net profits. Multiperiod models also allow decision makers to incorporate their own views about future trends, thus yielding, for instance, a decision to invest so as to take advantage of predicted changes in interest rates.

The solution obtained by the use of linear programming reveals the investment in each category that will yield maximum profits under the specific conditions in the model. The program may have to be run several times for several sets of assumptions, in order to test their sensitivity. For instance, a range of interest rates may be considered in order to see their effect on optimal allocation of funds. Moreover, the linear-programming solution would also show the opportunity costs of the constraints in the model. These opportunity costs can be used to increase profits, for example, by relaxing liquidity requirements or by raising funds through issuing capital notes.

The linear-programming model offers flexibility through the use of shadow prices associated with constraints and affecting profits or the value of the objective function. (A shadow price is the amount by which the objective function would increase if the constraint were decreased by one unit.) For instance, if the solution indicated that profit could be maximized by lending as much as possible in term loans, this could be accomplished through increased demand for such loans. If the maximum that could be invested were $10 million and the shadow price were .05, then each additional dollar of loan demand up to $10 million would generate $.05 of additional profit.

Shadow prices can be used in making policy decisions, especially when they show that profitable activities can be undertaken at less than shadow prices, or that the cost of additional activities is justifiable. In the latter case the information could, for instance, lead to a decision to increase bank funds by issuing notes with a net cost not exceeding the shadow price.

For banks that have computers and properly trained staff, the linear-programming model has several advantages. First, it helps to reveal the implication of decisions. Second, it can be used to test the sensitivity of decisions to errors or changes in economic conditions. Third, it can be used in summarizing the interactions of variables that affect the allocation of funds. Fourth, it helps to formulate bank objectives and have a clear statement of constraints. Fifth, it forces the examination of loan and investment portfolios in terms of types of investment, expected return, and costs.

Some of the factors that have limited the success of management science include difficulty of expressing constraints precisely, poor-quality data, and management preference for low-risk positions over profit maximization during changing economic conditions. For small banks, computers and trained personnel may be too costly in relation to the expected benefits. This problem is lessening as more bankers are receiving training in the use of the computer and as more banks install their own computer systems, join computer time-sharing networks, and provide personal computers to individual staff members.

IDENTIFYING LIQUIDITY NEEDS AND DETERMINING REQUIREMENTS

In its quest for an optimal allocation of bank funds, management is constantly confronted with the issue of making adequate liquidity provisions to meet customer demands for funds. A bank must maintain sufficient amounts of highly liquid assets and/or be able to raise funds quickly from money-market sources to meet deposit withdrawals and legitimate loan requests. Liability management for liquidity is generally relied upon by large money-center banks and some aggressive regional banks, whereas the vast majority of U.S. banks have traditionally relied upon liquid assets to provide for the varied demands for funds. The maintenance of liquid assets against deposit demands has been termed by some analysts "deposit liquidity" or "protective liquidity," as distinguished from "lending liquidity" or "portfolio liquidity," which applies to the maintenance of liquid assets for meeting the community's additional loan demands. Before discussing the nature of the assets that meet these liquidity needs, we will examine how banks go about establishing their liquidity requirements. This is all the more important because an excessive or deficient liquidity position can result in an unprofitable operation. Thus, for a bank to develop a comprehensive liquidity policy, it is first necessary to forecast the size and timing of its liquidity needs.

Analysts have developed various approaches to liquidity planning. Although there are differences among these approaches, they all consider liquidity in the context of prevailing economic conditions and their projected effects on deposit withdrawals and loan demands. Forces at work in the economy (local, regional, or national) impact the customer demand for funds (deposit withdrawals and loans), which directly affects a bank's liquidity position. These forces may be random, seasonal, cyclical, or secular.

Random forces are unexpected and unpredictable developments that affect the economy. They include natural disasters (such as earthquakes and hurricanes) and unanticipated human actions (such as widespread labor strikes or a sudden threat of war). Because of their unpredictable nature, random forces are difficult to take into account in liquidity planning. Seasonal forces recur in a regular pattern every year. They are therefore more predictable and are determined by such developments as planting and harvesting of crops, retail activity during holiday seasons, and stockpiling of inventory to take advantage of weather conditions (for instance, the accumulation of iron ore by Midwest steel mills during the summer months, when the Great Lakes are navigable). The great predictability of seasonal forces allows bankers to use them more effectively in liquidity planning. Cyclical movements are less predictable, and hence less useful for liquidity planning. They are, in simplest terms, alternations of expansive and contractive phases of economic activity. Since cycles do not occur at regular intervals, cyclical liquidity needs are difficult to predict. Past experience indicates that cycles are of unequal duration, and each has its own distinguishing features. Just as individual people differ even though they are members of the same family, so do business cycles. Nonetheless, there are some common repeating features: at the beginning of each cycle, economic growth rates and credit flows increase significantly; later they peak; and subsequently they fall quite rapidly. Thus, comparison with previous cyclical booms may, to some extent, provide helpful indications about the magnitude of a bank's cyclical liquidity needs.

Forces that influence the economy over a longer period than a business cycle constitute a secular trend. Changes in such magnitudes as savings, consumption, investment, technological developments, and population are examples of secular forces. Clearly these forces affect a bank's liquidity. However, though significant for long-range financial planning, they are of limited importance for shorter-run liquidity management. Thus, from a planning perspective, a bank's need for defensive liquidity stems basically from the seasonal and cyclical movements of the economy.

Since the outcome of future events cannot be predicted with complete certainty, no commonly agreed-upon forecasting technique exists for liquidity planning. Larger banks that possess greater resources and expertise have turned to computer models to develop quantitative forecasting techniques. Smaller banks, however, rely on a more judgment-based approach that uses the experience of their officers. Two methods frequently used to forecast liquidity needs are the *sources and uses of funds statement* and the *structure of deposits*. Both are valuable analytical tools well suited to smaller banks that have limited resources, but they are also used by larger banks with access to computers in order to generate more elaborate calculations and trace more detailed data. Use of these techniques is described in the section that follows.

Determining Liquidity Requirements

Bank liquidity serves two basic functions: meeting deposit withdrawals and potential loan requests. To estimate liquidity needs, management must determine potential future changes in current deposit and loan data. Realistic forecasts of loans are essential for efficient liquidity management, and such forecasts can be made only if the bank takes careful soundings of the activities and plans of major customers and follows local developments that may lead to such actions as bond issuance for community development, major construction projects, or the entry of new business into the local market. Bank officers directly involved in various market areas should gather this information, and there should be a mechanism for pooling and analyzing it.

How is this information gathered? It should be an ongoing part of the bank's relations with its customers and with the community at large. Although some officers are reluctant to appear to interfere in their customers' planning endeavors, asking about future financing needs—expansion, construction, capital acquisition, and so on—is in fact a part of the bank's service, because it allows the bank to stand readier to meet the customer's financing needs as they arise. A bank's active involvement in community affairs is also an important source of forecasting information.

In many cases bankers gather or are aware of information of this type but do not systematically use it to help forecast liquidity needs. One way to facilitate effective use of this information is to incorporate into each customer's credit file information on past borrowing and projected business activity, and tag it for easy retrieval for liquidity planning.

Projections of deposits must identify their overall behavioral pattern in response to various forces in the economy. For example, in planning for deposit liquidity, management may take into account the effect of market conditions and competitive pressures on deposit levels. It is usually found that in a period of rising interest rates, a bank's deposit volatility is due to the behavior of the large demand-deposit accounts, the unexpected or sudden withdrawal of which would cause relatively heavy pressures upon the liquidity position of a bank. Rising interest rates prompt holders of these deposit accounts to move their balances into interest-bearing assets as competition for deposit funds from nonbank financial companies (e.g., money-market mutual funds) heightens. When interest rates drop, as was the case in 1993, holders of these accounts seek the higher yields of bonds and stocks, causing important strains on bank liquidity. In the category of time and savings deposits, large CDs are also subject to fluctuations in response to changing interest rates, but their liquidity requirements are predictable because of their specified maturity dates.

Other considerations that may affect banks' deposit levels include changes in monetary policy (an increase or decrease in money supply will expand or contract the volume of deposits in the banking system) and developments in international financial markets (e.g., lower interest rates abroad may prompt an influx of funds and an increase in the amount of CDs issued by U.S. banks, and vice versa). Although a local economy tends to reflect the total economy of which it forms a part, it may have some characteristics that cause sharp fluctuations in a bank's deposits. As a result, local and regional economic considerations must be taken into account in refining deposit liquidity projections.

Determining liquidity requirements against deposit and loan demands by means of the sources and uses of funds is illustrated in Table 8.1. Although bank management may undertake such computations for any particular time

Table 8.1
Calculating Liquidity Requirements for a Hypothetical Bank (in thousands of dollars)

End of Month	Estimated Total Loans	Estimated Total Deposits	Change from Prior Month		Estimated Liquidity (Needs)/Surplus
			Loans	Deposits	
December	$15,000	$21,000	$ - - - -	$ - - - -	$ - - - - -
January	14,500	20,800	(500)	(200)	300
February	14,100	20,500	(400)	(300)	100
March	13,600	20,100	(500)	(400)	100
April	13,400	19,800	(200)	(300)	(100)
May	13,600	19,500	200	(300)	(500)
June	13,900	19,200	300	(300)	(600)
July	14,400	19,600	500	400	(100)
August	14,700	20,000	300	400	100
September	15,100	20,500	400	500	100
October	15,600	20,800	500	300	(200)
November	15,800	21,200	200	400	200
December	16,000	21,500	200	300	100

Source: Developed by the author.

frame, projected data in Table 8.1 cover a 12–month period. An increase in the demand for loans constitutes a use of funds, whereas a decrease in loans is a source of funds. The opposite is true for deposits; an increase in deposit levels is a source of funds, whereas a decrease in deposits represents withdrawals and is a use of funds. Combining or netting of projected changes in deposits and loans, in order to determine net liquidity requirements, assumes a direct relationship between the two trends—in other words, that a potential decrease in loan demand would, through loan repayments, release funds that could be used for deposit liquidity, or that a potential increase in deposits would provide loan liquidity. Thus, according to Table 8.1, the bank will have surplus funds in the first quarter and a shortage of funds in the second. This should prompt management to plan accordingly in meeting the bank's liquidity requirements.

The second method available to estimate future liquidity needs is the structure of funds. This method provides for the structuring or classification of bank deposits into categories according to the degree of their stability, or likelihood of withdrawal—and hence loss to the bank—especially because of movements in interest rates. Management must then assign a probability of withdrawal to each deposit category to determine the amount that will probably be removed from the bank within a specific time frame. Thus, low-risk, or stable, deposits (e.g., long-term large CDs) may be assigned a low probability of withdrawal (e.g., 15 percent or less) and hence will necessitate relatively low liquidity provisions compared with high-risk, or unstable, deposits (e.g., demand deposits), which may be assigned a high probability of withdrawal (e.g., 95 percent or less) and will hence call for more sizable liquidity reserves. Relatively stable deposits (e.g., medium-term, small time and savings accounts) may be assigned a modest withdrawal probability (e.g., 30 percent). By multiplying each deposit category by the assigned withdrawal probability, management can determine the combined amount of expected withdrawals, and hence total deposit liquidity requirements. The same process can be applied to the bank's nondeposit sources of funds. The principal advantage of this approach is that it focuses management's attention on the very cause of liquidity strains. A key weakness is its limitation to addressing a bank's expected loan liquidity requirements.

Whatever the method used, aggregate liquidity requirements will essentially reflect the effect of seasonal forces; additional liquidity provisions must therefore be made for a margin of error or for an extra margin of safety against unexpected or unforeseen circumstances. In such instances bank judgment alone can determine how much additional liquidity should be reserved and what the degree of this liquidity should be.

Funds management is an ongoing process and continual review is necessary, especially since cyclical and secular movements in the economy are largely unpredictable. Besides regular checks at least once a month to see that adequate liquid assets are available, an officer should keep an eye on the situation on a daily basis, so that quick adjustments can be made when necessary. Ideally, the level of liquid funds should match the bank's loan and withdrawal demands at any given moment. Excess liquid funds entail an opportunity cost because of forgone earnings. But if liquid reserves are too low to meet actual demand, the bank must engage in the costly process of purchasing funds immediately or converting assets to cash. In either case the bank is likely to sustain losses if adverse conditions prevail in the marketplace.

MANAGEMENT OF THE LIQUIDITY POSITION

A bank's overall need for liquidity may be classified into immediate, for day-to-day operations; seasonal, for deposit shifts and loan demands anticipated in the near future; cyclical or unforeseen, for longer-run deposit shifts and loan demands associated with the business cycle and/or extraordinary developments. Liquidity for a bank's immediate needs can be provided only in the form of cash. Primary reserves or cash assets are the most liquid form of assets and serve to meet a bank's day-to-day operational requirements. They include currency and coin to meet day-to-day transaction demands, cash items in process of collection, legally required reserves, and balances with correspondents as compensation for services rendered. To plan for all other needs, seasonal and cyclical, by means of adequate cash holdings would require the bank to forgo earnings needlessly. It can be just as safe for the bank to provide for its liquidity

requirements by holding secondary reserves or by the technique of liability management.

Secondary-Reserve Management

Historically banks have relied on secondary reserves (asset liquidity) to meet
cash demands. As indicated earlier in this chapter, secondary reserves is an
analytical, rather than an accounting, concept used extensively by bankers in
thinking about portfolio composition. The assets that make up these reserves are
found in the investment and, to a certain extent, the loan portfolios of a bank.
There is no hard-and-fast line of demarcation between a bank's secondary reserves and its investments and loans. What differentiates these reserves from a
bank's other income-producing assets is that they are held primarily to meet its
liquidity needs. A secondary reserve is one that may be drawn upon to replenish
the primary reserve whenever the latter becomes depleted. Withdrawals of deposits first encroach upon the primary reserves, but a bank cannot afford to
allow its primary reserves to be drawn down and remain below a desirable
operating level. Withdrawal demands, therefore, require rapid replenishment of
the primary reserves, and for this purpose the secondary reserves are used. Consequently, secondary reserves essentially constitute the real source of bank liquidity in meeting deposit and loan demands for funds.

Employment of funds within secondary reserves follows different patterns.
Liquidity of the seasonal type can be provided by assets that possess certain
important attributes: prime quality (minimum of default risk), less than a year's
maturity (minimum of interest-rate risk), and in general a high degree of marketability (rapid and certain salability). Short-term, high-quality, but nonmarketable assets can also be considered in this class, with liquidity in this case
based upon a flow of funds at maturity. In other words, the liquidity of these
assets, and hence bank liquidity, would inevitably rely upon the flow of funds
at a given maturity date rather than upon their flexibility as marketable instruments. Management should reduce the participation of these assets in the secondary reserves. Instead, it should place greater reliance upon readily marketable
assets, so that if the demand for funds comes earlier than anticipated, the bank
will not have to resort to substantial borrowing.

Obviously considered eligible as secondary reserves of the seasonal type are
money-market instruments that have the characteristics mentioned above.
Among the most widely accepted instruments in this category of secondary
reserves are bankers' acceptances, commercial paper, short-term obligations of
the U.S. Treasury and federal agencies, and in general any obligations of the
Treasury or the federal agencies that are coming up for redemption in less than
a year. Loans do not generally qualify, for they do not possess the aforementioned characteristics. About the only loans that could be considered eligible
would be those of a very short-term nature, such as the sale of federal funds
(which are one-day loans to other banks) and call loans (which may be termi-

nated at any time on very short notice, and are usually made to securities brokers and dealers for the purpose of purchasing or carrying highly marketable securities).

Secondary reserves of the nonseasonal or cyclical type are designed to supplement the secondary reserves of the seasonal type and facilitate the making of adjustments against cyclical or unforeseen demands; that is, they are designed to provide for a bank's protective and loan liquidity requirements that are of a cyclical or unforeseen nature. To provide cyclical liquidity, management must be generally aware of the way in which the business cycle affects the local economy or market served. This holds especially true during the contraction phase of the business cycle, when deposit and loan declines are accentuated. During such periods, banks partly offset declining loan outlets by placing idle funds into government securities. Management's past experience, coupled with knowledge of the bank's current deposit and loan makeup, are important determinants of the degree of cyclical liquidity needed.

The liquidity characteristics of the assets that may be included in this category fall short of the strict requirements placed upon the secondary-reserve holdings of the seasonal type, but still exceed those of the assets included in the "bond portfolio," the latter term used hereafter to refer to that portion of the investment portfolio outside of both the seasonal and the nonseasonal classes of the secondary-reserve category. In other words, with the potential need for liquidity further removed, a bank can accept somewhat greater interest-rate risk for income purposes. It follows, then, that secondary reserves of the nonseasonal type represent allocation of funds to high-grade marketable investments possessing a maturity of short-intermediate term (a maturity that ranges from one year, where the secondary reserves of the seasonal type leave off, to five years). Thus secondary reserves of the nonseasonal type may be selected from the promises to pay of the federal, state, and local governments and of corporations. In practice, many banks prefer to place the bulk of the funds available in this category in Treasury obligations maturing in from one to five years because of the high degree of marketability of these securities.

Each of the two distinct types of secondary reserves is designed, then, primarily to fulfill one function: to provide, respectively, short-range and longer-range liquidity. The basic asset characteristics of each of these two classes of secondary reserves should, therefore, be inviolate for all intents and purposes.

Because of the importance of secondary reserves in meeting a bank's liquidity needs, tests have been developed to measure the degree of commercial bank liquidity. The two most commonly referred to in this respect are liquid assets to total assets and liquid assets to total deposits. Liquid assets may, of course, be interpreted in broad or narrow terms. In the former instance, for example, liquid assets would be considered a bank's cash assets and secondary reserves of both seasonal and nonseasonal nature; in the latter case, liquid assets would be considered a bank's cash assets minus required reserves plus seasonal secondary reserves. This latter definition of liquid assets appears to be conceptually preferable in measuring the degree of bank liquidity. In this context, then, the ratio of liquid assets to total assets would reflect the relative importance of a bank's liquid assets among its total assets. In other words, this ratio reveals the liquidity quotient of a bank's asset account. The ratio of liquid assets to total deposits shows what percentage of a bank's deposits is held in liquid form. Both ratios are significant because they reflect the ability of a bank (or of the banking system) to honor depositor's withdrawal demands and to grant loans.

Liability Management

Liability management also generates funds to meet liquidity needs. As we have seen in chapters 6 and 7, liability management involves acquiring funds by issuing CDs, purchasing federal funds, or borrowing from the Federal Reserve. Using funds acquired in this way to meet liquidity needs can allow a bank to reduce its holdings of secondary reserves. Liability-management-oriented banks generally rely upon money markets to provide for liquidity needs on a routine basis.

Liquidity Strategy

In determining liquidity policy, banks must decide to what extent they will rely on secondary reserves or liability management. The former focuses on storing liquidity in assets; the latter, on the acquisition of funds through a variety of borrowing arrangements that are unique in interest, maturity, and service characteristics. Degree of risk and return (cost) are important considerations in determining to what extent to rely on each strategy. Reliance on liability management entails the risk of not being able to renew or replace maturing liabilities. Risk assessment must take into account the extent to which the bank may be able to roll over purchased funds to sustain expansion of its asset base. In periods of financial strain (such as during the failure of the Franklin National Bank in 1974), the availability of funds may be nil. In less extreme instances the quantity of funds available may be limited, thus creating a shortage. This risk and the constraints it imposes must be viewed in the context of the bank's overall risk exposure. Cost of liability management depends upon the specific borrowing arrangement employed and includes interest cost-adjusted, where applicable, for reserve requirements, processing costs, insurance fees, and other factors. If interest-rate forecasts are inaccurate, decreases in interest rates may leave the banks locked into high-cost funds, with a corresponding reduction in profits. On the secondary-reserve side of the coin, the selling of assets to provide for liquidity needs has as its cost the amount of income that the bank would forgo during the life of these assets, adjusted for any gains or losses realized from the sale of these assets, tax effects, and brokerage fees.

Clearly, liquidity management does not have to be a choice between the secondary-reserve approach and the liability-management approach, since a combination of both strategies is employed by many banks. The most common instrument used to raise funds for liability management is the large-denomination CD. Large, well-known banks are able to offer these on the open market in addition to selling them to customers or investment dealers. In addition, RPs and federal funds are widely used in liquidity planning. The most common assets sold by these banks to raise funds are short-term government securities.

In the final analysis, management philosophy determines the best course to follow. Generally, nonmoney-center banks maintain secondary reserves sufficient to meet projected liquidity needs for the next 12 months. If unexpected drains on liquidity occur and the bank does not wish to sell other assets to meet this need, it can turn to liability management on an ad hoc basis. Money-center banks and some other large banks are more likely to use liability management as an ongoing method of meeting liquidity needs. However, there is a limit on how much aggregate activity of this type can occur. If too many banks plan to purchase funds for liquidity at times when the Federal Reserve is tightening the money supply, some banks may get caught in the squeeze and experience liquidity problems.

NOTE

1. Roland I. Robinson, *The Management of Bank Funds*, 2d ed. (New York: McGraw-Hill, 1962), p. 4.

SUGGESTED REFERENCES

Cates, David C. "Liquidity Lessons for the '90s." *Bank Management*, April 1990, pp. 20–25.
Chirot, Cynthia K. "Liquidity Sources." *Bank Management*, October 1991, pp. 51–56.
Fraser, Donald, Benton E. Gup, and James W. Kolari. *Commercial Banking*. Minneapolis/ St. Paul: West Publishing Co., 1995.
Reed, Edward W., and Edward K. Gill. *Commercial Banking*. 4th ed. Englewood Cliffs, N.J.: Prentice-Hall, 1989.
Rose, Peter. *Commercial Bank Management*. 3rd ed. Homewood, Ill.: Irwin, 1995.

Chapter 9

Solvency

Liquidity is one objective of portfolio management. Another is the maintenance of solvency—that is, ensuring that the value of assets is sufficient to cover liabilities. The former constitutes a short-run objective for bank management, while the latter is a long-run objective. Indeed, as we saw, the maintenance of a sufficiently liquid position constitutes the most immediate and compelling obligation of bank management, since failure to meet all claims as they come through would leave management with no alternative but to close the bank's doors. Solvency, on the other hand, ensures the safe, and hence continued, existence of the bank. Unless this objective is constantly considered, the day will come when the short-run objective of liquidity cannot be met. That is, the ability of the bank to remain open depends upon the fulfillment of the immediate objective of liquidity, but the attainment of that objective depends largely upon the achievement of the long-run objective of solvency.

The basis of an attack on the issue of solvency is suggested by the statement of the problem. The objective of bank management is to keep assets at least equal to liabilities, excluding subordinate notes and debentures plus capital stock. As long as such equality exists, a banking concern is solvent. Since bank liabilities are expressed in fixed amounts of money, it is evident that the causes of insolvency lie in changes in the value of bank assets. As losses occur, the value of assets declines, and such losses are customarily charged against the bank's capital account. If losses persist and the bank's capital falls below the par value of its outstanding shares, then capital is said to be impaired, yet the bank is still solvent. Should the assets decline in value by an amount in excess of the bank's capital, then insolvency exists—that is, the value of assets is less than the total amount of the bank's liabilities. It is essential that we examine the causes of these losses and of the risk factors responsible for them.

RISKS IN THE BANKING BUSINESS

In the course of their operations, banks are exposed to risks. Some of these risks are specific to the banking business, while others are inherent in virtually any business activity. The former category includes the risks of default, bank runs, interest-rate risk, and unfavorable fluctuations in foreign-exchange rates. In addition, like other businesses, banks are exposed to the risks of defalcation (embezzlement) and theft. Each of these types of risk is discussed below.

Risk of Default

The most obvious hazard in banking is the risk of default, the possibility that the funds loaned or invested will not be repaid, with consequent loss to the bank. In their lending and investing operations few banks knowingly make poor loans and investments. It is what occurs after a loan or investment is made that will be decisive as to whether it will deteriorate in quality or go into default. Many unforeseeable developments can undermine a borrower's ability to meet contractual obligations as they come due. "Acts of God" (hurricanes, tornadoes, floods, and earthquakes) can lead to nonpayment of debt. And changes in consumer tastes can significantly affect the fortunes of companies. If consumers, for example, prefer soft drinks in bottles over those in cans, manufacturers of bottles would prosper at the expense of those producing cans. Boutiques and clothing manufacturers are affected by style changes. Technological advance can drastically alter the financial condition of a business firm. Mechanical calculators, for example, were rendered obsolete by electronic calculators. The swings of business cycles affect the profitability of businesses and influence their willingness to discharge their debt. Such diverse developments as prolonged strikes, construction of an expressway, loss of key management, entry of new competitors into the market, and additional future debt can lead to the nonpayment of debt.

The risk of default ranges from practically none, on instruments such as government obligations or the highest grade of corporate debt, through many gradations. Judging gradations of risk requires a considerable degree of skill. What may appear to be currently within a borrowing firm's ability to pay may, five years later, turn out not to be the case. The firm's prospects may have definitely turned for the worse because of developments such as the ones mentioned above. The further one looks into the future, the less certainty there is about the actual ability of the borrower to carry the debt. Even self-liquidating, short-term commercial loans get into difficulties during recession and may need many renewals or extensions before repayment is made.

Because of this uncertainty element the risk of default, and hence the risk to the quality of bank credit, is ever present. In the case of loans, this risk element is covered in the rate of interest charged, while in the case of securities it is reflected in their market value. In investing in securities, banks typically buy any debt that has only slight chance of default. Thus, the price differentials among various debt instruments, other factors being equal, presumably reflect the risk of default. This in itself presents the management of a bank with a problem. To maximize bank profits, the management needs high yields, but they are associated with the riskier opportunities. Thus, skill and judgment are required to evaluate the opportunities open to the bank, for if the loan or investment is defaulted, income suffers and solvency is impaired. To prevent and control losses resulting from default, banks seek to maintain high credit standards, diversify loan and investment portfolios, have a good knowledge of the borrower and understanding of his affairs, and pursue a vigorous collection policy. These are discussed in Part IV.

Bank Runs

Even if there is absolutely no question about repayment of principal and interest when due, a bank may be forced to sell or call in high-quality assets at a loss, thus undermining its ability to repay depositors and other creditors in full. Forced sale of securities or collection of loans occurs when customer demand for funds necessitates the liquidation of assets. A depositor's withdrawal demand is one that a bank must honor promptly; failure to do so would force the bank to go out of business. Demands for funds may occur at any phase of the business cycle—during recession or economic expansion. During periods of decline in economic activity, withdrawal demands originate mainly from depositors, who rush to convert their deposits into currency because of distrust of banks. In the depression of the 1930s, for example, hints or suspicions of bank losses and doubts about the ability of particular banks to meet withdrawal demands led depositors to converge on banks to obtain their funds before the banks ran short. There are many historical examples of bank runs (as this condition is called), and they often culminated in the downfall of the bank involved. As the depression intensified, the merest hint of a bank loss was enough to trigger a run on its assets. In both Nevada and Louisiana, state-declared bank holidays convinced depositors that the banks were on the verge of ruin. The governor of New York was forced to close banks statewide to prevent panicked withdrawals and the collapse of the state's banking system. By early 1933 commercial banking activity had virtually ground to a halt until President Roosevelt restored public confidence by declaring, on the morning of Inauguration Day, a national bank holiday.

The danger of such panics and the accompanying runs on banks has been greatly reduced, if not eliminated, by such banking reforms as the establishment of a deposit insurance system, stricter banking laws, and greatly improved bank supervision. These reforms contributed to strengthening the banking structure and the confidence of the public in banks. Public confidence in the banking system has been further enhanced by the FDIC's access to a line of credit with the Treasury for additional cash in the event that its funds become depleted in an emergency. The FDICIA of 1991 recapitalized the Bank Insurance Fund by increasing the FDIC's ability to borrow from the Treasury to $30 billion (up from $5 billion). The FDICIA also allowed the FDIC to borrow $45 billion for working capital, to be repaid as the FDIC sold the assets of failed banks.

When several large banks were on the verge of collapse in the 1980s and early 1990s—such as Continental Illinois National Bank and Trust Company (1984), First Republic of Dallas (1988), and Bank of New England (1991)—the FDIC provided them not only with financial assistance to enable them to continue as going concerns, but also with a blanket guarantee of all their deposit liabilities. Although this type of regulatory assistance is successful at preventing bank runs, its most serious drawback is *moral hazard*; that is, it induces bank managers to engage in highly risky activities. The FDICIA was instrumental in limiting brokered deposits and restricting the use of the "too big to fail" concept, thereby introducing "market discipline." This implies that uninsured depositors have an incentive to monitor the activities of banks; if management takes on too much risk, they may exert pressure by withdrawing their funds or demanding a higher rate of return. The FDICIA has resulted in losses to uninsured depositors, as planned, and has increased market discipline.

Over the years several suggestions have been advanced to eliminate moral hazard and reform the deposit insurance system. Some of the proposed changes include lowering, or altogether eliminating, the amount of deposit insurance; introducing coinsurance, whereby the uninsured depositor would suffer a percentage of the losses along with the deposit insurance agency; providing private deposit insurance to substitute, or complement, federal deposit insurance; and allowing federal insurance only on deposits at *narrow banks* (banks that place their funds in riskfree assets, such as, Treasury bills), leaving uninsured the deposits at *wider banks* (banks that will make loans). Although these proposals enhance market discipline and encourage little moral hazard, they increase the prospect of bank runs and instability in the banking system. For example, the problem with private deposit insurance is that if its providers fail, they can cause bank panics like the ones that occurred in Ohio, Maryland, and Rhode Island in recent years. Lowering or abolishing deposit insurance will not increase market discipline because small depositors are not necessarily well enough informed to monitor bank activities; instead, they are more likely to get nervous and precipitate a run on the bank. The same argument may be advanced against the coinsurance proposal and the wider bank concept. The key concern with market discipline is the potential for bank runs.

A series of regulatory measures introduced in recent years has brought about what some experts describe as "regulatory discipline." FDIC assessment of risk-based premiums, capital adequacy requirements, and the provisions for prompt corrective action are examples of bank-imposed regulatory discipline. Collectively, these measures reduce moral hazard and are an important psychological deterrent to public runs.

Interest-Rate Risk

Any time a bank is forced to sell or liquidate long-term securities in periods of increased economic activity, it exposes itself to interest-rate risk—that is, the risk that the sale of these securities will be realized only at sizable discounts from their face value. The prevailing level of interest rates in the market at the time of the sale is thus a critical factor in the extent of bank losses. It is a basic principle in finance that the market value of securities moves inversely to changes in the current market rate of interest. Thus, if, as a result of market forces, the going rate of interest moves up, the market value of debt instruments calling for fixed payments over time (based on some previous lower rate) will fall. Let us assume that a bond bearing an interest rate of 6 percent and maturing in 20 years is purchased. If the bond is purchased at par (100 percent of face value), its market price would be $1,000. Suppose that, subsequent to this purchase, the market rate of interest for bonds of comparable quality rises to 8 percent. Clearly the market value of this bond will be affected. The extent of the effect can be determined through an equation that is based upon the concept of present value (worth today of funds to be received in the future), and is used to determine the yield to maturity of debt securities. This equation is

$$P = \frac{R_1}{(1 + k)} + \frac{R_2}{(1 + k)^2} + \cdots + \frac{R_n}{(1 + k)^n} + \frac{M}{(1 + k)^n},$$

where

P = current price of bond or present value of payments
R = annual interest revenue ($) from bond (coupon payments)
n = number of years to maturity
M = principal ($) payable at maturity
k = market rate of interest or yield to maturity.

Applying the information available, we would have

$$P = \frac{\$60}{(1 + .08)} + \frac{\$60}{(1 + .08)^2} + \cdots + \frac{\$60}{(1 + .08)^{20}} + \frac{\$1,000}{(1 + .08)^{20}} = \$804.08.$$

Thus, as the result of an increase in the going rate of interest to 8 percent, the value of the bond will decline to yield a competitive rate of return. At the price of $804.08, this bond provides an annual rate of return of 8 percent. It follows that a change in interest rates inversely affects the value of a bond, with consequent effects upon its yield. A rise in interest rates depreciates the value of lower-interest-bearing bonds, causing their yields to increase, and vice versa.

This fall in price will be similar for all bonds of similar risk and maturity. If coupon rates of interest differ, market prices will tend to fall accordingly, to keep the yields in line with one another. The longer the period that the instrument has before it matures, the greater will be the fall in its market price. This point can be illustrated by making reference to the above example. Suppose, for example, that the initial purchase included two additional bonds of the same quality and bearing the same interest as the one described above, but of longer maturities. Let us assume that one of these had a maturity of 25 years, and the other of 30 years. In such a case the rise in interest rates to 8 percent will cause the value of the 25–year-maturity bond to decline to $786.50 and the value of the 30–year-maturity bond to decline to $774.48. Clearly, the effect of this rise in interest rates is accentuated by the longer maturity of the debt instrument. By the same token, a decrease in interest rates would cause the value of the longer-maturity bonds to appreciate more than that of the shorter-maturity ones.

Clearly, then, the longer the maturity of the securities owned by the bank, the greater the decline in their market value, and hence the larger the capital losses to be sustained by the bank, which is forced to convert them into cash. But even if the bank may not have to sell the bonds that have declined in price because of the change in the rate of interest, the bank is not realizing the same amount of income it could be receiving at the higher rate if it had not invested in the bonds it now holds.

The interest-rate risk, is, therefore, inherent in all contracts calling for fixed payments over time. Consequently, bonds that are free of any default risk are still subject to the interest-rate risk, since the future level of interest rates is uncertain. This fact could make a case for loading up on short-term securities by the banks, since such securities are insulated from wide fluctuations in value. This is another aspect of liquidity. Even a long-term bond may become part of a bank's secondary reserves as it approaches maturity. This means that the realizable price in the event of its liquidation is more certain, and differs from its stated redemption value by only a small amount. But, of course, by loading up on short-term securities the bank precludes much chance of capital appreciation if interest rates should fall. Moreover, it exposes itself to *reinvestment risk*— the risk that a decline in interest rates will lead to lower interest income when securities mature and the funds are reinvested at the going rates.

In recent decades management concern over interest-rate fluctuations has gone beyond their effect on individual securities. Since bank balance sheets are largely composed of financial assets and liabilities, bank earnings are, in varying degrees, sensitive to interest-rate fluctuations. Thus bank managers have sought to devise a policy for managing their asset/liability sensitivity. Efforts in this direction received prime attention in the late 1970s and early 1980s, as a result of the wide swings in interest rates, which sharply increased the volatility of bank earnings. The sections that follow highlight the more important asset/liability management strategies used by banks: matched book, spread management, gap management, duration, and interest-rate swaps.

Matched Book

An important approach to protecting a bank from interest-rate risk is to focus on matching the maturities of the asset and liability portfolios. In other words, by matching the timing of its cash flows, a bank may lock in the rate spread between its assets and its liabilities. By maintaining a matched book on the entire portfolio, a bank may thus protect itself from the consequences of interest-rate fluctuations.

Although the matched-book approach has a lot of merit, not every bank will choose always to insulate its operations from interest-rate risk. Often, management may wish to take a position in the market to benefit from an expected move in the future course of interest rates. Specifically, if management believes that it can forecast the market on interest rates, it may allow a deliberate mismatch on the portfolio and assume the desired degree of exposure. Alternatively, a matched book may be difficult to maintain on an ongoing basis. A bank's financial intermediation function is hampered if it constantly takes only those liabilities that match its asset maturities. While the bank does not assume much risk, neither does it add much to its economic value because of the narrow spreads associated with a matched book. In fact, by trying to attain its matching objective, the bank may be forced to quote off-market rates, which, in turn, would oblige its customers to take their business elsewhere. Thus, in the normal course of business a bank may have to accept a mismatched position on the portfolio and resort to its management.

Spread Management

Another approach to insulating an institution from interest-rate risk is to focus on the management of its gross profit spread. Spread management, as this technique has been referred to, focuses on the spread between the average yield from assets and the average cost of funds. Before deregulation most bank liabilities consisted of noninterest-bearing demand deposits and fixed-rate time and savings deposits; consequently, spread management responded mostly to rates that banks could charge for loans and security investments. As those rates increased, banks were able to improve their spreads between returns on assets and cost of funds. With the advent of deregulation, however, customers converted low-rate savings and time deposits to higher-rate CD liabilities. Also, banks began to bid aggressively for borrowed funds. These developments reduced the rate spread between the banks' assets and liabilities, and encouraged banks to pursue flexible loan-pricing and asset-funding policies consistent with cyclical trends in the economy. Figure 9.1 shows a spread-management strategy that can be used over the course of a business cycle as short-term interest rates rise and fall. For example, during the recovery phase of the business cycle, when short-term rates are increasing, banks should focus on variable-rate assets while relying on fixed-rate sources of funds. During the prosperity phase, they should shift to fixed-rate loans and investments to lock in high returns and rely upon

Figure 9.1
Spread-Management Strategies

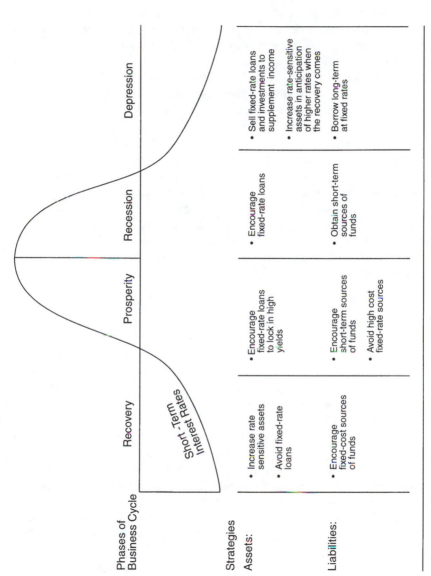

Phases of Business Cycle	Recovery	Prosperity	Recession	Depression
			Short -Term Interest Rates	
Strategies				
Assets:	• Increase rate sensitive assets • Avoid fixed-rate loans	• Encourage fixed-rate loans to lock in high yields	• Encourage fixed-rate loans	• Sell fixed-rate loans and investments to supplement income • Increase rate-sensitive assets in anticipation of higher rates when the recovery comes
Liabilities:	• Encourage fixed-cost sources of funds	• Encourage short-term sources of funds • Avoid high cost fixed-rate sources	• Obtain short-term sources of funds	• Borrow long-term at fixed rates

Source: Benton Gup, *Management of Financial Institutions* (Boston: Houghton Mifflin, 1984), p. 175. Reprinted by permission of the author.

rate-sensitive sources of funds in anticipation of lower costs when interest rates decline.

Gap Management

Gapping is a relatively new approach to risk management. Gap analysis is the analytical framework that relates the interest rate and maturity characteristics of assets and liabilities; gap management is the operating framework to manage these relationships.

To establish the rate sensitivity of balance-sheet items, gap analysis groups assets and liabilities into three categories. The first category consists of assets and liabilities with matched maturities and rates. The predetermined maturities and rate spread of these accounts render their profit margins immune to interest-rate fluctuations. The second category consists of fixed-rate assets and liabilities of long-term maturity (such as mortgages and long-term debt). To the extent that these items are matched, they are also immune to risk since they are relatively impervious to short-term fluctuations in interest rates. Their profit margin will fluctuate slowly over time as individual items mature or are rolled over. The third category consists of all assets and liabilities that are subject to variable rates either because of their short maturity or because of the periodic adjustment in their rate of interest. Variable-rate assets include such items as short-term loans and investments, variable-rate term loans, federal funds sold, and repurchase agreements subject to resale. Variable-rate liabilities include such items as short-term CDs, federal funds purchased, repurchase agreements, and other short-term borrowings.

The third category is the most critical one for gap management. To measure the extent of a bank's exposure to interest-rate sensitivity, variable-rate assets and variable-rate liabilities are each totaled and their dollar differential is established. This amount represents the gap. Illustration of an imbalance between variable-rate assets and variable-rate liabilities, and the resulting gap, is shown in Figure 9.2. When there are more variable-rate assets than there are variable-rate liabilities, a positive gap exists; when the volume of variable-rate liabilities exceeds the volume of variable-rate assets, a negative gap exists; and when variable-rate assets match variable-rate liabilities, the gap is equal to zero, in which case profit spreads can be maintained as rates rise or fall.* A bank will benefit from a positive gap when interest rates are rising because this means more assets than liabilities will be repriced at higher rates. Similarly, falling interest rates are beneficial when a negative gap exists because liability costs will fall faster than asset yields.

Depending upon the sources of funds relied upon, some institutions' rate-sensitive time horizon may be limited to a single period, while for others it may

---

*A positive gap implies that the excess amount of variable-rate assets is essentially being funded by fixed-rate liabilities; a negative gap, that the excess amount of variable-rate liabilities is used to fund fixed-rate assets.

Figure 9.2
Rate Imbalances, or Gap

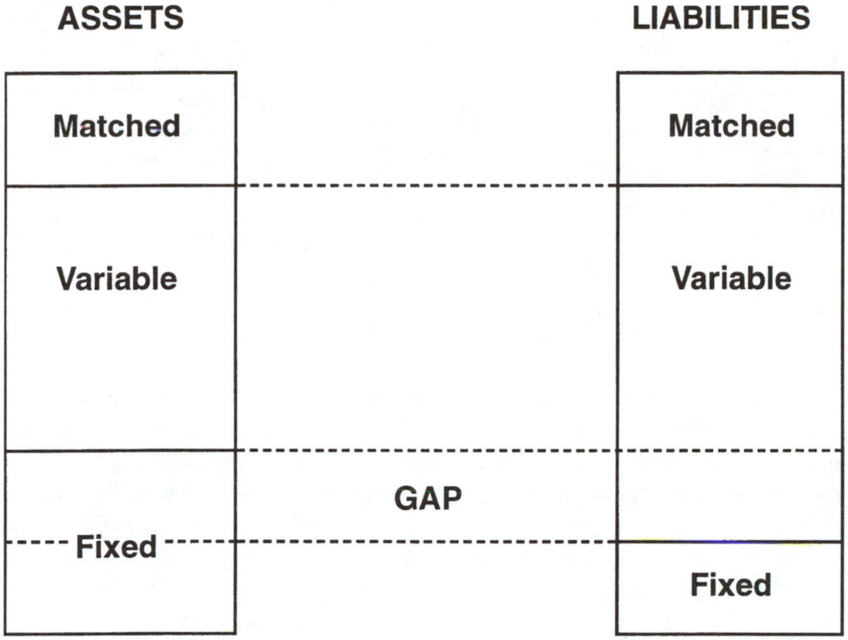

ASSETS　　　　　　　　　　　　　　　LIABILITIES

Source: Prepared by the author.

extend over several periods. In the latter instance the size of the gap changes with each period, thereby influencing the institution's cumulative gap. An illustration of gap measurement over several periods for a hypothetical bank is shown in Table 9.1. In this table, for an institution whose rate sensitivity extends over multiple periods, rate exposure may be determined by dividing all its interest-earning assets and liabilities into categories and computing the gap within each category—that is, the dollar difference between the assets and liabilities that either mature or are subject to a rate adjustment in that maturity interval.* Whether the gap of each particular time interval is positive or negative, it is reported under the gap column; accumulation of the gap figures helps derive the cumulative gap. In Table 9.1, the top four categories are associated with a positive gap; the last three, with a negative gap. Cumulatively, in the two-year period following the report, the institution's gap is a positive $40 million and drops to $10 million for the period in excess of ten years.

One can obtain a rough indication of the sensitivity of the present balance sheet to changes in interest rates from the present to some future time by looking at the cumulative gap up to that time. For example, if the cumulative gap up to one year is positive, this means that there are more assets than liabilities to be

*For items such as passbook savings, demand deposits, and credit card loans, a judgment of maturity is made on the basis of past experience.

Table 9.1
Rate-Sensitivity Gap over Several Periods (millions of dollars)

Repricing Schedule	Interest-Earning Assets	Interest-Bearing Liabilities	Gap	Cumulative Gap
Overnight - 1 month	20	10	10	10
1 - 3 months	40	20	20	30
3 - 6 months	30	20	10	40
6 - 12 months	10	0	10	50
1 - 2 years	30	40	-10	40
2 - 10 years	20	30	-10	30
Over 10 years	10	30	-20	10
Total	160	150		

Source: Developed by the author.

repriced within one year. This in turn means that the full balance sheet would benefit from higher interest rates one year out. Although interest rates on different balance-sheet items of similar maturity do not always move by similar amounts, large moves in one rate are almost always associated with large moves in the other. Thus, by multiplying the cumulative gap up to a particular point in time by a hypothetical change in interest rates, one can obtain a rough measure of the impact of such a change in interest rates on earnings up to that time. For example, if the cumulative gap up to one year is positive $50 million, this means that if interest rates increase immediately by 100 basis points, pretax earnings within one year will be roughly $500,000 higher. However, this is a very rough measure. The precise amount depends not only on the relationship between movements in different interest rates of similar maturity, but also on the detailed repricing pattern of the balance sheet within one year. That is, the impact will be different if the assets and liabilities that are repriced within one year are repriced at the beginning of the year, toward the middle of the year, or toward the end of the year.

Over the years different techniques have been developed to assist banks in gap management. The following sections describe three techniques: managing the gap over the interest-rate cycle, attaining gap targets using financial futures, and attaining gap targets by means of options.

Managing the Gap over the Interest-Rate Cycle. This strategy emphasizes the maintenance of a positive gap, with the size of this gap subject to manipulation over the interest-rate cycle. In a period of rising interest rates, banks benefit from an increasing positive gap. However, during such periods banks find it increasingly difficult to attract fixed-rate, long-term funds; yet some adjustments may be made on the liability side of the balance sheet through sale of capital notes and debentures and/or common stock. On the asset side, funds may be shifted to short-term investments and variable-rate term loans. These adjustments will change the maturity profile of the balance sheet and increase earning opportunities from positive gapping.

At the height of the interest-rate cycle, when the largest positive gap should occur, the bank should lock in high-yielding assets by shifting funds to long-term securities and fixed-rate loans. This portfolio adjustment may take time to effect as old loans come due and previously made short-term investments mature. More important, it may not come as easily because of borrower preference for variable-rate loans as interest rates fall. On the liability side, the bank should increase its reliance on rate-sensitive sources of funds to benefit from lower interest costs when rates fall. This funding pattern, continued throughout the recession phase, should narrow the gap until it reaches a minimum size at the bottom of the rate cycle (trough). At that point, emphasis should be shifted again toward increasing the positive gap as rates begin to rise. Thus, depending upon prevailing economic conditions, the gap should be managed according to the following guideline: the gap should be wide when interest rates peak and narrow when rates are low.

This strategy, like other methods of gap management, is generally practiced by large banks, which have the necessary talents to make realistic market predictions. However, even the most skilled forecasters cannot always make accurate predictions, and thus an element of risk is always present. In addition, some question the desirability of making rate structures for customers subservient to the bank's gap-management strategies.

Financial Futures and Gap Management. Increasingly in recent years large banks with sufficient resources in time and expertise have sought to limit their sensitivity to interest-rate fluctuations by trading in the financial-futures market. Banks trading in the futures market can hedge either the complete asset/liability portfolio (macro hedging) or individual asset or liability items (micro hedging). Hedging is the process of controlling the risk of a position or transaction by engaging in an offsetting transaction. In the futures market, buyers and sellers enter into contracts for the delivery of securities at a specified location and time and at a price that is set when the contract is made. The idea behind trading futures contracts is that buyers and sellers want protection against adverse movements in interest rates and prices. This protection is effected through investor adoption of equal and opposite positions in the spot (cash) market and in the forward (futures) market of the same or similar asset. By entering into such offsetting transactions, banks can effectively hedge their interest-rate exposure while transferring most of the risk of futures changes in the prices of securities to another participant in the futures market who is willing to bear that risk.

Originally transactions in the futures markets covered only agricultural commodities, such as wheat and corn. Producers and users of farm products, to protect themselves from the wide price fluctuations that resulted from seasonal surpluses and shortages of these products, entered into forward contracts calling for the future delivery of such products at a specified location and time, and at a guaranteed price. Futures markets evolved from forward contracts, and generally allow greater liquidity—that is, transacting parties can buy and sell at will, while in forward contracts the parties involved are locked in for the duration of the contract. Eventually futures contracts evolved and futures markets expanded to include metals (such as gold and silver) and wood products and, since 1975, such financial instruments as Eurodollar contracts and U.S. Treasury securities. The development of futures markets in these instruments was induced by deregulation as well as by the wide swings in interest rates and the value of securities that dominated the financial markets in the 1970s. Record high interest rates—under the pressure of tight money policies and inflation—drastically reduced the market values of securities and fixed-rate mortgages in the portfolios of financial institutions, threatening them with insolvency and ultimate failure. This was especially the case with savings and loan associations, whose assets consisted overwhelmingly of fixed-rate mortgage loans. Indeed, the rapid and sustained increases in interest rates in the late 1970s resulted in the decrease of the net worth of many associations to extremely low levels, which caused numerous failures or forced mergers with solvent institutions. This state of affairs elicited the favorable stance of some members of the regulatory community toward the growth of financial futures as a means of controlling the sensitivity of banks' and S&Ls' portfolios to interest-rate changes.

A transaction in the futures market can be in the form of a long hedge or a short hedge. A long hedge is the purchase of futures contracts today as a temporary substitute for the actual purchase of securities at a later date. Its purpose is to enable the transacting party to "lock in" a desired yield in the event that interest rates decline before the scheduled availability of funds and the actual purchase of securities in the cash market. Assume, for example, that today a bank purchases on margin Treasury bond futures contracts at their current market price, with cash payment on these contracts not due until the delivery date of the futures six months later. If later, as expected, interest rates fall and prices of securities increase, the gain realized in the futures markets from the sale of these contracts will help the bank offset the opportunity loss sustained in the cash market from the prevailing higher security prices at the time of the actual purchase (see Table 9.2).

Unlike a long hedge, which enables investors to benefit from falling interest rates (rising security prices), a short hedge guards investors against increasing interest rates (decreasing security prices). In other words, if a bank believes that interest rates are going to increase (security prices will decline) in the months ahead, it can protect itself against a reduction in the market value of its portfolio and the taking of losses upon the sale of securities by engaging in a short hedge. A short hedge involves the selling of futures contracts on selected securities until the actual sale is made at a later date in the cash market. Assume, for example, that in anticipation of higher interest rates (lower bond prices), a bank sells short Treasury bond futures contracts. Then, if interest rates do increase, the bank—to offset its short position—goes into the futures market and purchases, at the prevailing lower bond prices, an equal number of contracts to those sold short. The gain realized in the futures market would enable the bank

Table 9.2
Long Hedge of U.S. Treasury Bond Futures

Consider a trust department officer who manages a pension fund for a client. On April 1, he expects that in three months he will receive $1 million–an amount he plans to invest in Treasury bonds. He suspects that interest rates will fall and bond prices will rise. The course of action he will pursue until cash is available on July 2 is outlined below. On April 1 he will go long (purchase) ten September bond futures contracts. Assume that by July 2 rates have fallen and bond prices have increased. He will then sell his futures contracts, realizing a gain of $119,062.50. This gain partially offsets the opportunity loss sustained by his late entry into the cash market.

Cash Market	*Futures Market*
April 1 Wants to take advantage of today's higher yield level on 20-year 8.25% Treasury bonds at 68-14	April 1 Buys 10 September bond futures contracts at 68-10
July 2 Buys $1 million of 20-year 8.25% Treasury bonds at 82-13 (yielding 10)	July 2 Sells 10 September bond futures contracts at 80-07
Loss: $139,687.50 (Given an opportunity loss per contract of 13-31/32, each 1/32 equal to $31.25, and the number of contracts bought amounting to 10, total loss = 447/32 x $31.25 x 10)	Gain: $119,062.50 (381/32 x $31.25 x 10)

Note: This illustration does not include commissions and Chicago Board of Trade service fees.
Source: Chicago Board of Trade, *A Guide to Financial Futures at the Chicago Board of Trade* (Chicago: Chicago Board of Trade, 1983), pp. 41–42. Reproduced by permission of the Chicago Board of Trade.

to offset the capital loss from the actual sale of the securities in the cash market (see Table 9.3).

From the preceding it follows that a bank with a positive gap can hedge against an unexpected decline in interest rates by buying long 90–day T-bill futures. If such a decline materializes, the gains realized from the long position will offset some of the losses from the positive funds gap. If rates do not fall but continue to increase, the losses in the futures position will be offset by the gains from the positive funds gap. A negative gap is hedged by engaging in a short hedge. If rates increase, the gains realized in the futures market will offset some of the losses associated with the repricing of liabilities at higher rates. Of course, if interest rates decline, the losses in the futures position will be offset by the gains from the negative funds gap.

Although financial futures are an important tool of risk management, viable futures markets exist for only a limited number of financial instruments. If such

Table 9.3
Short Hedge of U.S. Treasury Bond Futures

Consider a trust officer who on October 1 manages a portfolio of $1 million, 20-year 8.75 percent Treasury bonds. He suspects that interest rates will rise and bond prices will fall. To protect the portfolio from a decline in value, he engages in a short hedge; that is, he sells U.S. Treasury bond futures contracts. Assume that by October 31, interest rates have risen and bond prices have declined. The officer offsets his previous futures sale by purchasing an equal number of contracts. Although his portfolio is worth $83,125 less as a result of the decline in bond prices, this loss is partially offset by the gain of $70,625 realized in the futures markets.

Cash Market	*Futures Market*
October 1	October 1
Holds $1 milllion, 20-year 8.75% Treasury bonds priced at 94-26 (yield 9.25%)	Sells 10 Treasury bond futures contracts at 86-28
October 31	October 31
Prices for bonds fall to 86-16 (yield 10.29%)	Buys 10 U.S. Treasury bond futures at 79-26
Loss: $83,125.00 (266/32 x $31.25 x 10)	Gain: $70,625.00 (226/32 x $31.25 x 10)

Note: This illustration does not include commissions and Chicago Board of Trade service fees.
Source: Chicago Board of Trade, *A Guide to Financial Futures at the Chicago Board of Trade* (Chicago: Chicago Board of Trade, 1983), p. 43. Reproduced by permission of the Chicago Board of Trade.

a market for a particular security does not exist, a future for another security can be used (a technique referred to as cross-hedging), assuming that the price movements of the two securities are similar. The historical relationship between the price movements of the two securities must be derived mathematically in order to determine what amount of the existing future is needed to hedge the security for which there is no futures market. However, such indirect hedging does not guarantee complete insensitivity to changing interest rates, because interest rates for different financial instruments do not always move in the same manner relative to one another.

Trading in financial futures is conducted in such high-quality financial instruments as 90-day Treasury bills, 90-day Eurodollar time deposits, intermediate-term Treasury notes (maturing between 6.5 and 10 years), and long-term Treasury bonds (with maturities in excess of 15 years at delivery date). Futures for 1-year Treasury bills; 30-day and 90-day commercial paper; 90-day CDs; GNMAs; 2-year, 4-year, and 4-6 year Treasury notes; and 15-year Treasury bonds were started, but these markets did not survive because of lack of trading interest. Three of the most active exchanges in futures trading in the United States are the Chicago Board of Trade (CBT); the International Monetary Market (IMM), a division of the Chicago Mercantile Exchange; and the New York Futures Exchange.

Options and Gap Management. Options on debt instruments represent another important strategy for managing risk. Just as with futures, a bank may hedge individual securities or its overall balance sheet. Options give holders the right to buy or sell securities at predetermined prices on or before a specified date. A call option is an option to buy securities, and a put option is an option to sell securities. The values of puts and calls are determined by the volatility of the market value of the underlying securities as well as by other market considerations. The high interest rates that prevailed in the late 1970s and early 1980s made put options on debt instruments an important hedging tool because they can protect fixed-rate assets in bank portfolios against rising interest rates and lower security prices without limiting the potential to benefit from lower interest rates and rising prices.

A bank with long-term, fixed-rate assets funded by short-term liabilities may hedge against rising interest rates by buying put options for these assets, or for securities of similar maturity and coupon in the absence of a market for the assets to be hedged. In the latter case such hedging can be effective only if the direction and size of price movements for both sets of assets are similar. The put option protects the bank against rising interest rates and declining security prices. Specifically, the put would give the bank the option to sell the underlying security at a predetermined price by a predetermined date with the prospect to profit if security prices drop in the interim. Under this scenario, the market value of the fixed-rate assets would go down, but the ensuing loss to the bank would be offset by the gain in the price of the put. On the other hand, if interest rates decreased, the market value of the assets would go up, and the bank would be free to sell them at the more advantageous price, losing only the cost of the put option.

On the other hand, if conditions in the marketplace indicate a trend toward lower interest rates and rising security prices, a bank with fixed-rate liabilities funding floating-rate assets may hedge its risk exposure through the purchase of debt call options. Assuming that this bank cannot buy back its fixed-rate liabilities, purchase of call options will help offset its losses from having to finance floating-rate assets in a falling-rate environment with high-cost, fixed-rate liabilities. The purchase of call options on the underlying securities, or on securities of similar maturity, protects the bank, in that if interest rates decrease, the value of the options will increase in response to increases in the market value of the underlying securities. While this hedge protects the bank if interest rates fall, it leaves it free to benefit from higher rates. This benefit would be reduced only by the cost of the call option.

It follows from the preceding that a negative gap can be hedged against interest-rate increases through the purchase of put options. If interest rates increase, the gains in the put options will offset some of the losses associated with the repricing of liabilities at a higher cost. By the same token, a positive gap can be hedged against a decrease in interest rates through the purchase of a call option. If rates fall, the gains in the call option will offset losses associated with the positive funds gap.

Investors hedging individual assets in the options market occasionally follow the practice of employing put and call options simultaneously for the same securities. This strategy can include one of two approaches: the selling of a call option and buying of a put option or vice versa. The former approach affords protection against the possibility of falling prices while reducing the cost of such protection by selling a call option. This strategy can be employed when the bank believes that the likelihood of declining security prices is greater than the likelihood of rising prices. In essence this practice allows the bank to protect itself against higher interest rates and covers the cost of this "insurance" through the sale of the call option on the same assets. On the other hand, a bank with fixed-rate liabilities can hedge itself by simultaneously buying a call and writing a put option against these liabilities. This practice can be employed when lower rates and rising prices are anticipated. In other words, if a bank believes that the likelihood of rising security prices is greater than the likelihood of declining security prices, it will sell a put option to cover the cost of purchasing a call option. The call option will increase in value as interest rates decline and security prices increase.

One important limitation on the implementation of an options strategy is that a viable cash options market exists only for Treasury bonds, which are traded on the Chicago Board Options Exchange. Options on futures exist for such instruments as 90–day Eurodollar time deposits, 90–day Treasury bills, Treasury notes maturing between 6 and 10 years, and Treasury bonds maturing over 15 years. The first instrument is traded on the Chicago Mercantile Exchange; the second, on the International Monetary Market; and the last two, on the Chicago Board of Trade.

Duration

An important tool through which banks have tried to manage their interest sensitivity is duration. The concept of duration originated in the 1930s when Frederick Macaulay wanted an alternative time dimension to the term to maturity for measuring a bond's life. Focusing on maturity ignores the fact that, for most securities, cash benefits are received before the maturity date.* These benefits may often be quite substantial. The time period over which the investor receives cash flows with relatively high present values is referred to as "effective" ma-

---

*This does not apply to zero-coupon instruments, such as a zero-coupon bond. This type of bond provides for no periodic interest payments; interest is built into the price of the bond. The bond is selling at a discount and the investor receives the face value when the obligation matures. Because it does not involve interim cash flows, the duration of a zero-coupon bond is equal to its maturity.

turity to distinguish it from the contractual, or legally stipulated, maturity. Duration is a measure of this effective maturity. It is defined as the weighted average time over which cash flows are expected, where the weights are the relative present values of the cash flows. The duration equation for a security j is

$$DUR_j = \frac{\sum_{t=1}^{n} \frac{C_t(t)}{(1+k)^t}}{\sum_{t=1}^{n} \frac{C_t}{(1+k)^t}}$$

where

$$C_t = \text{cash flow of security j in period t;}$$
$$k = \text{current market yield; and}$$
$$\sum_{t=1}^{n} \frac{C_t}{(1+k)^t} = \text{market value of the security.}$$

In recent years, duration has received considerable attention from both academicians and practitioners as a means of reducing interest-rate risk. The interest-rate fluctuations experienced in the late 1970s propelled the duration concept into an important asset/liability management strategy, relevant for almost every financial institution. Matching the durations of assets and liabilities is an important way to protect the value of an institution from interest-rate risk. The first step in the duration strategy is to figure the duration of the individual assets and liabilities. With many of these items similar to zero-coupon instruments, duration would be equal to maturity. For example, CDs on both sides of the balance sheet, T-bills, and demand deposits fall into this group because they do not involve interim cash flows. For the rest of the items (such as consumer loans and mortgages), durations would be calculated using the duration equation given above. The next step is to estimate the weighted average duration. To obtain this, each asset and liability is expressed as a percentage of total assets or liabilities; the duration of each individual item is weighted by its percentage; and weighted durations are summed to obtain the weighted average asset and liability durations. The last step involves comparing the weighted average asset and liability durations and undertaking the necessary adjustments in either side of the balance sheet—that is, engaging in outright sale or purchase of assets or outright purchase or retirement of liabilities.

Table 9.4 provides an illustration of duration analysis for a hypothetical bank. This institution has three types of assets—cash, investments (issues of same investment grade), and commercial loans. Its liabilities consist of negotiable CDs and time deposits of the same respective maturities. It is assumed that both earning assets entail equal annual interest payments, with annual compounding; furthermore, that there will be no defaults or prepayments, and in the case of liabilities, no early withdrawals. An example of a duration computation is pro-

Table 9.4
Calculating Balance-Sheet Duration

Assets	Market Value	Duration (in years)	Liabilities and Equity	Market Value	Duration (in years)
Cash	$100	0	Negotiable CDs	$600	2.74
Investments	300	4.04	Other time deposits	300	1.00
Commercial			Total liabilities	900	2.16
loans	600	2.62	Equity	100	
Total	$1,000	2.78	Total	$1,000	

Duration of assets = ($300/$1,000)(4.04) + ($600/$1,000)(2.62) = 2.78 yrs.
Duration of liabilities = ($600/$900)(2.74) + ($300/$900)(1.00) = 2.16 yrs.
Duration gap = 2.78 - ($900/$1,000)(2.16) = 0.84 yrs.

Example of Duration Computations: 3-yr. negotiable CDs at 10%

$$\text{CDs} = \frac{\dfrac{60(1)}{(1+.10)^1} + \dfrac{60(2)}{(1+.10)^2} + \dfrac{660(3)}{(1+.10)^3}}{600} = .091(1) + .083(2) + .826(3) = 2.74 \text{ yrs}$$

Source: Developed by the author.

vided in the lower part of the table; cash is assumed to earn no interest, and hence its duration is zero. The weighted average asset and liability durations are 2.78 and 2.16 years, respectively. This mismatch in average durations exposes the bank to interest-rate risk. Specifically, because the average maturity of assets is larger than the average maturity of liabilities, if interest rates rise substantially, asset values could decline enough to undermine capital adequacy; on the other hand, if rates fall, asset values will rise and the bank equity will increase.

The effect of a change in interest rates on the market value of equity depends upon the size of the duration gap (DGAP) and the specific interest-rate change. The formula for DGAP is

$$\text{DGAP} = \text{DA} - \left(\frac{\text{L}}{\text{A}} \times \text{DL}\right),$$

where DA and DL represent the weighted average asset and liability durations, respectively, and L/A, the ratio of total liabilities to total assets. In the example cited in Table 9.4, the bank has a positive duration gap of 0.84 years. With DGAP given, the expected change in the market value of equity (%ΔNW) because of a change in interest rates (Δi) can be measured, approximately, through the following formula:

$$\%\Delta NW = -DGAP \times \frac{\Delta i}{1 + i}.$$

Thus, if interest rates were to increase from 10 percent to 15 percent, this would lead to a change in the market value of net worth as a percentage of assets of

$$\%\Delta NW = -0.84 \times \frac{.05}{1 + .10} = -0.038 \text{ or } -3.8 \text{ percent.}$$

With assets totaling $1,000, this indicates a fall in the market value of net worth of $38. The greater the increase in interest rates, the larger the erosion of equity. If interest rates were to move in the opposite direction, the market value of equity would increase by the same amount. When the duration gap is negative (duration of liabilities is larger than duration of assets), an expected increase in interest rates would increase the market value of equity, while an expected decrease in interest rates would cause a decrease in the market value of equity.

To insulate the value of equity from the effect of changing interest rates, management may pursue a completely risk-averse position; that is, match the duration of assets and liabilities so that any changes in the market rates would affect both sides of the balance sheet equally. With DGAP equal to zero, the bank will be protected from interest-rate shifts and will not suffer a change in net worth because of them. An aggressive strategy calls for managing the gap by undertaking the necessary adjustments in either side of the balance sheet in anticipation of changes in interest rates. For example, if interest rates are expected to rise, management may shorten the average maturity of assets, lengthen the average maturity of liabilities, or employ hedging tools (e.g., financial futures). The prospect of a decrease in interest rates would justify the opposite course of action.

To be effective, duration gap management must be implemented on a continuous and ongoing basis. In addition to interest-rate changes, imbalances may be brought about by such factors as asset/liability fluctuations due to business transactions, increased complexity of the repayment and repricing features of many balance sheet items, and mere passage of time. As a result, duration gap management can be a costly and cumbersome process. These considerations have led some institutions to make use instead of a partial duration strategy commonly referred to as immunization. This strategy renders part of the balance sheet "immune" to interest-rate risk over a given holding period. The essence of this technique is to match the duration of designated assets and liabilities against unexpected changes in interest rates. An example would be to fund fixed-rate mortgages with deposits of equal duration (for instance, CDs of a certain maturity sold at a discount with no intervening interest payments). With the spread between particular assets and liabilities immunized, the interest-rate risk to which the institution is exposed would be limited to that of the remaining asset liability mix. That portion can then be managed by using techniques requiring active rate forecasting.

Duration strategy may also be applied to the bond portfolio alone. Investment officers can immunize the portfolio by acquiring securities with a combined duration equal to a bank's planned holding period. For example, if a bank plans to buy and hold securities in anticipation of an expected surge in loan demand, bonds with a duration matching the planned holding period will permit the immunization of the portfolio against both interest-rate risk and reinvestment risk. Specifically, if interest rates increase and securities are sold below cost, the loss sustained is offset by reinvesting the proceeds as well as future cash-flow payments at the prevailing higher market rates. Similarly, if interest rates fall and securities are sold at a gain, this gain is offset by the lower cash flow generated from reinvesting the proceeds and future coupon payments at the prevailing lower market rates. Capital losses and gains—or interest-rate and reinvestment risk—are counterbalanced when duration equals the bank's holding period. With changes in security prices offset by changes in reinvestment income, planned portfolio return remains unaffected.

An important limitation of immunization was the lack of investment instruments with a duration exceeding ten years. As a result, institutions desiring longer asset-holding periods were unable to use this strategy. This limitation was alleviated in 1982 when two major security firms—Merrill Lynch and Salomon Brothers—introduced a new security designed to meet the potential demand for zero-coupon bonds of all durations.* The generic term for these new financial assets is "stripped" securities. These are ordinary interest-bearing U.S. Treasury bonds transformed into zero-coupon instruments by stripping them of their coupon payments. Brokers may then sell one or more coupon payments or the par value separately to investors wanting single cash inflows at specified dates. Claims against only the principal payments are known as *PO* (principal only) securities, whereas claims against only the stream of interest payments are called *IO* (interest only) securities. Both PO and IO Treasury bond strips are essentially receipts for Treasury instruments held in trust by a bank.

To facilitate the issuance of stripped securities, in 1985 the Treasury Department introduced a program known as Separate Trading of Registered Interest and Principal of Securities (STRIPS). This program permits each individual coupon payment of specified Treasury issues to be registered in a separate name. Eligible issues are issued first to financial institutions, which may then sell each expected cash flow as if it were a separate security.

Since their inception in 1982, stripped securities have become so popular with institutions that the concept has been applied to other types of issues—mortgage-backed securities. Unlike Treasury bonds, however, mortgage-backed securities carry significant prepayment risk—some of the mortgage loans in the underlying pool may be paid off early as a result of amortization or prepayments. Stripping mortgage investments does not protect investors from this risk. Moreover, it

*As zero-coupon bonds involve no cash flows, they are free of interest-rate risk. Hence any portfolio of zero-coupon bonds is perfectly immunized.

makes it difficult to engage in matching the maturities of bank assets and liabilities because the maturity dates of the underlying mortgages are uncertain.

Interest-Rate Swaps

One of the newest tools in asset/liability management is an interest-rate swap. Institutions with mismatches in the maturities of their assets and liabilities may engage in an interest-rate swap to insulate their operations from interest-rate fluctuations. In other words, two institutions with opposite interest-risk exposures may get together—sometimes through an intermediary—and, in effect, exchange their interest payments. To illustrate this point, consider a savings and loan association (S&L) that has a portfolio of long-term, fixed-rate assets (such as mortgages) funded by short-term, interest-sensitive liabilities (such as money-market certificates repriced every six months). This S&L loses when interest rates rise unexpectedly, because the interest cost of its liabilities rises but the revenue from its mortgages remains the same. Conversely, the S&L gains from an unexpected drop in interest rates, because it reduces the cost of its funds. To hedge its position, the S&L will look for a swap partner that faces the opposite situation—a bank with a portfolio of floating-rate loans funded by long-term, fixed-rate liabilities. A rise in interest rates benefits the bank because its revenues rise faster than its cost of funds; but a drop in market rates undermines its profitability. When two institutions—such as those identified above—have opposite interest-risk exposures, the interest-rate swap allows them to effect a balance sheet restructuring. Interest-rate risk can be minimized for both institutions if yields on assets and cost rates on liabilities vary together, enabling them to lock in the spread. In the example cited above, the swap agreement permits the S&L to convert the interest payments on its liabilities from a floating-rate to a fixed-rate basis, and the bank to convert its liabilities from fixed to floating rate. The swap-agreement contract will thus provide for each party to make interest payments to the other. The two institutions will not actually exchange cash; instead, they will exchange the net difference in interest payments. That is, individual payments will be netted out so that only the net difference flows from one party to the other.

The interest-rate swap discussed above—exchanging fixed-rate for floating-rate debt—is the most common type of swap currently utilized in financial markets. Another widely used form, and one that preceded interest-rate swaps, is the currency swap, involving the exchange of cash flows denominated in different currencies. Both types are commonly referred to as "plain vanilla swaps" to distinguish them from various new types of swaps that the market has come up with in recent years.

In principle, a currency swap is much like an interest-rate swap. Consider a U.S. bank that holds fixed-rate assets denominated in dollars and financed in part with an issue of fixed-rate notes denominated in the pound sterling. At the other end consider a U.K. bank with a portfolio of fixed-rate assets denominated in pounds and financed in part with an issue of fixed-rate notes denominated in dollars. Each institution has the opposite currency exposure. Depreciation of the dollar against the pound will increase the cost to the U.S. bank of making interest and principal payments on its sterling notes. By contrast, appreciation of the dollar against the pound will increase the debt-servicing cost of the U.K. bank on its dollar issue. Each bank can hedge its foreign-currency risk exposure by engaging in a currency swap. Under a currency swap, the U.S. bank would make annual fixed payments in dollars to the U.K. bank so that it can cover its servicing cost on its dollar notes, while the U.K. bank would reciprocate with annual payments in pounds to the U.S. bank to cover the cost of servicing its sterling note issue. By swapping their future cash-flow obligations, the two banks are able to alter their currency holdings without incurring increased future currency exposure. In other words, the U.S. bank has transformed its fixed-rate sterling liabilities into fixed-rate dollar liabilities that match the dollar cash flows from its asset portfolio. By the same token, the U.K. bank has transformed its fixed-rate dollar liabilities into fixed-rate pound liabilities that better match the sterling cash flows from its asset portfolio. Payments would be swapped between the two banks at some prearranged dollar/pound exchange rate for a specified period of time (e.g., for the tenor of their notes). If in the course of the agreement, exchange rates change by more than a prespecified amount (e.g., 10 percent), an additional amount of the weaker currency might have to be advanced.

Interest-rate swaps were introduced in the Eurobond market in 1981 and have since taken the market by storm. Data from the Bank for International Settlements indicate that at the end of March 1995, currency swaps amounted to $2 trillion and interest-rate swaps, to $18.3 trillion. The interest-rate swap market has grown rapidly within the United States and between firms in this country and abroad. The increased popularity of this instrument is attributed to its unique advantages over other hedging techniques. Specifically, swaps are less expensive than debt refinancing. An institution wishing to adjust its exposure by refinancing its liabilities may find it very costly to enter the financial markets because of underwriting fees, disclosure costs, and differences in spreads between ratings for short- and long-term debt. Interest-rate swaps reduce the total funding cost by offering these institutions an indirect way of entering financial markets to restructure their balance sheets.

Also, swaps are more flexible than purchasing interest-rate futures. Futures contracts are standardized products traded on organized exchanges. By contrast, swaps are freely negotiated agreements between private parties and, therefore, can be customized. Clearly, this customization makes swaps more expensive to use than futures. On the other hand, futures contracts exist only with certain specific delivery dates: at 3–month intervals out to about 2.5 years. Interest-rate swaps, by contrast, have no such limits. Most swaps have a final maturity of three to ten years, thereby filling the gap left by futures in hedging against interest-rate risk.

Foreign-Exchange Risk

Just as in the domestic payments system, banks are at the center of the international payments system. They are the channels through which money transactions flow, and claims are settled, across national boundaries. Transacting over national borders usually requires some kind of exchange of money. Thus, banks have come to play an important role in foreign-exchange markets, in which they may operate for their own accounts and for those of their customers.

Although many U.S. banks handle foreign-exchange transactions, not more than 40 could be classified as major participants in this market. These banks are among some 200 institutions worldwide that are considered to be active market makers. The major players in this market trade a limited number of currencies, buying and selling them as warranted by market conditions. Transactions are carried out by specialized traders who use telephones, teletype equipment, and computer terminals to keep in touch with other foreign-exchange dealers and independent brokers. Each foreign currency is quoted in two prices. These prices, or foreign-exchange rates, are frequently referred to as "double-barreled." One quotation represents the "bid" (purchasing) price of the foreign currency, the other—which is slightly higher—the "offer" or "ask" (selling) price. Dealers and brokers in foreign exchange profit from the difference (spread) between the bid and ask prices.

To provide their clients with foreign-exchange services, U.S. banks maintain inventories of foreign currencies. These are held in the form of demand deposits, denominated in the currencies of other nations, in foreign banks. As might be expected, these inventories fluctuate. They are augmented as U.S. banks purchase credit instruments (drafts) denominated in foreign currencies from their customers. These instruments, once cleared abroad, are credited to their accounts in foreign banks. Their inventories decline when they sell credit instruments payable in foreign monies to their customers. Banks maintain large foreign-currency inventories in the currencies that are in greatest demand, such as the pound sterling, the German mark, the Swiss franc, and the Japanese yen.

U.S. banks' foreign-exchange transactions can be retail or wholesale. At the retail level they deal with individuals and businesses that use the market to effect a foreign commercial or investment transaction. This group includes tourists, importers and exporters, portfolio investors, and multinational corporations. At the wholesale level the foreign-exchange activity of U.S. banks is geared toward maintaining an interbank market. This market enables them to balance their positions in foreign currencies, depending upon their daily trading activity in these currencies. Based upon the daily volume of each kind of currency bought and sold, banks may experience shortages or overages in their inventories of individual currencies. To adjust their positions in particular currencies, banks use independent foreign-exchange brokers. These brokers, by operating among banks, play an important role in the negotiation of trades in the interbank market.

For a fee they put a bank with a shortage in a specific foreign currency in contact with one experiencing a surplus. The brokers preserve the anonymity of the transacting parties until the deal is closed, to prevent any influence of their names upon price quotations.

Use of an independent broker is but one method of temporarily adjusting a bank's shortage in a particular currency. Other methods include borrowing from a foreign correspondent bank appropriate amounts of the currency in shortage; using a "swap" arrangement with a foreign correspondent, whereby each party credits equivalent amounts of local currency to the other's account; and purchasing the needed amounts from a foreign correspondent, or through it, and paying accordingly in another currency. The basic characteristic of all these methods of adjusting shortages is that foreign-currency inventory is replenished through bookkeeping entries that transfer deposits denominated in various currencies from one holder to another. No money leaves the country of its origin; only the ownership of deposit balances changes.

Making or maintaining a market in foreign exchange entails risk. In 1973 the countries of the world shifted their currencies from a fixed rate of exchange to a system of floating rates. As a result exchange rates fluctuate on a daily basis, according to the forces of supply and demand in the marketplace. Because the exchange rates of currencies fluctuate, banks incur a risk of loss in the value of foreign currencies they hold. The international stability and value of a currency depend on several factors. The economic and financial conditions of a country, as reflected in its balance of payments, have a direct bearing on the value of its currency. Political instability or drastic changes in a country's political condition may cause its currency's position in the marketplace to deteriorate. Another significant factor is activity by speculators, who constantly seek to acquire undervalued currencies and divest themselves of overvalued ones. Still another force impinging on foreign-exchange markets is the action of central banks, such as the Federal Reserve System or the Bank of England. These may intervene to stabilize the value of their country's currency by shoring it up when it is weak or slowing its appreciation when it becomes too strong. Other important forces include multinational corporations and institutional investors. The extensive international operations of the former and the global dealings of the latter have been a decisive force on prevailing exchange rates.

Serious losses can be realized if a bank holds large inventories of a currency whose price drops significantly. Losses can also result from bank speculation in foreign exchange. In 1974 foreign-exchange losses precipitated the closing of the Bankhaus Herstatt in West Germany and contributed significantly to the closing of the Franklin National Bank of New York. Sizable foreign-exchange losses have, at one time or another, created crises for banks in England and Switzerland.

Banks guard themselves against foreign-exchange loss in part by realizing a spread between the bid and ask prices of currencies. In addition, the bank must conduct a sufficient volume of foreign-exchange business to allow gains and losses to offset each other. Moreover, close monitoring of events likely to cause changes in the values of currencies can help banks avoid losses. Finally, banks can hedge their foreign-currency positions by engaging in forward transactions. Foreign currencies are traded on a *spot* basis (for immediate delivery) or on a *forward* basis (for delivery on a specified future date, usually within 30, 90, or 120 days). The spot rate and the forward rate for a given currency will differ to the extent that the currency is expected to rise or fall in value. When the forward rate exceeds the spot rate, the difference is referred to as a premium; when the spot rate is higher, the difference is referred to as a discount. When a bank must make a large purchase in a particular currency, it hedges this position by selling that amount of the same currency in the forward market. In this way the bank is assured of being able to divest itself of that currency at a specified future date without incurring loss. By the same token, if a bank sells a particular currency to be delivered on a specified date, it can hedge this position by buying a similar amount in the forward market to protect itself against appreciation of this currency. These measures protect the bank from price fluctuations in the currency market but sacrifice the opportunity of realizing gains from unforeseen favorable movements in the price of currencies.

Forward exchange contracts are briskly traded wherever spot currency markets exist. These are found in the major international money markets: Amsterdam, Brussels, New York, Paris, Zurich, and London. These markets all trade in the world's major currencies; forward trading in currencies of less important countries is sporadic. For highly unstable currencies, forward contracts are costly because of the degree of risk involved.

Another form of hedging currency transactions is trading in foreign-currency futures contracts. These differ from forward contracts only in that the trading is done in organized exchanges instead of being negotiated directly between banks and their customers. As a result, in the former case the contracts are standardized, while in the latter, terms are determined by the negotiating parties. Foreign-currency futures contracts are of two basic types, long hedges and short hedges. A long hedge protects a bank's customer (e.g., an importer) from increases in the price of the currency he must eventually acquire; a short hedge protects the customer (e.g., an exporter) from decreases in the price of the currency he will receive payment.

Foreign-currency futures contracts are traded on the International Monetary Market (IMM), a division of the Chicago Mercantile Exchange. On the IMM contracts are available for pounds sterling, Canadian dollars, Dutch guilders, German marks, Japanese yen, Mexican pesos, Swiss francs, and French francs. The most actively traded among these are the pound, the mark, the yen, and the Swiss franc. Foreign-currency options contracts on cash instruments are traded in the Philadelphia Options Exchange. The IMM trades options on foreign-currency futures contracts.

Defalcation and Theft

Defalcation refers to the appropriation of bank funds by employees, whereas theft refers to such acts as forgery, burglary, and armed robbery performed by outsiders. Defalcation results from the continual exposure of bank employees and officials to large sums of money. It is a problem of surety. It is by no means unknown that bank employees and officials occasionally succumb to temptation and appropriate some of a bank's funds for themselves. As long as individuals are subjected to the financial, social, and moral pressures of our free society, the possibility of bank losses due to defalcation will be present. Yet it is in a bank's interest to take all necessary precautions to prevent, to the extent possible, the losses and embarrassment that result from the dishonest acts of its employees and officials.

Although legal prescription (e.g., the FIRREA of 1989) has expanded the powers of regulators in dealing with fraud, a bank may protect itself against loss resulting from defalcation by adequate fidelity insurance. In fact, losses from defalcation may be covered through a blanket bond that insures, in addition, the directors and the bank against many of the statutory and common-law liabilities, and against the various risks associated with the nature of bank operations. A bank may also protect itself through improvements in administration, such as using better protective equipment, clarifying the duties of officers and employees, and improving auditing systems. In the latter instance continuous checking (preauditing), staff cooperation, and frequent postaudits can deter fraud or detect it at a fairly early stage. The best that can be done, therefore, is to control the opportunities and to shorten the time between commitment of an offense and exposure.

Losses from theft by outsiders are insignificant compared with the magnitude of internal crime. Although theft losses can be covered by a blanket bond, banks have taken a variety of measures to safeguard against this risk. Some of the more important measures include the posting of guards in bank lobbies, installation of television and alarm systems, monitors, and limiting the amount of cash to tellers. ATMs present an additional exposure to theft that is protected against by making the machines physically strong enough to withstand break-in attempts and by placing them in highly visible locations.

With the growing use of computers in day-to-day operations, defalcation and theft have become more sophisticated. Experts on the subject place banks among the top victims of computer crime. Disgruntled or dishonest employees represent the greatest threat. Tellers, computer data-entry technicians, and even computer consultants have, through their positions of trust, succeeded in obtaining bank funds through various methods of computer manipulation. These include embedding unauthorized commands in programs, altering data, and making direct commands to the computer to transfer funds to a designated account in the bank (or perhaps in another bank), from which the employees can later withdraw them. Generally, computer theft involves a depositor who can successfully manipulate ATM codes and passwords, or an outsider who through sheer ingenuity uses a computer terminal to gain access to the bank's computerized money-transfer mechanisms.

Computer crime is often difficult to detect, especially since the computer can be programmed to erase all evidence of the act. In a notorious case of embezzlement by a bank computer consultant, exposure of the criminal occurred only after he bragged of his exploit.

Although no security measures are foolproof against computer theft, many preventive steps can be taken. These include careful use of codes and passwords that are frequently changed. Of course, such measures depend on human co-operation—for instance, not divulging passwords through carelessness. However, researchers are actively seeking additional safeguards. One possibility under review is a computer that memorizes the use routines of its authorized operators at each terminal and turns off if a user's behavior does not fit the established pattern.

REGULATING RISK EXPOSURE

Legal Prescription and Administrative Regulation

Regulatory authorities have sought to ensure bank safety through restrictions of different kinds. Although details differ between national banks and state banks, the general principles are similar. Some of the major rules covering national banks can be conveniently summarized under the following groupings.

One set of rules prohibits banks from holding certain kinds of assets either by explicitly proscribing them or by limiting bank acquisitions to certain expressly defined forms of assets. For example, national banks are forbidden to deal in real estate, commodities, and stocks. However, they are allowed to hold stocks if they have been acquired as collateral on defaulted loans, in which case they must be disposed of within a reasonable time (customarily interpreted as five years). Other exceptions are few. National, and member state, banks must own stock in the Federal Reserve bank of their respective district as a condition for membership in the Federal Reserve System. In addition, they may own stock in Fannie Mae, a U.S.-sponsored government agency that provides a secondary market for Federal Housing Administration (FHA), Veterans Administration (VA), and conventional mortgages; in corporations established to engage in foreign banking activity (such as Edge Act corporations); and in such subsidiaries as a safe-deposit company or a real estate concern that has been established to own the bank building. Furthermore, national banks are generally forbidden to grant loans on the security of their own stock, nor are they allowed to buy their own stock in the market, since this would, in effect, reduce the actual protection of the depositors. Moreover, national banks are prohibited from extending loans to their examiners—for obvious reasons.

A more moderate form of regulation does not prohibit, but sets ceilings on, certain types of assets. For example, a national bank may not extend personal loans to its directors and executive officers in excess of a stipulated amount. Loans to affiliates require designated types of securities as collateral. The loan size is subject to ceilings based on the type and amount of security the borrower can pledge. If the securities pledge are obligations of the U.S. government, the amount of credit extended cannot exceed the par value of the securities. If the securities pledged are municipals, their par value must exceed the amount of credit extended by a stipulated margin.

Another set of rules takes the form of quality standards. National banks may not acquire bonds that are regarded by the principal rating agencies as predominantly speculative, unless such bonds are acquired by way of settlement of a doubtful claim. Also, secured loans must meet various requirements to assure that the bank has a valid and enforceable claim. For example, loans on leaseholds can be made only if the lease has a stipulated maturity beyond the maturity of the credit. Real-estate loans must be secured by a mortgage, a trust deed, or any other instrument that gives the bank an enforceable lien on the property. Loans on securities can be made only if the securities are assignable, and provided the borrower gives the bank a power of attorney authorizing it to sell the pledged securities in the event of default.

Still another set of rules aims at promoting diversification. Many banks have long applied this principle in the management of their loan and investment portfolios, in an effort to reduce their overall risk exposure with little impairment of expected return. Regulatory authorities promote bank asset diversification by specifying the proportion of assets that may be held in certain form. For instance, the amount that national banks may lend to any one borrower on an unsecured basis cannot exceed 15 percent of tier 1 capital. For loans secured by a readily marketable collateral, this limit may rise to 25 percent of tier 1 capital. Also, holdings of securities of any one obligor (with the exception of U.S. government issues and general obligations of state and local governments) are restricted to 10 percent of a bank's capital and surplus. These are only a few of the areas in which bank loan and investment activities are constrained by legal bounds. Most of these regulations are designed to ensure that banks do not take undue risks in the use of their depositors' funds. These restrictions encourage diversification—compel it, in fact—in order to reduce the risk of asset depreciation. The rules also serve to strengthen the bank's independence from any one extremely large borrower.

Regulatory authorities also stipulate capital requirements at the time of a bank's establishment and capital-adequacy criteria in the course of its operations as a means of securing safety. (See chapters 4 and 5.)

Another important device for increasing bank safety is deposit insurance, available to commercial banks through the FDIC. Since 1993 the FDIC has been assessing banks with risk-based insurance premiums, as mandated by the FDI-CIA of 1991. This move has contributed to the establishment of a regulatory discipline for banks, as discussed earlier in this chapter in connection with Bank runs.

The Failure Record of U.S. Banks

For several reasons bank failure is considered more serious than the failure of most other kinds of businesses. As with any business, bank failure represents a loss of investment to stockholders. In addition, it means the loss of deposits to the bank's individual and business customers (although since the advent of the FDIC, balances up to $100,000 per depositor are insured against such loss). These funds may constitute the bulk of a family's savings or a business's operating capital. Thus the loss of a bank's aggregate deposits can have a devastating impact on a substantial segment of a community. Finally, a bank failure erodes public confidence in the banking system and, in extreme cases, may trigger other failures.

In the twentieth century most bank failures have occurred in the 1920s and 1930s as a result of economic conditions. Sharp recessions in the 1920s hit rural districts especially hard, and weaker banks in small towns and farm communities were forced to close. The Great Depression caused bank failures throughout the United States and in every economic setting. In an economic environment of this type, not only banks but other financial institutions as well encountered significant difficulties in remaining solvent.

In addition to unfavorable economic conditions, other causes of bank failures include mismanagement and criminal actions. Small banks have been especially vulnerable. They often lack the resources to attract highly skilled management and the resiliency to absorb losses. Such ill-advised practices as granting excessively high-risk loans, investing too heavily in promotion, jockeying for bank control, and operating with too small a capital base have contributed to their failures. Deregulation made things worse for mismanaged banks. Increased reliance on various forms of purchased funds and the advent of interest-bearing demand deposits have raised the cost of funds significantly and created especially acute problems for banks that lack the skills to manage interest margins effectively. Criminal actions leading to bank failure have included embezzlement and collusion with borrowers.

Figure 9.3 shows the pattern of failures of FDIC-insured banks since 1980. From the mid-1980s, relatively few banks failed, and losses to the deposit insurance fund were minimal. No more than 20 banks failed in any year. Enactment of DIDMCA in 1980 provided for the phaseout of ceilings on the interest rates that institutions could pay on savings and time deposits, and removed or weakened the barriers that separated commercial banks, thrift institutions, and credit unions. The ensuing increase in competition and the deep recession of 1981–82 combined to account for increasingly higher rates of bank failures. In 1982, 42 banks failed, and in each year thereafter failures rose until 1988, when they peaked at 221. After that the number of failures declined each year, and

Figure 9.3
Failures of FDIC-Insured Banks, 1980–94

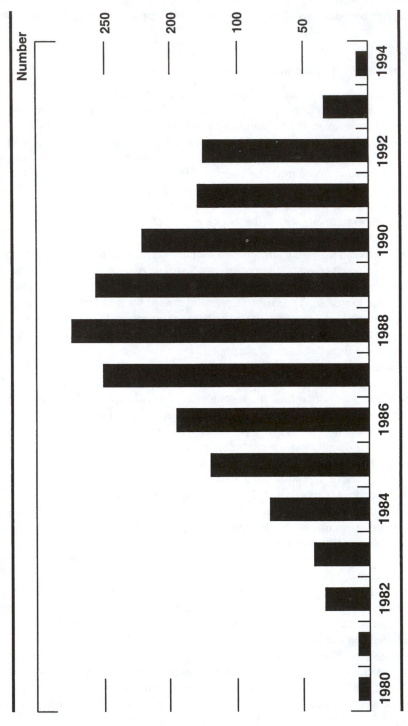

Source: Federal Deposit Insurance Corporation, *Statistics on Banking,* various issues.

by the end of 1994 they amounted to only 11. From 1982 through 1994, a total of 1,494 banks failed—more than 10 percent of all banks in the United States at the beginning of that period.

Many of the banks that failed in the 1980s and early 1990s had sizable numbers of poor-quality agricultural, energy, and real-estate loans. Some of the failed banks were rural banks in the Midwest, where farming activity suffered from declining commodity prices, shrinking export markets, and rising production costs. These conditions kept farmers from generating an adequate cash flow to service their bank debts. As the prices of farm products dropped, so did farmland values, thereby undermining farmers' ability to settle their debts by selling off their land.

Another group of failed banks was located in the oil-producing states of this country. These banks sustained severe losses in the mid-1980s when the oil boom of the preceding decade gave way to a bust. Declining oil prices had rendered many of the drilling, production, and distribution loans delinquent and nonperforming. As the economic plight of the oil industry permeated the local economies, commercial real estate suffered accordingly, causing additional losses to local banks.

Finally, the recession of the early 1990s and its severe effect on the real-estate industry contributed to loan losses and precipitated the failure of banks. Regulatory reports indicate that, notwithstanding the adverse effects of regional economic conditions in the 1980s and early 1990s, the blame for most bank failures during this period must be laid at the door of management (incompetent management and lax policies, director weakness, or insider abuse).

In protecting depositors' funds, and hence in fulfilling one of the most important objectives for its establishment, the FDIC is entrusted with significant authority. The courses of action open to the FDIC in this respect may be conveniently classified as preventive and remedial. Preventive measures offer the FDIC a variety of avenues to avert the adverse effects of bank failures. One major purpose of bank regulation is to prevent bank failure by assuring the soundness of banks. Regulatory examination is intended to assure the bank's health by providing an accurate picture of its activities and performance at all times. Thus, problems can be spotted at their inception and corrective steps taken before the problems grow large or serious enough to threaten the bank.

In addition to periodic examination, the FDIC tries to forestall failure by placing deposits with the bank in trouble, purchasing loans from it, extending loans, encouraging other banks to make loans to the bank, suggesting a merger with another bank, effecting management changes, and infusing capital through purchase of subordinated notes or preferred stock callable at the option of the bank. The most celebrated case involving most of these types of assistance was that of Continental Illinois National Bank and Trust Company of Chicago, in 1984. The bank received $4.5 billion in financial assistance, including loans from the Federal Reserve and other commercial banks. Mounting loan losses and deterioration in earnings had undermined public confidence in this institution, which at the time was one of the eight largest banks in the country, with assets of $47 billion. Part of the FDIC funds ($3.5 billion) went to buy a huge block of bad loans, and the balance ($1 billion) to purchase stock to shore up the bank's net worth. The FDIC guaranteed all of the bank's depositors and general creditors, and arranged for the bank to continue its operations under a new management. These measures averted the default of the bank on nearly $30 billion in uninsured deposits, part of which represented the accounts of 2,300 U.S. banks.

In recent years the FDIC has urged and facilitated mergers between weak banks and sounder ones in order to avoid bank closure and direct FDIC action on behalf of depositors. One such case was that of First Republic Bank of Dallas, which was acquired in mid-1988 by an affiliate of NationsBank (then North Carolina National Bank or NCNB). In that case, as well as in similar acquisition cases, the process followed is known as *purchase and assumption* (P&A). Under this method, the FDIC contacts healthy banks in an effort to solicit bids for the purchase of assets and the assumption of deposit liabilities of the failing institution. In evaluating the failing bank, interested buyers face a difficult task; although deposit liabilities are known, the value of some of the bank's assets is not. Specifically, while the value of fixed assets and of the investment portfolio can reasonably be derived from market data, the value of the loan portfolio is a matter of subjective judgment (e.g., establishing the liquidation value of the collateral supporting loans and determining the ability of borrowers to service their debts). If the total assets thus derived fall short of their book value, interested buyers would request the advancement of cash from the FDIC. This would be equal to the amount by which liabilities exceed the value of the failed bank's assets. The FDIC accepts the lowest-cost bid, absorbing part, or all, of the acquiring bank's losses from the merger transaction.

If the liquidation of the failed bank is unavoidable, the FDIC takes remedial steps, acting as a receiver and making direct payments to uninsured depositors. With a payoff, all insured depositors receive checks of up to $100,000 from the FDIC. Proceeds from the liquidation of the bank's assets are used for this purpose. Any remaining funds are paid to uninsured depositors and other creditors on a pro rata basis.

If closure of the bank would disrupt banking services to a community, the FDIC may organize a bridge bank—known as a deposit insurance national bank—to operate the troubled institution temporarily until a buyer can be found. Alternatively, if creditors stand to suffer sizable losses from the closure of a bank, reorganization—with or without regulatory help—may be allowed.

SUGGESTED REFERENCES

Bierwag, G. O., and George G. Kaufman. "Duration Gap for Financial Institutions." *Financial Analysts Journal*, March/April 1985, pp. 68–71.

Brewer, Elijah. "Bank Gap Management and the Use of Financial Futures." Federal
Reserve Bank of Chicago, *Economic Perspectives*, March/April 1985, pp. 12–22.

French, G. "Measuring the Interest Rate Risk of Financial Intermediaries." *FDIC Banking Review*, Fall 1988, pp. 14–27.

Gardner, Mona, and Dixie Mills. *Managing Financial Institutions: An Asset/Liability Approach*. Chicago: Dryden Press, 1988.

Gup, Benton. *Managing Interest Rate Risk*. Chicago: Probus Publishing, 1993.

Kareken, John H. "Deposit Insurance Reform: Or Deregulation Is the Cart, Not the Horse." Federal Reserve Bank of Minneapolis, *Quarterly Review*, Winter 1990, pp. 3–11.

Shaffer, Sherrill. "Interest Rate Risk: What's a Bank to Do?" Federal Reserve Bank of Philadelphia, *Business Review*, May/June 1991, pp. 17–27.

Chapter 10

Income

In addition to maintaining solvency and liquidity, a bank must achieve a sufficient income on its portfolio to pay operating costs and provide a competitive return on the capital ventured in the enterprise. In the quest for income, management must always keep in mind the need for maintaining liquidity and solvency. In fact, it should never subordinate the need for liquidity and solvency to the income function. While income is definitely important, and clearly essential for the successful performance of a continuing banking operation, the aggressive pursuit of income per se, without regard to these other factors, could rapidly precipitate the collapse of the bank. The employment of bank funds must, in the first place, be consistent with the bank's liquidity needs and, second, be within the limits of the amount of risk that capital available for the portfolio can bear. Within the confines of these two basic policy considerations, efforts may be directed toward the realization of adequate income. Management has some choice regarding the way in which income may be sought and the way in which profits are used.

The importance of profits to commercial banks is hard to exaggerate. They are a decisive factor for the continued existence of a bank and its success as a going concern. Profits represent the return on the capital funds invested in the bank. In fact, it is for this return that shareholders are willing to supply the capital that will enable the bank to fulfill its role as the chief credit-granting institution in the economy. If the return on existing capital is not comparable with the returns on other investments, capital will, in the long run, be attracted to other economic pursuits. Profits, moreover, constitute an important source of bank capital. It is a common practice of banks to retain a relatively large portion of their earnings for capital additions. To the extent that profits are used for the payment of dividends, they have favorable effects upon the marketability and value of bank shares, thereby rendering it possible for the bank to return to the market and raise additional capital to finance expansion and improvements in banking practices. Profits also make it possible to pay competitive salaries and attract competent management. But depositors, too, benefit from bank profits, since they result in a stronger and safer institution capable of absorbing losses and protecting against the risks inherent in the banking business. Borrowers also have interest, indirectly, in bank profits. Bank policy of plowing earnings back into equity capital results in a larger capital account, and therefore in an increased lending and investing ability. With an increase in the size of capital, banks can make larger loans to any single borrower and invest larger amounts in the securities of any single issuer. Even those economic groups that do not directly use commercial bank services benefit indirectly from adequate bank profits. The reason is that bank profits contribute to the strengthening of the banking structure, which results in the safety of deposits and the availability of credit to the economy, with consequences that are felt throughout it and are reflected in the nation's economic welfare. This chapter starts with a discussion of the profitability considerations at the level of the individual bank, then proceeds to review the performance record of the banking industry.

PROFITABILITY OF THE INDIVIDUAL BANK

Factors Affecting Bank Profitability

A number of studies have sought to identify the key elements in a bank's formula for profitability. They have selected groups of banks for examination and attempted to correlate degree of profitability with such factors as size, ownership, market concentration, bank structure, advertising expenditures, and management characteristics. In all cases the researchers concluded that the primary factor distinguishing successful or high-performance banks from the rest of the sample was effective management.

Although strong and able leadership is difficult to quantify, its effects are apparent in the composition of the balance sheet and the distribution of expenses in the income statement. These studies indicate that a bank's asset management and funding practices can contribute to superior balance-sheet management. Balance-sheet management, coupled with control of operating costs, has the most significant effect on bank profitability. Invariably these studies found that the asset portfolios of the most profitable banks were relatively inexpensive to service because they contained a high proportion of securities in relation to loans. On the liability side, successful banks held large volumes of demand deposits, thus incurring lower interest expenses, and relied heavily on equity funds, which entail lower accounting costs. Last, profitable banks had lower noninterest expenses than could be explained by differences in their asset and liability portfolios. This evidence suggested that the managers of these banks exercised more effective control over operating costs.

Table 10.1
Key Profitability Ratios for Banks

Name of Ratio	Formula for Calculation
Return on equity (ROE)	$\dfrac{\text{Net income}}{\text{Total equity}}$
Return on assets (ROA)	$\dfrac{\text{Net income}}{\text{Total assets}}$
Net interest margin	$\dfrac{\text{Total interest income-Total interest expense}}{\text{Earning assets}}$
Net noninterest margin	$\dfrac{\text{Total noninterest income-Total noninterest expense}}{\text{Earning assets}}$

Source: Developed by the author.

The importance of these findings for bank managers is apparent. Although asset and liability mix is significant, the efficiency of bank operations is no less important. In other words, managers should pay close attention to bank control over operating expenses.

Use of Financial Ratios to Assess Performance

Management and analysts have relied widely on the use of ratios in evaluating the financial performance of a bank. Though different ratios can be computed to track the different aspects of banking activity, a few are considered to be of primary importance in determining the financial soundness of an institution. These are the profitability ratios. In theory, stock price is the best indicator of a firm's performance because it reflects market evaluation of the firm. However, since the stock of many medium-size and small banks not actively traded in national markets, profitability ratios are a useful proxy for market evaluation of performance. The key profitability ratios in banking are presented in Table 10.1.

Two traditional indicators of bank profitability are the *rate of return on equity (ROE)* and the *rate of return on assets (ROA)*. ROE is, in the accounting sense, the true bottom-line measure of performance. ROE is calculated by dividing a bank's net income by its common equity. The ratio tells a bank's shareholders how much the institution is earning on their investment. The ratio is especially important because a key objective for any bank is the maximization of shareholder wealth.

The second profitability measure, ROA, is calculated by dividing net income by total bank assets. This measure gauges how well a bank's management is using the bank's assets. A low rate may reflect excessive operating expenses or conservative lending and investment policies. Conversely, a high rate may reflect operational efficiency or aggressive lending and investment policies. If the latter is the case, the bank may be assuming increased risk in order to attain higher returns on assets.

Another important profitability indicator is the *net interest margin* ratio, which expresses the difference (spread) between interest earnings and interest costs as a percentage of earning assets. Net interest margin is monitored closely by management, and if the spread between income and expense narrows, steps must be taken to boost interest income and effectively control interest expense (funding costs). Because changes in interest rates impact both a bank's interest income and its interest expense, management must position assets and liabilities to take advantage of rate changes. Thus, both the net interest margin ratio and the spread are indicators of a bank's ability to manage interest-rate risk.

A related indicator is the *net noninterest margin* ratio, which measures the spread between noninterest income (e.g., fees and service charges) and noninterest costs (e.g., salaries and maintenance expenses), expressed as a percentage of earning assets. Although increasingly in recent years banks have been emphasizing noninterest income, for many institutions this ratio may be negative because of high noninterest costs.

Decomposition Process

It is often useful to decompose the principal profitability ratios into their component parts for closer analysis. This approach helps narrow down the causes of bank earnings problems and suggests where management needs to look for possible cures. The decomposition process focuses on the ROE and its key components, ROA and the equity multiplier (which compares assets with equity). This relationship may be expressed in the following manner:

$$\text{ROE} = \text{ROA} \times \text{Equity multiplier}$$

or

$$\text{ROE} = \frac{\text{Net income}}{\text{Total assets}} \times \frac{\text{Total assets}}{\text{Total equity}}$$

The *equity multiplier* is also known as the *leverage multiplier* because it indicates the extent of bank reliance on leverage. That is, by identifying how many dollars of assets are supported by each dollar of equity, it reveals how much of the bank's resources therefore rest on debt. Together the two ratios indicate that a higher ROE can be attained by increasing either ROA or financial leverage.

A further step in this analysis would be to break down ROA into its key components, profit margin and asset utilization. ROE can then be expressed as

$$\text{ROE} = \text{Profit margin} \times \text{Asset utilization} \times \text{Equity multiplier}$$

or

$$\text{ROE} = \frac{\text{Net income}}{\text{Operating revenue}} \times \frac{\text{Operating revenue}}{\text{Total assets}} \times \frac{\text{Total assets}}{\text{Total equity}}.$$

The *profit margin* ratio identifies net income per dollar of total revenue. Management can increase earnings by maximizing revenues and successfully controlling expenses. This ratio provides information about expense-control efficiency—that is, management's ability to control expenses and taxes. A high profit margin implies low expenses, low taxes, or both. The *asset utilization* ratio shows how effectively assets are being employed in generating revenues. This is a real test of the success or failure of portfolio policy (e.g., size of portfolio, type of holdings, and yield). The two ratios (profit margin and asset utilization) provide key information about the magnitudes that determine the ROA.

The profit margin and asset utilization ratios may each be decomposed further. The profit margin reflects four ratios, each of which measures the relative importance of specific types of expenses as well as taxes on bank revenue. These are

$$\text{Interest expense ratio} = \frac{\text{Interest expense}}{\text{Total revenue}}$$

$$\text{Noninterest expense ratio} = \frac{\text{Noninterest expense}}{\text{Total revenue}}$$

$$\text{Provision for loan-loss ratio} = \frac{\text{Provisions for loan losses}}{\text{Total revenue}}$$

$$\text{Tax ratio} = \frac{\text{Income taxes paid}}{\text{Total revenue}}.$$

Careful control of expenses enables more dollars of sales revenue to become net income. The first two ratios thus identify the share of interest and noninterest expenses in total revenue. Interest expenses are affected by a number of considerations, including the rates paid by banks to attract funds, the makeup of these funds, and the volumes involved. Rates paid are a function of such factors as the timing of borrowings relative to the interest-rate cycle, the market's perception of institutional risk, and maturity differences in the funds raised. The composition of funds generally reflects management philosophy; banks that rely heavily on deposit liabilities incur lower interest costs than those that make extensive use of nondeposit, or purchased, liabilities. Whatever the liability mix, some banks make greater use of debt (as identified by the equity or leverage multiplier) than others, with corresponding implications for interest expenses.

Noninterest expenses reflect a variety of expense items, including salaries (and related benefits), data-processing costs, and occupancy expenses (at the head office and branches). Noninterest expenses have been the focus of many banks' efforts to cut costs. To this end, individual ratios may be calculated by dividing various expense items by total operating expenses for different expense categories. Alternatively, these expense items may be expressed as percentages of average assets to allow comparison with other banks. Whatever the approach, individual ratio analysis enables management to identify areas where cost efficiencies may be realized.

Provision for loan losses is a key element of a bank's operating expenses and represents an estimate of future loan losses. Loss provisions were responsible for fluctuating bank profits in the late 1980s and early 1990s. Its ratio to total revenue identifies the relative importance of this item. Similarly, the tax ratio measures the share of taxes in total revenue.

As indicated earlier, a component part of ROA is the ratio of operating revenue to total assets, identified as the utilization ratio (AU). This earnings measure may itself be broken down into two component parts, the interest return on assets and the noninterest return on assets, as follows:

$$\frac{\text{Operating revenue}}{\text{Total assets}} = \frac{\text{Interest income}}{\text{Total assets}} + \frac{\text{Noninterest income}}{\text{Total assets}}$$

Traditionally banks have emphasized interest income, which is derived from such income-producing assets as loans and investments. Interest income differs from one bank to another because of considerations similar to those identified with respect to interest expenses. In other words, the interest income of a bank reflects the key features of its portfolio—yield, makeup, and size. Portfolio yield is a function of such factors as timing of loans and investments relative to the interest-rate cycle, asset quality, and differences in loan and investment maturities. The type and proportion of holdings within each asset category (e.g., within loans and investments) affects portfolio composition and has a direct bearing on interest income. Whatever the asset mix, the size of the portfolio impacts the amount of income generated.

In recent years, in an effort to raise the net income flowing to stockholders, banks have been emphasizing noninterest income, namely fees, service charges, and other income from various services (e.g., deposit accounts, trust services, and customer use of electronic technology). Separate ratios may be calculated to provide information for revenue enhancement by dividing each income service by total noninterest income or total assets.

Other Tools to Monitor Performance

The process of analyzing bank revenues and expenses is usually called cost analysis. Until the late 1950s only large banks typically undertook the difficult job of cost analysis. Working from the general ledger, they allocated the various expenses and revenues to individual departments and to functions within those departments. In 1958, management and financial analysts received an important tool to aid them in analyzing bank performance. The Federal Reserve Bank of New York began the development of a cost-analysis system that was both feasible and affordable for banks. Today an expanded version of that system, called the Functional Cost Analysis (FCA) program, is available to all participating banks. Although many banks have their own approach to cost analysis, FCA is designed to help banks assess overall profitability and the profitability and efficiency of each bank function.

Participating banks are given instruction manuals and worksheets on which they enter expenses and revenue information. For difficult-to-allocate items (primarily salaries and wages), guidelines on how to make the allocations are provided. The Federal Reserve will make the more difficult allocations if the bank does not wish to or cannot. For this purpose, the Federal Reserve has designed a computer program that allocates items based on "experience factors" formulated from the information provided by participating banks. This technique has helped to minimize inconsistencies of interbank comparisons. The participating bank receives a report that summarizes and compares, in a standardized format, its current year's operations with those of the previous year. In addition, the report includes, for comparative purposes, average figures on overall profitability and on the profitability of specific functions for banks of similar deposit size and percent of time deposits to total deposits, and of similar functional activity (for instance, similar composition of the loan portfolio). Additional information is also provided, including per-item costs and break-even points in various service categories.

Table 10.2 is an example of the kind of information provided by FCA. It refers to banks that administered their own credit card plans or were a primary regional agent of a national credit card plan at the time of this report. The data provided identify, for different groups of banks, the average assets generated from credit card business; the amounts of income, expense, and earnings involved; the number of personnel employed; and related data.

Another important tool for analyzing bank performance is the Uniform Bank Performance Report (UBPR), a cooperative effort of the three federal regulatory agencies (Federal Reserve, Comptroller of the Currency, and FDIC). Published by the Federal Financial Institutions Examination Council, the UBPR provides a standardized presentation of individual banks' balance-sheet and income-statement data as well as financial ratios, along with peer-group figures for all institutions of the same size and average data for banks within the same state. This allows comparisons with banks of comparable size and comparable location.

Both the FCA and the UBPR yield standards for meaningful evaluation of bank performance. With performance constantly evaluated and monitored, senior management can more effectively plan a bank's future course of action. Armed with knowledge of current performance, senior management is in a better position to decide on the expansion, or perhaps contraction, of specific activities within the bank. In recent years concern over the cost of retail business, and the large volume required to make such business profitable, has led some large banks to consolidate their retail services or to concentrate on their corporate customers. A case in point is the State Street Bank and Trust Company, which in late 1990 sold its credit card portfolio because it was not a good strategic fit with the bank's long-term objectives. Another case is Bankers Trust of New York, which between 1980 and 1983 sold most of its city branches (76) and four subsidiaries in upstate New York in order to minimize its retail business and build its wholesale banking activities.

Bank Planning

Although certain factors affecting performance may be out of a bank's control, management has significant room to maneuver in controlling costs and improving profitability. One way to accomplish this is through planning. Planning is the activity through which the bank charts its future course of action. Profit planning can take the form of a budget or of a long-range plan.

Budgeting

A budget is a financial plan that forecasts the results of a bank's operations in the year ahead. It includes a bank's expected revenues, expenses, and profits, based on management's well-reasoned objectives for every item in the asset-and-liability statement. In other words, a budget is a reflection of management's expectations regarding the volume and character of bank assets and liabilities for the coming year.

Preparation of the budget must be a collaborative effort. A good budget system requires that those responsible for carrying out the budget be involved in its preparation. This approach contributes to better communication between top management and middle management, and helps guard against unrealistic targets and unattainable objectives. Participation of all the branch managers and department heads in the preparation of the budget has additional advantages. It increases managers' understanding of the complexity of today's economic environment and prepares them to react faster to developing events. It enables each departmental manager and unit supervisor to better comprehend the relation of his or her activities to the totality of the bank's operations and the extent to which he or she contributes to bank profits. It improves internal coordination and contributes to better cost control and increased operational efficiency.

For all of the above reasons, budget inputs must come from all the branches and departments of the bank, the units that are accountable for performance. These inputs usually reflect the previous year's experience, adjusted for anticipated changes in the year ahead. These initial budget data are then combined into an integrated forecast by the comptroller's department, which is customarily responsible for the formulation of the annual budget.

Once approved, the budget becomes an effective tool of control. Departmental and branch managers can be provided with budgets for their own areas of responsibility and can be asked to operate within the confines of their budget. This approach enhances the monitoring of the results of each department and

Table 10.2
Functional Cost Analysis: Credit Card Function

	19 Banks Deposits Up To $50M		53 Banks Deposits $50 - $200M		26 Banks Deposits Over $200M	
1 Total number of active accounts	239		668		6,425	
Composition	Percent of Credit Card Volume					
2 Outstandings	$ 165,800	97.70%	$ 478,782	92.86 %	$ 6,523,704	98.75 %
3 Cash advances	3,906	2.30	36,793	7.14	82,410	1.25
4 Total Volume	$ 169,707	100.00%	$ 515,575	100.00 %	$ 6,606,114	100.00 %
Income						
5 Gross merchant discount	$ 15,939	9.39 %	$ 65,863	12.77 %	$ 445,082	6.74 %
6 Finance charge interest	21,078	12.42	65,580	12.72	720,684	10.91
7 Net interchange and all other fees	4,602	2.71	16,135	3.13	227,650	3.45 %
8 Total Income	$ 41,619	24.52 %	$ 147,579	28.62 %	$ 1,393,417	21.09 %
Expense						
9 Officer salaries	$ 6,908	4.07%	$ 17,777	3.45 %	$ 87,568	1.33 %
10 Employee salaries	6,195	3.65	14,936	2.90	108,430	1.64
11 Fringe benefits	2,986	1.76	7,939	1.54	47,102	.71
12 Salaries and Fringe, Subtotal	$ 16,089	9.48%	$ 40,652	7.88 %	$ 243,100	3.68 %
13 Data services	15,105	8.90	29,744	.5.77	132,980	2.01
14 Cr card activity & franchise fees	5,480	3.23	31,359	6.08	125,190	1.90
15 Other operating expense	13,762	8.11	28,444	5.52	416,932	6.31
16 Total Operating Expense	$ 50,436	29.72%	$ 130,199	25.25 %	$ 918,203	13.90 %

248

Earnings							
17 Net Earnings Before Losses	$	8,817-	5.20-%	$ 17,380	3.37 %	$ 475,214	7.19 %
18 Net credit losses		2,158	1.27	5,300	1.03	78,667	1.19
19 Net fraud losses		895	.53	593	.12	20,780	.31
20 Net Earnings	$	11,870-	6.99-%	$ 11,487	2.23 %	$ 375,768	5.69 %
21 Cost of money		6,658	3.92	20,975	4.07	233,196	3.53
22 Net Earnings After Cost of Money	$	18,527-	10.92-%	$ 9,488-	1.84-%	$ 142,572	2.16 %

Miscellaneous Data

Number of Credit Card Personnel					
23 Officers	.18		.44		1.99
24 Employees	.34		.86		5.31
25 Total Personnel	.52		1.30		7.31
Other Credit Card Data					
26 Total number of accounts	326		913		9,333
27 Active accounts/total accounts	239	73.31 %	668	73.08 %	6,425	68.84 %
28 Active accts paying interest/active accts	150	62.74 %	443	66.30 %	4,248	66.12 %
29 Active account average size	$ 711		$ 772		$ 1,028
30 Cash advance average size	$ 9		$ 319		$ 334
31 Sales draft average size	$ 109		$ 81		$ 82
32 Average volume per merchant	$ 41,688		$ 46,931		$ 7,689
33 3-yr avg loan losses/credit card volume	$ 2,231	1.31 %	$ 5,654	1.10 %	$ 66,186	1.00 %
34 Total number of sales draft transactions	11,369		35,820		374,118

Note: Details may not add to totals due to rounding.

Source: Federal Reserve Bank of New York, *Functional Cost Analysis* (New York: Federal Reserve Bank of New York, 1995), p. 36. Based on data furnished by participating banks in 12 Federal Reserve districts. Available from the Federal Reserve Bank of New York.

makes it more likely that the bank's operations will approximate the overall plan. If actual results deviate appreciably from the budgeted targets, management investigates the reasons for the deviations. Depending upon the factors responsible for such deviation, management may either revise the budget to reflect changing circumstances or take action to bring operations into line with the plan.

Long-Range Planning

A growing number of banks, in addition to budgeting, have been making use of projections that cover periods longer than the next year. This kind of projection, commonly referred to as long-range planning, usually covers a five-year period. The planning process begins with a set of overall goals for the bank for the period under consideration. For example, a bank's long-range goals may include a combination of the following:

—To expand the sale of its services over a wider geographic area

—To increase its share of the market through improved services and more specialized, or perhaps a wider array of, banking products

—To train and develop successor management to ensure continuity of policies and direction

—To contribute as a responsible corporate citizen to its community's economic life and growth

—To identify its position in the light of ongoing changes in the banking industry (for instance, to extend its business across state lines, acquire other banks, become part of a multibank holding company, form its own holding company, and/or establish a physical presence in foreign markets)

—To increase annual profits by 10 percent a year over the next five years, or to set a profitability objective in terms of target rates of return (for instance, return on total assets in excess of 1 percent and on average equity capital in excess of 13.25 percent).

Once a bank's goals are defined, management must determine appropriate strategies to attain the set goals. The formulation of strategies or development of activities constitutes, in effect, the bank's long-range plan. In other words, this plan is a quantification of the ideas on how to get the bank where it wants to be five years later. The solicitation of business from local companies through personal calls (call program) or the introduction of credit cards, pay-by-phone services, bank-by-mail facilities, and preauthorized bill payments are only a few examples of strategies. Whatever the recommended strategies may be, they must be realistic; that is, their formulation should be based upon such considerations as the bank's human and physical resources, the size of its market, economic conditions, competitive and technological changes, and legal and regulatory developments.

Just as in the preparation of the budget, so here the component units within the bank are expected to contribute their inputs for the realization of the set goals. If, for example, management's objective is to increase annual profits (or assets) by 10 percent a year over a five-year period, this objective provides guidelines for profit planning by the bank's component units. Their inputs would be integrated and result in a long-range projection of revenues, expenses, and earnings. These projections, however crude, are valuable in determining a bank's future course of action and in calling management's attention to the need for solutions to perceived problems ahead. Frequent comparisons of actual results with projections permit management to take corrective action promptly or to modify the plan to reflect changes in the economic environment. Clearly, the planning process must be a continuous activity and not an intermittent one. Recognizing the importance of this activity, many large banks have planning departments that engage in long-range planning. Other banks assign responsibility for this activity to a management committee, while in many small banks this function is nonexistent, at least in a formal sense. Today's deregulated banking environment makes some form of planning essential if a bank wishes to maintain efficient operations and sustain a pattern of growth. This growth will ultimately benefit stockholders by increasing the return on their investment.

PROFITABILITY OF THE BANKING INDUSTRY

The performance of the commercial banking industry in 1995 generally reflected the state of the U.S. economy during this period. Slow recovery from the 1990–91 recession led in 1994 to a significant increase in the demand for loans. In spite of higher interest rates, loans grew at the fastest pace in more than ten years. Banks financed most of the increases in loans by issuing managed liabilities and reducing their holdings of securities. Rapid growth in assets caused banks' return on assets to dip even though profitability remained quite high by historical standards. Earnings performance was supported by a substantial reduction in loan-loss provisions. Banks were able to lower provisions as loan quality improved because of both their past efforts to tighten credit standards and the continued expansion of the economy. A decline in net noninterest expense as a share of assets also contributed to the high profitability. This improvement came largely as a result of industry efforts to control costs.

For a more detailed assessment of the performance record of commercial banks, the remainder of this chapter is divided into three sections. The first considers the composition of bank revenues, the second deals with the expense side, and the third with commercial bank profits. Each of these sections is presented in relation to the corresponding category of the income statement for all insured commercial banks found in Table 10.3.

Components of Bank Income

Table 10.3 identifies the interest and noninterest sources of operating income of all insured commercial banks for the period 1990–95. Operating income data

Table 10.3

Income and Expense of Insured Commercial Banks, 1990–95 (amounts in millions of dollars)

Item	1990	1991	1992	1993	1994	1995
Total Interest & Fee Income	320,476	289,214	255,224	245,058	257,843	225,242
Loans	234,407	209,745	180,927	175,163	187,118	165,510
Lease financing receivables	4,406	4,038	3,815	3,396	3,140	2,683
Balances due from depository institutions	12,696	9,182	7,447	6,178	5,079	4,667
Interest & dividend income on securities	51,126	52,535	51,936	48,883	48,585	38,447
Interest income on federal funds sold & repurchase agreements	12,462	9,044	5,789	4,745	6,388	7,639
Assets held in trading accounts	5,379	4,670	5,310	6,693	7,533	6,296
Total Interest Expense	204,952	167,302	121,805	105,742	111,266	110,081
Deposits	161,524	138,445	98,211	79,594	79,407	78,255
Expense of federal funds purchased & reverse repurchase agreements	22,744	14,325	9,268	8,486	12,590	13,909
Interest on demand notes issued to the U.S. Treasury & other borrowed money	18,683	12,260	12,298	15,345	16,666	15,462
Interest on subordinated notes and debentures	1,765	2,060	1,862	2,164	2,463	2,348
Interest on mortgage indebtedness & obligations under capitalized leases	236	202	165	153	140	107
Net Interest Income	115,524	121,912	133,419	139,316	146,577	115,161

Provisions for loan & lease losses & allocated transfer risk	32,087	34,314	26,048	16,812	10,912	8,804
Total noninterest income	54,899	59,739	65,647	74,961	76,222	60,810
Service charges on deposit accounts	11,439	12,814	13,978	14,919	15,337	11,991
Other noninterest income	30,226	32,024	35,597	40,182	42,992	35,000
Gains on securities not held in trading accounts	481	2,972	4,006	3,061	(570)	440
Total noninterest expense	115,768	124,795	130,965	139,689	144,196	111,076
Salaries & employee benefits	51,765	53,111	54,802	58,189	60,600	47,361
Expenses of premises & fixed assets, net of rental income	64,003	71,683	76,163	81,500	83,596	63,715
Pretax net operating income	22,567	22,542	42,054	57,777	67,691	56,092
Applicable income taxes	7,704	8,265	14,481	19,838	22,426	19,674
Income before extraordinary items	15,344	17,249	31,578	40,999	44,695	36,858
Extraordinary items, net of tax	647	686	409	2,070	(15)	24
NET INCOME	15,991	17,936	31,987	43,069	44,680	36,882

Note: Details may not add to totals due to rounding.

Source: Federal Deposit Insurance Corporation, *Statistics on Banking* (Washington, D.C.: FDIC, 1994). Data for 1995 are from *Call Report*, September 30.

may be conveniently grouped under three headings: income from loans, income from investments, and other income. The relative importance of each is discussed below.

Income from Loans

As Table 10.3 indicates, income from loans and leases is the largest source of income for commercial banks, amounting on September 30, 1995, to $168.2 billion. The recession of 1990–91 adversely affected this source of income until 1994, when it turned around because of the larger volume of loans made and the higher rates of interest experienced during this period. Two other income items are, in reality, products of lending transactions, even though the Federal Reserve does not classify them as such. The first, interest earned on "balances due from depository institutions," represents, to a large extent, income realized from the placement of interbank deposits in the Eurocurrency market. This source of income is especially important for the large money-center banks, which are very actively engaged in international lending. The second income item is a composite of income derived from two transactions: the sale of federal funds and the purchase of securities under agreements to resell. As indicated in Chapter 7, a bank can earn interest income by lending some of its excess reserves at the Federal Reserve bank to another bank or by purchasing securities from cash-strapped dealer houses and banks under agreements to resell. Technically, both of these transactions are loans, since neither is exposed to the risks associated with investments. Combining the income earned from all of these items with that of loans boosts the contribution of the latter to 63 percent of operating income.

Since one of the two factors responsible for growth in loan income is a higher lending rate, it is useful to identify the forces that determine these rates. Unlike rates on money-market instruments (such as Treasury bills), which are determined by the competitive climate of public markets, interest rates on bank loans are a product of direct negotiation between borrower and bank. This negotiated method of pricing credit arrangements is responsible for significant interest variation from one loan to another. Other considerations contributing to interest-rate variations include the degree of risk of a particular loan, the length of its maturity, the size of the loan, the cost of originating and administering the loan, the size of borrower balances brought to or maintained with the bank (compensating balances), and the existence of collateral.

In addition, bankers' outlook on the state of the economy and the future course of interest rates can affect the rates charged on specific loans. This outlook is in part affected by the Federal Reserve's actions to expand or contract the money supply. Interest rates tend to be higher in periods of tight monetary policy and lower in periods of monetary ease.

Income from Investments

Income from investments accounted for 13.4 percent of banks' operating income on September 30, 1995. This item constitutes the second largest source

Table 10.4
Rates Earned on Assets, All Banks, 1990–94 (percent per annum)

Item	1990	1991	1992	1993	1994
Investment account, total	8.66	8.22	7.11	6.06	5.78
U.S. government and other debt	8.91	8.39	7.17	6.06	5.79
State and local	7.37	7.25	6.81	6.26	5.87
Equity	7.32	6.19	5.31	4.77	4.79
Loans and leases, gross	11.47	10.36	9.19	8.67	8.61
Net of loss provisions	9.92	8.69	7.87	7.86	8.12

Source: Federal Reserve Bulletin, June 1995, p. 561.

of bank income. The relative importance of this source is a function of the amount and types of investment holdings and their yields. In 1995, for example, most of the investment income of insured commercial banks came from their holdings of U.S. Treasury issues and obligations of government agencies; these securities dominated bank investment portfolios. Next in importance was interest from municipal securities, whose major attraction for commercial banks is that their interest is exempt from federal income tax. The Tax Reform Act of 1986 limited the appeal of these issues for banks by eliminating the deduction from taxable income of 80 percent of the interest expense on deposits allocable to the funding and carrying of tax-exempt obligations. Bank purchases of tax-exempt instruments became less attractive. Thus, as the instruments held matured, the total holdings of tax-exempt securities contracted. Following in importance was the income from all other investment holdings, such as corporate bonds, foreign securities, and Federal Reserve bank stock.

Overall, the security income of insured commercial banks experienced a decrease in the period under consideration. A drop in market yields, in response to prevailing conditions, adversely affected the profitability of the investment portfolio. Table 10.4 shows the investment and loan yields for banks during the period 1990–94.

The income derived from the investment portfolio is of two types: interest income and capital gains. The interest income generated by the investment portfolio was addressed above. Securities may generate income in the form of capital gains. This is considered a different form of income because it is a function of the securities' value at the time of their sale. As seen in Table 10.3, from 1990 through 1993 banks realized gains that varied in amounts from $480 million to $4 billion. By contrast, 1994 was associated with securities losses of $570 million. A runup in interest rates that year pushed securities' values lower, causing banks to take losses as they sold securities to free funds for loans. Such losses, which occur during periods of tight economic conditions and high interest rates, are offset by loss write-offs and the higher yields of the loans.

Other Sources of Income

All other sources of income accounted collectively for 23.4 percent of banks' operating income. This category includes income from trust department activities, service charges on deposit accounts, and other noninterest income.

Trust departments have the advantage of generating income through the sale of services without utilizing bank funds. They can be highly profitable if they have a good list of profitable accounts—that is, accounts that produce high earnings relative to expenses. However, some trust departments, small ones in particular, lack enough profitable accounts to make the department as a whole profitable. The existence of these departments is justified by banks' desire to offer a full range of services in order to attract customers. Trust income amounted to $9.1 billion in September 1995, an increase of 153 percent over the amount earned in 1988.

Since deregulation of deposit rates of interest, banks have been charging customers for what services cost. Services once considered courtesies are now subject to specific fees. An account may be unprofitable because it is too small relative to the number of checks written, the number of deposits made, and the overhead costs involved. As a result, many institutions charge customers with small balances a flat amount per month as an overhead charge and a per-item fee for each check written. By contrast, customers with large balances pay the lowest fees and often get free checking and other implicit benefits. Presumably the value of large deposit balances to these banks more than compensates for the cost of servicing them; that is, the income earned from these deposits covers the cost of servicing them and provides a profit margin. In addition to the use of monthly service charges, institutions have also introduced special charges for special services, such as returned deposit items, stop-payment orders, overdrafts, and certification of checks. Income from service charges accounted for 3 percent of operating income in 1988, and increased to 4 percent by September 1995.

"Other noninterest income" is derived from an assortment of services such as correspondent banking, corporate cash management, securities held in trading accounts, underwriting, off-balance-sheet activities, and other income-producing activities not elsewhere classified (for instance, EFT-related products). Between 1988 and 1995, this category increased from 11.4 percent of operating income to 21.2 percent. As banks expand the range of their fee-based services to diversify from traditional lines of business, this category will grow further.

Distribution of Bank Expenses

Table 10.3 also identifies the composition and trends of operating expenses of insured commercial banks for the period 1990–95. Aggregation of the various expense items identified in Table 10.3 indicates that bank expenses fell faster than income during the time period under consideration. Specifically, between 1990 and 1995, while operating income decreased by 23.8 percent, operating expenses fell by 34.8 percent. Review of the expense items indicates that this decrease was mainly due to a drastic drop in banks' loan-loss provisions.

The paragraphs that follow examine the various types of bank expenses under three headings: interest expense, salaries and employee benefits, and other operating expenses.

Interest Expense

Interest expense has grown over the years to become a major, if not the dominant, expense category. On September 30, 1995, it represented about 48 percent of operating expenses. This figure can be broken down into interest on deposits (34 percent) and interest on nondeposit liabilities (14 percent). The dominant role of interest on deposits among bank expenses reflects the relative importance of deposits as a source of funds for banks. The phaseout of Regulation Q throughout the early and mid-1980s led banks to pay competitive rates on retail deposits and thus add to the cost of these funds. The phasing out of Regulation Q was initiated, as discussed in Chapter 6, with the enactment of the DIDMCA in 1980 and accelerated rapidly in 1982 with the passage of the Garn-St. Germain Depository Institutions Act. This act made possible the introduction of the money-market deposit account, which has since enjoyed significant popularity among consumers. Despite the increased reliance of banks on time and savings deposits, deposit interest expenses generally declined throughout most of this period because of a decrease in the market rates of interest.

Nondeposit liabilities, the other type of interest expenses included in this category, decreased, too, from their 1990 level in response to prevailing conditions during this period. However, since this drop was far less than the overall decrease in operating expenses, this item registered a modest rise of about 1.5 percent of operating expenses in the 1990–95 period. Larger banks generally tend to rely more than small banks upon nondeposit liabilities to meet expanded loan volume. This category includes such items as interest on capital notes and debentures as well as other borrowed money, and the expense of purchasing federal funds and selling securities under repurchase agreements.

Salaries and Employee Benefits

Between 1990 and 1995, salaries, wages, and fringe benefits increased from 14.7 percent of operating expenses to 20.6 percent. This increase generally reflected conditions in smaller banks. Indeed, small institutions generally have a high percentage of expenses in salaries and wages, demonstrating the traditional labor-intensive nature of banking. By contrast, very large banks have automated their operations and adopted electronic banking in the delivery of their services. With the cost of these technological changes prohibitively high for smaller institutions, employee expenses remain high.

Other Operating Expenses

An important operating expense is provision for loan losses, which represents current earnings used by banks to build or replenish their reserves for loan and

Figure 10.1
Reserves for Loan and Lease Losses, Loss Provisions, and Net Charge-offs as a
Percentage of Loans, 1980–94

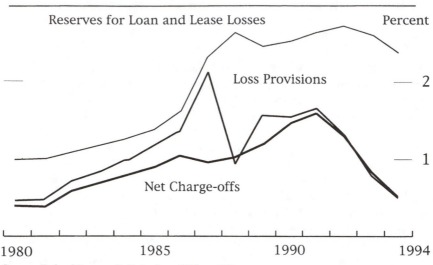

Source: Federal Reserve Bulletin, June 1995, p. 553.

lease losses. Between 1990 and 1995, loan-loss provisions dropped from 9.1 percent of operating expenses to 3.8 percent, thereby contributing to an improvement in banks' earnings performance during this period. Figure 10.1 presents reserves for loan losses, loss provisions, and actual loan losses or net charge-offs to outstanding loans, from 1980 to 1994. As seen in this figure, in the early 1980s loss provisions tended to follow charge-offs closely.* By the mid-1980s, however, banks started raising their provisions at rates in excess of charge-offs because of rising losses from foreign, agricultural, energy, and real-estate loans. By year-end 1987, provisions reached a record level, accounting for over 2 percent of outstanding loans, or $37 billion. In the 1990s, provisioning closely followed, and even dropped below, charge-offs in 1993 and 1994, causing a small decline in reserves. Charge-off rates started declining in 1991, and by 1994 they had reached their lowest level in more than a decade. The decline in charge-off and delinquency rates reflected an overall improvement in the quality of loan portfolios, which was attributed to two factors—the tightening of bank lending standards in the early 1990s and the growth of the U.S. economy. The improved quality of loan portfolios caused provisions to reach their lowest level in recent years. Brisker economic growth entailed stronger business

---

*Loan charge-offs reduce the reserve for loan losses on the balance sheet; thus, by making provisions generally in line with current-period charge-offs, banks are able to maintain the level of their outstanding loan-loss reserves.

and consumer borrowing, as a result of which the ratio of reserves to loans and leases outstanding fell to less than 2.5 percent.

Banks incur a variety of other expenses that collectively totaled 27.7 percent of operating expenses on September 30, 1995. One such expense is that of occupying bank premises and acquiring furniture and equipment. This includes maintenance, insurance, depreciation, and taxes on bank premises, in addition to salaries of all employees connected with the operating and management of the property. There are also some operating expenses not previously discussed that are essential for the functioning of commercial banks. These expenses include such outlays as fees for legal work and for directors, as well as expenses related to computer software, examination by regulatory agencies, publicity, and advertising. The competitive environment in which banks operate has increased their awareness of the need for advertising. Competition for the public's business in general and, recently, for the business of lower-income groups has produced a marked increase in outlays for advertising. Along with advertising expenses is a more common expenditure of day-to-day business, office supplies and printing. Banks use enormous amounts of drafts, notes, deposit and withdrawal slips, loan applications, and other forms.

Since banks deal with a great amount of risk in the course of their operation, the assessment made by the Federal Deposit Insurance Corporation to insure deposits, as well as premiums paid to insure other aspects of the banking business, are significant expenses. Banks carry far greater risks than one might assume. The possibility of burglary, robbery, embezzlement, and defalcation is uppermost in people's minds. However, losses from forged checks, losses of important documents, and errors and omissions in various documents are also possibilities that require insurance protection.

Along with these expenses is that of income taxes. Since banks are subject to the standard corporate income tax rates, these taxes become a significant expense incurred by commercial banks, accounting for 35 percent of pretax income on September 30, 1995.

Bank Profits

Figure 10.2 depicts the net income and dividends of all insured commercial banks for the years 1979–94. As seen in this figure, the net income of banks increased over the years except for 1987, when huge provisions ($37 billion) were made for possible loan losses. Strong loan demand, combined with reduced loan provisions, contributed to a remarkable recovery in bank profitability in 1988. Loan losses lowered net income until 1992, when it surged to record levels, sustained by the continued expansion of the U.S. economy.

Bank dividends also increased during this period. The trend was generally upward, including 1987. Indeed, despite the large loan provisions effected that year, banks paid dividends at a rate slightly above their 1986 pace, thereby contributing to sizable reductions of retained income. Counting on a turnaround

Figure 10.2
Net Income and Dividends of All Insured Commercial Banks, 1979–94

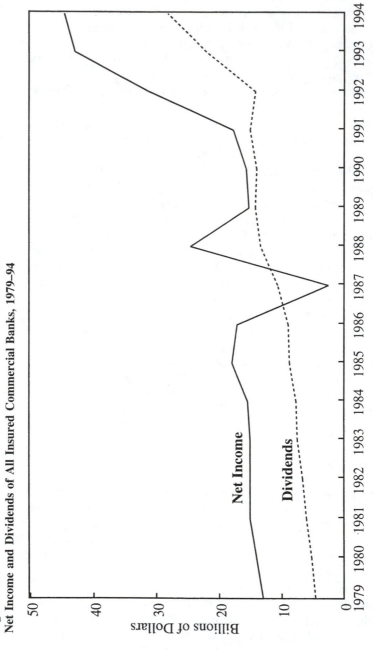

Source: Federal Reserve Bulletin, selected issues.

Figure 10.3
Return on Assets and Equity, All Insured Commercial Banks, 1970–94

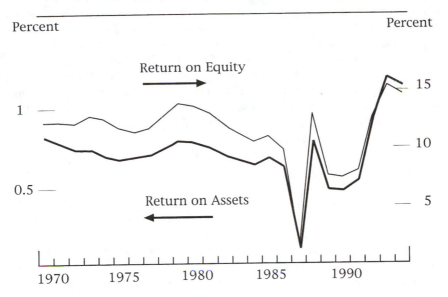

in profitability, banks continued to pay dividends, reluctant to further erode the price of their stock and, thus, their future ability to raise equity capital. From 1993 on, dividends surged higher in response to a highly profitable performance.

Though the dividend trend was generally upward, some banks have consistently followed a policy of retaining profits annually, while others have pursued a more liberal dividend payment policy. Small banks are generally typical of the former group. The stocks of small banks have a low payout and stockholders are more interested in the appreciation of the stock than in large dividend earnings. This is due mostly to the fact that stocks of small banks are family owned or held closely by a small group of investors.

Banks whose stock is widely held follow a more liberal dividend policy. It improves a bank's position in the equity markets and enhances its potential to raise funds when needed.

Profitability Measures and Trends

The profitability of the banking industry increased significantly in the 1990s, reaching record levels in 1993. Figure 10.3 portrays the industry's primary profitability measures, return on assets and return on equity, for the years 1970–94. As seen in this figure, the relationship between the two sets of rates was quite stable until the early 1980s, when they started declining, reaching a record low in 1987. Huge provisions made by large banks against loan losses cut the industry's return on assets and equity in 1987 to about one-fifth of the 1986 levels (return on assets and equity in 1987 stood at 0.12 percent and 1.94 percent, respectively). In the following year, both measures recovered dramatically as loan spreads improved, noninterest income increased, and provisioning for loan losses returned to more normal levels. In the years 1989–91, loan losses again increased sharply, forcing both measures to retreat once more from the high they reached in 1988. As loan losses eased, ROA and ROE increased significantly again through 1993. Bank profitability remained strong in 1994, although it was down slightly because of changes in accounting rules that caused a one-time increase in reported assets (marking securities to market and limiting the netting of off-balance-sheet deviratives to contracts with same counterparty).

To better evaluate the profitability record of the banking industry, it is necessary to compare it with other key sectors of the economy. Figure 10.4 shows the trends in the rates of return for commercial banks and manufacturing corporations from 1968 through 1994. The rate of return for manufacturing firms has at times exceeded or trailed that of commercial banks. Stated differently, the banking industry experienced more stable rates of return than did manufacturing corporations. The anomaly experienced in 1987 was due to the huge loss provisions made by banks in that year. With this exception, the profitability of commercial banking was relatively more stable than that of manufacturing corporations. This does not mean, however, that commercial banking is an industry that does not suffer from cyclical fluctuations. Bank profits are influenced by the business cycle, but a bank's ability to invest in loans when loan demand is high, and in securities when the demand for loans is low, reduces the variability of bank profits.

With the rising competition that banks are encountering from other financial institutions, and with their profit margins squeezed by deregulated interest rates, the banking industry faces the challenge of earning competitive rates of return and maintaining profit stability. Only through such performance can commercial banks maintain investor confidence and sustain an ongoing expansion of their capital base. Changes in banking in the 1990s and indications of further deregulation and broadening of banking powers are positive signs. These developments hold the promise of further consolidation in the banking industry and the emergence in the years ahead of banking organizations that will function more efficiently and effectively than at any time in U.S. history.

Figure 10.4
Rate of Return on Equity Capital of All Insured Commercial Banks and Manufacturing Corporations, 1968–94

Percent

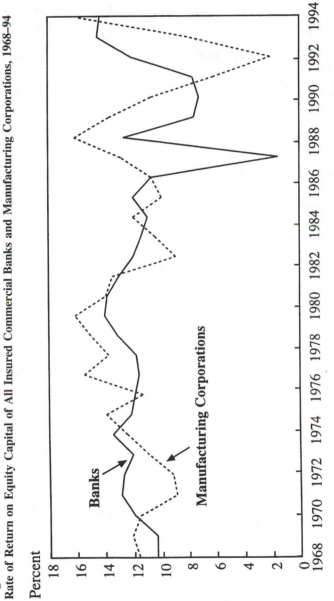

Source: Federal Deposit Insurance Corporation, *Annual Reports; Economic Report of the President* (Washington, D.C.: U.S. Government Printing Office, February 1996), p. 383.

SUGGESTED REFERENCES

Brown, Albert. *High Performance Banking: How to Improve Earnings in Any Bank.* Rolling Meadows, Ill.: Bankers Publishing Company, 1990.

English, William B., and Brian K. Reid. "Profit and Balance Sheet Developments at U.S. Commercial Banks in 1994." *Federal Reserve Bulletin*, June 1995, pp. 545–69.

Federal Financial Institutions Examination Council. *A User's Guide for the Uniform Bank Performance Report.* Washington, D.C.: Federal Financial Institutions Examination Council, 1984.

Federal Reserve Bank of New York. *Functional Cost Analysis: Average Banks.* New York: Federal Reserve Bank of New York, 1995.

Fraser, Donald, and Lyn Fraser. *Evaluating Commercial Bank Performance.* Rolling Meadows, Ill.: Bankers Publishing Company, 1990.

"Spotlight on Profitability." *American Banker*, June 7, 1995, pp. 8–11.

Woosley, Lynn W., and James D. Baer. "Commercial Bank Profits in 1994." Federal Reserve Bank of Atlanta, *Economic Review*, May/June 1995, pp. 11–31.

Part IV

Uses of Bank Funds

Chapter 11

Cash Assets

Part III indicated that in the employment of bank funds, management must be guided by the objectives of liquidity, solvency, and profitability. If a bank is to discharge its community obligations in a satisfactory manner and to continue as a going concern, it must seek to provide a rational solution to the fundamental conflict between liquidity and profitability. The manner in which management goes about resolving this conflict is the ultimate test of its efficacy and success.

Whatever management's approach may be in each individual case, this liquidity-profitability conflict underlies the increased diversification of bank uses of funds. These uses are customarily grouped into the following categories: cash assets, investments, loans, and other assets (a category covering a variety of items including fixed assets, such as buildings and land). The first three are the object of asset management—the process of allocating funds among alternative uses—on an ongoing basis. The last category is not normally dealt with on a daily basis, although when expenditures are planned for fixed assets, adequate cash provisions must be made. Part IV thus focuses upon the first three asset categories. While chapters 12 through 15 cover a bank's loan and investment portfolios, this chapter deals with cash assets and their management.

Cash assets are the most liquid resources a bank holds; they are immediately available with no risk of loss whatsoever. Although these assets produce no income, they perform a basic function for commercial banks. They enable them to meet their legal and day-to-day operating requirements. In the latter instance, cash assets ensure the ability of commercial banks to meet their customers' liquidity needs and cope with a volatile financial environment. Because they function as the first line of liquidity defense, these assets (as stated in Chapter 8) are also referred to as a bank's primary reserves.

It follows that banks need to maintain adequate primary reserves. Clearly, it is not possible to lay down fixed rules regarding the size of a bank's primary reserve account. What would be desirable for one bank might not be for another. Moreover, what would be desirable under one set of circumstances may not be desirable under another. Obviously, then, individual bank requirements should determine the size of the primary reserves, which must be sufficiently large to meet legal reserve requirements. Moreover, banks must carry additional funds, working reserves, which must be sufficient to meet day-to-day operational needs. The size of working reserves thus depends primarily upon the bank's operational requirements.

Primary reserves, as determined by legal and operational requirements, must be managed as efficiently as possible. Banks are profit-seeking enterprises, and maximum utilization of their resources is naturally desirable. Carrying sizable amounts of primary reserves means sacrificing income for liquidity. Since liquidity needs cannot be forecast with absolute precision, the size of primary reserves is a matter of judgment. Banks do not want to sacrifice income unnecessarily by holding idle reserves against possible liquidity needs that might not arise. They therefore should keep these nonearning assets to a minimum. The maintenance of minimum primary reserves is generally thought of as a test of good management. A skilled management shifts the burden of meeting all possible demands for funds to the investment portfolio, which is used by many banks to provide backup liquidity against their short- and intermediate-term needs while also serving as a residual haven for longer-term employment of bank funds.

TYPES OF CASH ASSETS

Cash assets are made up of the following accounts: cash items in process of collection, balances with correspondent banks and other depository institutions, balances with Federal Reserve banks, and cash in vault. These accounts make up a bank's money position. Each of them, depicted in Table 11.1, is discussed below.

Cash Items in Process of Collection

Cash items in process of collection include checks, promissory notes, and other matured items deposited at the bank by its customers for collection. The widespread use of checks in the U.S. economy contributes to rendering this account a major cash asset. As shown in Table 11.1, on September 30, 1995, cash items in process of collection accounted for 36.9 percent of cash assets of all insured commercial banks.

The size of this account varies significantly from one bank to another, and reflects in each case the volume of checks received and the time it takes for them to clear. Because these items represent nonearning assets, banks make every effort to speed their collection, in order to benefit from their conversion

Table 11.1

Cash Assets Held by All Insured Commercial Banks, 1995 (millions of dollars)

Item	Amount (millions of dollars)	Percent of Total
Cash items in process of collection	$101,543	36.9
Balances due from depository institutions in the U.S.	48,031	17.4
Balances due from banks in foreign countries	68,562	24.9
Balances due from Federal Reserve banks	22,740	8.3
Currency and coin	34,237	12.4
Total	$275,113	100.0

Note: Details may not add to totals due to rounding.
Source: Federal Deposit Insurance Corporation, *Call Report*, September 1995.

from nonearning to earning assets. As stated in Chapter 6, checks drawn on local banks are customarily cleared through the local banks are customarily cleared through the local clearinghouse. Checks drawn on out-of-town banks may be sent for collection to a correspondent bank or the Federal Reserve bank. In the latter case the individual bank receives credit in its reserve account within the time frame provided for by the Federal Reserve System. For some items credit may be received immediately, while for others (such as checks drawn on banks in distant parts of the country) credit may be deferred for up to three full business days. For items cleared through a correspondent bank, credit is received after the correspondent bank has received credit for the item(s) in question. However, some arrangements with correspondent banks provide for the immediate credit of the remitting bank's account.

While the Federal Reserve may defer crediting a bank's account for up to three business days, at the very most, many banks took as long as three weeks to make funds available to their depositors. This practice led consumer groups to lobby Congress for legislation limiting check holds. Congressional response was Title VI of the Competitive Equality Banking Act (CEBA) of 1987, the Expedited Funds Availability Act (EFAA). The Federal Reserve Board was assigned the task of implementing EFAA, which became effective in September 1988. Under this act, also known as Regulation CC, banks and thrifts must make funds available to depositors the next business day for checks drawn on the U.S. Government, state and local governments, U.S. postal money orders, and cashier's and certified checks. On local checks, Regulation CC provided for the initial availability of funds within three business days after their deposit, and on checks from out-of-town banks within seven business days after deposit. Effective September 1, 1990, this maximum hold period was shortened to two business days on local and five on nonlocal items. Banks can put longer holds for certain checks, but they must disclose the reason to customers in writing when the check is deposited. Special conditions cover checks in excess of a certain amount or checks for newly established accounts.

Balances with Correspondent Banks and Other Depository Institutions

As indicated in Chapter 2, banks maintain demand deposits with other banks for more efficient check clearing and to compensate correspondent banks for the provision of varied services (such as lines of credit, international banking services, loan participations, federal funds transactions, and investment counseling). The specialized talents of larger banks and the scope of their operations render correspondent banking a vehicle for substantial economies of scale for smaller banks. However, the correspondent relationship is profitable for the correspondent bank as well. Indeed, large banks in regional and national money centers compete actively for these deposits. Their attractiveness is obvious—they can amount to a substantial source of interest-free funds that can be loaned and invested for profit. Even though the profit realized is an implicit interest payment for services rendered to the respondent bank, the arrangement is still profitable, since correspondent balances subsidize activities that the correspondent would ordinarily have undertaken in the course of its operations.

The high rates of interest experienced in the late 1970s and early 1980s led many banks to review their correspondent relationships. The high opportunity cost of maintaining relationships with too many correspondents or of holding larger-than-necessary balances led to the streamlining of these relationships and the reduction of balances to more reasonable levels. On September 30, 1995, correspondent balances accounted for 17.4 percent of cash assets (see Table 11.1).

Balances with Federal Reserve Banks

Since enactment of the Federal Reserve Act of 1913, member banks have been required to maintain balances with their district Federal Reserve bank or branch equal to a specified percentage of their public deposits. This account, along with a bank's cash in vault, constitutes a bank's legal reserves. In addition to meeting reserve requirements, this account is used by banks to facilitate their financial transactions. For example, it is used as a channel for the payment of checks drawn on the bank and for the collection of incoming checks. This account is also used to effect payments to the U.S. Treasury and to other banks, or to collect from them. When banks borrow from the Federal Reserve or other banks, this account is credited with the loan proceeds, and then debited at the time of repayment. On September 30, 1995, all insured banks held 8.3 percent of their cash assets in the form of balances with the Federal Reserve banks (see Table 11.1).

Origin and Evolution

Wherever commercial banking has developed, the need for cash reserves has been demonstrated. At first the size of cash reserves held by commercial banks was merely a product of individual bank experience. The epidemics of bank failures in many nations proved, however, that banks were operating beyond the bounds of prudence. This fact led U.S. banking authorities to introduce prudent liquidity standards to ensure commercial bank ability to meet withdrawals of deposits in cash. Provisions for legally required reserves first appeared in the United States in 1863, with the passage of the National Bank Act. National banks located in central reserve cities were required to hold reserves equal to 25 percent of their deposits. Banks in reserve cities also had to keep reserves of 25 percent, but half could be in the form of deposits with national banks in central reserve cities. All other national banks, referred to as country banks, were required to keep reserves of 15 percent of their deposits, but 60 percent could be in the form of deposits with national banks in reserve and central reserve cities.

Because of the absence of a central bank in the United States, reserve regulations provided for a considerable degree of pyramiding—part of the reserves of country banks consisted of deposits with reserve city banks and part of these in turn were redeposited with central reserve city banks. The Federal Reserve Act of 1913 preserved the geographic classification of banks but modified reserve provisions, extending them to all member banks (national banks and state member banks), and required the maintenance of reserve balances with Federal Reserve banks. The Banking Act of 1935 authorized the Board of Governors to vary reserve requirements at its discretion over a substantial statutory range—an authority it has held ever since.

Although reserves were initially envisioned as a safeguard of bank liquidity, their original character has changed. Statutory regulations do not permit legal reserves to be depleted for any extended period of time. Indeed, the deviation allowed from legally required reserves is generally very little; excess or deficiency is limited to 4 percent of required reserves and can be carried forward up to the next statement period, but not beyond. Deficiencies in excess of this percentage are generally subject to a penalty equal to the discount rate plus two percentage points. Thus, required reserves can no longer be considered a significant source of liquidity, and hence a bulwark of protection. "Thus we find the paradox: in practice, a bank cannot depend on its legal cash-reserve requirement to meet deposit shrinkage; this must come mainly from other assets."[1]

In addition to possessing a low degree of liquidity, reserve requirements involve a loss of bank income. A bank's gross earnings, and in turn its net profits, are determined both by the amount of loanable and investable funds on hand and by the efficiency with which these funds are employed. Clearly, the required maintenance of legal reserves with regulatory authorities is a limiting factor on a bank's supply of loanable and investable funds, and hence on a bank's earnings prospects.

The function of legal reserves today is a very basic one. Their existence is justified not on the grounds of enforcing minimum liquidity standards of managerial prudence, but on providing a tool of monetary policy. Indeed, it is now generally recognized that reserve requirements serve primarily as a control device through which monetary authorities can influence the availability and cost of credit. By altering reserve requirements upward or downward, monetary authorities can effectively decrease or increase the ability of commercial banks to lend and invest, and therefore affect the volume of bank deposits, the major part of the money supply. This manipulation of reserve requirements is, of course, dictated by the objectives of monetary policy.

Current Structure of Reserve Requirements

In 1972 the Federal Reserve System abandoned the traditional criterion of geographical location (reserve city, city, or country) in the determination of member bank reserves. Instead, it adopted a system of reserve requirements that, depending upon the type of deposit involved, provided for a multitiered structure of required reserves. For demand deposits, reserve requirements were graduated according to deposit intervals and applied to those intervals of the deposits of each bank. For time deposits, the reserve schedule was based on the maturity classification.

Enactment of the DIDMCA in 1980 brought important changes in reserve provisions. To increase Federal Reserve control over the monetary system, this act introduced uniform reserve requirements for all depository institutions (including commercial banks, mutual savings banks, savings and loan associations, and credit unions). Recognizing that all depository institutions offer at least one type of transaction deposit that is part of the money supply, it subjected these deposits to a uniform reserve requirement. Of all other deposits, only certain types of managed liabilities were subjected to reserve requirements. Under the terms of the DIDMCA, reserve requirements were imposed on three categories of deposits:

- Transaction accounts (demand deposits, NOW accounts, share-draft accounts, ATS accounts, and any other account through which an automatic or telephone transfer of funds can be effected)
- Nonpersonal time deposits (time deposits of businesses and governments)
- Eurocurrency liabilities (deposit borrowings of U.S. banks from their offshore branches and foreign depository institutions).

Transaction accounts subject to reserve requirements are the total transaction accounts less cash items in process of collection and deposits due from banks. Cash items are excluded because they represent deposit liabilities, subject to

Table 11.2
Reserve Requirements of Depository Institutions (percent of deposits)

Type of Deposit	Requirement	
	Percent	Statutory Range (percent)
Net transaction accounts		
$0-52 million	3	3
More than $52 million	10	8-14
Nonpersonal time deposits	0	0-9
Eurocurrency liabilities	0	none

Source: Federal Reserve Bulletin, January 1996, p. A9.

reserve requirements, of other banks. Deposits due from banks are excluded because they are interbank deposits, which by definition are not part of the money supply. The derived net transaction accounts figure is subject to a two-tiered reserve requirement (see Table 11.2). At the present time the first $52 million is subject to a 3 percent requirement; amounts in excess of this figure, to a 10 percent requirement. Unlike the requirement for the first tier of accounts, which remains fixed, the act gave the Federal Reserve Board authority to alter the requirement on the remaining accounts within the range of 8–14 percent. The act also authorized the Federal Reserve Board to adjust the breakpoint figure annually, to reflect the growth in the transaction accounts held by all depository institutions. Thus, from the $25 million that was initially set by the act, the breakpoint has gradually been adjusted to the present $52 million level.

As implied by the current reserve requirement on transaction accounts, small deposit institutions are generally favored over large ones. The Garn-St. Germain Act of 1982 carried this further by providing for reservable liabilities subject to a zero percent requirement, with this amount adjusted every year by the Board on the basis of the total growth of bank deposits during the year. In December 1995, the zero percent bracket was $4.3 million. At the other extreme, institutions with net transaction accounts in excess of $52 million are subject to the highest reserve requirements. Clearly, the intent of the Federal Reserve Board is to control the larger institutions more effectively because of their growing role and importance in the financial system. These institutions, in addition to the private and public deposits they hold, are the depositories for many small and medium-size deposit-type financial intermediaries. Their failure would contribute to the collapse of these intermediaries and undermine the country's economic life.

The DIDMCA provided no reserve requirements for the time and savings deposits of individuals and households. However, it stipulated requirements for the time and savings deposits owned by a depositor that is "not natural person."

Clearly subject to this requirement are large CDs, which represent the major type of nonpersonal time deposits. The reserve requirement against these deposits with an original maturity of less than 1 1/2 years was reduced from 3 percent to zero in December 1990. For nonpersonal deposits with an original maturity in excess of 1 1/2 years, the reserve requirement has been zero since 1983. Here, too, the Federal Reserve Board was given the power to alter these requirements within the range of 0 to 9 percent, and to change them according to maturities.

On Eurocurrency liabilities the DIDMCA gave the Federal Reserve Board unlimited power, leaving the matter of reserve ratio or statutory range of permissible ratios to its discretion. The intent of this provision was to give the Board a free hand in preventing banks from relying on foreign deposit borrowing to fund domestic activities on a reserve-free basis. Required reserves against such borrowing were reduced from 3 percent to zero in December 1990.

The reserve requirements described in the preceding paragraphs do not exhaust the reserve provisions of the DIDMCA. This act also provided for supplemental reserves on transaction accounts of not more than 4 percent, if deemed essential by the Federal Reserve Board. However, unlike the basic reserves described above, supplemental reserves would earn interest at a rate to be determined by the average earnings on the Federal Reserve's portfolio. A final provision of the DIDMCA grants the Federal Reserve Board emergency powers in dealing with extraordinary circumstances, authorizing it to impose on depository institutions additional reserve requirements at any ratio on any liability. These reserves may be imposed for up to 180 days and require, because of their extraordinary nature, prior consultation with the appropriate congressional committees.

Calculating Reserve Requirements

To facilitate compliance with reserve requirements, the Federal Reserve has developed standard operating procedures for banks to follow. The actual computation of an institution's reserve liability depends upon its size, as measured by its depository liabilities. Institutions whose total deposits do not exceed the zero percent reserve-requirement provisions (currently $4.3 million) are exempted from any reporting ("nonreporters"). At the other extreme are institutions with the largest depository liabilities in the country. Currently, institutions with more than $57 million in deposits and more than $4.3 in reservable liabilities are required to report weekly ("weekly reporters"), while institutions with less than $57 million in deposits and more than $4.3 million in reservable liabilities are permitted to report on a quarterly basis ("quarterly reporters").* The threshold between the two categories is adjusted by the Federal Reserve Board each year by means of a formula.

*Institutions with smaller deposit bases and reservable liabilities are subject to eased reporting requirements.

Figure 11.1

Reserve Computation and Maintenance Cycle under the Contemporaneous Reserve Accounting System

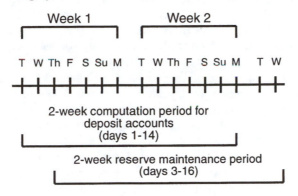

Source: Board of Governors of the Federal Reserve System.

For quarterly reporters, the required reserves are based on their daily average balance of reservable deposits during a seven-day period (also referred to as the computation period) that begins the third Tuesday of the last month of each calendar quarter. Required reserves are than determined by multiplying the daily average of each deposit classification—transaction accounts, nonpersonal time deposits, and Eurocurrency liabilities—by the appropriate ratios shown in Table 11.2. The daily average vault cash held during the computation period is deducted from the depository's reserve liability. Required reserves must then be maintained (maintenance period) from the fourth Thursday following the computation period until the fourth Wednesday after the end of the depository's next computation period.

The required reserves for institutions reporting weekly are computed on the basis of the contemporaneous reserve accounting (CRA) system. The CRA permits the Federal Reserve to exercise more effective control over the supply of money. A schematic presentation of this system is provided in Figure 11.1. As seen in this figure, the reserve computation period for deposit accounts stretches over a two-week period beginning on a Tuesday and ending on the second Monday hence. Required reserves are then calculated by multiplying the daily average balance of each deposit classification by the appropriate ratios shown in Table 11.2. The amount of reserves established by the application of these ratios must be maintained during a two-week period that begins on a Thursday and ends two weeks later on a Wednesday. By beginning shortly after the computation period, the reserve maintenance period affords banks only a two-day lag to make final adjustments in their actual reserve position and meet reserve requirements on the settlement date. An institution's daily average vault cash held during the computation period previous to the period used for deposit calculation is subtracted from its required reserve liability.

Table 11.3 provides an example of the process followed in determining required reserves under the CRA. This table identifies the daily volume of reservable liabilities, vault cash, and reserve balances for a hypothetical bank over a given period of time. With the bank closed on Saturday and Sunday, data for these two days are the same as those recorded the preceding business day—in this case, Friday. The same principle would apply for a holiday. Daily vault cash figures during the preceding two-week period (days 1–14) must be averaged before calculating required reserves. Specifically, suppose the average daily level of vault cash held during the 14-day period was $9,650,000; this cash—according to regulatory provisions—may be counted toward the bank's required reserves. Also, suppose the average daily level of nontransaction liabilities for the same period was $425,000,000.

Transaction account balances must first be netted out by deducting demand balances due from depository institutions in the United States and cash items in process of collection. The resulting net daily figures are then averaged before being subjected to the statutory reserve requirements. Suppose the net average daily level of transaction accounts for days 15–28 was $613,000,000. The computation period for these accounts is almost concurrent with the reserve maintenance period, which runs from days 17 through 30. Suppose the bank's average daily reserve balances for the first 12 days of the maintenance period amounted to $47,917,000. The bank has the last two days of the maintenance period to make final adjustments in its reserve holdings to satisfy the minimum requirement. To identify the need for any adjustment, we must determine the level of required reserves.

Table 11.4 identifies the steps involved in calculating the sample bank's required reserves. The starting point is the bank's average daily transaction balances during the given 14-day computational period, per Table 11.3. The first tier (tranche) of net transaction accounts ($52 million), adjusted for the prescribed exemption of $4.3 million, is subject to a reserve requirement of 3 percent (see Table 11.2); the excess in transaction accounts is subject to 10 percent. Once required reserves are determined for each tranche and for the total amount of transaction accounts, the next step involves subtracting vault cash to determine the average daily required reserves to be held at the Federal Reserve bank. In the example given in Table 11.4, the hypothetical bank must maintain average daily reserves of $47.881 million; on a cumulative basis, this would amount to $670.334 million. With the cumulative total reserve balances for the first 12 days at $575 million, the average balance required for each of the next two days would be $47.667 million. As this amount is less than the actual average daily balances ($47.9 million), the bank should have no problem in meeting the minimum requirement at the close of the settlement date (day 30).

Banks do not have to meet required reserves each and every day of the maintenance period. A shortage early in the reserve maintenance period can be offset by a surplus later on, and vice versa. Despite the flexibility afforded by the use of averages and lagged accounting, bankers do not always succeed in meeting

Table 11.3
Reservable Liabilities, Vault Cash, and Reserve Balances (millions of dollars)

Lagged Computation Period			Contemporaneous Computation Period			Maintenance Period		
Day Number	Calendar Day	Vault Cash	Day Number	Calendar Day	Transaction Accounts, Net	Day Number	Calendar Day	Reserve Balances
1	T	$9.9	15	T	$611.9			
2	W	10.4	16	W	612.2			
3	T	9.4	17	T	612.8	17	T	$47.900
4	F	9.6	18	F	613.0	18	F	47.800
5	S	9.6	19	S	613.0	19	S	47.800
6	S	9.6	20	S	613.0	20	S	47.900
7	M	9.5	21	M	612.9	21	M	47.900
8	T	9.8	22	T	613.2	22	T	48.000
9	W	9.2	23	W	613.2	23	W	48.100
10	T	10.6	24	T	613.4	24	T	48.000
11	F	9.4	25	F	613.3	25	F	47.900
12	S	9.4	26	S	613.3	26	S	47.900
13	S	9.4	27	S	613.3	27	S	47.900
14	M	9.3	28	M	613.5	28	M	48.300
						29	T	
						30	W	
Average		$ 9.65			$613.000	12-day Average		$47.917

Source: Developed by the author.

Table 11.4
Calculation of Required Reserves

Item	14-Day Averages of Daily Data (millions of dollars)	Reserve Requirements (percent)	Required Reserves (millions of dollars)
Transaction accounts			
Average transaction accounts	$613.00		
Low reserve tranche (initial amount subject to reserves)	52.00		
Less exemption	4.3[a]		
Adjusted tranche	47.7	3	$ 1.431
Accounts over tranche	561.0	10	56.100
Total transaction reserves			$ 57.531
Vault cash (lagged)			
Less average vault cash			(9.65)
Average daily balance required			$ 47.881
Reserve position			
Cumulative total required reserves (daily average x 14)			$670.334
Less cumulative total balances achieved (12 days)			575.000
Total amount required for remaining two days			$ 95.334
Average balance required for each day ($95.334/2)			47.667
Maximum negative carryover allowed:			
Daily balance required x .04			1.915

[a]Represents the current amount in reservable liabilities subject to zero percent reserve requirements.
Source: Prepared by the author.

their reserve target. Recognizing this difficulty, the Federal Reserve has followed the policy of providing for a carryover allowance, which permits banks to carry forward into the next reserve period a reserve deficiency limited to 4 percent of the average daily required reserves for the current maintenance period. In the example of Table 11.4, the maximum allowable carryover of reserve deficiency into the next reserve period would be $1.9 million ($47.881 million $\times$ .04). A deficiency cannot be carried forward to additional periods following the period in which it occurs. However, alternation of reserve excesses and deficiencies from one period to another is permitted, provided the amounts involved in the carryforward process are within the allowable range. In other words, a deficiency in one period can be offset by an excess in the next period, and vice versa.

A bank with reserve deficiencies in two consecutive periods, or a reserve deficiency of more than 4 percent in any reserve period, is subject to a penalty. As indicated earlier in this section, the penalty rate on the deficiency is two percentage points over the going Federal Reserve bank discount rate. If the bank is consistently deficient, the Federal Reserve bank may enforce reserve requirements through moral suasion (by suspending membership privileges or denying a bank holding company application, for example). Ultimately, the Board of Governors may revert to the courts and initiate cease-and-desist proceedings against the violators. To avoid the penalties and sanctions, banks try to manage their reserve positions in a manner consistent with prescribed reserve accounting procedures.

Cash in Vault

Banks hold relatively little cash in their vaults to meet their day-to-day operating requirements. Such cash usually represents only a small percentage of the bank's primary reserves and is held to meet daily requests for coins and paper money. As might be expected, vault cash requirements vary widely among banks, and at any particular bank they vary from season to season. Experience teaches each bank when the heavy drains come (that is, on an annual, monthly, or weekly basis) as well as the times when a heavy cash inflow may be expected.

Since banks are the public cash depots, management must look at it as a service function not only to keep on hand the cash that regular and exceptional circumstances will call for, but also to keep it in the denominations and form that are demanded. Most banks replenish their cash supplies from the nearest Federal Reserve bank or branch, though some still get direct shipments from their city correspondents. The amount of cash in vault, then, is frequently related to the distance between a bank and its cash source, distance being measured in terms of the length of time needed to acquire such cash.

During the early 1960s the reserve-requirements regulation changed to permit member banks to include vault cash in computing their required reserves. This seemed justified on two counts: currency, which is the main component of vault cash, is chiefly in the form of Federal Reserve notes, which basically are the same as reserves in the Federal Reserve banks; and banks located a considerable distance from the Federal Reserve banks must hold more vault cash than those closer to their source of new currency.

Although member banks can count vault cash in meeting reserve requirements, they frequently try to minimize these holdings. Not only is it a question of a nonearning asset; it is also a problem of surety (that is, the risk of armed robberies or defalcating tellers). The least-cash-possible principle has been gaining widespread acceptance among banks. Thus banks with excess vault cash resulting from favorable over-the-counter balances may use it to replenish their reserves with the Federal Reserve banks or with correspondent banks, to pay off their borrowings from the Federal Reserve bank, or to increase their earning assets. On September 30, 1995, vault cash accounted for only 12.4 percent of the cash assets of all insured commercial banks.

MANAGING THE MONEY POSITION

Since cash assets produce no income, every effort is made by banks to manage them as effectively as possible. Effective cash management involves keeping the amount of funds held to meet legal and day-to-day operational requirements at a minimum. In many banks this task has been assigned to the money manager. In well-managed banks the money manager will carefully evaluate the cost-benefit relationship of the demand-deposit balances held with correspondent banks. He or she will strive to process and collect cash items as rapidly as possible, so that the bank can benefit from their early conversion from nonearning to earning assets. The money manager will take into account seasonal fluctuations and the bank's proximity to the Federal Reserve bank when determining the amount of vault cash holdings at any specific time. The most time-consuming task, however, is to make sure that the bank meets its legal reserve requirements within the time constraints discussed in the preceding section. Controlling the volume of bank balances at the Federal Reserve banks is a demanding task. The manager must see to it that during any maintenance period, reserve balances are, on average, at the target level, given the 4 percent carryover provision— that is, neither too high (because excess reserves cause the bank to sacrifice earnings) nor too low (because a reserve deficiency would be subject to a penalty charge).

To attain this objective, the money manager must develop a reserve strategy. A basic component of this strategy is the bank's required reserves. Because of the contemporaneous reserve accounting system, the reserve computation period and the reserve maintenance period overlap by 12 days. As a result, the money manager can establish only a tentative reserve target through the maintenance period until the exact reserve requirement is known at the end of the reserve computation. Once the reserve target is known, the next step is to meet it—that is, to ensure that the bank's reserve position matches the current period's requirement. The difficulty of this task stems from the effect that daily transactions may have upon reserve balances as the settlement date approaches. As stated earlier in this chapter, reserve balances at the Federal Reserve bank are affected daily by all the transactions through which payments flow into or out of the bank. Obviously, the larger the bank, the greater the number of transactions affecting its daily reserve position, and hence the more complicated the task of the money manager. Indeed, in many large money-center banks the size and frequency of transactions are such as to warrant continuous oversight of these banks' reserve positions. By contrast, smaller banks generally experience transactions of more limited size and frequency, which reduces the need for constant monitoring of reserve balances.

Forecasting the Reserve Position

Because of the immediate and unpredictable effect of daily transactions upon reserve balances, many banks try to forecast their expected positions on a day-by-day basis during the maintenance period. The large money-center banks incorporate reserve management into their overall asset-planning process. As a result, the reserve position of these banks is forecast by econometric models and is controlled within the framework of their other activities and plans. Other banks try to forecast their reserve positions through use of simpler statistical techniques. One such technique involves identifying the various transactions affecting reserve balances daily, measuring their effect on the bank's reserve position carried forward from the preceding day, and deriving the bank's new net reserve position for each day. Since the outcome of future events cannot be predicted with complete certainty, probabilities may be incorporated into these computations. In other words, probability coefficients may be attached to the range of likely reserve positions for each day. The ensuing computations would determine the mean reserve position and deviations (weighted for probability) from that mean. On the basis of these data, the money manager will then plan the course of action to be followed in order to meet reserve requirements. Other smaller banks do not engage in any formal planning. The money manager has some idea of the seasonal and other influences on the bank's reserve position at particular times of the year.

However rigorous or lax the methodology used, the resulting forecasts or anticipations should be based on all the transactions that influence a bank's reserve position on a daily basis. These reflect all the different services offered by the bank and the scope of its operations. Some of the more important kinds of transactions deserve mention. The net clearing of checks is the principal factor influencing a bank's reserve position. Frequently this figure is forecast on the basis of known influences and recurring seasonal patterns. Loan contracts must be taken into consideration because they represent funds flowing out as loans and back in as scheduled payments. Maturity dates for securities and certificates of deposit are also noted.

Other transactions incorporated in these forecasts include the planned purchases and sales of securities, currency and coin orders, transfers of funds into or out of correspondent accounts, and Treasury calls on tax and loan accounts. The financial officers of important corporate customers may be contacted to provide information on their plans for large deposits or withdrawals. Some of these officers may be willing to cooperate with the bank and provide advance notice of future transactions on a regular basis.

This and other information is collected by the money manager's office or—as it is generally referred to—the money desk, and is used to estimate the resulting change in reserve balances from one day to another and to determine the bank's net reserve position for each day of the maintenance period. In time the money desk will have the opportunity to cross-check each day's forecast against actual figures and to test the validity of the underlying assumptions. Differences between actual and expected amounts can be studied, and the insights gained will contribute to more realistic forecasts in the future.

Adjusting the Reserve Position

However closely monitored and well-managed the reserve position may be, problems are unavoidable. Unforeseen inflows or outflows can occur at any time during the maintenance period, and it is up to the money desk to decide what course of action is warranted and when to put it into effect. Clearly, developments early in the maintenance period offer more latitude for adjustment than last-minute ones. In the latter instance any adjustment may be very costly, since other banks are in the market at the same time, trying to balance their reserves before the close of the settlement date. A need for corrective action frequently surfaces on Fridays. Since banks are closed during the weekend, the reserve balance that the bank achieves Friday afternoon will also be its balance for Saturday and Sunday. Thus, a large Fedwire inflow late on a Friday afternoon, assuming a reasonably balanced reserve position, would result in sizable excess reserves. If Monday is a holiday, the bank would be locked into a surplus reserve position for three days. Unless the money manager anticipates offsetting transactions during the remaining working days of the maintenance period (such as Tuesday and Wednesday), the bank will forgo income unnecessarily. In such a case the money manager may adjust the bank's excess reserve position by placing these funds profitably—by selling federal funds, purchasing securities through repurchase agreements, or purchasing securities outright (such as Treasury bills).

The opposite situation will arise if a bank sustains an outflow of funds. For example, an unexpected outflow on the settlement date, assuming a reasonably balanced reserve position, would result in a reserve deficiency and a need for immediate corrective action. The money manager of the bank will have a choice of alternatives in the final hours of the reserve period. A decision will have to be made and transactions executed in short-term liabilities or short-term assets. In other words, it is a matter of deciding between using liability-management or asset-management techniques in adjusting the bank's reserve position. In the former instance, funds may be raised quickly by purchase of federal funds, borrowing of Eurodollars, selling of securities under repurchase agreements, or borrowing from the Federal Reserve bank. Any of these techniques ensures the immediate availability of funds and makes possible the rapid adjustment of a bank's reserve position. Alternatively, the money manager may opt to sell short-term assets or use the proceeds of maturing short-term assets to adjust the reserve position.

Two of the considerations that weigh significantly in deciding which of the alternatives to use will be the duration for which the additional reserve funds are needed and the cost involved in choosing one alternative over another. It may, for example, be found more costly to sell securities than to borrow from another bank, particularly if the market price of securities has declined or if the additional funds to correct the bank's reserve position are needed only overnight. Again, it may be found more desirable to borrow funds than to call in outstanding loans. The methods more frequently used by money managers for short-run adjustments are the liability-management techniques mentioned above (other liability-management techniques are not customarily relied upon because they take more time to execute). But to effect long-run adjustments in the reserve position, money managers are more likely to liquidate short-term assets. In the final analysis, the choice between using asset or liability liquidity in adjusting the bank's reserve position is entirely up to the individual bank. Not infrequently such choice reflects the overall reliance of bank policy upon either type of management: asset or liability.

NOTE

1. Roland I. Robinson, *The Management of Bank Funds*, 2nd ed. (New York: Mc-Graw-Hill, 1962), p. 71.

SUGGESTED REFERENCES

Feinman, Joshua N. "Reserve Requirements: History, Current Practice, and Potential Reform." *Federal Reserve Bulletin*, June 1993, pp. 569–89.

Garber, Peter, and Steven Weisbrod. "Banks in the Market for Liquidity." National Bureau of Economic Research Working Paper no. 3381, June 1990.

Goodfriend, Marvin. "The Promise and Pitfalls of Contemporaneous Reserve Requirements for the Implementation of Monetary Policy." Federal Reserve Bank of Richmond, *Economic Review*, May/June 1984, pp. 3–12.

Roberds, William. "Changes in Payments Technology and the Welfare Cost of Inflation." Federal Reserve Bank of Atlanta, *Economic Review*, May/June 1994, pp. 1–12.

Sargent, Thomas J., and Neil Wallace. "Interest on Reserves." *Journal of Monetary Economics* 15 (1985): 279–90.

Chapter 12

Bank Lending: Evolution and Current Scope

The core function of commercial banks is the granting of credit. Although banks offer a wide spectrum of financial services, lending has traditionally been their main function. Banks profess experience, expertise, and flexibility in lending, which gives them a clear competitive advantage over all other financial institutions. Bank credit has been responsible for the development and growth of many small and moderate-size businesses that otherwise would have withered and died. By providing credit, banks have contributed to the growth of their respective communities and the advance of local economic well-being.

Aside from its public-service character, bank lending is a quite profitable activity. In fact, it is the most profitable activity of commercial banking, and hence the greatest contributor to bank profits. Income from loans and loan-related activities accounted on September 30, 1995, for 63 percent of total operating income. The remaining 37 percent was contributed by many other activities of commercial banks.

The loan function is important on other grounds. Lending is instrumental in creating and maintaining good deposit relationships, which are essential for the furthering of bank lending. The close and continuing contact established with the borrower is also instrumental in broadening the market for other bank services.

The above helps explain the prominent place of loans among bank assets and, more specifically, vis-à-vis investments, a bank's second major category of earning assets. There are distinctive differences between the acquisition of each of these assets. As noted earlier, investments constitute open-market purchases of securities, some of which serve as secondary reserves, while loans constitute direct customer demand for funds. Investments are evidences of interest-bearing debt offered for sale in the open market, and the acquiring bank does not anticipate establishing a continuous or permanent relationship with the issuing company. In other words, the acquisition of securities is generally conducted impersonally and is influenced by objective criteria, such as relative interest rate, quality of the issue (rating), maturity, and marketability. Banks purchase these securities either at the time they are issued or later on, by acquiring them from other investors in the open market. A loan, on the other hand, is arranged through direct, face-to-face negotiation between the borrower and the lending bank, and hence is personal. Bank lending is thus influenced significantly by subjective criteria, such as the borrower's character, the type and length of the borrower's relationship with the bank, and the new business potentially generated for the bank.

These differences between loans and investments make apparent the need for well-formulated loan policies and practices. Sound lending policies and practices are reflected in the quality of the loan account and, hence, in bank solvency. Throughout most of the history of commercial banking, the quality of the loan portfolios has been closely linked with banks' solvency. This traditional link between the quality of loans and banks' solvency exists because banks' loan portfolios contain the bulk of their assets. This chapter provides a historical overview of the evolution of loan portfolios, examines the current nature and scope of commercial bank lending, and describes securitization—the development of secondary markets for loans other than mortgages. The historical section is essential because it ties past experiences to the present and focuses upon the factors that have influenced and shaped loan portfolios then and now.

EVOLUTION OF THE LOAN PORTFOLIO: A HISTORICAL VIEW

Loan portfolios have existed since the early days of commercial banking, in response to theories of bank liquidity management. Four different theories of liquidity can be identified: the commercial-loan theory, the shiftability theory, the anticipated-income theory, and the liability-management theory. The first three relate to asset management, and the last focuses on the management of liabilities.

The Commercial-Loan Theory

The commercial-loan theory of credit—also referred to as the "real bills doctrine"[1]—dates back to the eighteenth century and is of English origin. Bank lending to merchants traditionally took the form of discounting commercial bills (the standard IOU used by merchants). The discounting of bills was viewed as a safe and liquid loan practice; it was backed by the goods involved in the transaction, the imminent sale of which would generate the proceeds to pay off the bank. This practice led to the development of the commercial bills doctrine or commercial-loan theory. Formulated by Adam Smith in *The Wealth of*

Nations, it influenced commercial banking activity in the United States from colonial times through the 1930s. It exerted significant influence on the National Bank Act of 1863 and the Federal Reserve Act of 1913, the cornerstones of U.S. banking legislation.

According to this theory, the earning assets of commercial banks must be in the form of short-term, self-liquidating loans extended to businesses for the financing of their inventory needs. In other words, banks should be financing the processing of goods and their movement from the production to the consumption stage. These loans were viewed as self-liquidating because they generated the means for their repayment—that is, the goods acquired or produced on credit, when sold, provided the funds to repay the loan. By financing this type of loan, banks, it was held, would possess the most liquid earning assets, and therefore would be able to meet their demand-deposit liabilities when called upon to do so. Banking was thus related to the financing of commerce, which helps explain the original reference to the institutions extending this kind of loan as "commercial" banks.

The commercial-loan theory has three basic weaknesses. First, it ignores other types of credit needs, such as loans to finance the acquisition of equipment and machinery, or the purchase of residential and nonresidential property and consumer goods. As a result, other kinds of financial institutions—such as savings and loan associations, credit unions, and finance companies—were formed to serve these credit needs of individuals and businesses. Second, it rests on an overly cautious view regarding deposit withdrawals. It assumes that all demand depositors will withdraw their funds at the same time. Experience has shown that demand deposits possess a higher degree of stability than is assumed by the theory. Since withdrawals are to a large extent offset by simultaneous deposits, the bank need not confine itself to short-term placement of these funds. Third, in periods of recession or depression, loans may not be self-liquidating because many borrowers have difficulty in repaying them. But under normal circumstances, too, short-term loans may not be self-liquidating. For example, a firm's continued need for working capital or use of the loan proceeds to purchase long-term assets may force the bank to renew the loan. Thus, what was officially characterized as a short-term loan may effectively become long-term.

Despite the limitations of the commercial-loan theory, many bankers still favor short-term, self-liquidating loans over other types. Risk exposure is easier to evaluate and is generally more limited than with other loans. Also, even though banks have numerous options for meeting their liquidity needs, these loans continue to represent an important source of liquidity.

The Shiftability Theory

This theory holds that as long as a bank's assets are shiftable (readily marketable), its liquidity is adequately maintained. For example, if loans can be discounted to the Federal Reserve bank or if their collateral can be readily sold in the event of default, they are deemed to be sufficiently liquid. Similarly, securities, which can easily be converted to cash, possess a high degree of liquidity. In essence, the shiftability theory considers the marketability of an asset to be the main source of liquidity, and hence to be the qualifying attribute for its acquisition by a bank.

Originated by H. G. Moulton in 1918,[2] this theory became increasingly popular during the long bull market of the 1920s. Entry of the United States into World War I and the need to finance the war led to the issuance of large—by contemporary standards—amounts of government bonds (the Liberty Loan bonds and later the Victory Loan bonds) that raised public debt from $1 billion to $26 billion. To encourage banks to buy these bonds, the Federal Reserve System amended the Federal Reserve Act and allowed banks to offer these securities as collateral against their borrowing from Federal Reserve banks. Advances collateralized by government securities were thus placed on an equal footing with the discounting of real bills at the Federal Reserve banks. This development, along with the growth of a national market for government issues, made these securities an attractive asset for commercial banks. Convinced that government securities were more marketable than loans, and hence a superior source of liquidity, banks were drawn into the government securities market.

Although prior to World War I it was considered inappropriate to purchase or hold securities, some banks held such securities among their assets. This was generally true of national banks, which were required by law to maintain securities as collateral against their issues of banknotes. In all other instances, holdings of securities were in violation of the prevailing principles of banking theory, if not of practice.

The booming securities markets in the 1920s led banks to include corporate bonds and foreign bonds in their investment holdings and to engage in investment-banking activities. Banks' investment excesses during this decade were criticized in the early 1930s and led to legislation that restrained many of their investment activities. The legislation of this era and, more important, the prevailing economic conditions led banks to expand their holdings of government securities to sizable proportions. Economic conditions were affected by two major events: the depression of the 1930s and World War II. In the 1930s the depression brought in most countries both a sharp decline in the private demand for loans and a substantial increase in government borrowing to finance budgetary deficits. Throughout World War II commercial banks bought substantial amounts of government securities, as a result of both a huge increase in government borrowing and a contraction in the demand for loans by private borrowers.

Commercial banks thus became important holders of government securities, which far outstripped the volume of bank loans. The paramount position of the Treasury among commercial bank borrowers is reflected in the relevant data of the era. In 1945 Federal Reserve member bank holdings of U.S. government securities reached an unprecedented height, accounting for 73 percent of the earning assets of all member banks. If all other securities held by these banks are taken into consideration, investments constituted 79 percent of their earning assets and loans but 21 percent. Drastic as it may have been, this change in the composition of banks' earning-asset portfolios was but a deviation from a historic asset distribution pattern in commercial banking. Indeed, throughout banking history loans have exceeded investments, usually by a wide margin. This normal asset pattern also characterizes the post-World War II period.

The Anticipated-Income Theory

With the end of World War II, the composition of the earning assets of commercial banks began to change as resources shifted back from the government to the private sector. The spectacular rise in the loan demand of the immediate postwar years provided commercial banks with strong incentives to expand their loan portfolios, and hence to increase bank earnings. However, the almost exclusive reliance of Federal Reserve policy throughout this period on bank credit restraint to promote a sustainable rate of economic growth and to counter inflationary pressures led commercial banks to monetize part of their holdings of government securities in order to meet the postwar credit needs of the nation's expanding economy. Thus banks began to make loans that were of longer maturity, covered a much wider variety of borrowers, and extended to many more purposes than originally envisaged. More important, however, this move reflected the ongoing changes in banking attitudes. The sharp decline in the demand for loans in the 1930s had generated substantial pressures upon banks to seek and consider new outlets for their funds. These pressures, accentuated by the banks' dwindling proportion of savings flowing into nonbank financial institutions, forced important changes in bank attitudes toward extending maturities in their loan portfolios. Moreover, bank management had acquired more experience in meeting deposit withdrawals and had gained more confidence in its ability to design portfolios that were only partly composed of short-term or highly liquid assets. In other words, they had found that through prudent asset management, a mixture of very liquid and not-so-liquid assets could achieve the desired degree of overall liquidity.

Thus, the loan portfolios of commercial banks in the postwar years have included such items as intermediate- and long-term loans to consumers, home owners, and business firms that would not qualify as liquid assets under the traditional theory of bank liquidity and would qualify only in part, if at all, under the shiftability theory. However, loans of this type do qualify under the "anticipated-income theory" of liquidity developed in 1949 by Herbert V. Prochnow.[3] This theory argues that a bank can maintain its liquidity if loan repayments are scheduled on the basis of the anticipated income of the borrower rather than the use made of the funds or the collateral offered. Thus, in making loans of the type cited above, this theory suggests that banks should rely on debtors' income and its coverage of debt-service requirements. This coverage is determined on the basis of inclusive cash-flow projections, which ordinarily provide a reliable indication of the quality of the loan being financed. Hence, the future cash flow of the borrower, rather than the nature of particular transactions being financed, assures the self-liquidating character of a loan because it will determine a borrower's overall ability to meet interest and principal payments as they fall due. If the debtors' anticipated income is estimated correctly, the bank will have a flow of funds that can be used to meet depositors' claims and/or other loan demands. During normal times, bank lending of this type would function in about the same way as bank lending based on the commercial-loan theory of liquidity.

The Liability-Management Theory

Since the early 1960s the loan portfolios of commercial banks have been affected by the emergence of a new theory, which became known as the liability-management theory. As stated earlier, liability-management banking was originated by large New York City banks under strong pressures at the time: growing demand for loans as the economy experienced recovery from the 1960–61 recession, plus an inadequate growth of deposits at these banks. According to this new doctrine, it is no longer necessary for a bank to observe traditional liquidity standards if it can go into the market and bid for funds whenever it experiences a need for liquidity. In other words, a bank can meet its liquidity needs by creating additional liabilities. There are a number of possible sources on which the individual bank may draw to meet liquidity needs during the last phase of periods of cyclical expansion, such as issuing CDs, purchasing federal funds, borrowing at the Federal Reserve, issuing short-term notes, and borrowing from the Eurodollar market. The importance of these sources and the impact of Federal Reserve regulation upon their effectiveness have been discussed in chapters 6 and 7.

Liability management has been viewed as a major banking innovation and, as such, it has significantly influenced the outlook of bankers. It is a far cry from traditional banking and the need for short-term, self-liquidating commercial loans. Bank lending is symptomatic of new attitudes that are becoming increasingly general in the banking industry. There is no longer such a thing as a standard bank loan or borrower. Although some classes of borrowers and loan arrangements are more characteristic than others, bank lending has been evolving in response to new opportunities. For the most part, opportunity has been the mother of innovation, to paraphrase an old saying. The fact that banks have been so alert to opportunities and so resourceful in exploiting them is a plus factor in any assessment of the U.S. financial system.

Table 12.1
Loans and Leases of All Insured Commercial Banks, 1995

Type	Amount (millions of dollars)	Percent of Total
Real estate	$1,070,946	41.8
Construction and land development	68,115	2.6
Secured by farmland	23,893	0.9
Secured by 1 to 4 family residential property	622,091	24.3
Secured by multifamily residential property	35,286	1.4
Secured by nonfarm nonresidential property	294,364	11.5
Other	27,197	1.1
Commercial and industrial	647,434	25.3
Loans to individuals, total	518,475	20.2
Credit cards and related plans	200,618	7.8
Other consumer loans	317,857	12.4
Loans to depository institutions	84,000	3.3
Loans to finance agricultural production and other loans to farmers	41,870	1.6
All other loans	146,395	5.7
Lease financing receivables	52,509	2.0
Total	$2,561,629	100.0

Note: Details may not add to totals due to rounding.
Source: Federal Deposit Insurance Corporation, *Call Report*, September 1995.

LENDING ACTIVITY OF COMMERCIAL BANKS

Although loans can be classified in a variety of ways, the most meaningful presentation of statistics on the lending activity of commercial banks is by borrower or purpose for which funds are used. This criterion is commonly employed by regulatory authorities in identifying the scope and magnitude of the lending activity of commercial banks. Table 12.1 presents information regarding the loans and leases of all insured commercial banks on September 30, 1995. Loans and leases outstanding totaled $2.6 trillion, compared with a mere $38 billion in 1947. The various types of loans and their relative importance are shown in Table 12.1 and reflect the current pattern of customer credit demands. The first three loan categories are the dominant ones, accounting for about 87 percent of the total. The various types of loans made by banks are discussed below.

Commercial and Industrial Loans

One-fourth of all loans granted in late 1995, according to Table 12.1, were commercial and industrial loans. These loans are usually much more important, both relatively and absolutely, for large money-center banks than for middle-size and small banks. Part of the rise in large money-center bank lending came from foreign business borrowing. These loans involved the financing of plant expansion or working capital needs of businesses located in less-developed countries, where credit has generally been tighter and, hence, relatively expensive.

Some of the loans extended to businesses are secured and others are not. The businesses that can borrow on an unsecured basis usually have an adequate capital base, a record of meeting their financial obligations promptly, a good earnings performance, a potential for growth, and, above all, an efficient and effective management. These firms generally constitute the elite of their respective business communities and are a bank's most creditworthy customers. As a result these firms—customarily referred to as prime borrowers—are charged the lowest rate of interest, or prime rate, on short-term loans.

Loans to businesses take different forms, depending upon the needs being financed. Some of the more important financial arrangements that banks have traditionally extended to businesses are discussed in the following paragraphs.

Open Line of Credit

Assume that a company that has been a regular customer of a bank determines from its cash-flow forecast a need for a certain amount of funds at the low point of the season. The company may request a seasonal loan in the form of a line of credit for a period usually not exceeding 90 days, supporting this request with current and forecast financial statements. If the request is approved by the bank, the company will have access to a credit facility that it can use as needed during the specified period. Open lines of credit are unsecured and are usually made available on a floating-rate basis; that is, the rate charged is tied to the bank's prime rate. In essence the open line of credit is an informal arrangement, oral or written, whereby a bank agrees to lend up to a stated maximum amount to a firm for a specified period of time. The bank is not legally bound to supply the funds. For example, the bank has the legal right to refuse the loan request in the event of an extreme shortage of loanable funds resulting from tight credit conditions. Although this arrangement is not a binding contract, banks tend to feel a moral obligation to honor requests made under open lines of credit.

Standby Commitment

This is a more formal and binding arrangement. Here the bank enters into a formal contract with the borrowing company and commits to extend to it the agreed-upon amount for a specified period of time. For this commitment the borrower pays a fee (commitment fee) that ranges between 0.25 and 0.75 percent (on an annualized basis) of either the unused portion of the commitment or the entire amount, regardless of usage. The agreement customarily contains provisions covering the amount of the facility, the time availability of funds, the rate of interest charged (which is usually floating), and security.

Working-Capital Loans

Many businesses have credit needs that cover a period longer than a season. For example, a manufacturing concern with a long production cycle may need to borrow working capital to acquire raw materials and to finance the production process until the goods are sold. Such a company needs a working-capital loan to draw upon. Repayment of the loan will be made from the current sales of the firm and the conversion of accounts receivable to cash. Some banks require the borrowing company to stay out of debt to the bank for at least one or two months during the year. This "annual cleanup" provision is intended to ensure that the facility is not used as a means of permanent financing through continuous renewals. It also gives the bank the opportunity to reevaluate the borrower periodically and to decide whether to continue its financing.

Bridge Loans

Bridge loans extend temporary financing on the assumption that repayment will be made with funds from a prearranged source. Because they bridge a gap in a borrower's financing, these loans are also known as *gap financing*. For example, a business may obtain interim financing from a bank to construct a new manufacturing facility until the old facility can be sold. Similarly, a firm may obtain a short-term loan from a bank to cover the time lag between redemption of a bond or a commercial-paper issue, and its replacement by another issue. The quality of bridge loans depends on the certainty of the timing and the amount of the anticipated funds from the prearranged source(s).

Revolving Credit

This arrangement has some similarities to the standby commitment. Like standby credit, this is a formal, contractual agreement that obligates the bank to make funds available to the borrower on demand. The borrower pays a fee for this commitment ranging from 0.50 to 0.75 percent of either the unborrowed amount or the entire commitment. Unlike the standby credit, however, the revolving credit represents a specialized arrangement that provides for both the seasonal and the longer-term working-capital needs of businesses. Revolving credits usually run for three to five years and represent a form of intermediate credit. The following example identifies the sort of circumstances that give rise to a revolving-credit facility. Assume a firm is planning to expand its operations on a regional scale. Uncertain of the precise amount of funds needed or the timing of their disbursement, it may apply for a revolving credit. If the request is approved, funds will be taken down as needed and repaid at the borrower's option, with the bank committed to continue lending up to the maximum amount stated in the revolving-credit agreement until its expiration. The details covering the revolving credit are customarily spelled out in the agreement, which contains provisions on amount of credit, rate of interest charged, maturities of the notes, and security. At maturity, the revolving credit may be paid off or rolled over, in response to the particular needs of individual borrowers. Often, revolving-credit agreements include a provision that at their expiration, the entire amount borrowed will be incorporated into a term loan.

Term Loans

This is an intermediate type of credit. A term loan is usually defined as a loan to a business firm with an original maturity of more than one year. In the early and experimental period of term lending, maturities tended to be short—from one to five years. As banks became more confident of their ability to provide such credit safely, term-loan maturities were extended up to ten years, and not infrequently they now exceed this limit.

Most term loans are amortized regularly (monthly, quarterly, semiannually, or annually), according to an installment schedule. In some cases repayment provisions may call for a large portion of the loan (such as 15–20 percent of the principal) to be paid at the end in the form of a balloon payment. The purpose of such a provision is to permit the borrower an increased cash flow in the early years of the loan and thus afford greater financial flexibility. Occasionally repayment provisions may call for installments of irregular size and timing, based on the borrower's cash-flow projections. Term loans are thus easily adapted to financing the credit needs of a business whose ability to repay is related to its anticipated earning power.

Term loans have been sought by and made to businesses that are either too small to raise money in the capital market by the sale of bonds and stocks, or have access to such markets but find term borrowing more advantageous for a variety of reasons: loan maturity or repayment schedule is tailored to borrower's needs; there is greater flexibility in dealing with a single lender than with a large number of bondholders; capital-market conditions may be unfavorable for the issuance of securities. Looked at from the side of the bank, term loans replace intermediate- and long-term corporate bonds, which a bank would otherwise be buying and carrying in its bond portfolio, and have the added advantage of protective provisions in the loan agreement that permit the bank to exercise more control over the debtor and its activities than would be true if it carried bonds. Term loans are usually made to businesses that have heavy fixed-capital requirements (e.g., petroleum refining, mining, chemicals and rubber, and public utilities). Term loans are used for a number of purposes, including the financing of working-capital increases and the purchase or improvement of fixed assets (plant, equipment, and machinery). They represent one of the few means available for the financing of fixed capital by small and medium-size firms.

A special type of term loan is the bullet loan. This loan provides for regular interest payments throughout the life of the loan and a single principal (balloon) payment at maturity. In this respect it resembles a bond issue. Bullet loans mature between five and ten years, and are usually made on a floating-rate basis. These loans may be repaid, in whole or in part, prior to maturity without penalty.

Project Loans

These loans are among the most profitable loans made by banks. Project loans usually finance the construction of high-risk, high-cost projects that are beyond the financial capacity of a single creditor. Such multibillion-dollar projects include refineries, pipelines, and mining facilities. In some instances these projects are undertaken by private interests that contribute equity capital to create a new legal entity that will own and operate the facility. The sponsor-owners then approach various banks to secure a project loan, which usually accounts for 80–90 percent of the venture's capital. The lender assumes several significant risks in the financing of a project. These are highlighted below and reflect the experiences of both domestic and foreign banks in the financing of major international projects.

In the first place, the lender assumes a credit (default) risk, the risk that the borrower will fail to meet contractual obligations when due (make timely payments of interest and/or principal). In evaluating this risk a bank encounters a number of difficulties. The borrower has no financial history. Moreover, the project being financed is new, which means that the merit of the loan must be based solely on long-range forecasts. One such forecast is the project's cash flow, which will determine amortization of the loan. Since projects typically require a long time to complete, the project's cash flow during the construction period will be nil. As a result, the bank should allow a grace period in loan amortization. What this means is that the bank should fund (accrue) interest payments throughout the construction phase. From the moment the project is completed and operations begin, any estimates of cash flows for debt service are based on subjective judgment, since the market prices for end products or services are difficult to forecast and the borrower has little, if any, control over them. Regardless of prices, however, if operations prove unprofitable, the bank will have a difficult time selling the physical facilities and avoiding any losses on the loan.

Completion delays are another risk lenders must face, since such long-term projects are frequently subject to delays and disruptions. This risk is higher in projects that are a part of an extended system. For example, if a project provides for the financing of a plant designed to supply chemicals, delays in the construction of the plant or in the transportation facilities may delay operation of the project over an extended period of time.

There can also be an interest-rate risk if the project is financed at a fixed rate of interest. This risk can be shifted to the borrower by financing the project on a floating-rate basis. Thus, an increase in interest rates is passed on to the borrower. If the project's profit margins are significant, the added interest cost will be absorbed without difficulty. Otherwise, an undue burden is placed upon the project, undermining its financial viability.

If the project is in a foreign country, the bank is also exposed to country risk during both the construction phase and the subsequent operation. This risk refers to the political, economic, and social conditions in the country of the borrower that may adversely affect repayment of the loan. For example, the host government may nationalize the venture, or its operations may be disrupted by political tensions, civil unrest, violence, or rebellion. The profitability and eventual viability of the venture may also be affected by such economic factors as heavy taxation, price controls, and government red tape. Moreover, religious, tribal, linguistic, or other social differences may eventually lead to political and economic tension and undermine company operations. These and other forces (such as foreign-exchange controls and currency devaluation) may make it impossible for the company to meet its obligations on time. A bank's country risk exposure is moderated if the project is owned by the government or if the government is one of the project's sponsors.

These risks, though seemingly formidable, can be reduced in a number of ways. Banks can shift the risk to sponsors by requiring their guaranty of debt servicing. Guaranties by the parent companies are particularly common. Banks also limit their exposure by forming, or participating in, a syndicate that assumes the financing of the project. It is a common practice for banks to form a syndicate to participate in a large loan to a borrower, regardless of whether the borrower is a domestic or a foreign concern. As a result, a bank's risk exposure is limited to the amount of the participation in the syndicated loan. In addition, banks try to reduce their exposure by diversifying their credits. In the case of foreign loans, they try to spread them over several countries rather than concentrate them in a single country. If the loan is denominated in a foreign currency, the bank may manage its foreign-exchange risk by hedging in the futures market (e.g., sell futures contracts in that currency to avoid a major loss in loan proceeds). Of course it is not always possible to hedge with futures contracts because there is no futures market in many currencies; or if it exists, the maturity of the contract is limited, in which case the bank may have to enter into successive hedging transactions over the life of the loan.

Letters of Credit

Businesses that engage in international activities make frequent use of letter-of-credit financing. This financing may take the form of a commercial letter of credit or a standby letter of credit. The commercial letter of credit relies on a bank's substituting its own reputation for that of a buyer who is unknown to the seller. The seller then looks to the bank for payment, which is made either immediately or within a specified number of days after the date of the draft. The international effectiveness of this form of financing has encouraged its increasing use in domestic transactions.

The standby letter of credit is a bank's guarantee of payment to a third party should the client (in whose favor the letter is issued) fail to meet his financial obligations or perform according to a contract. The issuing bank is not ordinarily expected to make any payments; however, if it does, the borrower is obligated to repay the bank promptly. In domestic transactions, standby letters of credit are used, as stated in Chapter 7, as backup for the issuance by companies of commercial paper and other obligations. Standby letters of credit also have application in international transactions. This type of credit has been used extensively by large banks to guarantee the performance of American companies under contract to foreign concerns. Standby letters are customarily requested by these concerns (such as foreign governments) as evidence of good faith in fulfilling the terms of the contract. These contracts may call for the construction of dams, military installations, or even villages. Although some transactions involve a higher degree of risk than others, letter-of-credit financing is popular with banks because of the income derived from fees.

Loan Participations

An outgrowth of correspondent banking has been the development of loan participations, which involve the purchase or sale of commercial loans to other banking institutions. Various reasons have given rise to the development of this practice. Certain banks, because of the strong loan demands in their communities, resort to selling some of the loans in their portfolios to other banks to replenish their liquidity. Another reason is the unavailability of local loan outlets, which induces banks to acquire loans originated by other banks. In addition, the credit needs of a business may exceed the legal lending limit of a bank (15 percent of the bank's capital and surplus for unsecured loans). Rather than turning down the loan request, with potentially adverse implications, the bank may sell the amount in excess of its credit limit (known as overline) to a correspondent bank. A final reason for loan participation is the need to control risk in the portfolio by spreading loans among different borrowers and over different geographic areas.

In recent years nonbank financial institutions have become increasingly involved in loan participations. Insurance companies and pension funds are significant buyers of loans originated and packaged by commercial banks. Since these institutions generally prefer longer-term credits than banks do, frequently they join a bank and fund a loan together. For example, in a 15-year loan to a business, it may be agreed that the principal payments made in the first seven years go to the bank and the payments made in the last eight years go to the insurance company. The interest rate charged may differ for each portion of the loan because of differences in the degree of risk assumed. For example, the rate of interest paid to the insurance company may be higher than the rate paid to the bank.

When considering a loan participation, a bank should always review all information available about the borrower, just as with any other loan request. Some participants have sustained losses because they failed to exercise their independent judgment, relying instead on the credit experience of the originating bank. Such was the case with many of the leading U.S. banks, which in the early 1980s bought $2 billion of energy-related loans originated by the Penn

Square Bank.* The drastic decline in gas and oil prices experienced during these years precipitated the failure of the bank and sizable losses in the portfolios of the participant banks.[4]

Consumer Loans

Consumer credit is defined by the Federal Reserve's Board of Governors as loans to individuals for household, family, and personal expenditures (except for real-estate mortgage loans). Consumer credit is of two types, noninstallment and installment. Noninstallment is all consumer credit that is scheduled to be repaid in one lump sum. Service credit (such as doctors' bills), nonrevolving charge accounts granted by merchants, and all single-payment loans to individuals are examples of noninstallment credit. Banks generally dominate this type of credit, essentially because other consumer-credit suppliers prefer to lend on an installment basis in order to obtain a rate of return high enough to cover the cost of their funds and operating expenses. Installment credit consists of all consumer credit that is scheduled to be repaid in two or more payments. Clearly, the convenience to the borrower of repaying a portion of the debt each month or payday, rather than at one time, has contributed to the phenomenal use of installment credit, which on September 30, 1995, amounted to $966.5 billion (91 percent of the total consumer credit outstanding from all sources). Banks are the primary source of installment credit, surpassing retailers and all other financial institutions supplying such credit. In September 1995, banks' installment loans amounted to $300 billion, which represented 45 percent of the total installment credit outstanding. Some of the more important types of installment credit are described below.

Automobile Loans and Loans to Finance Other Consumer Goods

The dominant type of installment credit extended by banks is the auto loan, financing the purchase of a new or used automobile. Other consumer goods financed through installment loans include mobile homes, household appliances, boats, and furniture. Banks handle this type of financing in two ways: lending directly to the borrower or purchasing dealer installment contracts. The chief benefit of indirect lending is that it provides a means of acquiring a substantial volume of loans without incurring the costs in money and manpower of attracting and assessing each individual borrower. However, there are several drawbacks to this type of financing. Because the bank forgoes the opportunity to evaluate the individual customer, it must rely on the judgment and standards of the dealer who extends the credit. As a result, there may be a greater possibility of failure, fraud, or forgery. Since the credit transaction is in effect secured,

---

*Some of the banks involved, and the corresponding amounts of energy-related loans bought, were Continental Illinois Corporation ($1 billion), Chase Manhattan Corporation ($200 to $300 million), Seafirst Corporation ($400 million), Michigan National Corporation ($200 million), and Northern Trust Corporation ($125 million).

from the dealer's point of view, by the item purchased, the dealer may be less than meticulous in appraising a customer's creditworthiness, reasoning that if payments stop, the item can be repossessed. Similarly, the customer may not take seriously the obligation to meet the installment schedule, reasoning that the only risk is the repossession of the item purchased. Finally, the bank, by purchasing paper in volume, cannot build a customer relationship with the actual beneficiaries of the credit.

Revolving Credit

Another type of installment credit is the revolving credit, which includes credit cards and check credit plans. Banks began to issue credit cards in the early 1950s, following entry into this field by other major issuers, such as oil companies, department stores, and travel and entertainment firms. Although they were relative latecomers, banks played a decisive role in the success of credit cards in the United States and abroad.

Each cardholder has a preauthorized line of credit with the bank issuing the credit card. When making a purchase with a credit card, the buyer signs a sales draft of a retail merchant, who presents the draft to the bank for full payment minus a service charge of 3 to 4 percent. In essence the bank is financing the merchant's accounts receivable at a cost significantly lower than the cost of operating a credit department, which has been estimated at between 5 and 6 percent of sales. The cardholder is billed by the bank that issued the credit card. The cardholder has the option of paying the draft in full, typically within 25 days, or paying only a portion, with the remainder paid in installments. Banks' income from these operations consists of the service charges and the interest-rate charges to consumers on the unpaid balance.

Over the years two distinct types of cardholders have emerged, depending upon the pattern of credit card use. The *convenience users* pay the amount owed in full when billed and consequently incur no monthly interest charges. By contrast, the *revolving credit users* rarely pay off their entire outstanding monthly balances and use the credit card as a source of credit. The former group uses the credit card because it minimizes the need to carry cash, defers payment for the goods and services purchased for a little while, and builds a favorable payment record. The latter group realizes the same benefits, plus an increased ability over time to finance purchases without the red tape of a personal loan. Convenience users generally account for 10–20 percent of a given portfolio of receivables. The remaining 80–90 percent actually revolves each month and is hence subject to finance charges. The presence of convenience usage reduces the expected yield on a credit card portfolio. For example, a credit card portfolio with an 18 percent annual percentage rate (APR) and a 20 percent convenience usage will yield 14.4 percent annually in gross interest income (that is, 80 percent of the receivables are subject to an 18 percent finance charge). When considering typical annual membership fees, the effective portfolio yield may increase by as much as 3–6 percent.

For high-risk customers banks have introduced the secured credit card. The cardholder is usually an individual with little or no credit history or a bad credit record. To obtain a credit card, he or she must deposit at the bank an amount equal to the desired credit limit. The bank may or may not pay interest on this deposit. Chase Manhattan Bank, for example, introduced its secured credit cards in late 1993, charging an annual fee and a fixed rate of interest of 17.9 percent. The credit lines offered ranged from $450 to $5,000. Currently there are some 450,000 secured cardholders in this country, and experts predict that this number may eventually increase to 30 million.

The increased popularity and use of credit cards has greatly diminished the other type of revolving credit, check credit plans. Check credit plans involve only two parties, the bank and the consumer. After appropriate screening, the bank provides a consumer a preauthorized line of credit that is utilized when the individual writes checks above the limits of his or her account. These plans are customarily referred to as overdraft accounts. A similar type of plan involves the use of specially coded or denominated checks that are used to purchase goods and services. The bank sets up a special checking account to pay these checks and charges the individual interest on the unpaid balance.

Consumer Protection Laws

In recent years there has been a tremendous increase in legislation that provides protection for the consumer.* The first, passed by Congress in 1968, is known as the Consumer Credit Protection Act or, more commonly, the Truth-in-Lending Act, enforced under the Federal Reserve System's Regulation Z. One part of this act extends consumers the right to rescind, within three business days, any credit transaction in which their residence is used as collateral. This provision allows consumers time to think about the transaction and make up their minds. Another part of this act regulates the advertising of credit terms and provides for full disclosure of details to enable consumers to reach intelligent decisions. The most important section of this act, however, requires lenders to provide borrowers complete information concerning the cost of credit. Lenders are required to disclose to borrowers the annual percentage rate (APR) of the finance charge on a consumer loan. The finance charge includes all the various charges that are incidental to the extension of credit: interest, loan fee, finder's fee or similar charge, transaction or service charge, points, premium for credit life or other insurance, and investigation or credit report fee. The annual-rate equivalent of the finance charge constitutes the loan's rate. The intent of

---

*Bank compliance with consumer legislation is customarily determined by bank examiners. In addition, consumer complaints against the practices of individual banks are brought to the attention of the appropriate supervisory agency by the Consumer Banking Affairs Units, which were established by the Federal Reserve banks to function as complaint clearinghouses. Complaints against state member banks are investigated by the Federal Reserve Banks, while complaints against insured nonmember banks are national banks are investigated by the FDIC and the Office of the Comptroller of the Currency, respectively.

this provision is to have the cost of credit presented to borrowers in a standard-ized way so that they can shop for the best credit terms.

Prior to this law, when buying a car or obtaining an installment loan, bor-rowers were frequently quoted "add-on" rates of interest. For example, on a $6,000 four-year loan, the consumer knew that the rate applied on the loan was a "low 8 percent annual interest rate" and the finance charge $1,920 ($6,000 × .08 per year × 4 years). The monthly payments, according to the add-on method, came to $165 ($6,000 + $1,920 = $7,920 ÷ 48 months). Clearly, the effective annual percentage rate is higher than the quoted 8 percent rate, since the borrower does not have full use of the amount borrowed for the whole time period. The equation used to determine the effective rate, or APR, is the familiar present value of an annuity:

$$PV_a = \sum_{t=1}^{n} \frac{PMT}{(1 + k)^n} = PMT\left[\frac{1 - (1 + k)^{-n}}{k}\right],$$

where

   PV_a = present value of an annuity—the amount borrowed
PMT = the constant dollar amount to be paid per period—the monthly payments
    k = interest rate per period—internal rate of return (the rate that equates the present value of expected cash flows to investment outlay, which is the amount borrowed in this case)
    n = number of periods.

Therefore, the value of k that satisfies the expression

$$6,000 = 165\left[\frac{1 - (1 + k)^{-48}}{k}\right],$$

or k = 1.20 percent per month, is the effective rate. Multiplying the monthly rate by 12 gives us an APR of 14.4 per cent.

If the loan is discounted and the interest is deducted in advance, the effective rate paid would be even higher (20.5 percent). This example helps explain why lenders are required to quote all installment loans on an APR basis. Detailed interest tables enable loan officers to provide consumers with instant APR quotations.

Another protection extended the consumer by the Truth-in-Lending Act is in the case of lost or stolen credit cards. The consumer is responsible only for the first $50 of charges made by unauthorized users before the loss is reported. The Fair Credit and Charge Card Disclosure Act of 1988 amended the Truth-in-Lending Act and required credit card issuers to disclose the annual percentage rate, fees, grace period, and method of calculating balances.

The Fair Credit Billing Act, implemented in October 1975, is an earlier amendment to the Truth-in-Lending Act. Also enforced under Regulation Z, it requires merchants and banks to inform consumers of their rights and the procedural steps to follow in filing complaints about billing errors. Consumers are given 60 days after billing to file a written complaint, and during this period no interest can be charged on the disputed amount.

This act also protects consumers who purchase defective merchandise, so long as the transaction is over $50 and the customer lives in the same state or within 100 miles of the place where the transaction occurred. According to this act, the consumer may refuse to continue paying the seller, or any third party that purchased the debt contract, until the complaint is resolved.

The Fair Credit Reporting Act of 1970 deals with the protection of the consumer against obsolete or inaccurate information provided by consumer reporting agencies. These agencies are responsible for safeguarding the privacy of the consumer, and restrictions are placed upon the distribution of information. If a loan request is denied because of information contained in a credit report, a bank must disclose to the consumer the substance of the information and the name of the credit reporting agency.

The Equal Credit Opportunity Act was implemented in 1975 as a guarantee that credit is extended fairly and impartially. It prohibits discrimination against credit applicants because of race, color, religion, ethnic origin, sex, marital status, or receipt of income from public assistance programs. If credit is denied on these grounds, creditors are liable to the aggrieved individual for actual and punitive damages. The provisions of this act are implemented by the Federal Reserve System's Regulation B.

The Home Equity Loan Consumer Protection Act of 1988 amended the Truth-in-Lending Act to impose specific requirements on home equity lenders. Specifically, this act calls for certain disclosures in applications for home equity loans; requires lenders to provide applicants with a brochure developed by the Federal Reserve describing home equity accounts and their advantages and disadvantages; prohibits a lender from unilaterally modifying the terms of a home equity account contract, except under certain specified conditions; and imposes new advertising requirements for home equity accounts.

Real-Estate Loans

Real-estate loans constitute the largest category of loans made by commercial banks and accounted in September 1995 for 41.8 percent of total loans (Table 12.1). These mortgages represented the financing of ownership, construction, and remodeling of both housing and commercial and industrial facilities. Real-estate loans are also made to farmers for the purchase of farmland. This type of real-estate credit, however, is relatively insignificant. Banks have become important real-estate lenders over the years. Their relative importance as a source of real-estate credit can be sensed from the following data. In mid-1995 total mortgage credit from all sources amounted to $4.5 trillion, of which 41 percent was provided by financial institutions (including banks) and 59 percent by U.S. credit agencies and individuals. Banks were the largest institutional mortgage-credit supplier, accounting for 23 percent of the market.

Mortgage loans are a typical example of a long-term credit, the maturity varying between 10 and 30 years. Real-estate loans also exemplify secured credits, since the owner has some equity in the property that is offered as collateral for the loan. Thus, even if the value of the property declines, the owner's equity provides a margin of safety against losses.

Residential Mortgages

Over half of banks' mortgage loans are for residential properties—that is, they are secured by one-to-four-family residential properties and multifamily properties. The former, single-family mortgages, are the principal type of residential mortgage held by commercial banks because of the high risk involved in the financing of multifamily mortgages (such as apartment buildings). Most of the residential mortgages in banks' loan portfolios are "conventional"—that is, they are not backed by a government agency. However, banks also hold a sizable number of residential mortgages that are insured by the Federal Housing Administration (FHA) or guaranteed by the Veterans Administration (VA). In case of default, the ownership of the property is shifted to the government agency and the bank is reimbursed for its losses. Yet most banks favor conventional loans over FHA and VA loans for a number of reasons. Since government-backed mortgages require minimal (FHA loans) or no (VA loans) down payment, the borrower tends to be more prone to nonpayment and default during difficult economic times. In addition, much less red tape is involved in extending, supervising, and foreclosing on conventional loans. There has also been an increase in the availability of private mortgage insurance modeled after that of FHA. The principal reason for the preference for conventional mortgages is that banks earn more money on these mortgages than they do on VAs and FHAs, whose rates generally trail other market rates. However, one distinct advantage that government-backed mortgages have over conventional mortgages is that the secondary market for FHA-insured and VA-guaranteed mortgages is widespread among various types of financial institutions.

The Secondary Mortgage Market

The functioning of a secondary market for residential mortgages enhances the liquidity of the mortgage portfolios of banks and other real-estate lenders. Three financial intermediaries form the basis of the secondary market: the Federal National Mortgage Association (FNMA or Fannie Mae), the Government National Mortgage Association (GNMA or Ginnie Mae), and the Federal Home Loan Mortgage Corporation (FHLMC or Freddie Mac).

Established in 1938, Fannie Mae was transformed into a private corporation in 1968. Functioning under the supervision of the Secretary of Housing and

Urban Development (HUD), Fannie Mae holds auctions at regular intervals in which it buys (or commits to buy) government-backed and conventional home mortgages. Fannie Mae also makes some mortgage purchase commitments outside the auction system for longer terms. Such commitments can be made on hospitals, apartment complexes, and nursing homes. Whether made through or outside the auction system, these commitments enable institutions short of loanable funds to continue their mortgage lending activities in periods of tight money. Fannie Mae sells the mortgages bought to institutions in regions where there are surplus funds and limited mortgage outlets. The recessionary state of the economy in the early 1980s had an important effect on the operations of this organization. As few institutions were willing to invest in long-term mortgages at that time, Fannie Mae followed the lead of its sister agencies—that is, it formed pools of mortgages and issued securities against them. These securities were backed by conventional mortgages and were guaranteed by Fannie Mae against default. For the most part, these "mortgage-backed securities" (MBS) have been issued in swaps with institutions in return for mortgages that underlie the securities, although there have been some public offerings of the securities. Fannie Mae activities are financed from commitment fees, mortgage repayments from its portfolio, and the sale of short-term notes, debentures, and mortgage-backed securities.

Ginnie Mae, created in 1968, is part of HUD. One of its activities includes the purchase of mortgages of low- and middle-income projects (tandem plan). Ginnie Mae buys these mortgages on the basis of a prior commitment to the originating institutions, and sells them to private investors, absorbing any loss in the differential between the purchase and sale prices. In this way it subsidizes and supports low-income housing. In 1970 Ginnie Mae initiated a "pass-through" program, which supports private organizations that pool government-backed home mortgages and issue securities against them. GNMA guarantees the payment of interest and principal on the securities of the pool. The private creators retain responsibility to collect all payments and prepayments, which are "passed through" each month to the holders of the securities.

Freddie Mac was established in 1970, its capital subscribed by the 12 regional Federal Home Loan banks. It supports the mortgage market by purchasing residential mortgages that it pools, then selling shares or participation certificates (PCs) in the pool. PCs range from $100,000 to $5 million in value. In addition it sells guaranteed mortgage certificates (GMCs), which also are issued against mortgage pools and—like Ginnie Mae pass-through securities—appeal to bond investors.

In 1983, Freddie Mac developed a new mortgage-backed security by effectively dividing the cash flows generated by the entire mortgage pool into separate categories and issuing several classes or *tranches* of securities with claims on these specialized cash flows. These securities, termed *collateralized mortgage obligations* (CMOs), are issued with a staggered maturity schedule to meet the needs of investors with different maturity preferences. The shortest class may have a stated maturity of two to five years, while the longest maturity class may be between 15 and 25 years. Investors who want a quick return on capital can buy the shorter maturities, while those seeking a long-term investment can buy in the 15–25-year pool. Each maturity class is retired sequentially; all securities in one class are paid off before any payment is made on the next class. In this respect a CMO differs from the standard pass-through security, for which every security holder in a given issue receives a pro rata share of all cash flows generated by a pool of mortgages. The issuer of the CMO continues to own the mortgages and the CMOs are direct obligations of the issuer, as would be true of any other bonds. Another important difference is that unlike pass-throughs, where every investor has an equivalent share of the total prepayment risk in the pool, in a CMO the specific tranches bear the prepayment risk of the specific parts.

Some of the mortgage-backed securities mentioned above were so successful in attracting investors into the mortgage market that before long, private institutions began duplicating them. In 1977, BankAmerica sold the first privately issued pass-through mortgage securities without a government guarantee. Since then, they have been issued by an increasing number of commercial banks, thrift institutions, and, more recently, private ''conduit'' firms that purchase regular mortgages from smaller lending institutions. The Tax Reform Act of 1986 established a new vehicle for restructuring the cash flow of mortgage pools—the *real-estate mortgage investment conduit* (REMIC). A REMIC, which can be a corporation, trust, association, or partnership, assembles mortgages into pools and issues pass-through certificates, multiclass bonds, and other securities to investors in the secondary market. Although a REMIC can qualify for exemption from federal taxes, the income earned by investors is fully taxable.

Interest Rates on Mortgages

Some states have enacted legislation imposing ceilings on interest rates for mortgages. When market rates for these mortgages rose above the ceiling rates, the supply of funds dissipated and new mortgages declined sharply. Because of this the DIDMCA of 1980 overruled state usury ceilings on mortgage loans, unless states reenact them within three years.

The removal of ceiling rates permits banks' mortgage loan rates to fluctuate in response to other capital-market rates. Considering the sharp increases in interest rates and the costs of housing experienced in recent years, many observers have expressed concern that young people can no longer afford to buy homes. However, the impact of these trends has been moderated by the proliferation of an ever increasing number of mortgage repayment plans, a smorgasbord of mortgage loan instruments from which the borrower can select according to his or her particular needs and expectations. These plans differ from the traditional fixed-rate mortgage, which is characterized by equal fixed monthly payments for the life of the loan.

One such mortgage instrument is the *graduated-payment mortgage* (GPM), which has a fixed interest rate and maturity and a specified schedule of monthly payments. These payments are purposely set at a low level in the initial years of the loan and increase gradually to cover the interest and fully amortize the loan. Thus, the GPM is particularly attractive to young, first-time home buyers who cannot afford the initial payments of a traditional mortgage but whose income and debt-servicing capacity is expected to grow over time. A related plan is the *flexible-payment mortgage*, which in the early years of the mortgage (for instance, the first five years) provides for low monthly payments covering only the interest on the loan. Later payments increase to cover the remaining interest and retire the principal of the loan by its maturity. The *deferred-interest mortgage* is also associated with low initial mortgage payments because of a lower interest rate; in return the lender receives the deferred interest plus a fee upon sale of the house. This plan is attractive to families that expect to live in a house for a limited number of years (such as five years) and plan to repay the lender out of the appreciation realized at the time of the sale.

The *balloon-payment mortgage* is typically made for a period of three to five years without any commitment by the lender to renew it at maturity. Monthly payments are based on a regular amortization period (such as 25 to 30 years) and a fixed interest rate. When the loan matures, the entire balance must be paid in one lump sum, a balloon payment. Since the lender is under no obligation to refinance, the borrower must secure a new loan for all or a portion of the balloon payment. Recent experiences in California indicate that borrowers who fail to receive new financing are forced to sell their homes at a sacrifice.

The *growing-equity mortgage* (GEM) is a relatively new instrument that provides for increases in monthly payments at the rate of 4–7.5 percent a year. As a result the loan is fully amortized in a shorter period than otherwise (for instance, in less than 15 years). Because of the accelerated payback, most lenders are willing to give borrowers a break on the interest rate. The appeal of this plan to the borrower stems from the fixed interest rate; the nominal increases in payments, which are known with certainty; and the relatively smaller amount of total interest paid on the loan because of its shorter average life.

The *shared-appreciation mortgage* (SAM) is a fixed-rate loan, usually for a period of ten years. Mortgage lenders make these loans at rates below market levels in return for one-third of the gains realized upon the sale of the property. The *reverse-annuity mortgage* (RAM) is a fixed-rate plan that enables retired people to use the equity in their homes to supplement their retirement income. Under this plan the lender, instead of advancing the borrower a lump sum, pays a fixed annuity each month over the life of the loan (for instance, over ten years). The debt (cash advances and accumulating interest) is to be repaid out of the borrower's estate. One drawback of this plan is that if the property value declines in the meantime, the value of the collateral may be less than the amount of the loan. Also, problems arise if the borrower outlives the loan and the value of the house has not increased enough for a new reverse annuity to be issued.

The *renegotiable-rate mortgage* (RRM) or *rollover mortgage* (ROM) is written with a fixed rate for a fixed period. Its renewal is guaranteed every three to five years, with the interest rate determined each time according to market trends. One drawback to this type is the possibility of a sharp increase in monthly payments after a renewal.

The *adjustable-rate mortgage* (ARM) provides for upward or downward adjustment in the interest rate over the life of the contract, in response to variations in a specific reference rate or index. Among the most commonly used indexes are the market rates of interest on U.S. Treasury securities (such as Treasury bills and Treasury issues of one, three, and five years' maturity) and the national average mortgage contract rate, computed monthly by the Federal Home Loan Bank Board. Whatever the index may be, some lenders try to entice borrowers by setting the interest rate on ARMs, for an initial period, below the rate for conventional, fixed-rate mortgages. After the initial period, rates are adjusted according to fluctuations in the key rate. The lower rate is commonly called a *teaser rate*. The Competitive Equality Banking Act (CEBA) of 1987 requires lenders to set in each individual case a cap on how much the rate can change at each adjustment period or over the life of the loan. For example, the rate cap might dictate that the interest rate can change no more than two percentage points annually nor more than six percentage points over the life of the loan. Clearly, the purpose of this provision is to protect borrowers from steadily escalating monthly payments in a period of rising interest rates. However, when a negative amortization occurs (that is, when interest rates in any given year rise above the cap, and hence loan payments do not cover the increased interest cost), the unpaid interest may be treated in a number of ways. ARM financing offers home owners a number of options: pay off excess interest in a lump sum upon sale of the house; have the loan's maturity stretched beyond the original date; authorize adjustments in both the maturity of the loan and monthly payments. From the lender's point of view, the ARM offers returns that vary with the overall level of interest rates. More important, it permits lenders, especially thrifts, to match the variable-rate nature of some of their liabilities with a portfolio of correspondingly variable-rate loans. This contributes to rendering earnings from lending activities reasonably stable.

There is no certainty as to which of the alternative mortgage instruments, if any, will prevail. The default record of alternative mortgage plans and the ongoing consolidation process in the financial sector will refine lender preferences among the various types of mortgages.

Regulations Protecting the Borrower

In addition to the credit laws discussed in the preceding section, consumers are protected by legislation specifically related to mortgage loans. These are summarized below.

The Real Estate Settlement and Procedures Act (RESPA) was enacted in 1974 and amended the following year. Administered by HUD, this law requires a lending institution, including a bank, to provide mortgage-loan applicants with good-faith estimates of all the settlement costs that will be incurred in a given transaction. The lender retains the settlement statement along with a signed receipt from the borrower acknowledging disclosure of such information.

The Home Mortgage Disclosure Act (HMDA) was passed by Congress in 1975 to discourage *redlining*, the practice of refusing mortgage loans in blighted or declining neighborhoods. This law requires banks and other lending institutions to compile, and make public, information on the geographical locations of the properties on which they have made mortgage loans. The objective of this legislation was to provide depositors with information about the lending activities of banks and, through public pressure, to discourage redlining. This act has a major limitation. Although disclosure of information about the lending activity of an institution is important, it is nevertheless incomplete, since it is not accompanied by information about the demand for loans in the various geographic areas under consideration.

In 1977 Congress passed another important piece of legislation, the Community Reinvestment Act (CRA). This act requires federal regulatory agencies to determine whether banks and thrift institutions attend to the credit needs of the communities in which they are chartered. Thus, according to this legislation, banks are required to formulate explicit CRA statements outlining their willingness to meet their community's credit needs and the types of loans they will extend. These policy statements are periodically reviewed by bank examiners from the federal supervisory agencies (the Federal Reserve System, the FDIC, and the Office of the Comptroller of the Currency), to ensure that low- and moderate-income individuals are not being systematically discriminated against. In addition to the periodic reviews conducted by examiners, regulatory agencies determine institutional compliance with CRA provisions when a lender applies for a branch, office relocation, merger, or acquisition. This power of enforcement allows the CRA more far-reaching authority than that of the HMDA, and necessitates adherence on the part of bankers to the evaluation criteria set up by federal agencies.

The Competitive Equality Banking Act (CEBA) of 1987 provides that any adjustable-rate mortgage loan originated by a creditor shall include a limitation (cap) on the maximum interest rate that may apply during the term of the mortgage loan. The Federal Reserve Board amended Regulation Z to incorporate this law, which has since been applicable to all "dwelling-secured" consumer credit.

The FDICIA of 1991 mandated federal banking regulators to provide for uniform real-estate lending standards. In this context, promulgated regulations include maximum loan-to-value ratios deemed prudent for the various real-estate loan categories. For example, a bank could lend no more than 65 percent of the appraised value of raw land, 75 percent on land development projects, 80 percent on nonresidential construction, and 85 percent on one- to four-family residential construction. For owner-occupied one- to four-family and home equity loans, any loan equal to, or exceeding, a 90 percent loan-to-value ratio requires enhancement in the form of private mortgage insurance or easily marketable collateral.

Loans to Depository Institutions

On September 30, 1995, this category of loans accounted, according to Table 12.1, for 3.3 percent of all bank loans. Recipients of these loans were such institutions as correspondent banks, foreign banks, mutual savings banks, savings and loan associations, and credit unions.

Loans to Farmers

For a great number of U.S. banks, this type of loan constitutes a dominant loan portfolio category. Indeed, for many rural banks, farm loans account for a sizable portion of total loans. Farmers generally borrow from banks to finance recurring seasonal expenses and intermediate-term investments. The former are such items as seeds, fertilizers, sprays, and feed for livestock. In the latter instance farm loans finance land improvements and the purchase of machinery and equipment, trucks and automobiles, and other consumer durable goods.

Despite the importance of farm loans for rural banks, for the banking industry as a whole, farm loans accounted for only 1.6 percent of the total loans outstanding on September 30, 1995 (see Table 12.1). This means that commercial banks are not the primary source of funds for farm credit. Indeed, banks are exceeded in importance by lenders that specialize in farm credit and offer farmers loans at subsidized rates. These lenders are federal agencies—Farm Credit Banks and Banks for Cooperatives—and make up the U.S. farm credit system.

All Other Loans

This last category of bank loans, accounting for 5.7 percent of total loans on September 30, 1995, is made up of various types of credits, such as loans to foreign governments and official institutions, loans for purchasing and carrying securities, and loans not elsewhere classified. Prior to the international debt crisis of the early 1980s, loans to foreign governments represented a major class of loans. Following the dramatic rise in oil prices and the recession of 1974, an increasing number of foreign governments entered the credit markets and borrowed from U.S. banks for a number of purposes. Some of the more important needs for which governments borrowed money include acquiring foreign exchange to finance seasonal export/import variations and funding infrastructure projects, such as highway or railroad construction. From a legal perspective American bankers distinguish four different levels of foreign government borrowers:

- Governments at the national (federal), provincial (state), and local levels
- Ministries of the national government and central banks
- Statutory authorities and agencies at all government levels

• Public-sector industries, development banks, and other banking institutions owned by the government.

This classification system permits a more realistic evaluation of the prospective borrower by readily identifying its importance in the government hierarchy, and by recognizing the supervisory authority responsible under law or policy in the event of nonpayment. These considerations play a decisive role in evaluating the quality of the loan, and dispel the notion that the government nature of the would-be borrower automatically assures repayment.[5]

The other component of this loan group is loans to official institutions. These include such international and regional organizations as the International Bank for Reconstruction and Development, the Inter-American Development Bank, and the Asian Development Bank.

Loans for purchasing and carrying securities refers to credit extended to individuals for the purpose of purchasing corporate stock and other securities. Because of the excessive speculation of the late 1920s and the stock market crash, the Securities Exchange Act of 1934, with amendments, authorized the Board of Governors of the Federal Reserve System to apply selective credit controls over this type of loan. As a result, Regulation U has since been applied to loans made by lenders on all securities listed on national stock exchanges and selected over-the-counter securities. According to Regulation U, purchase of these securities on credit is subject to margin requirements. The term "margin" refers to the proportion of the total value of the securities that represents the buyer's equity. In 1972 the margin requirement for stock was set at 65 percent; it was lowered to 50 percent in 1974 and has been since maintained at this level. The Board of Governors of the Federal Reserve has the power to change minimum margin requirements within the range of 25 to 100 percent. The securities acquired on margin are pledged as collateral at the time the loan is made. Banks also make loans to brokers and dealers for the purpose of financing customers' margin accounts and dealer security inventories, which must be carried in order to make a market in them.

The third group of loans included in the "all other" loans category is an assortment of credits not elsewhere classified, such as loans to nonprofit organizations: churches, hospitals, educational and charitable organizations, clubs, and similar associations. Also included are loans to individuals for investment purposes and unplanned overdrafts on checking accounts. The last approach to extending credit was quite rare in the United States until the introduction of credit cards and check credit plans. By contrast, this form of financing has been very popular in Great Britain and other European countries, and often is the predominant form of lending. Both tradition and the absence of well-developed European capital markets contributed to making these overdrafts "evergreen"; that is, they are not called in for payment and the bank charges interest on the negative balances in the borrower's account. In essence, then, overdrafts are functioning in these countries as a means of financing businesses' medium-term needs for capital.

Leasing

Lease-financing receivables accounted for 2 percent of total bank loans and leases on September 30, 1995. Instead of lending funds to a firm to buy the needed asset, a bank may lend the asset itself in exchange for specified regular payments. Leases are used to finance a variety of tangible assets, such as construction equipment, machine tools, medical equipment, cars and trucks, computers, and commercial aircraft. A lease is a contractual agreement that extends to a party (the lessee) the right to use an asset over a specified period of time in exchange for periodic payments to the owner (the lessor). Three important forms of leasing are the operating lease, the financial lease, and the leveraged lease.

Operating leases, also known as service leases, cover a period considerably shorter than the expected economic life of the leased asset. In other words, the asset is not fully amortized over the term of the lease; as a result, the lessor expects to recover all investment costs through subsequent renewal payments, subsequent leases to other lessees, or sale of the asset. Operating leases can be canceled; if the cancellation option is exercised, the lessee returns the asset to the lessor and ceases to make payments.

Financial leases differ from operating leases in that they are not cancelable (at least not without a significant penalty) and are fully amortized—that is, rental payments cover the full price of the leased asset and in addition offer a return on investment. In a typical financial lease arrangement, the lessee selects the specific asset it requires and negotiates the price and delivery terms with the manufacturer. The asset is purchased by the lessor at the request of the lessee and the latter assumes virtually all responsibilities of ownership, including insurance, maintenance, and taxes. The lessor collects the rentals and enjoys the tax benefits of ownership (accelerated depreciation); and in the event of default the asset can be repossessed.

Leveraged leases, also known as third-party leases, are financial leases where the lessor borrows a substantial fraction of the cost of the leased asset, say 80 percent, from one or more lenders. The lessor makes an assignment of the lease and lease rental payments to the lender, who is entitled to repossess the asset if the lessee defaults. A leveraged lease is a true lease for tax purposes because in addition to the rentals, the lessor—as owner of the asset—is entitled to all of the benefits of ownership (depreciation and deduction of interest expense on the long-term debt). Banks are active in financial leases, and in the case of the leveraged type they may function as either owner (equity participant) or lender (debt participant).

SECURITIZATION OF LOANS

Securitization refers to the transformation of financial assets into securities tradable in secondary markets. In other words, assets that would otherwise be held to maturity may be converted into forms acceptable to secondary market purchasers. Mortgage finance has been in the forefront of this financial innovation. Whereas the individual mortgage is a unique asset, mortgage pools are quite homogeneous and subject to the standardization necessary for the issuance of securities tradable in secondary markets. As a result, several types of mortgage-backed securities have been developed since 1970. Issued first by governmental and quasi-governmental agencies (for instance, Ginnie Mae and Freddie Mac), mortgage-backed securities proved so successful in attracting investors that banks and other lenders rushed to offer them. Investor reaction to private issues was so favorable that by 1988, over $100 billion in securities was outstanding, while securitized mortgages (including all Ginnie Mae issues) totaled well over $600 billion in outstandings.

In 1982 securitization began to spread to other loans. Commercial and industrial loans were first securitized in 1982. Consumer loans began to be securitized only in 1984, but the volume of these instruments grew quickly. Marine Midland Bank of New York was the first bank to securitize automobile loans, which it marketed in 1985 with the assistance of Salomon Brothers. The securities were aptly named certificates for automobile receivables (CARs). These securities were followed by others backed by loans on cars, trucks, and computers. A limited number of securities were, moreover, backed by consumer credit card receivables. For example, in February 1987, BankAmerica pioneered the first public offering of $400 million of securities backed by credit card loans. This issue had a maturity of about two years and offered 65 basis points over the Treasury bill rate for the same maturity. The size of reserves committed by the bank to cover any default on the underlying loans was deemed so adequate that Standard and Poor's awarded the issue an AAA rating. Prior to this public issue, Bank One of Columbus, Ohio, had made a private offering of credit card receivables.

The 1990s witnessed a drastic increase in the volume of securitized assets. In 1990 and 1991 the impetus came from banks which used securitization to get assets off their balance sheets to improve their capital ratio. In recent years however much of the momentum came from corporations which used securitization to access capital markets instead of relying on bank lines of credit and other forms of financing to expand their business. At year-end 1994, $75 billion of securities, generically called "asset-backed securities" (ABS), were issued in U.S. financial markets. ABS offerings in 1995 rose to $108 billion and were on track to attain a record $140 billion in 1996. At this pace, ABS offerings were growing at nearly twice the rate of corporate bonds.

To comprehend how securitization works, it is essential to identify the various facets that characterize this process. Securitization involves the following six functions:

1. Originating the loan. This stage is associated with the initial creation of the loan—that is, all the steps taken by a bank up to the time the loan is placed on its books. In the case of a mortgage, the origination process includes appraising the property, doing a title search, negotiating the terms of the loan with the borrower, and recording the documents in accordance with applicable real-estate laws.

2. Servicing the loan. This stage involves the collection and processing of borrower payments as they come due.

3. Forming a portfolio of loans and creating securities. Individual credits are collected to form a portfolio (pool) of loans against which securities are issued.

4. Guaranteeing the cash flows from these securities (credit enhancement). In some cases, a third party, such as an insurance company or a large bank, promises to continue payment to the investors should the original borrowers default. In other cases, the issuer provides its own limited guarantee or pledges collateral in excess of the security principal. The type of credit enhancement affects the rating classification assigned to a security issue.

5. Selling securities to investors. Securities are sold to a handful of investors (private placement) or to the public (public offering), with the assistance of an investment banking firm.

6. Maintaining a secondary market. For securities offered to the public, this function is performed by a dealer, who thus ensures the liquidity of these instruments. The investment banking firm that sells the securities and/or other institutions may operate as dealers in the market for the securitized loans.

The stages identified above are highlighted in Figure 12.1, which illustrates the securitization of General Motors Acceptance Corporation (GMAC) car receivables in October 1987.

A key facet in the securitization process is that of credit enhancement. As stated, credit enhancement may be provided by a third party or the issuer; often more than one type of credit enhancement may be deemed appropriate to support an issue. Third-party enhancement has taken the form of a letter of credit from a bank with a high rating or an insurance bond from a high-rated company. Enhancement by the issuer can take different forms: recourse, over-collateralization, spread account, or senior-subordinated structure. *Recourse* holds the issuer liable for any defaults in the securitized loans. In *overcollateralization*, the value of the collateral (loans) backing the issue is greater than the face value of the securities at the time of issue. The investor is thus protected against declines in the value of the collateral due to such factors as defaults, delinquencies, and prepayments. In fact, if the collateral falls below some predetermined amount during the life of the debt, the issuer may have to add collateral. A *spread account* is a fund established by the issuer at the beginning through an initial advance. If, throughout the life of the issue, the cash flows generated from the securitized assets exceed payment to investors and servicing fees, the value of the spread account increases; conversely, if cash flows are insufficient (e.g., due to defaults) to pay investors, the value of the spread account falls as it is drawn upon to supplement payments to investors. In a *senior-subordinated structure* two classes of securities are issued, the senior and the subordinated (junior). The issuer holds on to the junior class and sells only the senior. Citicorp has often made use of this type of enhancement in the securitization of its credit card receivables, retaining 10 percent of the securities issued.

The next stage, sale of securities, is also an important facet. As stated, the issuer may opt for private placement or a public offering. In the former case, the investment banker functions as an agent for the issuer in seeking to place the issue, while in the latter he purchases the securities from the issuer for resale and assumes the underwriting risk. Private placements are usually quicker and less expensive to arrange because of lower issuing costs—they are exempted from registration with the Securities and Exchange Commission (SEC) and the investment banking fee is generally lower. On the other hand, because they are relatively illiquid, the issuer must pay an interest-rate premium on these issues. If the issue is offered to the public, a secondary market must be maintained in these securities.

Some of the securitization functions (such as originating and servicing loans) have traditionally been performed by commercial banks, while others (such as creating and distributing securities and providing liquidity) have been the domain of investment banks. This functional segmentation has been a product of the Glass-Steagall Act of 1933, which forced banking firms to divest themselves of their securities operations. Increased pressure to repeal this act resulted in the late 1980s in the authorization by the Federal Reserve of the holding companies of major money-center banks (such as Bankers Trust, Citicorp, Morgan Guaranty, and Chase) to engage in the underwriting and trading of corporate issues, municipal revenue bonds, and securities backed by mortgages and consumer debt. This authorization was granted subject to certain conditions, including the establishment by these holding companies of subsidiaries to engage specifically in these activities. As a result, money-center banks and their affiliates have played a significant role in the underwriting and private placement of asset-backed securities.

Attributes

Securitized credit is superior to traditional lending on the following grounds: it is more cost effective; it provides for higher asset liquidity; it offers opportunities for income; it creates a diversity of roles for market participants; it is a better diversifier of credit risk; and it shifts interest-rate risk to investors. Each of these attributes is addressed below.

In pricing a loan, a bank takes into account a number of considerations that

Figure 12.1
Securitization of GMAC Car Receivables, October 1987

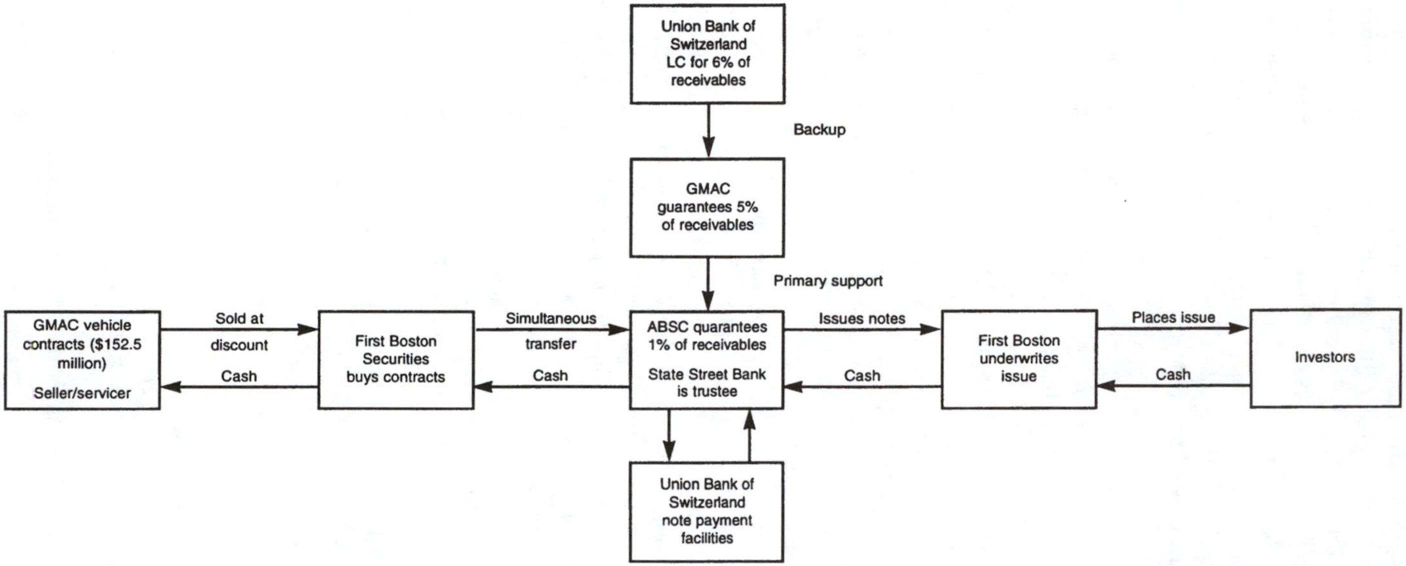

Transaction Summary

Sale date: July and September 1987

Buyer: First Boston Securities Corporation, a wholly owned subsidiary of First Boston Corporation, bought from GMAC, at two different dates, a pool of recently originated automotive installment-sale contracts. On October 27, 1987, Asset Backed Securities Corporation (ABSC), itself a subsidiary of First Boston Securities, purchased the contracts from its parent simultaneously with the issuance and sale of its own notes.

Trustee: State Street Bank & Trust Co.

Underwriter: First Boston Corporation

Securities offered: $142.7 million; 9.4% ABSC; notes series 5

Rating: AAA

Credit enhancement: First loss coverage provided by limited guarantees from GMAC (5%) and ABSC (1%), both of which were backed by a 6% letter of credit issued by Union Bank of Switzerland (UBS).

Note payment facilities: Minimum principal payment agreement with UBS to maintain scheduled principal payments on the notes. UBS provided to reinvestment agreement pursuant to which contract principal prepaid faster than scheduled note payments would be reinvested at a given yield.

Pool data: The annual percentage rates of contracts ranged from 5.75% to 7% and their original maturities from 36 to 48 months; contracts subject to dealer recourse, 12.3%.

Source: Developed by the author based on information obtained from First Boston Corporation.

315

are discussed in the next chapter. For the sake of our presentation, however, reference may be made here to three cost aspects: the cost for required reserves, the cost for FDIC insurance, and equity costs. Regardless of all other costs a bank may have, these costs—frequently referred to as regulatory costs—are products of the current regulatory environment, and as such they cannot be reduced or eliminated under the traditional lending system. For example, when a bank is funding a loan to a business borrower with transaction accounts, it must put up reserves against them, provide for their FDIC insurance coverage, and commit equity capital in accordance with capital adequacy requirements. We will assume the following cost structure: 30 basis points of cost for required reserves, 10 basis points for FDIC insurance, and about 1 percent in equity costs. Since these costs are in addition to all other costs, the bank's loans must earn a minimum pretax interest markup of approximately 1.4 percent, net of all other costs, to keep the price of the stock equal to its book value. If a bank securitizes its credit, these costs may be saved. In this respect, securitization enables a bank to be more cost-efficient.

Another attribute of securitization is that it makes assets more liquid. Under the traditional credit system, once a loan is made to a borrower, it must be held by a bank in its portfolio until maturity (or prepayment). With the exception of mortgages, there is no secondary market for most loans. This lack of liquidity adversely affects a bank's ability to manage its assets efficiently. This issue does not arise with securitized credit because securities are a liquid asset. As a result, a bank may at any time change its operating strategy and alter the composition of its portfolio; take advantage of new and more attractive investment opportunities as they arise; readily invest excess loanable funds that its local market cannot absorb; and liquidate securities to fund existing assets when new deposits are not forthcoming. None of these options is available to a bank when there is no secondary market for its assets. The above options are equally important for thrifts. Credit unions, for example, may now sell loans to increase liquidity. Moreover, any thrift that desires to broaden or build up its loan portfolio may now accomplish this immediately (for instance, by investing in asset-backed securities) instead of having to originate the loans itself.

Securitization creates opportunities for income. For banks that securitize and retain the servicing of the pooled loans, the process creates riskfree fee income. Indeed, the servicing institution earns fees for collecting and passing on interest and principal payments to the investors and for monitoring loan performance. In addition, the securitizing bank can capture a portion of the spread between the average yield of the packaged loans and the coupon rate on the securities sold to investors. Any residual interest income, after payment of all fees and payment of the coupon rate, accrues to the securitizing institution. Other banks have been able to benefit indirectly from securitization by providing such services as guarantee of cash flows to investors (credit enhancement), backup liquidity to the securitizing institution in case it suffers a temporary shortfall in cash and cannot fulfill its contractual obligations to investors, and expertise to institutions interested in securitizing their loans.

Securitization creates diverse roles for the various market participants. Traditionally banks and thrifts pursued parallel activities and evolved similar capabilities and ways of operating. Since the deregulation process is eliminating traditional barriers, these institutions find themselves competing against each other in offering the same undifferentiated product. Securitized credit changes this situation by creating a diverse number of roles for market participants. Specifically, each of the distinct functions that characterize securitized credit may be provided by a different firm. For example, a commercial bank may originate a loan; the loan may be acquired by another bank and placed in a portfolio; an investment banking firm may create and distribute a security backed by that portfolio of loans; a separate bank or insurance company may provide a guarantee against default on the loans; and a number of investment banking firms, as well as other types of institutions, may operate as dealers in the market for these securitized credits.

Securitized credit is, moreover, a better diversifier of credit risk. Under the traditional credit system, credit risk is geographically concentrated where a bank is located. In the securitized credit system, the originating institution must assume the responsibility of covering two or three times the amount of a possible credit loss on the portfolio. Then another financial institution, the credit enhancer, will guarantee emergency losses five to ten times the amount of expected loss. This institution may be a bank or an insurance company that, in turn, will syndicate the expected loss to other institutions. The credit enhancer reviews credit assessment skills, the servicing capacity, and the documentation of the originating institution before agreeing to participate. The credit enhancer is legally obligated to pay off if a loan it guarantees defaults; hence, it has a strong incentive to monitor the origination process of the lender whose loans it guarantees in order to ensure that every effort or resource was expended to reduce the risk of default. The next step would be for the rating agencies to evaluate the issue, including the enhancer's guarantee, and assign it a rating. This stage adds an additional layer of scrutiny in the credit evaluation process. The end result is the distribution in the secondary market of high-quality securitized loans. Securitization thus offers originating institutions strong economic incentives to maintain high standards in the underwriting of loans. Weak creditors will either have to upgrade their skills or remain outside the securitized system.

Another advantage of securitized credit is that no single bank will have to deal with a significant interest-rate risk exposure. In recent years, interest-sensitive deposits have dominated bank deposits. Commercial banks have responded to the increasing sensitivity of the liability side of the balance sheet by making more floating-rate loans. Yet these loans do not yield as high profit margins as fixed-rate loans do. Fixed-rate loans are subject to interest-rate risk. This exposure in interest-rate risk cannot intrinsically be remedied under the traditional credit system. Securitized credit enables banks to offer fixed-rate loans to customers and yet avoid interest-rate exposure by transferring the loan to the end investor.

The attributes identified above have provided strong incentives to bankers to focus on securitized credit as a means of funding growth while remaining competitive. Until recently the majority of asset-backed securities were issued by very large banks and finance companies. However, regional and community banks are becoming increasingly aware of the benefits of the process. At year-end 1995, the total volume of asset-backed securities outstanding amounted to $250 billion. Credit card receivables, accounting for nearly 50 percent of the total, were the most popular type. Securities backed by car loans and home equity loans trailed in importance with 33 percent. Asset-backed securities weathered the 1990–91 recession well, with no losses to investors.

LOAN SALES

Sales of loans differ from securitization in that no new securities are created. The loans sold may be either new loans or loans that have been on the bank's books for a while. The contract may provide for the sale of all or part* of the expected stream of cash from specific loans, thereby causing removal of these loans from the bank's balance sheet. Most loan sales—and securitizations—are made without recourse. That is, the buyer bears all the credit risk if the loan eventually goes bad.

The characteristics of the loan sales market resemble those associated with securitization. Loan sales—as long as they are without recourse—remove or limit a bank's credit risk and interest-rate risk, which are passed on to a third-party investor; they slow down asset growth and consequently ease a bank's capital requirements; limit loan concentration in any one sector or market and enable greater diversification of portfolio holdings; allow a bank to replace lower-yielding loans with higher-yielding ones when interest rates rise; increase cost efficiency by saving on regulatory costs (reserve requirements and deposit insurance); create an opportunity for profit because the high interest rate on these loans makes them attractive investments to other institutions; and the selling bank retains servicing rights, thereby earning income by collecting interest from the loans and monitoring their performance.

Two important concerns are associated with this activity. First, the commercial clients may not view the sale of their loans favorably because it would involve the sharing of vital financial information with other institutions. Moreover, it may undermine customer relationships with the bank. A second concern

---

*An example of a partial sale is loans guaranteed by two government agencies, the Small Business Administration (SBA) and the Farmers Home Administration (FmHA). These agencies typically provide up to a 90 percent guarantee on term loans to small and, in the case of the FmHA, moderate-sized businesses. Many banks follow the practice of selling the guaranteed portion of the loan in the secondary market and retaining the rest.

is that packaging the best-quality loans for sale may leave lower-quality loans in the portfolio, thereby exposing the bank to more volatile earnings.

The loans sold by banks are usually of short maturity (e.g., 90 days), although loans of medium-term maturity have also been the subject of such transactions. The market grew significantly during the 1980s, as a result of a spectacular growth in mergers and corporate buyouts during this period. The need to finance highly leveraged transactions (HLT) led to a drastic increase in the volume of loans made, and propelled loans sales to record levels (between 1980 and 1989, loan sales grew from $20 billion to $285 billion). Another important development that contributed to the growth of the market was the international debt crisis of the early 1980s. This development caused the creation of a secondary market for Third World (or LDC) debt.

Originally the domain of large banks, the market has expanded in recent years to include a variety of participants. Some of the more important sellers of loans are money-center banks, foreign banks (downsizing their U.S. loan portfolios), and, until recently, the Resolution Trust Corporation, a government agency established in 1989 to dispose of the assets of problem thrifts. The principal buyers include other banks (seeking to diversify their portfolios), foreign banks (trying to build or strengthen their presence in the domestic market), insurance companies and pension funds, U.S. and European nonfinancial corporations, mutual funds, and large investment banks. Investor appeal of these loans is based on their relatively high yields compared with bonds, their collateral backing and strong covenant protection, and their floating-rate pricing. Clearly these considerations do not apply to vulture funds, a specialized group of buyers interested only in distressed loans.

Loan Sales to a Bad Bank

An innovative way to handle the sale of delinquent and nonperforming loans was developed in 1988 by Mellon Bank, a Pittsburgh-based institution. The approach has been known as the good bank-bad bank strategy. A bad bank—also known as a collection bank—is a special-purpose corporation, usually established as a subsidiary of the parent holding company, for the purpose of acquiring the low-quality and nonperforming loans of the good bank. To this end, the bad bank raises funds directly from the capital markets through issuance of bonds and stocks. The proceeds are then used to buy the nonperforming loans of the good bank at a discount. The sale removes the assets from the books of the good bank at a loss, and results in a charge against income. Since this transaction usually affects capital, the bank may need to issue more stock.

The bad bank then attempts to collect all or a portion of the troubled loans it has purchased. Mellon's bad bank—Grant Street National Bank—paid 41 cents on the dollar, or $577 million, for Mellon's $1.4 billion in bad loans. Employing 75 workout specialists, Grant Street unloaded bad loans and property; within five years it had completed its mission at a cost of more than $100 million in expenses and liquidation losses of about the same amount. This strategy made it possible for Mellon to clean its balance sheet, focus on business development, and increase shareholders' wealth within that period. Mellon made a remarkable turnaround, and since the early 1990s it has expanded its operations through a number of acquisitions that included Dreyfus, one of the largest firms in the management of mutual funds.

NOTES

1. Lloyd W. Mints, *A History of Banking Theory* (Chicago: University of Chicago Press, 1945), p. 9; see also pp. 27–29.

2. On the "shiftability" theory of liquidity, see H. G. Moulton, "Commercial Banking and Capital Formation, III," *Journal of Political Economy* 26, no. 7 (July 1918): 723; Waldo F. Mitchell, *The Uses of Bank Funds* (Chicago: University of Chicago Press, 1925), pp. 15–17, 19ff.; Rollin G. Thomas, *Modern Banking* (New York: Prentice-Hall, 1937), pp. 161–69.

3. Herbert V. Prochnow, *Term Loans and Theories of Bank Liquidity* (New York: Prentice-Hall, 1949).

4. Christian Hill and Richard B. Schmitt, "Energy-Loan Losses, Bigger Than Expected, Figure to Climb Higher," *Wall Street Journal*, November 14, 1983, pp. 1, 13.

5. Emmanuel N. Roussakis, ed., *International Banking: Principles and Practices* (New York: Praeger Publishers, 1983).

SUGGESTED REFERENCES

Avery, Robert B., and Allen N. Berger. "Loan Commitments and Bank Risk Exposure." *Journal of Banking and Finance* 15 (1991): 173–79.

Booth, James R. "The Securitization of Lending Markets." Federal Reserve Bank of San Francisco, *Weekly Letter*, September 29, 1989, pp. 1–3.

Canner, Glenn B., and Wayne Passmore. "Home Purchase Lending in Low-Income Neighborhoods and to Low-Income Borrowers." *Federal Reserve Bulletin*, February 1995, pp. 71–103.

Canner, Glenn B., Wayne Passmore, and Monisha Mittal. "Private Mortgage Insurance." *Federal Reserve Bulletin*, October 1994, pp. 883–99.

Cantor, Richard, and Rebecca Demsetz. "Securitization, Loan Sales, and the Credit Slowdown." Federal Reserve Bank of New York, *Quarterly Review*, Summer 1993, pp. 27–83.

Crockett, J. "The Good Bank/Bad Bank Restructuring of Financial Institutions." *The Bankers Magazine*, November/December 1988, pp. 32–36.

Garwood, Griffith L., and Dolores S. Smith. "The Community Reinvestment Act: Evolution and Current Issues." *Federal Reserve Bulletin*, April 1993, pp. 251–67.

Goodman, John L., and Charles A. Luckett. "Adjustable-Rate Financing in Mortgage and Consumer Credit Markets." *Federal Reserve Bulletin*, November 1985, pp. 825–38.

Lederman, Jess, ed. *The Handbook of Asset-Backed Securities*. New York: New York Institute of Finance, 1990.

Lipin, Steven. "Corporate Loans Are Cashing in on Wall Street." *Wall Street Journal*, September 14, 1993, p. C1.

Saunders, Anthony. *Financial Institutions Management*. Burr Ridge, Ill.: Irwin, 1994.

Chapter 13

The Loan Account: Policy Considerations

Within the confines of law and regulation, the board of directors of each individual bank tries to create a framework for safe, sound, and profitable lending. As with all other aspects of banking activity, the board of directors ensures uniformity in lending practices through the formulation of a formal lending policy. This policy is in written form and is periodically reviewed, as warranted by changing economic conditions. Some of the key questions addressed by this policy are the size of the loan account, desirable maturities, types of loans, and the terms under which loans may be made. Once the loan policy has been formulated, the board must provide the administrative framework for its implementation. This chapter reviews the factors relevant to policy formulation, and describes the organizational structure and the procedures whereby loan policy is implemented.

SIZE OF THE LOAN ACCOUNT

Bankers continually face the question of how large the loan portfolio should be, a question that is especially significant because loans represent the bank's most lucrative activity. Banks may be tempted to increase the size of the loan portfolio in order to increase profitability, but the too liberal granting of loan requests can lead to losses through failure to collect. On the other hand, a conservative stance on the size of the portfolio may cause the bank to forgo earnings unnecessarily. There is no formulaic answer regarding the size of the portfolio; each bank must determine portfolio size for itself. The starting point is the accurate assessment of the credit needs of the community or market a bank serves or intends to serve. It has long been recognized that the basic responsibility of a bank lies in serving the credit needs of its community. There is no greater service that a bank can perform for a community than to provide the loans needed by creditworthy businesses and individuals.

In small communities this need for credit can be assessed by the actual demand for loans. In such communities bank officers and directors are usually in a position to have an intimate knowledge of most of the economic activity of the area and the developments that may be shaping up. In large communities such knowledge can be obtained through formal forecasting of expected credit needs. Loan officers of banks in such communities customarily provide this information after contacting their principal corporate clients and identifying their future credit needs. This information is then evaluated within the framework of the economic growth of the community. Large money-center banks frequently rely on national econometric models forecasting the sources and uses of funds for the entire economy. Private-sector estimates help identify the expected demand for and supply of funds in the year ahead. Since it is the role of banks to bridge the gap between the supply of and demand for funds by extending loans, this information sets the parameters within which the bank can determine its own share of the market. In whatever type of community a bank may operate, its management must know the credit needs of its present and potential customers, both for the short and for the long run, as a basis not only for establishing loan policies but also for determining the bank's liquidity needs and investment policy.

When bank management has a fairly clear concept of what volume and character of loan demands the bank will be called upon to meet, it must appraise its own willingness and ability to meet those demands. In some communities local demand for loans is strong and practically insatiable, while in more developed and stable communities, bank management may have to seek out opportunities for sound loans. In either case the controlling principle should be the community's credit needs and the bank's capability to meet those needs.

Once liquidity provisions have been made (primary and secondary reserves) and there is adequate capital for absorbing loan losses, a bank should be in a position to make all the sound loans it can. In other words, given adequate liquidity and capital protection, a bank's ability to expand its loans is limited only by its resources. If a bank's resources are inadequate to meet the full volume of loan demands, management may proceed to fill them indirectly. Bank management may provide for the financing of specific loan demands by participating in or negotiating placement of the requested loans with correspondent banks or other financial institutions, itself retaining the servicing of such loans as a means of sustaining continuous relationships with its own customers. A bank's ability and willingness to accommodate local loan demands directly or indirectly is the most important factor in creating and maintaining depositor relationships. In addition, such ability and willingness to lend contribute to the economic well-being of the community and thereby broaden the market for bank services, so that the bank shares in the prosperity it has helped to bring about.

Over the years management has developed certain criteria that assess the overall loan commitments of a bank in terms of its capacity to lend. These criteria identify a key balance-sheet relationship expressed in the form of a ratio, the loans-to-deposits ratio. As implied, this ratio aims to show the relationship of a bank's loans to its deposits. Because it is readily computed and compared, this ratio is in general use as a yardstick for asset management. Specifically, it is used to demonstrate the extent to which available resources have already been used in accommodating the credit needs of customers. The presumption is that the higher the ratio of loans to deposits, the less able a bank will be to make additional loans.*

Commercial bank managements have come, at various times, to accept a certain ratio of loans to deposits as being an acceptable determinant for the size of the loan portfolio desired. As might be expected, this ratio has experienced considerable variation over the years, reflecting the prevailing economic conditions and, more specifically, the credit demand of these years. Since 1914, for example, the average loans-to-deposit ratio for all commercial banks in the United States has varied from a high of 80 percent of loans in 1920 to a low of 17 percent in 1944.

The loans-to-deposits ratio has become a critical guide for commercial bank managements. Not infrequently a bank's management may feel uncomfortable when its ratio gets too far out of line with that of other banks regarded as comparable in size and character. The attitude has thus developed that whenever the ratio approaches what is considered the maximum acceptable for all banks or for banks of a certain size and character, management should try to become more cautious and selective in its lending policies.

However important this ratio concerning limits to overall lending capacity may be, it must not be taken to imply that it is in any sense a magic number. True, some element of tradition clings to a particular value for this ratio; such tradition, however, must be flexibly interpreted in the light of the current situation. This ratio becomes especially meaningful if interpreted in the light of such relevant magnitudes as the composition of the loan portfolio (by maturities and by major loan types), the size and composition of the bond portfolio, business expectations, management philosophy, and respectability in comparison with all commercial banks or with other banks of the same size and character.

LOAN MATURITIES

Because loan maturities have implications for both bank liquidity and risk exposure, it is important that the board of directors formulate a clear policy defining an acceptable distribution of maturities in the loan portfolio. In terms

---

*This ratio is frequently used by management as a liquidity indicator because, by showing the relationship of a bank's loans to its deposits, it also reveals the amount of funds still readily available for liquidity purposes.

of maturity, a bank's loan portfolio may be classified into short-term, intermediate-term, and long-term loans. Short-term loans are usually defined as those with a maturity of one year or less, intermediate-term loans are from one to eight (or occasionally ten) years, and long-term loans are in excess of ten years.

Short-term loans are of two types: demand and time. Demand loans are those that the borrower may repay, or the lender may demand payment of, at any time. The most common example of demand credit is loans to brokers and dealers for financing their inventories of securities and their customers' margin accounts. Because the bank can call the loan at any time, on one day's notice, these loans are also known as call loans. Rate quotations on these loans are customarily made by large money-center banks.

Time loans are extended for a definite period, up to one year. The traditional type of such credit, as we saw in Chapter 12, has been self-liquidating loans to businesses. In its pure form this loan is customarily employed to finance the seasonal inventory needs of businesses and is repaid from the sale of the inventory and the conversion of accounts receivable into cash.

Intermediate-term loans, by definition, are those whose maturities fall between the short-term and long-term categories. One example of intermediate credit is consumer loans, which are usually made for a period of two to three years. Term loans to businesses are another example of intermediate credit. (Both types of loans were discussed in Chapter 12.)

Loans with a maturity of ten years or more when contracted are characterized as long-term. The most common type of long-term loan is the real-estate loan. Originally, lending on the security of real estate was considered unduly illiquid, and hence inappropriate for commercial banks, whose liabilities were so largely payable on demand. Indeed, before the Great Depression mortgage loans were made with lump-sum maturities. These loans were seldom paid at the initial maturity and were renewed frequently. The monthly amortization feature came with the establishment of the Federal Housing Administration (FHA) in 1934 and with the initiation by this agency of a mortgage insurance program. The improved liquidity of mortgages that resulted from the monthly payments, along with the backing of real-estate loans by federal agencies (FHA and VA) and the creation of a secondary market, contributed to making real-estate loans more popular. In the years immediately after World War II, banks entered this market, and they have since become important real-estate lenders. Real-estate loans are a basic outlet for the time deposit funds of commercial banks.

Because of both quality and liquidity considerations, a few banks have adopted policies limiting their total term loans and real-estate loans combined in relation to their time deposits, to their capital, or to the sum of both. Because of similar concerns, banks may also wish to limit the maturity of their loans for the purchase of new automobiles to only 48 months, for example, or even less. Whatever the management philosophy regarding loan maturities, it should be expressed in writing to serve as a guide for the loan officer.

TYPES OF LOANS

The types and proportions of loans carried in the portfolio vary greatly from bank to bank. This variation generally reflects factors both external and internal to a bank. These factors include the economic character of the area in which the bank is located, the kind and stability of deposits held, the background and evolution of a particular bank, and the preferences of management within the framework of current opportunities and pressures.

Economic Character of the Community

The economic character of the area in which a bank is located largely determines the fields of lending in which it will specialize. Unit banks are more closely tied to a single community than is the case with branch banks. Thus unit banks located in areas where the economy is predominantly agricultural inevitably find themselves engaged primarily in agricultural and real-estate loans. In consequence, banks in these areas have far greater proportions of these types of loans in their portfolios than do banks located in large urban centers. The latter banks build loan portfolios predominantly with commercial and industrial loans, consumer loans, and mortgage loans. And if one of these centers functions as the national money market, then its larger banks can reasonably be considered money-market banks—a fact that would account both for the great proportion of loans for the purchasing of securities found in their loan portfolios and for the importance of correspondent bank accounts among their deposit balances.

Under the branch-banking system, banking is generally conducted through branches that operate in local, regional, or national markets. This characteristic of branch banking contributes to a highly diversified commercial bank loan portfolio with risks spread over different companies, industries, occupations, individuals, and geographical areas. At the same time, however, branch banking renders loan portfolios impersonal—that is, less representative of the specific needs of local communities and groups of individuals.

Banks whose communities include blighted or declining neighborhoods are torn between the desire to meet the credit needs of their communities and the need to make prudent loans. Increasingly in recent years bank boards have become sensitive to charges of redlining, the practice of using geographic location as a criterion to reject loan requests. As was discussed in Chapter 12, existing legislation discourages discriminatory loan policies. Bank boards must formulate policy that defines the bank's role in meeting the community's credit needs.

Stability of Deposits

The types of loans in a bank's portfolio reflect, in part, the composition of maturities and the stability of bank deposits and other liabilities. A general practice that banks have sought to follow over the years in the employment of their funds is to match the maturity of their liabilities with assets of corresponding maturity. This principle underlies the commercial-loan theory of lending, which, as we saw in Chapter 12, argues in favor of short-term, self-liquidating loans in recognition of the demand-deposit character of bank liabilities. Since the end of World War II, the gradual increase in banks' time and savings deposits and their importance, relative to total deposits, have led banks to increase their intermediate-term and long-term lending. Business term loans and many consumer loans constitute examples of the former, while mortgage loans exemplify the latter. These loans are generally financed out of the more stable savings deposits, while the more volatile demand deposits are used to finance short-term loans to businesses. Clearly a fluctuating deposit base, which is typical of banks in rural areas or single-industry communities, is less susceptible to longer-term financing.

Background and Evolution of Bank

Given the economic characteristics of its market and the stability of its deposits, a particular bank's opportunities to make loans also depend on the established patterns of business contacts and loan practice that its management has developed over the years. These patterns—which may have been the result of special talents or tastes of the bank's leading loan or executive officers, or of incidentally useful connections or conditions—also tend to develop institutional roots in highly trained and specialized lending officers, special reputations, and the like, which bestow upon the individual bank a particular character that is shown in the type of business it does and is expressed in the composition of its loan portfolio.

This helps to explain how some banks have become known as, for example, shipping, textile, electronics, or oil banks. Specialization of this type can be profitable, particularly where a degree of expert knowledge not common in the banking industry prevents other banks from competing effectively. It does, however, open the bank to a potential peril. Clearly, substantial loan concentration in the portfolios of such banks would be unavoidable. Such concentration, however, can be partly offset by seeking credit outlets in contrasting industries or in industries not subject to the same cyclical influences. This move, coupled with good income investment policy, geographically and/or industrially diversified, can hold the risks of loan concentration within tolerable margins.

Management Preferences

The foregoing influences set the framework of possibilities within which bank management makes policy decisions pertaining to the composition of the loan portfolio. Not only is there ample choice within this framework, but the framework itself is not unalterable and may be changed gradually and within limits by the additions to established patterns fostered by current policy. The preferences of management with respect to loan portfolio composition, as these are affected by such considerations as yield, risk of loss, and liquidity (average rate of loan payoff), have a strong effect upon the actual composition at any time. This is especially true during a period of monetary restraint. During such a period the general demand for credit is so strong that banks are confronted with more loan requests in practically every category than they can possibly accommodate. Then, more than in any other phase of the business cycle, management exerts a decisive influence upon the types and volume of loans to be made.

Management's preferences for proper balance in the portfolio among the various loan types are expressed in the form of limits upon various loan categories. These limits are not firmly fixed for all time, but are flexibly adjusted or altogether eliminated in line with changing conditions. Limits on specific categories take the form of absolute magnitudes or of percentage relationships that broaden loan categories, or of relationships to time (including savings) deposits or to capital accounts. These limits become especially important when the initial phases of a restrictive credit policy set in, for it is during this time that management adopts a more cautious and selective approach in the extension of loan funds. The implementation of such an approach affects all loan categories and all borrowers. However, there are significant differences in the degree of this effect and in the manner of its transmission for major loan categories and for the individual borrower.

The categories that are the first to feel the impact of credit restraint vary, depending on the character of the loan market in which the bank finds itself. A restrictive lending policy primarily affects the bank's major lending categories (those that constitute the overwhelming bulk of the loan portfolio). Regulation of such categories is both an effective and a necessary instrument of general loan policy.

The loan categories that usually feel the impact of credit restraint most are real-estate loans, consumer loans, and loans to brokers and dealers. By contrast, commercial and industrial loans, unless they constitute the overwhelming bulk of the loan portfolio, tend to feel the effects of a restrictive policy less. This must not be taken to imply that commercial and industrial loan applicants will not be required to meet the higher standards that are progressively imposed as credit tightens, or that they will receive priority over others seeking loans. The great diversity among borrowers within loan categories does not permit such a generalization to hold. But it does imply that commercial and industrial borrowers who can meet the high standards will be the last to be turned down as a bank's lending limit is approached. There are a number of reasons for this privileged position of commercial and industrial borrowers. The cost of administering large business loans is generally low. There are certain economies of scale achieved in making a $1 million loan rather than 50 small mortgage loans or even a larger number of consumer loans. Another reason for their preference over other types of loans is that they are considered essential in maintaining the bank's lending base in the form of commercial deposits. It is basically the deposit balances (compensating balances) provided by the borrowers that place commercial and industrial loans first in management preference vis-á-vis the loans in the other categories during a period of credit stringency.

TERMS OF LENDING

Although there is significant variation in the terms of provisions of loan contracts, some generalizations may be made regarding this domain of lending policy. Some of the more important loan terms covered by bank policy, as determined by the board, include the rate of interest, compensating balances, provisions to protect against defaults, and repayment schedule.

Rate of Interest

The rates of interest that banks charge on loans at any given time generally reflect the state of the economy—that is, of monetary and fiscal policies and the demand for credit. These forces provide the background against which individual banks define their interest-rate policy. This policy does not identify the specific rates that should be charged on the various kinds of loans made by a bank; instead, it provides guidelines to be taken into account by loan officers in the pricing of loans. The objective is, clearly, to treat the borrower fairly and earn a reasonable rate of return for the bank. If the rate quoted is too low, the bank will be forgoing income unnecessarily, while if it is too high, it may drive its customers to borrow elsewhere. Any consideration of the factors that enter into loan pricing must start with a discussion of the prime rate, which forms the basis on which other lending rates are formulated.

Role of the Prime Rate

The prime rate is the interest rate that banks charge their largest and most creditworthy customers. Large, preferred corporate clients have traditionally been granted short-term loans at the prime rate. It is considered an administered rate because it is adjusted by banks according to prevailing money-market conditions. This rate was first introduced in 1933 and represented the efforts of certain large banks to prevent the emergence of a price war among themselves in meeting the slack demand for bank loans that characterized the 1930s. Equally concerned about the adverse effects of a price war, the U.S. Congress allowed large banks to post a 1.5 percent prime rate as a minimum acceptable return on loans to creditworthy customers. Thus, the concept of a bank-imposed "floor" loan rate became an important feature of U.S. commercial banking, with rate changes initiated at various intervals by the leading banks. Once a change was announced, other major banks, and then smaller banks, followed suit. The rationale for this reaction was that if a large money-market leader deemed this change appropriate, it must be both needed and warranted by market conditions.

Changes in the prime rate were given significant coverage in the financial press and the financial community, for they signaled changes in short-term bank lending rates in general and a possible movement in longer-term lending rates.

From the late 1960s on, two developments reduced the significance of the prime rate. First, the increased reliance of banks on money markets to finance their loan demands caused greater volatility in the cost of funds and resulted in greater and more frequent changes in the prime rate. This development, along with an apparent desire for publicity, led an increasing number of banks to join in the act of announcing prime-rate changes. The resulting diversity reduced market sensitivity to rate changes and mitigated the importance of prime-rate changes by the larger and more influential money-center banks.

Second, beginning in 1977 and continuing through the early 1980s—a period of record high prime rates (in mid-December 1980 the prime rate reached an unheard-of 21.5 percent)—there were widespread reports of loans to preferred customers at rates below prime. Recipients of these loans were generally large corporations with impressive credentials and access to alternative sources of funds, including the open market (such as borrowing through issuance of commercial paper). The practice of lending below prime quickly spread throughout the country, and in the early 1980s many medium-size and small banks regularly offered their corporate customers discounts from the announced prime rates. As a result, the following trend developed: high-quality borrowers obtained loans at a discount from the prime rate while medium-quality borrowers received loans at prime. This practice was an important deviation from the traditional definition of the prime rate, and soon gave rise to a rush of lawsuits and congressional criticism. The rising controversy led banks to adopt one of two strategies: delete the term ''prime rate'' from their loan documents and operational language, and replace it with the term ''base rate,'' or keep the term but change its formal connotation as the ''lowest'' or ''best'' lending rate. Citibank and the First National Bank of Chicago are in the first group; Morgan Guaranty, Bank-America, and Chase Manhattan are in the latter. Wherever used, it is simply a reference rate: the rates are set up as a markup over prime.

Introduction of Floating Rates

Traditionally loans to businesses were made at fixed rates—that is, the rate charged did not change over the life of the loan. However, the higher cost of funds experienced in the late 1960s and its effects on profitability were instrumental in bringing about a change in banks' pricing strategies. To keep a profitable spread between their revenues and their cost of funds, in the late 1960s banks began to shift gradually to floating rates. When the rate is floating, it will usually be set at a certain number of percentage points over the prime rate, the commercial-paper rate, the T-bill rate, the T-bond rate, or the London Inter-Bank Offered Rate (LIBOR), which is the rate of interest offered by the largest and strongest London banks on deposits of other large banks of the highest credit standing. Then, when the rate to which the loan is indexed goes up or down, so does the rate charged on the outstanding balance of the loan. Rates may be adjusted annually, semiannually, quarterly, monthly, or on some other basis, depending on what the contract specifies. In 1995, about 60 percent of the dollar amount of all term loans made by banks had floating rates, up from virtually zero in 1970.

Variable-rate lending has also made headway in the area of mortgage financing. Indeed, as seen in Chapter 12, adjustable rates have become a common feature of mortgage instruments. Since the mid-1970s, when they made their first appearance in California, variable-rate mortgages have gained increasing acceptance among lenders because they offer returns that are competitive with going market rates. In addition, they provide greater flexibility in adjusting these long-term assets to the changing cost of funds.

The floating-rate concept of loan pricing acquired new impetus in the early 1980s. With profits undermined by competition, and a recessionary economy, banks began to make floating-rate consumer loans. The floating rate on these loans made them a perfect match for banks' floating-rate money-market deposit accounts. To enhance the acceptability of these loans, banks were advertising them at rates that were below the corresponding fixed-rate loans. For example, in July 1983, the BankAmerica marketed floating-rate auto loans priced at 12 percent, 2.5 percentage points less than its fixed-rate auto loans; rates were adjusted quarterly, in line with the yield of three-month Treasury bills. Floating-rate pricing has since expanded to other types of consumer credit, such as home equity loans and credit card financing. Borrower acceptance of floating-rate consumer loans has been better than that of variable-rate mortgages. With the maturity of consumer loans much shorter, borrower exposure to rate fluctuations is more limited.

With the advent of the floating-rate loan, the profitability of loan portfolios has been enhanced. In addition, the flexibility of the floating-rate loan gives bankers an important tool for coping with the increasingly competitive environment in which they must operate.

Compensating Balances

A customary feature of a short-term unsecured business loan is the compensating-balance requirement, which obligates the borrower to maintain demand or time deposits with the lending bank as part of the loan agreement. Alternatively, this requirement may be applied against the credit facility; that is, borrower balances are expected not to drop below an agreed-upon percentage of the loan amount. The way this requirement is applied varies. In some banks it is applied rigidly: borrowers' balances are expected to be maintained at the minimum or not to fall below it throughout their indebtedness to the bank. Frequently, however, borrowers are given more latitude—the deposit balance must equal the specified minimum on the average or over the course of the year. Clearly, the former rule is much more burdensome to the borrower. Average-balance requirements vary among banks and are influenced by prevailing money-market conditions. Generally, however, they run from 10 to 20 percent, with 15 percent being most common.

The requirement of maintaining compensating balances has an important effect on the cost of the loan. If the requirement is 20 percent and the borrower needs $80,000, the loan raised must amount to $100,000. Assuming that the interest rate charged is 15 percent, the effective cost of the portion of the loan usable by the borrower is 18.75 percent ($15,000 ÷ $80,000). The underlying assumption is, of course, that the borrower will use the entire amount of the loan. Since businesses frequently maintain some funds in their loan accounts, however, there is redundant borrowing (the difference between the level of these funds and the compensating-balance amount).

Banks place more emphasis on compensating balances as qualification for loan accommodation in a period of credit stringency. During such times a borrower's legitimate claim on a bank for a loan is expected to be a multiple of his or her average balance, a figure that is gradually reduced (thus increasing the compensating-balance requirement) as the bank's credit-granting capacity approaches its maximum. Although the compensating balance increases the effective rate of interest on a loan, this does not constitute the full explanation for management's concern. The deeper significance of the compensating balance lies in the relationship of a bank's lending capacity to its deposit base. In order for a bank to be able to lend, it must have deposit funds, and borrowers must be disciplined to contribute by giving the bank lending power. Finally, the compensating balance constitutes a protective device for the bank in dealing with borrowers whose credit is not above reproach. Thus, if a borrower's default appears imminent, the bank can apply the balance on deposit against the loan, thereby offsetting a portion of it. This legal practice (right of offset) enables a bank to obtain a slightly better settlement than would otherwise be possible; that is, it enables the bank to become a general creditor for the remainder of the loan rather than being a general creditor of the bankrupt customer.

The popularity of compensating balances has been affected adversely in recent years by banks' growing reliance on profitability analysis. Cost-benefit analysis of corporate accounts focused on two inefficiencies of compensating balances as a pricing mechanism: the need to maintain legal reserves against these balances and to pay FDIC assessments. As a result, a number of large banks have replaced compensating balances with fees or higher loan rates. This move is a departure from the traditional belief that lending is primarily a tool for developing a bank's current and potential deposit base.

Loan Pricing

Several factors must be taken into account in pricing a loan. First and foremost is the cost of funds to the bank. Bank overhead expense must also be considered in determining the rate charged. Another element is the credit risk involved. Small businesses have a higher rate of failure than large businesses and usually are charged more. The maturity of the loan is also considered, since the longer the loan period, the greater the interest-rate risk exposure. All of the costs involved in originating and servicing the loan—the costs of checking the borrower's credit history, of appraising collateral, and other administrative costs—must be covered by the interest charged. Consumer loans have relatively high rates of interest compared with most other bank loans because of the high administrative costs per dollar lent, in addition to their small size and greater risk. In order to entice borrowers, the bank must offer loans at rates that are competitive with the costs of alternative sources of funds available to the borrower (such as other domestic or foreign banks or the money and capital markets). The bank must also weigh the opportunity cost of the loan by comparing it against other possible uses for the same funds. Another consideration is the bank's desired return on stockholders' equity. Finally, the applicant's relationship with the bank must be considered. Evaluating a business loan application goes beyond estimating the profitability of the individual loan. It also entails assessing the overall profitability of the applicant's relationship with the bank. The loan is but one element in that relationship, which may include maintaining deposits and using other bank services. The essence of a banking relationship, after all, is that business customers expect banks to meet their credit needs and banks expect loan customers to use the bank's other services.

Ignoring the benefits derived from the long-standing relationship with the corporate customer means risking loss of the customer's other business, then and in the future. Further, that customer may be responsible for attracting other customers to the bank, thus contributing to an expansion of the bank's business. For these reasons, banks try to accommodate their steady customers' credit needs whenever possible.

A widely used approach to assessing the overall profitability of a corporate customer to a bank is called customer profitability analysis (CPA). This analysis is similar in principle to the standard account analysis (SAA), which determines the revenue generated by an account, the expenses of servicing it, and the resulting net profit or loss. The SAA is used primarily to determine appropriate compensating-balance requirements for nonborrowing customers who use the bank's other services (such as wire transfers and lock-box services) for which it charges fees. The CPA goes further, considering in addition such services as loans, data processing, and trust services in order to gauge a customer's overall profitability.

When the business loan applicant is a new customer, the bank has less information on which to base its profitability assessment, but the same issues apply: the bank forecasts the future profitability of the customer as a whole in deciding whether to grant the loan. Occasionally loan officers may extend loans to young and struggling businesses that other banks consider marginal credits. These loans constitute promotional lending. Several large U.S. companies owe their development and growth to aggressive and imaginative loan officers who recognized their potential and took greater-than-average risk to assist them in their modest beginnings. These companies never ceased to patronize the bank that extended them their first loan.

With loans constituting the largest source of income, loan policy must provide complete guidelines in determining rates for all the different categories of loans. In business loans there is a variety of loan-pricing models; no single model works for all banks. Some banks price commercial loans by considering the marginal cost of funds—that is, the cost of raising funds to loan to the clients (e.g., the rate paid on the CDs issued for that purpose). To this cost they add a markup of one or more percentage points to compensate for the risk of default, operating expenses (originating, servicing, and collecting the loan), and a return on stockholders' equity. This model, known as *cost-plus* loan pricing, may be expressed in the following manner:

$$\text{Loan rate} = \text{Marginal cost of funds} + \text{Markup}.$$

This formula, though simple and easy to understand, may understate the bank's risk exposure, funding costs, and operating expenses. Moreover, it does not take into account rates charged by competing institutions. These limitations are addressed by the *price leadership* method, which uses an index or reference rate, such as the prime or base rate. Because this rate includes a return on equity in addition to covering costs, the second component of the formula is a risk premium to compensate for the bank's risk exposure. This method may be presented as

$$\text{Loan rate} = \text{Reference rate} + \text{Risk premium}.$$

If the loan is for a period longer than a year, the premium would be adjusted to include term risk. When the prime is used as the reference rate, this method is also referred to as "prime plus." Some money-center banks developed an alternative approach to this formula known as "times prime," whereby the rate is set at some percentage (e.g., 125 percent) of prime.

In the 1980s, competition from the commercial-paper market and foreign banks prompted some institutions to offer short-term business loans to large corporate clients at rates below prime, hence the name of this practice: *below-prime market pricing*. The loan rate was based on the interest cost of borrowing in the money market (e.g., federal-funds rate) plus a markup to cover risk, operating costs, and return on equity. Hence,

$$\text{Loan rate} = \text{Costs of borrowing in money market} + \text{Markup}.$$

Some banks use models that compute the yield generated from a loan in determining whether it is adequate to compensate for the costs and risk involved. One such model considers the income to be generated from a discount interest loan, given a certain usage of the credit facility, a commitment fee, compensating balances (deposits pledged by the client), and the legal provision for required reserves.[1] The formula used for the loan yield is

$$y = \frac{uk + F(1 - u) - (C_T + C_u u)r}{u - uk - (C_T + C_u u)(1 - R)}.$$

The variables are defined as follows:

1. A fixed proportion, C_T, of the credit line will be maintained by the borrower in the form of demand deposits.

2. When the borrower borrows a fraction, u, from the credit line, he/she must maintain another fraction, say C_u, of u in the form of demand deposits.

3. The lending institution will pay an annual rate of interest, r, on the demand deposits.

4. The institution will charge a commitment fee, F, on the unused portion of the credit line.

5. The stated (nominal) rate of interest on the loan is k.

6. The institution lends the money in the form of a discount interest loan, that is, if an amount u is loaned, interest expenses equal to uk are deducted from the principal.

7. R represents the legal reserve requirement for deposits.

For example, suppose that a bank guaranteed a $10 million revolving line of credit to a corporate client under the following terms. A fixed commitment fee of 0.75 percent on the unused portion of the loan will be charged by the bank. The customer will maintain a compensating balance of 10 percent on the total line of credit and of 5 percent on the used portion of the credit line. The bank will pay 6 percent on its demand deposits, and the reserve requirements are 15 percent. The loan will be a discount loan and the rate of interest charged will be equal to the prime rate (currently 10 percent) plus a premium of 1 percent. The bank uses the ''actual/360'' accrual method to adjust for the nominal rate. The loan officer estimates that during the year the client will use, on the average, $7.5 million.

In the computation of the effective yield, the first step would be to determine the adjusted nominal rate of interest, considering that the bank uses the ''actual/360'' accrual method. In other words, since the interest on the principal is charged for 360 days of use, instead of 365 days of use with the usual ''365 days'' method, the adjusted nominal rate of interest is

$$\frac{365}{360} \times (\text{prime rate} + \text{premium})$$

$$\frac{365}{360} \times (.10 + .01) = 0.1115278$$

The other information is as follows:

$$u = 0.75$$
$$r = 0.06$$
$$k = 0.1115278$$
$$C_T = 0.10$$
$$C_u = 0.05$$
$$_F = 0.0075$$
$$_R = 0.15$$

Therefore, the yield for the bank is

$$y = \frac{(.75)(.1115278) + (.0075)(1 - .75) - (.10 + .05 \times .75)(.06)}{.75 - (.75)(.1115278) - (.10 + .05 \times .75)(1 - .15)}$$

$$= \frac{0.0772709}{0.5494792} = 0.1406257, \text{ or } 14.06257 \text{ percent.}$$

If the bank did not use the "actual/360" accrual method, the interest rate on the loaned funds would be 11 percent and the yield to the bank, 13.8252 percent.*

Other pricing models are variations of the above formulas or take into account additional information, such as the total business relationship with a particular customer. Whatever the method used, bank policy must offer complete guidelines for determining the loan rate applied in each case. Increasingly in recent years, banks use systems for loan pricing and profitability analysis that assist the loan officer in the performance of these tasks.

PROTECTION AGAINST DEFAULT

In extending a loan, a bank is always concerned with its ultimate collectability. If the borrower's current financial condition and past record of repayment are good, and loan collectability is expected from the liquidation of the transaction being financed or from anticipated profits, the bank will make the loan on an unsecured basis. Contrary to what is generally believed, large loans to businesses are frequently made on an unsecured basis. Moreover, consumer loans may be made on an unsecured basis because of borrower integrity, income, and past record of repayment. However, in a great many cases concern over the applicant's weak credit history may lead the bank to ask the borrower to pledge a specific asset or offer some other form of protection. Also, loans to rapidly expanding enterprises or to small or new businesses present a greater amount

---

*This would be derived as follows:

$$y = \frac{(.75)(.11) + (.0075)(1 - .75) - (.10 + .05 \times .75)(.06)}{.75 - (.75)(.11) - (.10 + .05 \times .75)(1 - .15)}$$
$$= 0.138252, \text{ or } 13.8252 \text{ percent.}$$

of risk and, therefore, necessitate bank protection. Long-term loans, because of the degree of uncertainty and potential risk involved, may require an extensive loan agreement to protect the lender.

There are various forms of protection available to a bank. The most common type is the direct pledge of assets. Lending against collateral is customarily referred to as *asset-based financing*. Various types of assets may be pledged as collateral, including real estate, equipment, corporate stocks and bonds, and accounts receivable. Since the purpose is to lessen the possibility of a loss if the loan is not repaid, banks have adopted certain criteria that determine the suitability of the collateral. First, the asset must be marketable—that is, it should be readily convertible into cash. A second desirable feature is that the asset has a relatively stable market value, so that the lender can ascertain in advance the approximate amount that can be realized should foreclosure become necessary. Further, the asset should not be perishable or subject to obsolescence due to changes in style or technology. Also, it is desirable that the asset entails a minimum of administrative expenses in maintaining control of it. Finally, the bank should obtain a first claim on the asset and its value should be greater than the face value of the loan it secures. The purpose of this safety margin is to protect the bank if it is forced to liquidate the asset because of borrower default. If the value of the collateral is not sufficient to cover the loan, the bank will have to obtain—in the event of a liquidation—a deficiency judgment and become a general creditor for the difference.

Frequently a loan applicant may substitute the *guarantee* of payment by another party for collateral. For example, when the loan request comes from the subsidiary (such as the production or marketing unit) of a corporation, the latter may offer its guarantee in support of the loan. Parent support is ordinarily justified on the ground that the operations of the subsidiary are financially an integral part of the parent's. Assuming the explicit guarantee of the parent, the bank's risk is no different from that assumed in a direct loan to the parent itself.

Guarantees are also sought and received by lenders in support of loans to veterans and small businesses. In the former instance, as stated in Chapter 12, the Veterans Administration guarantees all real-estate loans to former servicemen. Small businesses may obtain loans with the guarantee of the Small Business Administration (SBA). One of the conditions for such a guarantee is inability of the borrower to obtain funds from commercial banks on a reasonable basis. Rural businesses and farmers also may obtain loans from banks with the guaranty of another governmental agency, the Farmers Home Administration.

In addition to collateral and guarantees, there are other forms of protection. One is the incorporation of *covenants* into the loan agreement, especially common in term loans to businesses. These covenants are of three types: affirmative, negative, and restrictive. An affirmative covenant, for example, requires the borrower to submit audited financial statements at the end of each year and unaudited statements at more frequent intervals. Other affirmative covenants may require the borrower to maintain minimum balance-sheet ratios; to hire an officer (such as a vice president for finance) to ensure efficient financial management; and to carry "key-man" insurance on senior management personnel who cannot be easily replaced. Negative covenants restrain the borrower from certain actions, such as pledging assets while the loan is outstanding, entering into a merger with another concern, or offering a guarantee on loans to third parties. Restrictive covenants limit the latitude of management action, such as restricting dividend payments and potential borrowing, and setting ceilings on salaries, bonuses, and advances to officers and employees.

Still another form of protection normally required in loans to proprietorships and partnerships is securing a *cosigner* (comaker), which will render principals legally liable for the debt of the firm. In the cases of small or closely held corporations whose owners have also extended loans to the business, banks customarily request *subordination* of this debt to the bank's loan. The amount owed to principals thus serves essentially as additional capital protecting the bank's claim in the event of liquidation.

A final form of protection for the bank consists of the *default provisions* customarily included in loan contracts. Failure to comply with contractual obligations (such as to pay principal and interest when due or to observe the provisions of the loan agreement) makes the loan immediately due and payable. Term-loan agreements customarily include a clause, known as an acceleration clause, that provides for the immediate repayment of the loan if certain provisions are violated.

Loan Repayment

The time of loan repayment is a basic feature of a bank's lending policy. Loan repayment is generally agreed upon prior to the extension of the loan and should represent a realistic evaluation of the customer's ability to repay. The objective is to secure repayment through liquidation of the transaction being financed or the scheduled flow of earnings, rather than through forced foreclosure and subsequent sale of the pledged collateral.

When a bank is forced to sell collateral at a price below the market level, both the borrower and the community as a whole suffer. This effect is especially acute when the economy is already sluggish. The collapse of the real-estate market in the 1930s is generally blamed on just such a trend. Mortgage loans extended in the 1920s were based on collateral values rather than on a realistic appraisal of the customer's ability to repay. As a result, defaults occurred in the 1930s, forcing foreclosures in large enough numbers to depress the real-estate market as a whole.

Repayment terms exhibit significant variation, depending on the type of transaction being financed. Loan repayments may range from a few weeks to 25 or 30 years, as in the case of mortgage loans. The terms may require a lump-sum repayment or repayment according to an installment schedule. Lump-sum loans, usually called straight loans, require complete repayment of principal on an agreed-upon date, with interest being paid at maturity or at various intervals during the life of the loan. More common, however, are installment loans, which require incremental repayment at fixed intervals: monthly, quarterly, semiannually, or annually. This type of loan is less formidable for an individual to manage and aids in the budgeting of income.

Although installment terms are seen most often in consumer and real-estate loans, businesses also avail themselves of this type of arrangement. At times banks will offer different terms of installment repayment, such as a larger, balloon payment at the end. This often necessitates the arranging of a new loan to cover repayment of part of the balloon payment. A balloon payment is normally set up to allow the borrower more flexibility at first, trusting that he or she will be able to pay off the full loan when it reaches maturity.

Another form of installment loan calls for payments at irregular intervals or in varying amounts. Agricultural loans are frequently of this type. Because of its dependence on weather, size of crops, and control of insect infestations, agricultural financing does not lend itself to a regular method of loan payment. Regular and equal payments similar to those in consumer credit are found only in loans financing dairy and poultry activity.

Borrowers often opt to repay their loans before they come due. Banks are usually in favor of such actions because they indicate the borrower is financially stronger. However, banks do not favor repayments made from funds borrowed elsewhere at lower interest rates. In such a case they may impose a stiff penalty for prepayment. This is especially true for term loans to businesses.

ADMINISTRATION OF THE LOAN POLICY

The administrative framework for carrying out the lending function is an integral part of loan policy. In other words, loan policymaking extends to the establishment of an effective lending organization and the adoption of the necessary procedures for the proper execution of the lending function. Specifically, the directors must determine the organizational structure of the lending function, set procedures for the review of loan applications, and identify the steps to be taken when the borrower fails to meet contractual responsibilities.

Organizing the Lending Function

The lending organization varies considerably from one bank to another, reflecting, among other things, differences in the sizes of the banks, the types of loans made, the quality of management, and the attitude of the boards of directors toward the delegation of authority. Generally speaking, the legal responsibility for bank lending rests with the entire board of directors. It is customary, however, to assign responsibility for supervising the lending function to a loan committee or to a senior management member to ensure that loans are made in accordance with the law and the bank's own policies. If a loan or discount committee is placed in charge of the lending function, this body would be responsible for effecting the bank's lending policies. In such banks it is customary for the loan committee, which would be composed of senior loan officers, to handle all loan requests above the lending officers' limit. Members of the board may participate in this committee. If the responsibility for supervising the lending function is assigned to an individual, in large banks this would probably be a senior vice president, while in small ones it would be the president. The president of a small bank is at the same time the principal lending officer, and therefore handles all types of loan requests, whether for consumer, business, or real-estate purposes. Other officers may be charged with performing limited lending functions along with their other activities. Under no circumstances however, should the outside directors be actively involved in the granting of loans. Such involvement is poor loan policy, not only because of their lack of technical or specialized knowledge but also because of their community affiliations with political, social, and business interests.

In very large banks there is significant delegation of authority and lending specialization. These banks, in response to specialized loan demands, usually have the lending function carried out by such specialized departments as consumer, real estate, agricultural, and business or commercial. These departments may be broken down further according to the industrial diversity of the market served. Business loans, for example, may be divided by industry, with a loan officer in charge of each industry or group of related industries. If loan committees are an integral part of the lending organization, these committees would be organized along departmental lines; that is, each committee would be composed of officers of the same loan department (intradepartmental committee). With an organization of that kind, very few, if any, loan requests would be referred to the board of directors for action.

The delegation of lending authority by the board of directors extends beyond the establishment of a loan committee. The board, at the recommendation of management, also assigns maximum dollar lending limits, for both secured and unsecured loans, that authorize loan officers to decide independently of the committee on requests within their assigned limits. These limits are subject to periodic review by the board and generally vary according to the size of the bank and the experience of the loan officer. A generally accepted approach is to assign lending limits by title. For example, the assigned limits may be scaled as follows: commercial loan officer, $50,000; assistant vice president, $100,000; vice president, $500,000; senior vice president, $1,000,000. To expedite the loan decision process, some banks allow banking officers to combine their lending limits. Thus, two bank officers with loan limits of $100,000 each might jointly approve a $200,000 loan request. Combinations of lending limits are especially useful in situations requiring fast responses.

The lending organization of branch banks exhibits an important variation from that of unit banks insofar as it concerns the lending authority of the branches. It is not uncommon for branch officers and managers to have limited loan authority. In such instances loan requests above these limits must be referred to the head office for consideration by the branch's regional supervisor. If the specific request is higher than the supervisor's limit, it is referred to the bank's loan committee. Clearly, a high degree of centralization in lending authority is undesirable because of its detrimental effects. Such centralization results in significant delays; drastically reduces the element of personal contact, which is so important in credit evaluation; and gives rise to poor customer relations.

Assessing Loan Requests

In deciding upon loan requests, lending officers must have all relevant information about the applicant. While in small banks the loan officer must evaluate the creditworthiness and debt-repayment capacity of the loan applicant, in larger banks this task of credit analysis is performed by the credit department. The functions of the credit department are basically the same in all banks: it assembles, records, and analyzes credit information, with the objective of ascertaining the degree of risk associated with each loan request and determining the amount of credit the bank can prudently extend in each case. In some banks the credit department may make recommendations on a credit request; in others it may not. In any case the final decision is left to the lending officer and/or the loan committee.

Scope of Credit Analysis

In analyzing a loan request, the loan officer or credit analyst (depending upon who performs the credit analysis) will examine a variety of factors, commonly referred to as the five C's of credit: character, capacity, capital, collateral, and conditions.

Character implies not just a willingness to pay off debts but also a strong desire to settle contractual obligations in accordance with the terms of the contract. When the borrower is an individual, character is largely a function of moral qualities, personal habits, style of living, business and personal associates, and general standing in the business and social communities. When the borrower is a company, character is a function of management integrity and reputation and standing in the business and financial communities. In the final analysis the reputation, integrity, and standing of a company's management are primarily a reflection of the character of the individuals responsible for the formulation and execution of company policies. Whether the borrower is an individual or a business, the previous record of meeting financial obligations plays a major role in evaluating character.

Capacity has both legal and economic connotations. From a legal perspective, lenders are interested in knowing whether the party requesting the loan can legally obligate itself. In lending to a partnership, the loan officer should ascertain that the signing partner has legal authority (such as a power of attorney from the other partners) to obligate the partnership. Similarly, in lending to a corporation, it is advisable to examine the corporate charter and bylaws to determine who has the authority to borrow for the corporation. In the absence of any explicit statement, a bank may accept a corporate resolution, signed by the board of directors, that identifies the person who has authority to negotiate for the company and sign the loan contract.

From an economic perspective, capacity implies the ability to meet loan payments as they come due. The analytical measure utilized to determine a borrower's debt repayment capacity is cash flow, defined as net income plus depreciation and other noncash charges, minus other noncash income. The essence of cash-flow lending is that it enables a bank to analyze a company's financial projections and, if they are acceptable, develop a repayment schedule that reflects its ability to generate cash. An outgrowth of the anticipated-income theory, cash-flow lending has been extensively relied upon in the evaluation of loan requests. If the borrower is an individual, ability to generate income depends in part on business experience, education, good judgment, ambition, maturity or age, and shrewdness. For a corporation, its power to generate income depends upon the quality of goods and services sold, cost and availability of raw materials and labor, competition, profit sensitivity to cycles, effectiveness of advertising, and company location. In recent years, however, it has been increasingly recognized by banks that the single most important income-generating factor for a company is the quality of its management. Studies have concluded that inexperience, incompetence, neglect, and fraud are among the chief causes of business failures. Thus management should be able to adapt to changing conditions, replace inefficient practices with more efficient ones, take advantage of opportunities as they arise, and ensure that the company's products have price and/or quality appeal.

A company with a sizable capital base is a more acceptable credit risk than one that is highly leveraged. The utilization of capital to purchase quality assets is an important factor in determining the financial strength of the company. A borrower's ability to obtain credit would thus be greatly affected by the amount and quality of the assets owned. For example, a manufacturer that owns modern machinery and equipment will be more certain of obtaining credit than will its counterpart with obsolete machinery and worn-out equipment. Similarly, a retailer with attractive premises and adequate stock will be favored over a counterpart with run-down premises and inadequate stock.

A bank may request a would-be borrower to provide collateral for the loan. In some cases collateral is pledged because the loan is longer-term, which increases the risk factor for the bank; in other cases security is requested in order to increase the borrower's sense of responsibility. In most cases, assets are pledged because they improve a lender's claim against a borrower. Broadly speaking, the proper function of collateral is to minimize the risk of loss to a bank if, for unforeseen reasons, the borrower's income or profits fail to materialize sufficiently for repayment of the loan. In other words, the purpose of the collateral is to provide a bank with a second way out of a loan, and not to be the primary source of repayment. This view is exemplified by the axiom that collateral does not make a bad loan good but makes a good loan better.

A final factor to be considered by the loan officer in deciding on a loan request is conditions—the economic environment within which the borrower operates. To properly evaluate this factor, the loan officer must become familiar with the characteristics of the industry with which the firm is associated. This aspect of credit analysis has become increasingly difficult in recent years as more companies have grown into multiproduct and multinational concerns.

The kind of information for which the loan officer should look includes effect of economic conditions upon the industry (cycle sensitivity), the industry's output relative to gross national product, market structure, impact of technology (and technological changes) on the demand for the industry's product or its capital requirements, distribution methods, trends in industry profits, and the extent to which the industry is regulated by the government. Answers to these and related questions will enable the loan officer to obtain a comprehensive understanding of the dynamics of the industry, a basic input for a more pragmatic appraisal of the relative strengths and weaknesses of the firm.

Sources of Credit Information

Any evaluation of the applicant's creditworthiness has to rely on information. The bank certainly needs to accumulate information that will be used to evaluate the borrower's character, capacity, capital, collateral, and industry characteristics. Collecting information is the function of credit investigation, the scope of which varies from case to case, depending upon such considerations as type of loan, size, maturity, and collateral offered. Although a bank may draw upon several sources of credit information, some of the more important ones include an interview with the party requesting the loan, the bank's credit files, external sources, an in-person visit to the applicant's premises, and the applicant's financial statements.

It is customary for a loan officer to interview a would-be borrower for the purpose of developing credit information. During the interview the loan officer has the opportunity to inquire—or obtain additional information—about the history of the company, experience and background of the principal officers, the nature of the business, profitability of operations, extent of competition in the marketplace, and availability of resources for the smooth functioning of the business. Other information that the loan officer can obtain during the interview pertains to the purpose for which the proceeds of the loan are to be used. Knowledge of the purpose of the loan is important not only because of risk considerations but also because it enables the loan officer to relate repayment to the nature of the transaction being considered for financing. For example, project loans (for instance, to finance the development of raw materials, oil, mineral, and other resources) call for repayment provisions tailored to the cash flow of the project being financed. The interview, moreover, provides the loan officer with an initial impression of the sincerity, integrity, and capability of the party requesting the loan. Finally, the interview is an appropriate time for asking the loan applicant to submit financial statements and any other additional information, and to arrange for a visit to the company.

A bank's credit files can be an important source of information for a loan officer. Banks establish for each borrower a file containing detailed information on the credit relationship with that client. By studying a prospective borrower's file, the loan officer can see how well the customer complied with the terms and conditions of previous loans and can assess the bank's overall credit experience. The information contained in these files, though confidential, is customarily shared with other banks when they consider extending credit to the same client. Even if the borrower approaches the bank for the first time, a credit file may exist if the borrower is a sizable concern in the area in which the bank is located (a ''prospect file'').

Apart from the loan interview and the bank's own records, a loan officer may also make use of external sources of credit information. One such source is other banks; although banks compete vigorously among themselves, they share credit information when approached by the same customer. Another source of credit information is credit-reporting agencies. Payment and employment information on individuals is customarily supplied by credit bureaus that may be local, regional, or national. For businesses there are various credit-reporting agencies. One of the best-known is Dun and Bradstreet. This agency collects information on businesses in the United States and abroad, and publishes it on a firm-by-firm basis. Dun and Bradstreet also issues written credit reports that provide more detailed information on individual firms. These reports contain a brief history of the company, its principal officers, the nature of the business, ownership, operating data, and other financial information. Other external sources of credit information are the suppliers and customers of the prospective borrower; public records (where reference is made, for example, to pending lawsuits, bankruptcy proceedings, and transfers of property); trade journals, which report developments and trends in the particular industries in which bank customers are engaged; public accounting firms; commercial publications (such as Moody's and Standard and Poor's); and newspapers, magazines, circulars, bulletins, and directories.

The financial status of a loan applicant and the quality of its management can often be determined by the loan officer through a visit to the applicant's business. Such a visit will give the loan officer first-hand information on the condition and efficiency of its physical facilities; the extent of management sophistication in terms of nature and method of operation, and financial planning; and employee attitudes toward management policies.

One of the most important sources of credit information is the applicant's financial statements. Because financial statements identify the expected ability of a would-be borrower to repay indebtedness, their submission is generally required. A firm usually must submit audited condition and income statements, covering the last three to five years, so that the loan officer can obtain a feeling for company direction. In analyzing current financial statements, the loan officer will need to determine whether the figures cited represent a fair and accurate statement of the values involved. Clearly, such evaluation may result in the trimming or adjustment of items from what was originally reported by the applicant.

This approach provides a pragmatic picture of the prospective borrower's financial position. A generally accepted practice was to record the applicant's financial information on standardized forms known as spread sheets. These permitted consistency in the presentation and organization of financial data, and facilitated comparisons of several annual financial statements. In recent years, financial analysis software assists the credit analyst in organizing the information, making calculations, and comparing data. Analysis of financial information is effected through certain widely used techniques, which are presented in the appendix to this chapter.

As stated earlier, credit analysis does not involve decision making; at best it is a recommendation to loan officers and/or the loan committee, which will review the credit information and decide on the action to be taken. As is implied, in arriving at such decisions, loan officers are always expected to consider what is good for the bank. After all, the purpose of the lending policy is not to serve as an end in itself but to promote the objectives of the lending function.

Loan Monitoring

A necessary part of the loan officer's responsibility is to keep abreast of the loans outstanding. That is, once a loan has been made, the loan officer is usually responsible for supervising it. Loan supervision implies keeping in close contact with the borrower and monitoring his financial activities. This may include plant visits, securing the borrower's periodic financial statements, and reviewing requests for renewal or additional funds.

Many banks have a separate unit (department) that is entrusted with the loan-review function. The loan-review staff engages in periodic audits of the loan portfolio to ascertain compliance with laws and regulations, and bank policy. Large loans are routinely examined; small ones, on a random basis. The key features of each loan are checked, such as borrower's current financial condition, record of payments, quality and condition of collateral, and completeness of loan documentation. Loan review helps the bank maintain a sound lending program by identifying problem loans quickly and acting as a continuing check on officers' adherence to the bank's loan policy.

Despite a bank's best care in the granting and monitoring of loans, some borrowers inevitably will be unable or unwilling to meet their repayment schedules. Some borrowers may present minor problems for the bank from the very beginning, some may develop gradually and become chronic problems, and some may develop all of a sudden, without any prior indication of trouble. What are the underlying causes of problem loans? Figure 13.1 identifies some of the

Figure 13.1
Causes of Problem Loans

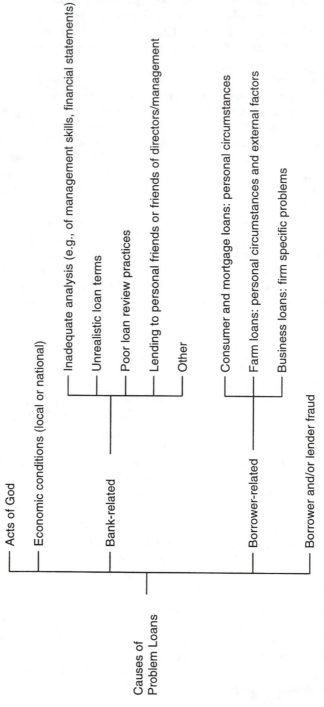

Source: Developed by the author.

most important causes of problem loans. As seen in this figure, the causes of problem loans include acts of God, such as earthquakes, hurricanes, and floods; economic conditions (such as recession or depression); flaws in bank lending policies and practices; borrower-related difficulties resulting in inability to reduce or repay loans as agreed; and borrower and/or lender fraud.

It seems that the major reason by far for problem loans and possible losses is borrower-related and stems from the inability to realize sufficient income to meet contractual obligations. For consumer and mortgage loans, personal circumstances (for instance, unemployment, divorce, sickness) weigh heavily in borrowers' ability to repay their debts. In the case of farm loans, external factors figure prominently in the servicing of these loans. Farming is a risky enterprise because of such factors as unfavorable weather, crop disease, infestation, and oversupply. Business loans can develop into problem loans and losses as a result of many factors, most of which are directly related to management. Studies by Dun and Bradstreet attribute over 90 percent of business failures to management inexperience and incompetence. Although strong and able leadership is difficult to quantify, its effects permeate all aspects of business activity: selection of company goals, definition of organizational structure, formulation and implementation of policies, control over the production process, and efficient and profitable operation of the business firm.

The first explicit sign that a bank receives of a loan in distress is usually an indication from the borrower of inability to comply with the original repayment terms. Early signs of financial problems with business borrowers include one or more of the following developments: decline in deposit balances and occurrence of overdrafts, slow or delinquent loan payments to the bank, delays in the submission of financial statements, delays in arranging for plant visits, new indebtedness, and deterioration in the original rapport with the borrower. With the first indication of customer delinquency, a bank should take appropriate action. Commercial banks have two broad choices, and within each choice there are various alternatives. Figure 13.2 identifies these choices in the handling of problem loans: "work out" arrangement and liquidation. "Work out" is a process of working with the borrower to enable repayment of the loan in part or in full. Liquidation is the process of employing every legal means to enforce loan repayment.

Banks usually want to avoid legal action because it consumes resources and time. The attitude of the borrower toward the debt and the financial condition of the company may justify the handling of the loan on a "work out" basis. A "work out" arrangement may take any form that best suits a particular situation. For example, the bank may work closely with the borrower to renegotiate the terms of the loan, and may even advance additional funds if warranted by circumstances. Other important steps to restore the financial health of the borrower may include advice and counsel to improve operations, restructuring the business, or even taking an active part in the management of the firm (for instance, handling all financial and accounting functions).

Figure 13.2
Handling of Problem Loans

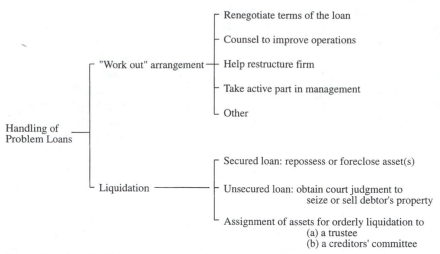

Source: Developed by the author.

If a "work out" is tried and proves unsuccessful, or the prospects for such an arrangement are poor, liquidation may be the only way of handling a loan that has become a collection problem. If the loan is secured, the bank will repossess or foreclose the asset and sell it at a price that will possibly cover the debt. For an unsecured loan, a judgment is issued from the proper court to permit the seizure and selling of debtor property. If the bank is one of a number of creditors, the borrower may assign its assets voluntarily to a trustee or a creditors' committee for an orderly disposal of the assets and distribution of the proceeds on a prorated basis.

Generally, liquidation occurs if the company is deemed to be too far gone to be saved—if it is worth more dead than alive. Liquidation is one form of relief for debtors; the other is reorganization. The decision to force a firm to liquidate or to permit it to reorganize depends on whether the value of the reorganized firm is likely to be greater than the value of the firm's assets if they were sold off piecemeal. Unlike liquidation, which is addressed by Chapter VII of the Bankruptcy Act of 1978, reorganization is provided for by Chapter XI of this act. In a reorganization, a committee of unsecured creditors is appointed by the court to negotiate with management on the terms of a potential reorganization. The reorganization plan may call for a restructuring of the firm's debt, such as lengthening the maturity of the debt, reducing the rate of interest, or exchanging a part of it for equity. The objective is to reduce financial charges to a level that can be covered by the firm's cash flow. The court may appoint a trustee to oversee the reorganization, or the existing management may be allowed to retain control. Although a reorganized business firm is of more value than a failed one, there is no assurance that a bank will recoup the funds advanced, or that it will do so within a reasonable period of time. Indeed, banks may have to settle for less and wait for several years before they can collect.

When delinquencies arise, they should promptly be brought to the attention of the loan committee or the board of directors. Detailed reporting is especially warranted when delinquent loans are large (as is the case in many commercial loans), with such reporting containing information on the cause of the delinquency and the subsequent measures instituted by the loan officer. On the other hand, small loans (consumer loans) may be referred to in the delinquency reports in a more generalized manner—in terms of aggregate amounts per type or class of loan. Many large banks follow the policy of assigning delinquent loans to a separate department staffed by trained personnel with significant experience in the handling of problem loans. The fresh look at the loan by an officer other than the one who originally made it is highly desirable. Unbiased analysis of the situation and firmness in handling the loan are important attributes of this approach.

Loans that perform well are classified as "nonrated." However, those loans with problems must be classified according to the level of risk they represent. Loans considered unduly risky, and therefore calling for careful monitoring to avoid loss, are labeled "substandard." "Doubtful" loans are those expected to result in partial loss. Loans judged to be uncollectible are classified as "loss" and may no longer be listed among the bank's assets—that is, they are charged off (they are removed from the loan portfolio and are charged against the allowance for loan losses). Although loans are charged off, the bank may be able to recover all or part of the funds involved, thereby reducing its net charge-off amount (recoveries are added back into the allowance account). Comparative data on charge-offs, recoveries, and net charge-offs by type of loan or by state for banks of different asset size are provided by the FDIC. The direct comparison of these data with individual bank figures should provide a reasonable index of the soundness of a bank's lending and collection policies.

APPENDIX: TECHNIQUES OF ANALYSIS

Although inquiring about the nature and determining the true worth of accounts in financial statements are essential to intelligent analysis of the prospective borrower's business, item-by-item evaluation does not identify any key relationships between accounts or groups of accounts, nor does it make possible any judgment on the stability of the company's operations or the efficiency with which it is being managed. To address these and related questions, the loan officer must turn to such tools of financial analysis as cash flow, ratios, sources and uses of funds, and common-size analysis. Use of these tools helps the officer recognize exceptional situations quickly and distinctly, and encourages him or her to seek additional information, or clarification, from the would-be borrower.

No single tool is complete; rather, each tool gives a different perspective on the prospective borrower's financial condition. Therefore, each of these tools should not be viewed as an end in itself, but as a means of reaching a reasoned decision. A brief description of some of the basic techniques used in the analysis of financial statements is provided below.

Common-Size Analysis

One of the simpler methods that the loan officer may use in analyzing financial statements is the common-size analysis, which expresses all related items as a percentage of a basic magnitude. For the purpose of this analysis, the basic magnitude is given the rating of 100 percent. Thus, all items in the income statement are expressed as a percentage of net sales, and all balance-sheet items are expressed as a percentage of total assets or liabilities and equity. Once this is done and is extended to the financial statements of preceding years, the loan officer will be able to compare the relative importance of similar figures for previous periods and to identify any situations that appear to be out of line.

Trend Percentage Method

A related technique is the trend percentage method of comparison. This approach calls for establishing as base year the earliest year for which financial statements are submitted by the would-be borrower, and giving each item appearing in that statement a rating of 100 percent. If the corresponding accounts in subsequent years' statements are related to the base year, the lending officer will be able to detect the extent of the increase in each statement account, or group of accounts, over the base year and the revealed trend over the period under consideration. In some accounts the trend may be upward; in others, downward; in still others no definite trend may be evidenced. In addition to the direction of the trend, the loan officer will be able to compare the trends of individual accounts, or groups of accounts, over the period under consideration.

Sources-and-Uses Statement

Another method useful in investigating financial statements is the sources-and-uses-of-funds statement. Preparation of a sources-and-uses-of-funds statement is based on the computation of the net changes in the asset, liability, and net-worth accounts from one balance-sheet date to another. The net change in each individual balance-sheet item is listed under separate "source" and "use" columns, depending upon what such a change represents. Changes that reflect increases in assets and decreases in liabilities and in net worth are recorded under the "uses of funds" column; decreases in assets and increases in liabilities and net worth, under the "sources of funds" column. The purpose of this method is to readily identify the sources tapped by the would-be borrower to meet the need for funds during the period under consideration.

Cash Budgets

Cash flow is still another technique of value to the loan officer in the credit analysis function. Since borrowers are expected to pay off loans out of income rather than out of the sale of assets or through refinancing from another lender, the loan officer must look to their future income for debt retirement. Cash flows are thus prepared, for the most part, from information contained in projected income statements and balance sheets. Hence the importance of always checking the reasonableness of the borrower's projected data against the economic and industry forecasts for the period that the loan will be outstanding. Since the accuracy of a cash flow depends heavily on the assumptions underlying pro forma financial statements, the loan officer may wish to develop cash flows under best, worst, and most likely assumptions when deciding the borrower's ability to service the debt.

Cash flows are normally requested from would-be borrowers for each year that the loan will be outstanding. These cash flows, in addition to predicting loan repayment, provide important insights into management competency. In other words, a company's sources of cash and its cash needs, and the relative amounts involved, project a clearer picture of the degree of efficiency with which the company is being managed. If, for example, the company's net cash generation is poor because of a rapid growth pattern, this raises questions about the soundness of credit practices, requirements for additional working capital, inventory policies, and payables policies.

An example of a cash-flow analysis for a business firm is presented in Table 13.1. This table cites two cash-flow versions: one submitted by the credit applicant and the other developed by the bank's credit analyst. The format is made up of the following components: total cash generated from operations, which includes net income plus depreciation and other sources of cash (such as decrease in noncurrent assets or increase in senior liabilities); total uses of cash, which includes capital and other expenditures as well as changes in net working investment (as determined by separate analysis of current accounts); changes in short-term debt, which may—or may not—constitute an additional source of cash, depending upon the direction of the change; servicing of already contracted long-term debt; and the resulting excess or deficit, which identifies the prospective borrower's ability to service the loan requested.

Ratio Analysis

A final technique in financial-statement analysis is ratios. The objective of ratios is to highlight the internal relationship between figures reported in financial statements. If discriminately calculated and wisely interpreted, ratios can be

Table 13.1
Cash-Flow Analysis

	Company's Estimate of Most Likely Cash Flow					Bank's Estimate of Most Likely Cash Flow				
	1998	1999	2000	2001	2002	1998	1999	2000	2001	2002
Net income	-1	22	37	48	69	-5	-1	6	18	26
± depreciation	51	56	60	63	57	48	51	52	55	58
Operating cash flow	50	78	97	111	126	43	50	58	73	84
± other sources	11	8	12	13	1	11	8	11	10	1
Total operating cash flow	61	86	109	124	127	54	58	69	83	85
Change in net working investment	-69	48	-1	3	5	24	-6	-17	8	12
Capital expenditures	56	34	36	34	52	56	34	36	34	52
Other uses	7	6	0	1	11	1	12	0	0	1
Total uses	-6	88	35	38	68	81	40	19	42	65
Excess/(deficit)	67	-2	74	86	59	(27)	18	50	41	20
Change in short-term debt[a]	-29	-8	-7	5	-7	-29	-8	-7	5	-7
Available to service long term (LT) debt	38	(10)	67	91	52	(56)	10	43	46	13
LT debt repayments	84	64	73	130	71	85	65	73	130	71
Excess/(deficit)	(46)	(74)	(6)	(39)	(19)	(141)	(55)	(30)	(84)	(58)

[a]Reduction in short-term borrowing as anticipated by loan applicant.
Source: Provided by a large New York bank.

Table 13.2
Summary of Financial Ratios

Type and Name of Ratio	Formula for Calculation
1. Liquidity	
Current	$\dfrac{\text{Current assets}}{\text{Current liabilities}}$
Quick, or acid test	$\dfrac{\text{Current assets - inventory}}{\text{Current liabilities}}$
2. Debt Management	
Debt to total assets	$\dfrac{\text{Total debt}}{\text{Total assets}}$
Debt to equity	$\dfrac{\text{Total debt}}{\text{Common equity}}$
Interest coverage	$\dfrac{\text{Earnings before interest \& taxes}}{\text{Interest charges}}$
Fixed charge coverage	$\dfrac{\text{Earnings before fixed charges and taxes}}{\text{Fixed charges}}$
3. Asset Management	
Inventory turnover	$\dfrac{\text{Cost of goods sold}}{\text{Average inventory}}$
Average collection period (days)	$\dfrac{\text{Accounts receivable}}{\text{Annual credit sales/360}}$
Fixed assets turnover	$\dfrac{\text{Sales}}{\text{Fixed assets}}$
Total assets turnover	$\dfrac{\text{Sales}}{\text{Total assets}}$
4. Profitability	
Net profit margin	$\dfrac{\text{Net profit}}{\text{Net sales}}$
Return on assets (ROA)	$\dfrac{\text{Net profit}}{\text{Total assets}}$
Return on equity (ROE)	$\dfrac{\text{Net profit}}{\text{Common equity}}$

Source: Prepared by the author.

of considerable assistance in the analysis of these statements. In other words, ratio calculations are helpful when the figures selected are reliable and come from accounts that bear a fundamental and important relevance to one another. Thus, though a large number of ratios can be computed, only a few are considered basic in analysis work. Table 13.2 lists the commonly used financial ratios, grouping them according to type.

Ratios are meaningless if analyzed in isolation. To provide insights regarding a company's performance, they must be compared against certain standards. Ratios lend themselves to two kinds of comparative analysis: time series and cross-sectional. The former provides for interyear comparisons of borrower performance to determine the general direction in which the company's financial condition is moving; the latter, for comparisons with other firms in the same industry over a common period of time.

There are several sources of comparative financial ratios for both time series and cross-sectional analysis. Probably the source of industry average ratios most widely known and used by bankers is the *Annual Statement Studies*, published by Robert Morris Associates (RMA). This publication provides financial data on more than 425 lines of business activity, based on the financial statements of a sample of over 120,500 different firms. The data, which consist of 16 ratios and a common-size balance sheet and income statement, are presented on an industry-by-industry basis, with each industry subdivided into size categories. A standard page from the *Annual Statement Studies* is reproduced in Figure 13.3.* Another source of ratios is Dun and Bradstreet's *Key Business Ratios*, which provides various ratios calculated for a large number of industries. The *Almanac of Business and Industrial Financial Ratios*, published annually by Prentice-Hall, is still another source. Ratios cover many lines of business activity and are based on samples of corporate tax filings with the Internal Revenue Service. Although quite accurate, these data have a drawback—they are available with a lag of two to three years. Ratios pertaining to banks may be found in the *Index of Bank Performance*, published annually by the Bank Administration Institute, and in the *Bankbook Report on Performance*, published by the investment firm Keefe, Bruyette & Woods, Inc. Both are excellent sources of industry averages for banks.

Apart from their use for comparative analysis purposes, ratios may be used for predicting the insolvency of business firms. In a multiple-discriminant analysis model developed by E. I. Altman for publicly traded U.S. manufacturing firms, it is possible to use a set of ratios that, based on past experience, best predicts impending corporate bankruptcy.[2] Altman's discriminant function takes the form

$$Z = .012X_1 + .014X_2 + .033X_3 + .006X_4 + .999X_5,$$

where

$$X_1 = \text{net working capital/total assets (in \%)}$$

---

*RMA cautions that the *Studies* should be regarded only as a general guideline and not as an absolute industry norm. This is due to limited samples within categories, the categorization of companies by their primary Standard Industrial Classification (SIC) number only, and different methods of operations by companies within the same industry. For these reasons RMA recommends that the figures be used only in addition to other methods of financial analysis.

$X_2=$ retained earnings/total assets (in %)
$X_3=$ EBIT/total assets (in %)
$X_4=$ market value of equity/book value of debt (in %)
$X_5=$ sales/total assets (times).

The critical Z value that discriminated between bankrupt and nonbankrupt firms is 1.81. That is, a firm with a Z score greater (less) than 1.81 is classified a nonbankrupt (bankrupt) firm. Use of the Z analysis, as this approach has been formally referred to, can be helpful in the screening of commercial loan applicants and in the early detection of any financial deterioration among existing borrowers.

LOOKING BEYOND ANALYTICAL TOOLS

Although analytical tools are important in evaluating the financial condition of a would-be borrower, it is necessary to supplement them with specific pertinent facts and direct contact with the borrower. After all, credit analysis is not cut-and-dried. It is as unique as each individual borrower. If a borrower's character is poor, the probability of respect for the terms of a loan agreement is low. Arriving at a reasoned decision thus requires use of analytical tools combined with intuitive judgment.

Figure 13.3
Industry Statistics for Retailers: Groceries and Meats (SIC #5411)

Comparative Historical Data — columns 10 | 36 | 31

Current Data Sorted By Sales — 207 statements (4/1–9/30/94); 402 statements (10/1/94–3/31/95)

	4/1/92-3/31/93 ALL	4/1/93-3/31/94 ALL	4/1/94-3/31/95 ALL	0-1MM	1-3MM	3-5MM	5-10MM	10-25MM	25MM&Over
# Postretirement Benefits	10	36	31		5	1	3	7	15
Type of Statement									
Unqualified	111	105	101		6	3	8	9	75
Reviewed	96	109	107		7	7	17	34	42
Compiled	171	195	197		42	22	44	40	35
Tax Returns	23	41	27		4	4	8	4	2
Other	143	173	177		33	24	32	36	48
NUMBER OF STATEMENTS	544	623	609	24	93	60	109	123	200
ASSETS	%	%	%	%	%	%	%	%	%
Cash & Equivalents	9.7	10.6	10.8	4.9	8.7	10.0	11.3	13.4	10.7
Trade Receivables - (net)	4.9	5.4	5.1	4.6	4.8	4.6	3.9	5.4	5.8
Inventory	33.7	32.1	32.1	32.6	33.4	35.7	37.4	30.5	28.6
All Other Current	2.4	2.0	2.1	1.5	1.2	.8	3.1	2.6	2.3
Total Current	50.7	50.1	50.1	43.6	48.2	51.1	55.6	51.8	47.4
Fixed Assets (net)	36.3	36.9	37.0	44.8	39.1	32.9	30.5	34.9	41.0
Intangibles (net)	2.4	2.6	3.0	8.2	2.5	4.1	2.5	2.9	2.6
All Other Non-Current	10.6	10.4	9.9	3.4	10.2	11.9	11.4	10.3	9.0
LIABILITIES									
Notes Payable -Short Term	4.9	5.0	5.0	14.2	5.9	7.2	4.7	4.7	3.1
Cur. Mat.-L/T/D	4.8	4.9	4.4	2.2	4.1	4.9	4.2	5.2	4.2
Trade Payables	20.8	19.6	19.9	8.6	14.1	16.0	21.0	22.7	22.8
Income Taxes Payable	.4	.9	.4	.3	.4	.1	.3	.2	.8
All Other Current	9.1	10.1	9.1	6.0	7.0	12.9	9.5	8.1	9.7
Total Current	40.0	40.4	38.7	31.4	31.4	41.1	39.6	41.0	40.5
Long Term Debt	25.7	24.4	24.4	22.7	36.4	33.4	16.6	22.9	21.4
Deferred Taxes	.5	.4	.4	.4	.2	.0	.2	.2	.9
All Other-non-current	2.9	3.3	3.3	5.2	2.5	3.6	3.8	3.9	2.8
Net Worth	31.0	31.4	33.2	40.4	29.5	21.9	39.9	32.1	34.4
Total Liabilities & Net Worth	100.0	100.0	100.0	100.0	100.0	100.0	100.0	100.0	100.0
INCOME DATA									
Net Sales	100.0	100.0	100.0	100.0	100.0	100.0	100.0	100.0	100.0
Gross Profit	22.9	23.4	22.9	26.9	25.0	22.4	22.8	21.8	22.4
Operating Expenses	21.9	22.2	21.6	23.2	22.6	21.5	21.8	20.8	21.2
Operating Profit	1.0	1.2	1.4	3.7	2.4	.9	.9	1.1	1.2
All Other Expenses (net)	-.1	-.1	-.1	.8	.1	.0	-.3	-.3	.0
Profit Before Taxes	1.1	1.2	1.4	2.9	2.3	.9	1.2	1.4	1.2
RATIOS									
Current	1.9	1.9	2.0	4.7	2.8	2.3	2.3	1.9	1.6
	1.3	1.3	1.3	1.5	1.7	1.5	1.5	1.3	1.1
Quick	(533) .6	(618) .7	(601) .7	(91) .6	(58) .9	(107) .9	.9	(198) .8	.6
	.3	.4	.4	.2	.4	.4	.4	.5	.3
	.2	.2	.2	.0	.1	.2	.2	.2	.2
Sales/Receivables	1 666.6	1 665.6	1 634.8	0 UND	0 999.8	0 961.3	0 999.8	1 553.2	1 409.6
	1 249.0	2 233.5	2 230.3	1 565.0	1 285.7	1 377.8	1 352.8	2 226.7	2 181.0
	3 112.5	4 101.6	3 113.5	3 120.0	4 97.4	3 116.7	2 151.9	3 117.4	4 98.5

	17 23 31 / 8 14	16 23 31 / 8 14	18 24 31 / 9 14	17 28 45 / 0 7	22 30 41 / 5 10	21 28 33 / 6 10	18 24 30 / 7 12	15 20 2 / 9 13	18 20 27 / 12 17
Cost of Sales/ Inventory	21.0 16.2 11.8	22.2 15.7 11.9	20.2 15.5 11.6	21.3 13.0 8.1	16.8 12.0 9.0	17.7 13.9 11.2	20.2 15.2 12.0	24.8 18.5 14.2	22.3 16.1 13.7
Cost of Sales/Payables	46.9 28.6	46.4 28.9	41.8 25.2	UND 50.7	68.7 37.4	58.2 36.9	53.3 31.5	39.1 29.2	29.8 22.0
Sales/Working Capital	22.4 54.8 -229.3	25.9 52.7 -213.4	22.8 63.1 -169.0	11.6 63.7 -24.0	15.3 31.2 391.9	22.5 36.2 -248.9	17.9 43.9 -613.3	24.8 65.2 999.8	29.5 101.9 -166.7
EBIT/Interest	(545) 7.9 3.3 1.6	(563) 6.8 3.0 1.1	(493) 5.6 2.7 1.1	(19) 12.0 3.1 1.2	(86) 8.7 3.3 1.4	(56) 5.7 1.9 1.2	(91) 12.1 37 1.4	(108) 7.2 3.7 1.8	(185) 7.5 3.2 1.8
Net Profit+Depr.,Dep., Amort./Cur.Mat.L/T/D	(200) 4.0 1.9	(234) 3.4 1.9 1.2	(206) 4.3 1.9 1.0		(17) 2.9 1.3 -.0	(16) 1.9 1.4 .7	(32) 3.4 1.7 1.1	(40) 3.4 1.9 1.1	(94) 4.5 2.4 1.5
Fixed/Worth	.6 1.2 3.1	.6 1.4 3.2	.6 1.4 3.4	.4 1.2 11.6	.4 1.5 15.0	.6 1.9 8.9	.3 .7 1.9	.6 1.1 3.1	.8 1.3 2.6
Debt/Worth	1.0 2.1 6.6	1.0 2.3 6.6	1.1 2.3 7.2	.3 1.2 119.9	.9 2.0 25.6	1.4 3.9 16.5	.6 1.4 3.7	1.0 2.3 6.2	1.1 2.1 4.3
% Profit Before Taxes/ Tangible	(531) 43.9 20.3 8.4	(541) 37.3 18.2 5.5	(487) 37.2 17.2 4.2	(19) 79.0 27.5 12.3	(75) 65.4 30.8 13.4	(50) 52.1 20.1 4.7	(95) 33.7 15.7 44.8	(105) 56.7 26.8 10.3	(187) 32.8 18.8 9.2
% Profit Before Taxes/Total Assets	13.4 6.2 1.7	12.6 5.4 .7	11.8 5.3 .3	17.2 9.9 1.9	17.1 7.8 2.0	7.9 3.9 .3	13.0 6.1 .9	16.0 8.4 2.5	10.9 5.4 2.2
Sales/Net Fixed Assets	36.0 17.0 9.3	38.5 17.1 9.4	36.7 18.3 9.4	30.4 8.1 3.4	34.8 15.5 6.2	56.4 22.4 9.3	63.3 24.6 12.0	35.6 18.1 11.8	26.4 16.0 8.6
Sales/Total Assets	8.1 5.8 4.1	8.3 5.9 4.2	8.4 5.9 4.4	5.7 3.4 2.1	6.7 4.8 3.2	8.2 5.6 3.9	9.1 6.4 4.6	9.0 6.5 5.0	7.7 5.8 4.6
%Depr.,Dep.,Amort/ Sales	(553) .7 1.1 1.6	(579) .7 1.1 1.6	(500) .7 1.1 1.5	(18) .7 1.8 3.8	(80) .7 1.2 2.1	(52) .6 1.0 1.4	(103) .5 .8 1.3	(118) .7 1.1 1.5	(182) .8 1.2 1.5
% Officers', Directors', Owners' Comp/Sales	(230) .9 1.4 2.7	(257) .8 1.4 3.0	(214) .8 1.4 3.0		(38) 1.5 2.6 5.4	(27) 1.1 2.1 3.0	(57) .8 1.3 2.5	(52) .6 1.2 1.6	(47) .7 .9 .2
Net Sales ($)	32069673M	38476971M	31564710M	13981M	166441M	239747M	801614M	1930893M	28914022M
Total Assets ($)	7013147M	8646989M	7208512M	98773M	43319M	49527M	147430M	339375M	6334723M

M = $ thousand   MM = $ million

Source: Robert Morris Associates, *Annual Statement Studies* (Philadelphia: Robert Morris Associates, 1995), p. 575. Reprinted by permission of Robert Morris Associates.

NOTES

1. Gordon V. Karels and Arun J. Prakash, "Loan Pricing and Loan Yields on Commercial Lines of Credit," *Review of Research in Banking and Finance* 5, no. 1 (Spring 1989): 29–39.

2. Edward I. Altman, "Managing the Commercial Lending Process," in *Handbook of Banking Strategy*, R. C. Aspinwall and R. A. Eisenbeis, eds. (New York: John Wiley, 1985), pp. 473–510.

SUGGESTED REFERENCES

Altman, Edward I. "Valuation, Loss Reserves, and Pricing of Commercial Loans." *The Journal of Commercial Lending*, August 1993, pp. 8–25.

Erdivig, Eleanor H. "Lender Liability Under Environmental Law." Federal Reserve Bank of Chicago, *Chicago Fed Letter*, September 1991, pp. 1–3.

Eyring, Joseph R. "Five Key Steps for a Successful Workout Program." *The Journal of Commercial Bank Lending*, December 1984, pp. 28–35.

Gup, Benton E., D. R. Fraser, and J. W. Kolari. *Commercial Bank Management*. New York: John Wiley, 1989.

Nakamura, Leonard I. "Lessons on Lending and Borrowing in Hard Times." Federal Reserve Bank of Philadelphia, *Business Review*, July/August 1991, pp. 13–21.

Pollock, Ellen Joan. "Second Lenders Can Lose Place in Line." *Wall Street Journal*, June 20, 1991, p. 38.

Rose, Peter S. "Loan Pricing in a Volatile Economy." *The Canadian Banker* 92, no. 5 (October 1985): 44–49.

Sinkey, Joseph F. *Commercial Bank Financial Management—In the Financial Services Industry*. 4th ed. New York: Macmillan, 1992.

Tighe, Roger. *Structuring Commercial Loan Agreements*. Boston: Warren, Gorham & Lamont, 1984.

Walter, John R. "Loan Loss Reserves." Federal Reserve Bank of Richmond, *Economic Review*, July/August 1991, pp. 20–30.

Chapter 14

Investment Securities and Regulation

From a functional point of view, the investment account may be said to straddle the lending operations of commercial banks. On the one side it provides the necessary degree of bank liquidity in the form of short-maturity, money-market instruments (secondary reserves). On the other side it employs whatever funds cannot be loaned to provide income for the bank in the form of long-maturity, capital-market instruments (bond portfolio). Liquidity, in the first instance, and income, in the second, thus constitute the determining factors in the acquisition and holding of securities. This dual role of the investment account is not, however, identifiable in a bank's balance sheet, where reference to investment holdings is made only according to issuer. Since statistics also do not distinguish between secondary reserves and the bond account, discussion of banks' investments is kept at the general, or aggregate, level. This chapter thus identifies the different types of securities that banks may purchase and describes the regulations that govern such purchases. The last part of this chapter deals with the underwriting function and related investment activities of commercial banks.

ELIGIBLE INVESTMENT SECURITIES

Securities eligible for purchase by commercial banks may be classified according to obligor into the following categories: U.S. Treasury securities, agency obligations, state and local government issues, corporate debt, and other securities. These are discussed below.

Table 14.1
Total Gross Public Debt of U.S. Treasury, 1995 (billions of dollars)

Item		Amount Outstanding
Total gross public debt		$4,951.4
By holder		
Held by U.S government agencies & trust funds		1,316.6
Held by Federal Reserve banks		389.0
Held by private investors		3,244.6
Commercial banks	305.6	
Money-market funds	58.7	
Insurance companies	260.0	
Other companies	227.7	
State and local treasuries	415.0	
Individuals	344.2	
Foreign and international	783.7	
All other[a]	850.4	
By type[b]		
Marketable		3,252.6
Bills	748.3	
Notes	1,974.7	
Bonds	514.7	
Nonmarketable[c]		1,695.2
Savings bonds and notes	180.1	
Foreign issues	41.4	
Held by U.S. government agencies and trust funds[d]	1,322.0	
Other	121.2	

[a]Includes savings and loan associations, nonprofit institutions, credit unions, mutual savings banks, corporate pension trust funds, dealers and brokers, certain U.S. Treasury deposit accounts, and federally sponsored agencies.
[b]Excludes $3.6 billion of noninterest-bearing debt.
[c]Includes (not shown separately) securities issued to the Rural Electrification Administration, depository bonds, retirement plan bonds, and individual retirement bonds.
[d]Held almost entirely by U.S. Treasury and other federal agencies and trust funds.
Source: Federal Reserve Bulletin, January 1996, p. A30. Data for 1995 are as of July 31.

U.S. Treasury Securities

Types

When its revenues from taxation are not large enough to cover its expenses, the federal government must make up the difference. On various occasions the Treasury Department, as fiscal agent of the government, has sold securities as a means of borrowing. As shown in Table 14.1, in mid-1995, the total gross public debt of the U.S. Treasury was $5 trillion. If allowance is made for the portion of the debt held by accounts of the federal government itself, the net indebtedness of the U.S. Treasury was actually much less. Not all of the U.S.

Treasury debt was "in the market." There are three major forms of nonmarketable debt: U.S. savings bonds sold to households, special dollar-denominated and foreign-currency-denominated Treasury issues held essentially by foreign central banks, and issues held by U.S. government agencies and trust funds. Thus, the marketable portion of the U.S. Treasury debt amounted in mid 1995 to $3.2 trillion, 65.7 percent of total debt.

As indicated in Table 14.1, there are three types of marketable Treasury debt: bills, notes, and bonds. In mid-1995, Treasury bills amounted to $748 billion, 23 percent of the total marketable debt. Treasury bills (T-bills) are short-term obligations with original maturities of 3, 6, or 12 months.* Each issue is advertised and sold on an auction basis through the Federal Reserve banks and their branches, which perform the role of agents for the Treasury. Unlike the 12–month bills, which are auctioned once a month, the 3- and 6-month issues are auctioned every Monday at 1:30 P.M. New York time, with payment made on the following Thursday. Interested investors, primarily financial institutions, submit their bids for particular quantities of specific denominations. The Treasury awards bids in full, starting with the highest price and going down to the one that exhausts the amount available of that issue, which is the total to be issued less the amount for which noncompetitive tenders have been received. Noncompetitive tenders (normally less than $5 million each) from small investors are accepted in full, with such investors paying the average of the accepted competitive bids in the weekly or monthly bill auction.

The automation of the government securities market has resulted in the marketing of T-bills on a computerized book-entry basis. T-bills are customarily quoted on the basis of 100, even though the par, or face, value of each bill is $1,000. They are sold in denominations of $10,000 to $1,000,000, and are issued on a discount basis. In other words, the rate of return to an investor is determined by the difference between the par value of the bills and the price paid for them. For example, if an investor pays the Treasury $9,500 for a $10,000 T-bill maturing a year later, he or she will earn $500 (5.3 percent) on the investment if it is held to maturity.† Since there is an active secondary market in bills, the

---

*A nine-month bill was issued in 1966, but the sale of this maturity was discontinued in late 1972.

†For T-bills of less than a year's maturity, the discount rate (D_r) may be determined on the basis of the bank discount method, which uses a 360-day year for simplicity. This formula is

$$D_r = \frac{\text{par value} - \text{purchase price}}{\text{par value}} \times \frac{360 \text{ days}}{\text{no. days to maturity}}.$$

The yield to maturity for this instrument is always higher because of consideration of the amount invested rather than the principal, and of a 365–day year rather than the 360 used in the above computation. Thus,

$$Y = \frac{\text{par value} - \text{purchase price}}{\text{purchase price}} \times \frac{365 \text{ days}}{\text{days to maturity}}.$$

investor may sell them at any time before their maturity, receiving the current market price of the bills (which will be less than the par value).

The principal utility of Treasury bills for banks and other investors is liquidity. T-bills are liquid not only because their maturity is near but also because the secondary market in these obligations is very large. In fact, it is so large that a $100 or $200 million sale of T-bills can be made almost casually, with minimal, if any, pressure exerted in the market. T-bills have thus evolved into the most popular money-market instrument. Commercial banks are large investors in T-bills, which they hold as part of their seasonal secondary reserve requirements.

As seen in Table 14.1, the largest concentration of marketable Treasury debt in mid-1995 was in Treasury notes (60.7 percent of marketable debt). Treasury notes range in original maturity from one to ten years. With the passage of time, of course, the maturities of outstanding notes fall to five years or less, which renders them ideal for banks' cyclical secondary-reserve needs. These notes bear a fixed rate of interest that is paid semiannually and is slightly above that on T-bills. They are also quite marketable and may be purchased in denominations ranging from $1,000 to $1,000,000. Treasury notes are available in either a registered or a book-entry form.

Treasury bonds, the government's typical instrument for long-term debt, have a maturity at issue of more than ten years. They are also very marketable and are issued in denominations of $1,000 to $1,000,000. Bonds, like notes are available in registered or book-entry form and pay a fixed rate of interest sem-iannually. In mid-1995 the value of bonds outstanding was $515 billion, 15.8 percent of the Treasury's marketable debt. The limited importance of bonds vis-à-vis the other forms of marketable debt outstanding is partially explained by interest costs. Short- and intermediate-term financing is customarily associated with lower rates of interest than is long-term debt, thus contributing to a reduction in the Treasury's interest expense. Most important, however, the maturity structure of the federal debt has been affected by legislative constraint on the interest rates that the Treasury can pay on long-term debt. Since the late 1910s Congress has restricted the interest rates that may be offered on Treasury bonds*

Thus the discount rate on a three-month, $10,000 T-bill that costs $9,800 is

$$\frac{\$10,000 - \$9,800}{\$10,000} \times \frac{360}{90} = 8 \text{ percent.}$$

The yield to maturity of this bill is 8.277 percent.

*The statutory interest-rate restriction on Treasury bonds originated with the Liberty Bond acts of 1917 and 1918, which introduced a ceiling interest rate of 4.25 percent. This ceiling did not cause any controversy for several decades because government bond yields in the secondary market rarely rose above it. In 1965, however, bond yields began to exceed the ceiling, placing the Treasury at a competitive disadvantage vis-à-vis other borrowers in the capital markets. Recognizing this problem, the U.S. Congress has on various occasions waived the interest constraint and exempted certain long-term debt issues of the U.S. Treasury from interest-rate ceilings. More important, however, it authorized the extension of the maturities of Treasury notes to ten years (instead of the earlier five years), to enable the Treasury to tap funds at competitive rates.

while leaving unregulated the rate that may be paid on short- or intermediate-term securities. Thus, during periods of high interest rates the Treasury, in view of its ability to compete effectively for funds in capital markets, relies extensively on short- and intermediate-term issues.

Investment Characteristics

As seen in Table 14.1, commercial banks are a major private investor in Treasury issues. Several features make Treasury obligations attractive to commercial banks. Government securities are unique in that they offer investors safety of principal and interest. The constitutional right of the federal government to tax and to print money assures its current and future capacity to service its debt. Because these debt instruments are so safe, their yields are generally lower than those obtained from corporate issues. An additional corollary of safety is that bank holdings of Treasury securities require less supervision, and hence administrative costs in managing them are relatively low. Another attribute of these securities is their availability in almost any desired maturity consonant with bank investment policies. In addition, they enjoy a high degree of marketability. The secondary market in which Treasury securities are traded is a very large one with great absorptive capacity. The average trading volume in Treasury securities in October 1995 approached $190 billion a day (see Table 14.2). The number of dealers in this market is unknown, but it is estimated to be from 300 to 500. At the heart of this market is a relatively small number of dealers, known as primary dealers, who purchase large amounts of Treasury issues at auctions and stand ready to trade in these issues in the secondary market. Some of the primary dealers are money-center banks, and the rest are nonbank dealers.

These qualities have expanded banks' use of government securities beyond the traditional domains of liquidity and income. One alternative use of U.S. Treasury obligations is as collateral for advances obtained from Federal Reserve banks. Another is their use in repurchase agreements. Still another is their use in meeting the pledging requirement on public deposits. More specifically, commercial banks that accept federal government deposits are required to secure such deposits by pledging U.S. government securities against them. These securities, whether from the bank's liquidity account or the bond portfolio, are typically pledged with the bank's trust department to ensure the safety of these deposits in the event of insolvency. Their replacement by other types of securities is possible, although the Secretary of the Treasury reserves the right to require amounts in excess of 100 percent of the value of the deposit if the collateral is deemed to be of great potential risk.

This pledging requirement extends to state and local government deposits, with U.S. government securities, and sometimes the securities of state and local governments, usually pledged to ensure the safety of these deposits. Although this requirement is important, the extent to which it is enforced by local governments is more a matter of local custom than of careful consideration of the potential hazards involved.

Table 14.2
U.S. Government Security Dealers' Transactions for the Week Ending October 25, 1995 (average of daily trading)

Item	Volume of Transactions (billions of dollars)	Percent of Total
By maturity		
Bills	$ 41.3	21.9
Five years or less	98.7	52.5
More than five years	48.1	25.6
Total	$188.1	100.0

Note: Details may not add to totals due to rounding.
Source: Federal Reserve Bulletin, January 1996, p. A31.

All business decisions normally are accompanied by constraints on the range over which action can be taken. The alternative uses of Treasury securities described above constitute one such dimension of decision making for a bank. Money-market instruments, and more generally investment securities used in any of the above capacities, cannot be readily sold. Thus, to the extent that these securities are held for other purposes, their efficiency as media of liquidity is thereby lessened.

At year-end 1995, U.S. Treasury issues accounted for 24.4 percent of the investment holdings of all insured commercial banks.

Agency Obligations

Another popular type of security traded in financial markets is the debt of government agencies. Established to support the financial needs of disadvantaged sectors of economic activity, government agencies issue their own debt securities and compete effectively for funds in financial markets. The activities of these agencies have expanded significantly over the years, as evidenced by the size of the agency debt outstanding. From a modest existence in the early 1950s, the market for agency debt has grown to a major component of the U.S. financial system, with close to $800 billion of securities outstanding in mid-1995. This debt encompasses the entire spectrum of maturities, ranging from short- to long-term. Like most Treasury issues, many agency obligations enjoy an active secondary market, and price quotations are made available for many of these to banks on a daily basis by the financial press.

Types

Federal agencies issuing debt include the Export-Import Bank, the Federal Housing Administration, the Postal Service, and the Tennessee Valley Authority.

The securities of these agencies accounted for only 5 percent of the total agency debt outstanding in mid-1995. The public debt of these agencies was gradually reduced because of the activities of the Federal Financing Bank (FFB). Established in 1974 and operating under the Treasury Department, the FFB finances the activities of federal agencies by borrowing funds from the Treasury. FFB securities issued to the Treasury have thus replaced federal agency debt outstanding. Government-sponsored agencies, which cannot borrow through FFB, are the only agencies tapping the markets for funds.

Government-sponsored agencies are in essence corporations sponsored, but not owned, by the U.S. government. These agencies account for the bulk of the agency debt outstanding (95 percent in mid-1995). These agencies are active in two markets, the residential mortgage market and the market for farm credit. The agencies included in this group are the Federal National Mortgage Association (FNMA or Fannie Mae) and the Federal Home Loan Mortgage Corporation (FHLMC or Freddie Mac), which provide a secondary market for mortgages; the Federal Home Loan Banks, in essence the equivalent of the Federal Reserve Banks for savings and loan associations; the Student Loan Marketing Association (SLMA or Sallie Mae), which supports the student loan program by purchasing insured student loans from, and making advances to, eligible lenders; and the Farm Credit System, which issues securities and then uses the proceeds to make loans to farmers. Several of these agencies were formerly part of the federal government structure. However, to spare them the political and economic constraints of the federal budget and to allow them to achieve their full potential, the government converted these agencies to private ownership.

Investment Characteristics and Bank Holdings

Since agency securities do not constitute the direct obligations of the federal government, they tend to offer somewhat higher yields than those available on U.S. Treasury securities. Nevertheless, agency debt is extremely safe and is regarded by the investment community as having credit quality similar to that of U.S. Treasury issues. For it is the general belief that the federal government would not allow the default of any of these obligations. Agency issues have thus been treated as noncredit-risk assets and are usually reported in bank statements separately from other risk assets. Agency securities can be pledged as collateral by commercial banks for securing public deposits. At year-end 1995, all insured commercial banks held $426 billion of agency securities, which accounted for 52.6 percent of their total investment holdings.

A significant portion of these holdings consist of mortgage-backed securities. The preferential treatment of these issues by the risk-based capital standards has induced many banks to acquire large amounts of mortgage-backed securities. Indeed, with certain of these issues requiring no capital backing and others in the 20 percent risk category (which is lower than that for many other instruments), mortgage-backed securities have become a significant component of banks' investment portfolios. The most common type of mortgaged-backed security is the pass-through.

As stated in Chapter 12, pass-throughs are certificates representing shares of ownership in a pool of residential mortgages bearing the same interest rate and maturity. Originated by the Government National Mortgage Association (GNMA or Ginnie Mae) in 1970, pass-throughs are issued against mortgage loans insured by the Federal Housing Administration (FHA) or guaranteed by the Veterans Administration (VA). When guaranteed by GNMA, itself a government-owned agency, these certificates bear the ''full faith and credit'' pledge of the federal government, and are consequently free of the risk of default like Treasury issues.

Pass-through certificates are also issued by the FHLMC, with such certificates backed by a pool of conventional mortgages. Although these certificates are guaranteed by the FHLMC, its guaranty does not bear the full faith and credit of the federal government because this agency is not government-owned. Thus, because they entail more risk than GNMA issues, FHLMC pass-throughs offer a slightly higher yield.

FNMA is another government-sponsored agency that issues pass-throughs with features similar to FHLMC's participation certificates. FNMA, too, backs payment of principal and interest with its guarantee. However, being a sponsored agency like FHLMC, its pass-throughs entail more risk than GNMA issues. Because of the perceived low risk of default, FNMA pass-throughs offer a slightly higher yield than those of GNMA pass-throughs.

Collateralized mortgage obligations (CMOs) were introduced by FHLMC in 1983 in an effort to reduce the prepayment risk associated with traditional pass-through securities. CMOs are essentially classes of bonds (tranches) of different maturities issued against a single mortgage pool. Banks usually prefer first-tranche securities because their short-term maturities are a better match for their deposit liabilities. Because each maturity class is retired sequentially, early classes of bonds are overcollateralized. Moreover, the mortgages backing the bonds are generally government-backed. As a result, most CMOs enjoy high ratings and are priced at a spread over Treasury issues.

Some issues of real-estate mortgage investment conduits (REMICs) have been also included in bank portfolios. Whether structured in pass-through form or bond form, these issues are usually backed by a pool of agency-guaranteed mortgages.

State and Local Government Issues

Population pressures (increases in, and movements of, population) and the soaring costs of providing services have driven an increasing number of state and local governments to financial markets in order to finance their capital projects and budgetary deficits. These bodies include not only state, county, and municipal governments but also school districts and special districts, such as water or transportation authorities. The securities issued by these entities have come to be known as municipal bonds or "munis."

The major distinguishing feature of these securities compared with all other securities in the financial markets is that the interest paid to investors is exempt from federal income taxes (hence the reference to these securities as tax-exempts). Most states exempt their own securities from state income taxes as well. Exemption of the interest income of these securities from federal taxation dates from the late nineteenth century, when Congress passed a law to this effect. The implication of the federal income-tax exemption of these securities is that state and local governments can raise funds at lower interest costs than the federal government, since investors gain from the lack of taxation. These securities are thus appealing to investors who are subject to a high marginal tax bracket (such as commercial banks, casualty insurance companies, and wealthy individuals). By contrast, these securities do not appeal to such investors as pension funds, thrift institutions, and life insurance companies, which are subject to either relatively low or zero marginal tax rates.

Issues of state and local government debt were affected adversely in recent years by two developments: the Tax Reform Act of 1986 and a Supreme Court ruling in 1988. Passage of the Tax Reform Act affected both the demand for and the supply of funds in the municipals market. On the demand side it eliminated or restricted the ability of certain municipal entities to issue tax-exempt debt; as a result, some of these entities were forced to issue taxable securities to raise the funds needed. On the supply side, it affected the appeal of these issues to banks by introducing important changes in tax provisions. Banks were no longer allowed to deduct the interest cost of funds used to purchase municipal issues, which essentially eliminated the tax-shelter benefits of these issues.

The second development was a ruling by the Supreme Court in April 1988 to the effect that Congress is free to tax interest on state and local government securities.* This ruling upheld a 1982 federal law requiring state and local governments to issue their securities in registered form (as against the previous practice of issuing them payable to the bearer). Bond registration was viewed by investors as an important requisite to taxation of interest income on these bonds. If the tax exemption were eliminated, as has been suggested in many reform proposals, the bonds would sell on a yield basis allowed by the credit position of the issuing authority operating in a competitive capital market, just like other bonds.

The effect of the aforementioned developments has been a drastic shrinkage of the municipal securities market. For example, while between 1950 and 1980 state and local debt expanded from $24.7 billion to over $300 billion, by June 30, 1988, it regressed to $51.4 billion.

---

*In *South Carolina* v. *Baker*, the U.S. Supreme Court ruled that the Constitution does not prohibit federal taxation of the interest paid on state and local government issues.

Types

State and local government debt is both short- and long-term. Short-term borrowing by state and local government units is basically of three types: tax anticipation notes (TAN), which are used to bridge the gap between actual expenditures and anticipated tax receipts; public housing authority notes (HAN), which provide local housing agencies with working capital for public housing projects until permanent financing is secured through long-term bonds; and bond anticipation notes (BAN), which are used as temporary sources of financing particularly if credit markets are tight or interest rates are expected to fall. These notes are generally backed by the "full faith and credit" of the issuing government unit. Housing authority notes are, in addition, guaranteed by the full faith and credit of the federal government, according to the Housing Act of 1949. These issues are thus especially attractive to investors because they are both tax-exempt and guaranteed by the federal government—that is, virtually free of credit risk.

The bulk of state and local government financing is on a long-term basis. There are two major types of municipal bonds, general-obligation bonds and revenue bonds. General-obligation bonds are the most common type of state and local government debt. From the investor's point of view, general obligations are generally safer than revenue bonds because they are backed by the full faith and credit of the issuing government; that is, the full taxing power of the issuer is pledged to assure payments of interest and principal when due. Despite this safeguard, the tangled financial problems of many large cities caused investors to reassess the credit standing of general obligations. The financial crisis of New York City and its default in 1975 led the federal government to step in and guarantee loans to the city. In December 1978, the city of Cleveland defaulted on its debt. In 1991, the city of Bridgeport, Connecticut, filed for bankruptcy. In December 1994, Orange County, California, defaulted on $110 million in general-obligation bonds as a result of losses sustained in its investment fund. To protect itself against creditors, Orange County proceeded to file for bankruptcy on December 7, 1994.

In addition to the financial crisis of cities and countries, the "taxpayer revolt" of the late 1970s increased investor sensitivity to the creditworthiness of borrowing governments. This revolt started in California in the summer of 1978 with the passage of Proposition 13, which introduced limitations on real-property tax rates. The effect of this law was to limit the taxing authority of the state, and hence its ability to finance new bond issues through tax increases. The success of the taxpayer revolt in California resulted in the creation of taxpayer lobbies in other states, and the passage of similar legislation.

Revenue bonds, the other major group of state and local obligations, lack any government backing and are payable only from the revenues generated by the project being financed through their issue. For example, dormitories and universities are frequently financed with revenue bonds, and student fees are used to pay them off. Also, roads and bridges may be financed with revenue bonds, to be repaid with tolls. The risk assumed by investors is that the revenues generated may not be sufficient for the payment of interest and principal, in which case the bonds will go into default. Since investors cannot foreclose on a university or a bridge, their only course of action is to wait and hope for a possible resumption of payments in the future.

Over the years various new types of revenue bonds have appeared in financial markets. One type is industrial development bonds, which finance the purchase of land and the construction of plants to attract new industry to an area. The new businesses lease the plant, and the rental payments are used to service the bonds. The benefits to the area are twofold: an increase in the number of local jobs and an increase in local tax revenues. Another type is hospital revenue bonds, issued to finance the building of hospitals. Once completed, these hospitals are leased to private or public agencies, with the lease income used to amortize the debt. Still another type is mortgage revenue bonds, whose proceeds are loaned to low- and moderate-income families for the purpose of buying a home. The home buyers' monthly mortgage payments go to service these bonds. A similar type is life-care bonds—or retirement community bonds—which finance housing for the elderly, with lease income going to servicing the bonds. Last, public housing bonds are issued to finance the construction of public housing projects, with rental revenues servicing these bonds. If revenues are inadequate to meet principal and interest payments, the Public Housing Administration makes up the difference through payments to the local authority that issued the bonds. Like HANs, these issues are tax-exempt and guaranteed by the federal government.

Investment Characteristics and Bank Holdings

With banks subject to high marginal tax rates, the tax-exemption feature of state and local government debt has a powerful appeal. Although the Tax Reform Act of 1986 eliminated banks' interest-cost deduction in carrying municipal issues, some exceptions were introduced. Banks are allowed to continue to deduct 80 percent of the interest expense for funds used to carry issues that finance traditional governmental projects or hospitals, and university projects, as long as the issuing authority does not issue more than $10 million in debt per year. This enables small issuers to continue to sell securities to some banks, but it largely eliminates banks as purchasers of other issuers' securities. At year-end 1995, all insured commercial banks held $74 billion of state and local government securities, which represented 9 percent of their total security holdings, placing state and local issues next in importance to banks' U.S. government security holdings. These securities qualify as collateral for securing fiduciary, trust, and public funds.

Unlike U.S. Treasury debt and agency obligations, state and local government issues exhibit a significant variation in quality; some issues are free of credit risk (such as those guaranteed by the federal government), while others contain different degrees of risk. In the case of general obligations, the degree of risk involved is determined by the ability and willingness of the issuing government to service its debt. The ability and willingness are, in turn, a function of such factors as the economic base of the community, the stability of employment, per capita income, and the current as well as future pattern of revenues available to service the debt. For revenue bonds, risk exposure is a function of the profitability of the project being financed and debt service requirements.

The prime-credit issues of large, well-known state and local government units enjoy a national market. The great majority of tax-exempts, however, trade only on a regional or a local basis. Trading in these issues is rather inactive, and price quotations for most of them are not available on a regular basis. The thinness of the market for local issues has contributed to spreads (between the bid and asked prices) usually of 1.5 points, which in periods of tight money conditions may rise to 3 or more points. The dealers who are making a market in various state and local government issues and the inventories they carry are advertised in a daily publication, *Blue List*. Other sources of information on related financial matters include Standard and Poor's monthly *Bond Guide* and Moody's monthly *Bond Record*.

In order to improve the credit ratings and marketability of their securities, municipal issuers frequently make credit or liquidity enhancement arrangements. Agreements, for example, with banks and insurance companies, ensure, for a fee, the availability of funds if the issuer is unable or unwilling to make payment to the security holders when due. In essence, these agreements substitute the credit or liquidity of a bank or insurance company for that of the municipal security issuer. Banks are the principal providers of credit enhancement in the form of an irrevocable letter of credit; insurance companies provide such enhancement through municipal bond insurance. Most liquidity enhancements are provided by large U.S. and foreign banks and take the form of a standby letter of credit, a bank line of credit, or a standby purchase agreement for outright purchase of these issues.

State and local government debt is issued in various maturities. Most issues, especially general obligations, have serial maturities. That is, a single bond issue is split into several different maturities. Coupon rates are lower on the shorter-term securities and gradually increase as maturities lengthen. Serial bonds thus offer banks and other investors a wide choice of maturities and yields. This approach contrasts with the practices of most corporate borrowers and the federal government of having all securities in the same issue come due on the same date (term bonds). The multiple-maturity approach is in essence a vehicle ensuring the gradual amortization of state and local debt.

Corporate Debt

Corporate debt is both short- and long-term. The former consists of commercial paper; the latter, of bonds, notes, and debentures. As we have seen in

Chapter 7, commercial paper is the unsecured promissory notes of large, well-known financial and nonfinancial businesses with impeccable credit ratings. Issued on a discount basis, commercial paper matures anywhere from a few days to a maximum of 270 days. It is sold either directly to investors or through commercial-paper dealers.

Bonds, notes, and debentures are the most common forms of long-term financing by corporations. Although this terminology is often used interchangeably, bonds are long-term, usually secured promises to pay, bought and sold on the open market; notes are similar to bonds except for shorter maturities; and debentures are unsecured long-term promises to pay. Prior to the early 1930s, corporate debt was of principal importance in the investment portfolios of commercial banks. Its primacy over all other security holdings stemmed from the limited availability of federal and municipal issues and management emphasis upon income. At the end of 1930, corporate issues accounted for over 50 percent of banks' investment holdings. In the following decades these issues declined in importance, and by year-end 1995 they accounted for 7 percent of the investment holdings of all insured commercial banks.

The reduced attractiveness of corporate issues for commercial banks is essentially attributed to several considerations. First, corporate issues entail a higher credit risk than is true of state and local government debt. Indeed, corporations can go into bankruptcy and disappear; however, examples of state and local governments disappearing are much less frequent. Second, with banks operating under higher tax rates, the after-tax yield of corporate issues is ordinarily lower than that of municipals of the same quality. Third, banks prefer to deal personally with their corporate customers and grant them loans tailored to their needs rather than finance them indirectly through the highly impersonal bond market. Last, the secondary market for corporate issues is rather limited compared with that for municipal bonds. Trading volume is low even for issues of some of the largest corporations with strong credit standing and reputation. Insurance companies and pension funds are the major institutional investors in this market.

Some of the larger U.S. banks include among their security holdings a less-known type of corporate debt, equipment trust certificates. These certificates are issued to finance the purchase of industrial equipment or rolling stock (such as locomotives, railroad cars, airplanes, and trucks), with such equipment pledged as collateral. Specifically, a corporation may contract for the purchase of equipment by arranging for a trustee to receive it from the manufacturer and to sell it conditionally to the corporation in return for a series of certificates. When sold to investors, these certificates provide the funds to pay off the manufacturer. As the equipment is used and cash flow is generated, interest payments are made by the company to the trustee, which passes them on to the certificate holders. In time the certificates are retired by the purchasing corporation, and ownership of the asset becomes final and complete. Although the collateral is generally of excellent quality and can be readily moved, the market for some of these assets may at times be quite soft, contributing to sizable investor losses in the event of borrower default on the certificates. Such, because of the world recession, was the state of the market for used planes in the early 1980s, when Braniff Airlines and Freddie Laker's Skytrain went bankrupt. As a result, many secured creditors—including banks—were unable to collect in full.

Other Securities

This category is of limited importance and includes the obligations of international organizations and foreign governments as well as equity securities.

Issues of International Organizations and Foreign Governments

The growing financing needs of the world economy have led many international financial organizations to rely increasingly on international capital markets for funds. Through international bond issues these organizations are able to raise sizable amounts of funds to fulfill their objectives. Foremost among these organizations is the International Bank for Reconstruction and Development (IBRD or World Bank), which, established in 1945 under the Bretton Woods Agreement, makes loans to member countries in order to assist in the development of their resources. The World Bank is the primary institution of the World Bank Group, which includes two other institutions—both of which are financially assisted by, and are affiliated with, the bank—the International Finance Corporation, formed in 1956, and the International Development Association, set up in 1960. A sizable portion of the bonds issued by the World Bank is dollar-denominated. These bonds are backed in full by the commitment of the U.S. government because they represent the portion of subscribed capital for which the United States is subject to call (callable capital). For practical purposes, therefore, these bonds belong in the federal debt category. Their yields are slightly above those of direct government obligations of the same maturity.

Other international financial organizations whose bonds are eligible investments for commercial banks are the Inter-American Development Bank, established in 1959, and the Asian Development Bank, formed in 1966. These institutions duplicate the functions of the World Bank Group in a particular region of the world and fund their activities through international bond issues. These bonds are backed in full by the callable capital, and hence the commitment, of the member countries of these organizations. Thus the bonds of the Inter-American Development Bank and the Asian Development Bank are considered of high quality, being rated Aaa by Moody's Investors Service.

Foreign governments and their political subdivisions have in many instances tapped U.S. financial markets through issuance of dollar-denominated bonds, frequently referred to as "Yankee bonds." Although U.S. investors sustained significant losses in the past with such issues, the record has improved greatly since World War II. Under current laws all foreign issuers—like domestic private borrowers—must comply with the registration requirements of the Securities and Exchange Commission (SEC) prior to the public offering of their bonds. Although domestic investors cannot take any legal action in the event of borrower default on these bonds, foreign public debtors usually make adjustment offers to U.S. creditors (for instance, exchange of an old issue for a new one with longer maturity or one paying lower interest). Most of the foreign public issues currently in the market are of high quality. For example, the bond issues of the governments of Australia, Canada, Norway, France, and Sweden are rated Aaa by Moody's. The issues of the European Economic Community and the European Investment Bank have a similar rating.

At year-end 1995, foreign debt securities amounted to $37.6 billion and accounted for 4.6 percent of the investment holdings of all insured commercial banks.

Equity Securities

This category amounted to $18.5 billion or 2.3 percent of the investment holdings of all insured commercial banks at year-end 1995. The general rule is that a national bank, or a state member of the Federal Reserve System, may not purchase or acquire common stock except as permitted by law in special cases. Some of the special situations that account for stock ownership by commercial banks include the following:

- Member banks are required to purchase stock in their district Federal Reserve bank, upon their admission to Federal Reserve membership, in an amount equal to 3 percent of their capital and surplus.

- A bank may own stock in an amount equal to its capital in a corporation organized to own the building in which the bank is located.

- With the approval of the Board of Governors, a bank may invest no more than 10 percent of its capital and surplus in a foreign banking corporation.

- A bank may purchase unlimited amounts of stock in government-sponsored agencies (such as Fannie Mae and Sallie Mae).

- A bank may hold corporate stocks if such stocks served as collateral on defaulted loans. However, these stocks are to be disposed of as soon as can reasonably be done without undue loss. A reasonable holding period for these stocks is generally viewed as up to five years.

In recent years, regulators allowed banks to include in their holdings shares of mutual funds that invest in eligible securities (e.g., U.S. Treasury and agency debt, mortgage-backed securities, and corporate issues). The objective was to allow small banks to minimize their exposure to credit risk by owning shares in a pool of securities rather than owning the individual securities themselves. Holdings of mutual-fund shares were limited to 10 percent of a bank's capital and surplus.

Initial interest in this investment vehicle in the late 1980s had faded by the mid-1990s due to regulatory implementation of Statement 115 issued by the Financial Accounting Standards Board (FASB). The requirement that all securities for sale—and hence mutual-fund shares—be marked to market rather than be reported at book value was exposing investment portfolios to significant fluctuations as a result of changes in interest rates. Concerned that such volatility would give investors and depositors the impression of a risky portfolio, banks have reduced their holdings of mutual-fund shares to a negligible amount.

REGULATORY FRAMEWORK

Banks' investment activities are subject to a host of regulatory controls for the same reason that all other aspects of commercial banking are: safety of deposit funds. The main objective of investment regulations is to minimize bank losses resulting from the default risk inherent in certain securities. As part of his regulatory powers, the Comptroller of the Currency has issued investment regulations that apply to national banks and all state banks that are members of the Federal Reserve System. Some of these regulations were reviewed in the preceding section in connection with corporate stock, which banks are allowed to acquire only exceptionally. A more important part, however, deals with debt instruments, which constitute the core of banks' investment portfolios.

The regulations promulgated by the Comptroller of the Currency require all national and state member banks to diversify their securities holdings among various issuers, and for this purpose they identify three classes of marketable instruments eligible for bank investment. Type I securities are essentially risk-free, and a bank "may deal in, underwrite, purchase and sell for its own account without limitation." This category includes U.S. Treasury obligations, debt issues of federal agencies, and general-obligation bonds of any state or political subdivision within the state. In light of municipal defaults, such as Cleveland's, some Type I securities pose a limited risk. Therefore, even with Type I securities the Comptroller's caveat that the banks must exercise "prudent judgment" applies.

Riskier than Type I bonds, Type II securities include those issued by international organizations, such as the Asian Development Bank, the World Bank, and the Inter-American Development Bank, as well as certain bonds issued by local governments. The latter include state obligations for public housing projects and university buildings and dormitories. Regulations permit a bank to "deal in, underwrite, purchase and sell for its own account" Type II securities, subject to a 10 percent capital and surplus limitation per obligor.

Type III securities are made up of all other issues that possess a higher degree of risk than those of the preceding two categories. Unlike Type I or II securities, banks may "neither deal in nor underwrite" Type III securities. A bank's portfolio may not contain Type III securities in excess of 10 percent of its capital and surplus accounts. The category includes state and local revenue bonds, corporate debt instruments, and foreign corporate or government bonds. Banks are expected to exercise a considerable amount of judgment with Type III securities because they are exposed to greater risk. In particular, a bank should consider the issuer's historical operating record and/or reliable estimates concerning the likely success of new projects. The bank must maintain a complete file on these and all other securities not backed by the U.S. government. This file allows the investment officer and the bank examiners to determine that a security is investment-grade.

INVESTMENT-BANKING ACTIVITIES

As stated in the investment provisions cited above, in addition to holding securities in their portfolios, banks also can deal in and underwrite securities within certain prescribed limitations. Since enactment of the Glass-Steagall Act of 1933, banks have been confined to dealing in and underwriting Type I and Type II securities, as provided by administrative regulation. Banks are required to have these functions handled by separate units within their investment departments and to keep the underlying securities (trading-account securities) separate from the investment account. However, a series of court rulings in the 1980s proved instrumental in removing major barriers to banks' securities powers. In 1987, and again in 1989, the Federal Reserve granted limited authority to money-center banks to deal in and underwrite Type III securities, such as commercial paper, corporate bonds, municipal revenue bonds, mortgage-backed and consumer-paper-backed securities, and equities. A key feature of this authorization is that their activities must be funneled through an affiliate institution (that is, a bank holding company subsidiary) that engages in traditionally non-banking business. The Federal Reserve interpreted Section 20 of the Glass-Steagall Act to allow bank holding companies to establish such subsidiaries, which are known as "Section 20 subsidiaries." To date, over 40 bank holding companies have received approval and operate investment banking, or Section 20, subsidiaries.

Under the rules laid down by the Federal Reserve, trading and underwriting in eligible Type III issues were limited to 10 percent of the subsidiary's gross revenue. This volume limitation was of concern to large money-center banks because of the heavy involvement of their subsidiaries in securities trading and underwriting. In December 1996, however, the Federal Reserve gave banks more leeway by raising the limit to 25 percent of gross revenue.

In addition to trading and underwriting eligible securities, banks' investment-banking activities include private placements. Each of these functions is presented in the remaining pages of this chapter.

Dealing in Securities

A bank, or a Section 20 subsidiary, may function as a dealer by standing ready to buy or sell a security at an established bid or asked quotation. The difference between the two prices is known as the spread. The spread realized by a dealer bank in specific transactions varies over time in response to fluctuations in the market prices of the securities owned. Banks dealing in securities maintain a "trading account," which represents an inventory of securities held for resale. Such securities are listed separately on the bank's balance sheet as trading-account securities. In making a market, a dealer rarely sells as much as is bought. In some instances the dealer may have a negative inventory, having sold (short) more than is owned, in which case additional securities will have to be purchased. In any case, the individual spreads and the frequency of transactions are determinants of the revenues dealer banks realize from this kind of activity.

Traders also may engage in arbitrage. Arbitrage is the coordinated purchase and sale of two securities in which there is a relative market imbalance. The objective of such activity is to obtain earnings by taking advantage of changing yield spreads. Arbitrage opportunities take many forms and can exist whenever segments of the securities markets are subject to a yield variance.

An activity that may be classified as trading is known as "bond swapping." Securities that have declined in market value because of a rise in interest rates may be sold and replaced with other issues of comparable maturity. The loss sustained from the transaction enables the bank to realize tax savings without significantly altering the composition of its investment holdings. For the bank to claim this tax loss, however, it is important that the securities purchased are neither the same nor essentially identical to the ones sold.

Banks dealing in securities generally concentrate on U.S. Treasury and agency issues because they are the most marketable of all investments. As a result of initiatives by the Federal Reserve System and the U.S. Treasury, the markets for federal government securities and agency debt have been automated since the 1970s. The Federal Reserve issues, maintains, and transfers ownership of the debt securities of the U.S. Treasury, most federal agencies, and certain international organizations in a computerized book-entry, instead of a physical, form; that is, transactions are effected through entries in the Fed's computer system. This automated program offers many advantages to both the Treasury and investors. It cuts the printing costs of the Treasury and eliminates the problem of counterfeiting. At the same time it protects the investors from loss and theft of the certificates, and reduces handling and storage costs. Progress has also been realized toward the automation of the municipal and corporate securities markets. Four privately owned book-entry depositories handle transactions for these securities. The Depository Trust Company (DTC), the largest such depository, is owned and operated by participating (member) banks.

In reporting trading-account securities, banks have been following market-value accounting rules. That is, securities held for trading are marked to market on the balance sheet, with unrealized gains and losses included in income. This approach does not apply to a bank's other investment securities. Specifically, the Financial Accounting Standards Board's Statement 115 (FASB 115), which became effective in January 1994, requires banks to assign to all their investment holdings one of three designations: held for trading, held to maturity, and available for sale. FASB 115 did not affect the reporting of securities designated as held for trading, which continue to be marked to market. Securities held to maturity can be carried at book (or historical) value with no consequent effect on bank statements; securities available for sale are carried at book value or market value, whichever is lower, with unrealized gains and losses reflected directly in bank equity. The purpose of market-value accounting is to enhance the ability of investors and regulators to evaluate the worth of a bank. Moreover, it is intended to force banks to monitor closely the exposure of their investment portfolios to interest-rate risk. Since a rise in interest rates would adversely affect the value of securities, and consequently a bank's net income and equity capital position, it is expected that banks will choose to take less risk by shortening the maturity of their investment holdings.

Underwriting Activities

The term "underwriting" refers to the process of selling newly issued securities. The underwriter customarily agrees to buy from the issuing concern (such as a government entity) its entire new issue of securities for a specified amount of money, with the intention to resell such issue publicly for profit. Failure to sell the securities or adverse price fluctuations at the time of the public offering impose significant losses on the underwriter, who still must pay the issuer the agreed-upon sum of money.

Just prior to 1930, banks and their investment affiliates were responsible for the retailing of over half of all new debt issues coming into the market. The domination of the security business by commercial banks seemed almost certain until interrupted by the Great Depression. Failure of a large bank in 1931, triggered by the failure of its investment affiliate, aroused congressional concern over the tie between commercial banking and investment banking. As a result, the Glass-Steagall Act of 1933 gave commercial banks one year to divest themselves of their investment affiliates and introduced important limitations on banks' underwriting functions. Thus, banks were permitted to underwrite only Type I and Type II securities.

Commercial banks are actively involved in the underwriting of U.S. Treasury obligations through their participation in the auctions of Treasury bills, notes, and bonds. Banks are also underwriting eligible municipal issues. Bidding for municipal securities is usually competitive as a safeguard against connivance. The announcement of a new municipal issue by the issuing unit of government is made through a published solicitation of bids. If the issue is small, large commercial banks in the area may bid individually to buy the issue. Large issues, however, require the formation of an underwriting syndicate. A syndicate is a temporary association of a group of banks and other underwriters who join together to spread the risk of underwriting and assist in the marketing of a specific issue. A large commercial bank in the area may lead or manage the syndicate formed to bid on the given issue. Prior to submitting any bids, the syndicate members agree in advance on their responsibilities and liabilities in the event that the bid is successful.

The broadening of banks' securities powers has led Section 20 subsidiaries underwrite Type III securities subject to the 10 percent revenue limitation stated earlier. Since the Glass-Steagall Act does not apply outside the United States, many U.S. banks have been quite active in underwriting and in other securities business overseas.

Private Placements

Although the Glass-Steagall Act prohibits the underwriting of corporate bonds and stocks by banks, it cannot prevent a bank's assisting a borrower in obtaining funds from other financial institutions, such as insurance companies or pension funds. A bank's role in private placements is much more limited than in underwriting. Private placement of new issues involves bringing together the securities issuer and one or several large institutional buyers. The intermediary earns a finder's fee, but does not take even brief possession of the securities. Both the Fed and the Comptroller have ruled that private placement is not underwriting under Glass-Steagall, and have permitted commercial banks to earn private placement fees. The fees charged have been, for obvious reasons, lower than the fees usually charged by investment bankers. For the borrowing concern the private placement is associated with lower costs, since it eliminates the underwriting fees and entails fewer legal restrictions than a public offering.

Another service provided by a bank involves aiding corporate clients in finding and negotiating merger opportunities.

SUGGESTED REFERENCES

Benston, G. J. *The Separation of Commercial and Investment Banking: The Glass-Steagall Act Revisited and Reconsidered.* New York: St. Martin's Press, 1989.

Chari, V. V., and Robert J. Weber. "How the U.S. Treasury Should Auction Its Debt." Federal Reserve Bank of Minneapolis, *Quarterly Review*, Fall 1992, pp. 3–12.

Fortune, Peter. "The Municipal Bond Market, Part I: Politics, Taxes, and Yields." *New England Economic Review*, September/October 1991, pp. 13–36.

Parkinson, Patric et al. "Clearance and Settlement in U.S. Securities Markets." Special Study no. 163, Board of Governors of the Federal Reserve System, March 1992.

Reinhart, Vincent. "An Analysis of Potential Treasury Auction Techniques." *Federal Reserve Bulletin*, June 1992, pp. 403–13.

Rose, Peter S. *Money and Capital Markets*. 5th ed. Burr Ridge, Ill.: Richard D. Irwin, 1994.

Stigum, Marcia. *After the Trade: Dealer and Clearing Bank Operations in Money Market and Government Securities*. Homewood, Ill.: Dow-Jones Irwin, 1988.

Chapter 15

The Investment Account: Policy and Management

The regulatory provisions discussed in Chapter 14 constitute the framework within which a bank's board of directors formulates investment policy. Whether in detail or in general terms, this policy is put into writing to ensure consistency by all those involved in its implementation. To guard against the inflexibility of the investment function over a period of time, it is imperative that investment policy be periodically reviewed in the light of changing economic conditions.

Formulating a bank's investment policy generally implies the setting up of standards and the establishment of procedures for the management of a bank's investment account. Developing an investment policy offers a bank's board of directors a wider framework than for loans. Unlike the loan portfolio, the distributional character of which reflects local conditions and therefore can be controlled only within limits, a bank's investment account can be planned in advance and consequently can be tailored to bank wishes. Investment policy, therefore, has a unique element: it can be designed around the types of investment instruments that are available in the open market.

The basic considerations that underlie the liquidity aspect of a bank's investment account have already been considered in discussing a bank's secondary reserves (see Chapter 8). A notable part of investment activity, however, is still to be discussed, and this pertains to the other aspect of a bank's investment account, the residual employment of bank funds—the bond portfolio. A bank's bond portfolio may be defined as those securities not held as secondary reserves. This chapter identifies the objectives of the bond portfolio, outlines the basic criteria established by the board for the selection of securities, and reviews the organization of the investment function.

OBJECTIVES OF THE BOND PORTFOLIO

The objectives of the bond portfolio, as defined by the board, are basic to the determination of a bank's investment activity. They are generally the same for all banks: to provide supplementary liquidity and to generate supplementary income.

Supplementary Liquidity

Although banks try to forecast their liquidity needs over the next year and to maintain adequate secondary reserves, there is always the possibility of some unaccounted-for developments that may cause important deviations between the actual and the forecast liquidity needs. In addition, the bank must always be prepared for contingencies. For example, a natural disaster might cause a rapid decline of deposits and a delay in repayment of loans. A bank that experiences such unexpected demands on its liquidity positions may be forced to sell securities from its bond portfolios in order to increase the amount of funds raised from borrowing and selling of secondary reserves.

Supplementary Income

Except for tight money periods, when loan demand exceeds available resources, banks usually have residual funds that can be profitably invested in securities. These investments can be the determining factor in assessing a bank's profitability.

A bank's investments, as we saw in Chapter 14, are generally restricted by law to debt instruments. The income generated by these instruments is in the form of interest and capital gains (or losses). The interest income consists of explicit cash flows received periodically from the issuer over the lifetime of the bond. The size of these flows is determined by the bond's coupon rate, which is established at the time of its issue. A $1,000 bond bearing a 6 percent coupon rate would pay the investor $60 per annum until its maturity, regardless of the state of the economy. That is, regardless of whether the market rates of interest go up or down in the future because of changes in economic conditions, the bond will continue to generate $60 per year until its maturity. Capital gains (or losses) are realized if the bond is sold prior to its maturity and at the time of its sale the going market rates are lower (higher) than the bond's coupon rate.

Both interest income and capital gains (or losses) determine the yield a bank earns from a bond. There are two measures of a bond yield, the current yield and the yield to maturity. The current yield is derived by dividing the annual interest income of a bond by its market price. In other words, a bond with three years left to maturity, paying $60 per year, and bought for $948.62 offers a current yield of 6.3 percent. The current yield formula is $Y_c = R/P$, where Y_c

stands for the current yield, R for the annual interest income from the bond, and P for its current market price. Current yield quotations for listed bonds are customarily provided by financial newspapers and are helpful for investors who finance their purchases through borrowed funds and wish to determine whether their borrowing cost is being covered.

Otherwise, the importance of this measure is limited because it assures that payments will continue forever. Moreover, it ignores that at maturity the investor will receive the face value of the bond, which is different from the market value. For these reasons the yield-to-maturity concept is considered a more meaningful and useful measure of a bond's rate of return. The equation for the yield to maturity is the one that was used in Chapter 9 to determine the effect of interest-rate changes on the value of a bond:

$$P = \frac{R_1}{(1+k)} + \frac{R_2}{(1+k)^2} + \frac{R_3}{(1+k)^3} + \cdots + \frac{R_n}{(1+k)^n} + \frac{M}{(1+k)^n}.$$

Here R_1 through R_n represents the annual income from the bond until it matures; M, the principal of the bond payable at maturity; P, the bond's current market price; and k, the yield to maturity—that is, the rate of discount that makes the present value of the expected future stream of revenue equal to the cost of the asset. We can illustrate the application of this formula by making reference to the data of the example cited above. The equation would be

$$\$948.62 = \frac{\$60}{(1+k)} + \frac{\$60}{(1+k)^2} + \frac{\$60}{(1+k)^3} + \frac{\$1,000}{(1+k)^3}.$$

Solving for k, we find that the rate that makes the total present value of future income equal the cost of the asset is 8 percent.

An approximate yield-to-maturity estimate can be derived by means of a simple arithmetical computation. The formula that may be used in this respect is

$$\text{Yield to maturity} = \frac{\text{annual dollar coupon interest} \begin{array}{c} + \text{ annual accumulation} \\ \text{or} \\ - \text{ annual amortization} \end{array}}{\dfrac{\text{current market price} + \text{par value}}{2}}$$

Using the information of the example illustrated above, we can calculate the approximate yield to maturity. The example mentioned a three-year bond, bearing a 6 percent rate of interest, acquired at the price of $948.62. Since this bond will be redeemed at maturity for $1,000, the investor will receive an appreciation of $51.38, which corresponds to an annual gain of

$$\frac{(\$1,000 - \$948.62)}{3} = \frac{\$51.38}{3} = \$17.127 \text{ per year.}$$

To determine the yield, we also need to ascertain average investment, which can be established by averaging the cost of the bond ($948.62) and the par value at maturity ($1,000). Using this information in the above formula, we have

$$\text{yield to maturity} = \frac{\$60 + \$17.127}{\dfrac{\$948.62 + \$1,000}{2}} = \frac{\$77.127}{\$974.31} = 7.916 \text{ percent.}$$

If the bond was bought at a premium, the above calculation would differ in that we would need to amortize the premium on an annual basis, and hence charge it off to annual interest income.

Once the yield of a security has been determined, a bank's decision to acquire it will be based upon the spread, or difference, between that yield and the bank's cost-of-funds rate. As was indicated in Chapter 5, if an investment promises a rate of return exceeding the bank's cost of funds and cost of servicing the asset, its acquisition will make a positive contribution to profits and will enhance the wealth of stockholders. By contrast, investments that are expected to produce a return equal to, or less than, the bank's cost of funds will not be undertaken. Thus, among alternative investment opportunities a bank will undertake only those offering the highest spread possible for the same degree of risk.

CRITERIA IN THE SELECTION OF SECURITIES

The degree of detail by which the board of directors sets bond portfolio policy varies from bank to bank, and indicates the margin of latitude for maneuvering in the application of such policy. However detailed such policy may be, the basic issues covered include the quality of the securities to be bought, market-ability guidelines, extent of diversification desired, tax considerations, and max-imum maturities. Each of these is discussed below.

Quality

Although the bond portfolio is an important source of income, aggressive pursuit of income could undermine the bank's continued existence. To ensure the safe employment of funds in banks' bond portfolios, regulatory authorities have introduced certain qualitative standards for banks to follow in security purchases. In regulations promulgated by the Office of the Comptroller of the Currency and extended to state banks that are members of the Federal Reserve System, banks are allowed to buy only *investment-grade securities*.

Banks thus refer to the published opinions of rating agencies to identify the rating classification assigned to a specific security. Considered eligible for a bank's portfolio are the general obligations that are readily marketable and are rated within the top four classes by leading agencies in their investment-rating manuals.

Two highly respected agencies that rate debt issues are Standard and Poor's and Moody's Investors Service. They do not rate all the issues, but only those that are subject to default risk (municipalities and corporates) and enjoy a rel-

Table 15.1
Bond Ratings

Standard & Poor's		Moody's	
AAA	Highest grade	Aaa	Best quality
AA	High grade	Aa	High quality
A	Upper medium grade	A	Higher medium grade
BBB	Medium grade	Baa	Lower medium grade
BB	Lower medium grade	Ba	Possess speculative elements
B	Speculative	B	Generally lack characteristics of a desirable investment
CCC		Caa	Poor; may be in default
CC	Outright speculation	Ca	Speculative to a high degree; often in default
C	Income bonds	C	Lowest grade
DDD	In default; rating		
DD	indicates relative		
D	salvage value		

Note: Moody's applies numerical modifiers, 1, 2, and 3 in each generic rating classification from Aa to B. The modifier 1 indicates that the company ranks in the higher end of its generic rating category; the modifier 2 indicates a midrange ranking; and the modifier 3 indicates that the company ranks in the lower end of its generic rating category.

The S & P uses modifiers for bonds rated below triple A. It uses a plus and minus system; thus, A+ designates the strongest A-rated bonds and A− as the weakest.

Source: Moody's Bond Record, July 1995; *Standard and Poor's Bond Guide*, January 1996.

atively broad market. Table 15.1 shows the rating system of each agency. Both systems attribute high ratings to securities of high quality (low risk) and lower ratings to issues of poorer quality (high risk).

A national bank or a state bank member of the Federal Reserve System can hold securities down through Moody's Baa or Standard and Poor's BBB. Double-B and lower bonds are speculative, or junk, bonds; they have a significant probability of going into default. If a bank holds a bond with a low rating, examiners will advise the bank to sell it. The FDIC and state banking authorities maintain similar quality standards for banks under their jurisdiction.

Often banks may consider buying securities that are not rated (such as securities of small face value or of small localities)—for example, the nonrated obligations of a local governmental unit that holds deposits with the bank. Unrated securities are eligible for purchase by member banks, even though they enjoy limited marketability. The responsibility for proving the quality of these securities, however, rests with the bank's top management. Whether the securities are rated or unrated, the Comptroller of the Currency requires that every "bank maintain in its files credit information adequate to demonstrate that it has exercised prudence" in making its investment determination.

Although banks emphasize high-quality securities in their bond portfolios, some credit risk is unavoidable with state and local debt as well as corporate issues. Moreover, all intermediate- and long-term obligations entail significant interest-rate risk. Hence the question of what amount of risk is appropriate for the bond portfolio. The framework for risk-taking is, to a great extent, determined by the amount of capital available for application against the portfolio. Acceptance of risks beyond the ability to absorb them (in the form of capital adequacy) should be avoided, as being outside the framework of a realistic and productive investment policy.

Marketability

Regulatory agencies view marketability as a criterion for quality. The reasoning is that if an obligation possesses quality, investors will be eager to purchase it, and vice versa. This approach raises the question of defining marketability. Although there are differing degrees of marketability, in general a marketable instrument is one that is actively traded and hence can be readily converted into cash through the securities market mechanism. A more refined approach would be to consider the differences between the bid and asked quotations for a security. Financial experts suggest that a margin of one point or more between such quotations is an indication of limited marketability.

Banks have every reason to emphasize marketability in their portfolios. With deposits providing the overwhelming portion of loanable and investable funds, marketability ensures promptness in the disposition of the securities held and availability of supplemental liquidity in periods of financial strain. In these instances marketability can be ensured by holding nationally known issues that are capable of attracting buyers under any market conditions.

Of the various securities available in the market, obligations of the U.S. government enjoy the highest marketability. Their riskless character and the highly organized market available enable the holder to convert them into cash with minimal loss. These attributes have rendered U.S. government securities the most common and convenient type of security desired. Also of significant marketability are the obligations of U.S. government agencies and government-sponsored corporations that are traded in the same markets as the direct obligations of the federal government. Of the municipal and corporate securities, only those of the larger and more creditworthy issuers enjoy a national market.

Diversification

With most of the investment holdings of insured commercial banks consisting of U.S. government securities (Treasury and agency obligations), the principle of diversification has application to their holdings of corporate debt as well as state and local government issues. A generally accepted method of reducing risk in the investment account to manageable proportions, diversification may be defined as a process of spreading risk, prompted by the need to minimize the effect of poor judgment and the impact of economic conditions on the investment portfolio. Diversification is effected through the purchasing or holding of investment issues consistent with the regulatory provisions discussed in Chapter 14. The holding of an assortment of securities in the portfolio, rather than a limited number of issues bunched at one time or in one place, tends to reduce losses by averaging them out over the long run.

Proper diversification can be ensured by providing in the investment policy of a bank that certain percentages of the investment portfolio be invested in particular types of securities or by establishing a ceiling on the funds that may be placed in specific types of securities. Diversification may take various forms, two of which stand out in banking practice: diversification by industry and by geographical area.

Diversification by industry has significance only with respect to holdings of corporate securities. When corporate debt was the dominant investment in the portfolios of commercial banks, securities were classified into industrials, transportation, public utilities, and miscellaneous.* Each of these groupings was further divided into subgroupings. Clearly, the degree of detail in the classification of corporate securities depended to a large extent upon the size of such holdings and the feasibility of such classification. Because of the minor amounts of corporate securities in the investment portfolios of commercial banks, diversification in corporates is currently of limited significance.

Diversification by geographical area is used for state and local government securities. As stated earlier, municipal securities represent debt of the various states and their political subdivisions. This debt has grown considerably over the postwar years, reflecting the increasing use of debt financing by state and local governments. Because of the large number of issuers and issues, there is a wide variation in the type of securities available. This variation is, of course, to be expected, since each issuer has a different economic base not only vis-à-vis other issuing governments, state or local, but also over time. Some states or localities are agriculturally oriented, some industrially, some commercially, while others are fairly diversified. In some the pace of economic change is slow; in others, faster. Some issuing governments are heavily indebted; others are less so. Differing portions of this debt are in the form of revenue obligations, supported by the earnings of some business venture, and in the form of general obligations, with the full taxing power of the issuing body pledged to assure repayment.

In building up its portfolio of state and local government securities, a bank should seek to purchase—over and beyond such local issues as are required for

---

*In the late 1890s and the early years of the twentieth century, railroad bonds were almost the only ones listed on the New York Stock Exchange.

reasons of good customer and community relations—securities that are dependent upon areas of the country beyond the local community. With the loan portfolio consisting basically of local credits, a large position in local municipals in the bond portfolio would only accentuate the concentration in assets subject to adverse developments in the local economy. In planning investment operations, therefore, management may offset concentration in the loan account by following a policy of not duplicating it. In other words, the bond account must be viewed as complementary to a bank's loan account. This type of relationship constitutes an important test of diversification.

Tax Considerations

Tax considerations play an important role in the formulation of a bank's bond portfolio policy. Federal income-tax laws affect the profitability of the bond portfolio and its contribution to the bank's net income in two ways. First, tax reform has had a major impact on the relative attractiveness of state and local government securities as bank investments. Second, interest and capital gains income are taxed at the same rate.

Importance of Tax-Exempts

In the 1970s and early 1980s, state and local government securities constituted the dominant type of investment in the portfolios of commercial banks. Their exemption from federal income taxes (as well as from state income taxes in the issuing state) made them an attractive investment for banks in the upper tax brackets. For example, for a bank in the 34 percent marginal tax bracket, an 8 percent coupon-rate municipal bond was equivalent to a before-tax rate of 12.1 percent, calculated from the following formula:

$$\text{Tax-equivalent interest rate} = \frac{\text{Coupon rate}}{(1-\text{marginal tax rate})}$$

Applying the information provided,

$$\text{Tax-equivalent interest rate} = \frac{.08}{(1-.34)} = .121 \text{ or } 12.1 \text{ percent.}$$

The pretax yield of municipal issues was often more attractive than the pretax yields of U.S. government and corporate securities.

Until 1982, the federal tax code had allowed banks to fully deduct (100 percent) from their taxes the interest expenses incurred on the funds used to finance their holdings of munis. Passage of legislation in that year (Tax Equity and Fiscal Responsibility Act of 1982) reduced the interest deduction to only 85 percent of the interest expense and provided for a further adjustment of the interest deduction to 80 percent by 1985. Enactment of the Tax Reform Act of 1986 eliminated this tax break, rendering munis a much less attractive asset for top-earning banks to hold. Exception was made for munis that meet essential public requirements, provided that the issuing local government issues no more than $10 million in securities per year. Banks purchasing these securities—often called ''bank-qualified''—can continue to deduct 80 percent of the interest cost of funds used to carry these issues. Thus, to compare the yield of a qualified municipal with that of a taxable security, allowance must be made for the carrying cost, which limits the loss in interest deduction to only 20 percent. The formula to determine the tax-equivalent interest rate for a qualified municipal is

$$\frac{\text{Coupon rate} - (.20 \times \text{average cost of funds} \times \text{marginal tax rate})}{(1 - \text{marginal tax rate})}.$$

Given a 20 percent nondeductible interest expense, assume a qualified municipal bond bearing a coupon rate of 8 percent, an average cost of bank funds of 6 percent, and the bank's marginal tax rate of 34 percent. The tax-equivalent interest rate would be

$$\frac{.08 - (.20 \times .06 \times .34)}{(1 - .34)} = .1150 \text{ or } 11.50 \text{ percent.}$$

If the municipal bond is nonqualified, 100 percent of the interest expense is nondeductible. Thus, replacing .20 in the numerator by the factor of 1.0 will produce a tax-equivalent interest rate of 9.03 percent. This lower tax-equivalent rate reflects the loss of interest deduction compared with the qualified municipal, which yields more because the bank loses only a portion of the interest deduction. Clearly, the tax-shelter benefit of a qualified municipal for a bank will depend upon the coupon rate of the security, the bank's average cost of funds, and its marginal income-tax rate.

The yields on tax-exempt bonds have varied over time. Figure 15.1 shows the average yields of municipal securities (Aa), and their relationship to other bond yields, for the period 1984–94. As seen in this figure, yields exhibited significant variation during this period in response to prevailing economic conditions in the course of the last two decades. During the 1970s and early 1980s there was a considerable fluctuation in the yield of tax-exempts, consistent with the general trends of the market. For example, in 1971 the yield to maturity for these securities was about 5 percent; it rose to an unprecedented 12.6 percent in 1981 before going back down to about 6 percent in 1995. There was a comparable fluctuation in the yields of other instruments during the same period, with corporate Aa-rated bonds rising to 15.9 percent in 1981 before declining to 7.7 percent in 1995. A corresponding trend was exhibited by the 30–year U.S. Treasury bond, which between 1981 and 1995 decreased from 13.4 percent to 6.9 percent.

Figure 15.1
Bond Yields, 1984–94 (monthly averages)

Percent

Source: U.S. Department of the Treasury, *Treasury Bulletin*, December 1989, p. 68.

The fluctuations of this period, as was generally true for preceding decades, reflected prevailing economic conditions in financial markets. The inflationary pressures and tight monetary policy pursued in the late 1970s produced high rates of interest, which led to increases in the yields of outstanding securities. A decrease in inflation by the mid-1980s and the monetary ease of the early 1990s caused lower rates of interest and corresponding decreases in yields. In addition to the prevailing economic climate, the yield trends of this period reflected demand and supply forces in specific markets. For example, when many state and local governments simultaneously seek funds through the issuance of bonds, the large volume of municipals being sold drives up the yield of these instruments.

In addition to showing the fluctuation in yields, Figure 15.1 shows the yield relationship between instruments of different risk. For example, Aa-rated corporate bonds yielded more than riskfree U.S. government securities. The lowest yield in the market was that of municipal bonds, because of exemption of their interest from taxes. The gaps between the yields on the three types of bonds

varied over time, indicating that the cost differentials, or risk premiums, fluctuated from year to year, reflecting the extent of investors' risk aversion.

Tax Treatment of Capital Gains and Losses

Federal income-tax laws affect the profitability of a bank's investment portfolio through their treatment of capital gains and losses, whether actual or resulting from the mark-to-market rules pertaining to dealer securities. Both short-
and long-term gains from the sale of securities are taxed at the same rate as
ordinary income. Short- and long-term capital losses cannot be used as offsets
to taxable ordinary income; they can only off-set capital gains.

Like other corporations, banks must carry capital losses back against the capital
gains they realized in the three preceding taxable years. This entitles the bank to
receive a cash refund of taxes paid in the past three years, beginning with the earliest year in the period. If the prior years' capital gains are less than the current
loss, the unused portion of the capital loss must be carried forward for five years.
By applying this provision, the bank will be able to reduce its exposure and pay
lower taxes on its potential income than it would otherwise pay.

Maturity

An important supplement to quality and diversification considerations in the
selection of securities is the factor of maturity. In the employment of funds in
the bond portfolio, the policymakers are faced with the problem of determining
the maximum maturity of the securities to be acquired. To maximize income,
bank managers need to invest in long-term securities with high yields. However,
if these securities are held to maturity, the bank will be exposed to a considerable
amount of risk. The longer the maturities of the securities acquired, the greater
the bank's exposure to credit and interest-rate risks.

With an investment involving credit risk (such as municipal and corporate
issues), the likelihood of quality deterioration over time is greater than the
chance of improvement. No such bond is good enough to buy and then forget.
There is always the possibility that the credit standing of the obligor may change,
with consequent implications for the credit quality of the outstanding debt. If
the issuer is a state or local government unit, various developments (such as
natural disaster, increased indebtedness, loss of industry) can undermine its ability to make the requisite periodic payments. By the same token, the sizable
losses of a corporate obligor may affect its intention to make prompt payments
of principal and interest when due.

These developments will affect the credit quality of the issues outstanding,
and rating agencies are prompt to lower their quality rating. This, in turn, reduces
investor appeal of the securities, with consequent implications for their marketability. In the late 1970s, as the financial condition of Chrysler Corporation
began to deteriorate, the rating of its bonds was lowered accordingly. This had
a negative effect on the price of Chrysler's bonds and their marketability. An-

other example of change over time in the credit standing of the obligor is the case of railroad companies. At the turn of the twentieth century, many investors viewed favorably the purchase of railroad bonds with maturities of 100 years. The decline of the railroad industry in subsequent decades made apparent the danger involved in such long commitments.

Even though a bond may be free of credit risk, it is still subject to interest-rate risk. As stated before, this phenomenon is a result of the contractual rate of interest that bonds carry when issued, and of changes in the level of interest rates. When interest rates are low and the demand for loans is weak, banks usually have surplus funds for employment in the bond portfolio. Consequently, when banks enter the market to buy bonds, these bonds, reflecting the prevailing interest-rate trends, carry a low contractual rate of interest. Banks that purchase bonds when interest rates are low face the risk of a depreciation in the bond account when interest rates subsequently increase, for such an increase will adversely affect the market value of these bonds. Banks cannot, of course, afford to dispose of their bonds at such times, because they will sustain capital losses. They will try instead to hold them until maturity or until bond prices increase again, as a result of a reversal in interest-rate trends, and reach a level that will permit them to sell without realizing substantial losses. If, however, in response to unusual withdrawals or intense customer loan demands, banks are forced to sell a portion of their bond portfolios at low prices, they will sustain sizable losses.

There is, therefore, always uncertainty over the prospective level of interest rates both at the time when the obligation falls due and the funds are available for reinvestment, and (more so) throughout the period that the security is held. The longer the maturity, the greater the possibility that market value (and income) over the long run will be (favorably or unfavorably) affected by changes in the level of rates. An investment, for example, in a 30–year U.S. Treasury bond at 5.91 percent is tantamount to accepting that the average return on one-year funds will not exceed 5.91 percent over the next 30 years.

It is apparent that the longer the term of maturity, the greater the potential for quality deterioration and market vulnerability. The question, therefore, that the policymaker faces is how far the maturities should be extended.

As depicted in Figure 15.2, it was not until the mid-1960s (Vietnam war) that the general movement in interest rates turned upward. With the end of the war in the early 1970s, inflation dipped a bit, but then high oil prices led to high inflation rates and sharply higher interest rates by the early 1980s. Since then a decrease in inflation has produced lower interest rates, with high-quality corporate bonds yielding about 7.60 percent at year-end 1995. Based on the interest rates that the market has shown since the mid-1950s, the general level of future interest rates will move up or down, depending primarily on what happens to the rate of inflation.

Bank experience with longer-term bonds has not been favorable; a number of banks have found themselves with substantial depreciation on holdings of such bonds acquired 20 to 25 years ago. Obviously, forecasting the state of the

Figure 15.2
Long- and Short-Term Interest Rates, 1960–94

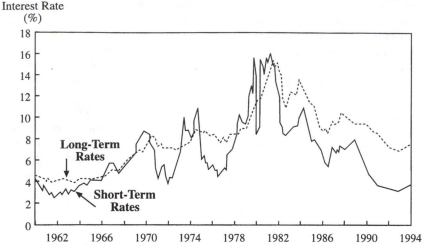

Source: *Federal Reserve Bulletin*, various issues.

market and the demand for bank loans in the decade ahead, in planning for bond portfolio maturities, is a hard task. In light of the uncertainties involved in a rapidly changing world, many banks limit the maximum maturity of securities in the bond portfolio to 10 or 15 years, even though this may be considered a long time. Although there is important variation from one bank to another on this subject, establishing a maturity limit generally reflects a fundamental issue, a bank's investment strategy.

As stated in Chapter 9, a bank can manage the exposure of its bond portfolio to interest-rate risk through use of duration analysis. Immunization of the bond portfolio can be effected by purchasing securities with a combined duration equal to the bank's planned holding period. However, duration analysis is only a tool in the management of portfolio risk. Alternative information and risk-management strategies offer additional perspective on the overall control of risk in the bond portfolio.

Interest-rate fluctuations and their effect on bond portfolio profitability have led to the emergence of three basic strategies for structuring or scheduling maturities: spaced or staggered maturities, riding the yield curve, and the barbell maturity structure.

Spaced or Staggered Maturities

Although there are variants, the concept of a strictly spaced maturity structure provides for the even allocation of funds among various bond maturities within the established maximum maturity limits. For example, if, because of the uncertainties involved with long-term investments, the bond portfolio manager of a given bank wants to limit maturities to no longer than ten years, the funds may be spread evenly within this maturity range. This approach to allocating funds gives the bond portfolio the appearance of a ladder of maturities, hence the reference to this strategy as "laddered portfolio." As securities approach their maturity, the bank is provided with a convenient source of supplemental liquidity on an ongoing basis. The proceeds of maturing securities are reinvested at the longest maturity admitted to the account. The even spacing of maturities assures the bank of an average portfolio maturity of half the maximum and an income of average yields over an interest-rate cycle. This yield performance is true as long as banks continue their investment pattern (such as reinvesting maturing issues) over the course of the business cycle. To the extent that securities are sold, or the proceeds from maturing securities are not reinvested (because of a strong demand for credit), the rate of return of the bond portfolio will be lower than the average market returns over a complete interest-rate cycle.

The spaced approach is simple and requires little investment expertise. As a result, a large number of banks are using it in their portfolio operations. Some apply this treatment only to a sector of the investment portfolio, such as the secondary reserves, while others apply it to the entire portfolio. In the former instance a bank has little choice to act differently. However, to apply this approach to the entire investment account undermines its profitability potential. For bank managers who are not sufficiently versed in a more flexible portfolio policy or do not wish, for one reason or another, to introduce and frame such a policy, the results of maturity spacing are doubtless better than those of intuitive judgment. Maturity spacing is an acceptable portfolio approach for small banks. But for the banks that are willing to replace a static rule with an analytical procedure and informed judgment, it will certainly make no sense, for instance, to reinvest the funds derived from maturing securities at the longest end of the maturity schedule when the economy is sluggish and monetary authorities pursue a policy of easy money. For if they do, they will find themselves with sizable book losses in their portfolios when the economy eventually recovers and interest rates start rising.

For management to adhere to the spaced maturities method rigidly and in all kinds of economic weather is to close its eyes and ignore the market opportunities that exist for portfolio improvement and added long-run income for the bank.

Riding the Yield Curve

This approach, also referred to as flexible investment policy, provides for an aggressive employment of funds by taking advantage of interest-rate movements. The essence of this approach is that if managers believe that interest rates will decline, they should lengthen maturities in their portfolios in order to "lock in" some of the currently high long-term rates and to generate potential capital gains when interest rates fall and security prices increase. If they anticipate that interest rates will increase, they should shorten portfolio maturities to avoid potential capital losses. This is tantamount to saying that it is advisable to hold short-term securities when business activity starts picking up slowly and the credit demand is expected to grow, and to lengthen maturities when the first indications of an approaching recession start setting in and the credit demand is expected to fall.

As implied, aggressive employment of funds in the bond portfolio relies heavily upon management ability to forecast interest-rate movements. The most useful predictive device available is the yield curve, which depicts the maturity distribution of yields (often called the term structure of interest rates) in the market at a particular time. A yield curve for U.S. government securities is published regularly in the *Treasury Bulletin*, a monthly publication of the U.S. Department of the Treasury. Yield curves for agency securities, municipal obligations, and corporates are published on a regular basis by various major investment-banking houses.

Since the yield curve represents the pattern of yields in the market at a specific point in time, it is a useful tool in investment decision making because it permits investors to spot any deviations of individual securities from such curves. If a security's rate of return lies above the curve, this implies that the particular security is underpriced relative to others of the same maturity. This is a buy signal that many investors will try to take advantage of. The strong demand for the security will drive its price up and bring its yield down in line with others in the yield curve. By the same token, a yield below the curve would indicate an overpriced security; investors holding it will be quick to sell it, thus driving its price down and raising its yield toward the curve.

More important, the slope of the yield curve is critical for the planning of investment strategy. Its shape depicts the influence on financial markets of such forces as Federal Reserve monetary policy, maturity preferences of borrowers, and investors' expectations. Study of the shape of the yield curve thus enables portfolio managers to prepare their own interest-rate forecasts and attempt to pattern their activities in financial markets accordingly. There are three distinct types of yield curves: increasing, flat, and decreasing. Examples of each of these types are depicted in Figure 15.3.

Figure 15.3 illustrates an increasing or upward-sloping yield curve for U.S. government securities for March 1994. An increasing yield curve is typical of a period of slow, or negative, economic growth and a low demand for funds relative to the supply. Consequently the entire rate structure is at a lower level than during other phases of the business cycle. Although rising yield curves vary in degree of steepness, they are invariably characterized by lower short-term rates vis-à-vis other rates prevailing in the market. This reflects investor expectation that interest rates will be rising in the near future. Banks and other investors, in anticipation of the lending and investing opportunities during the ensuing expansionary phase of the business cycle, are unwilling to buy long-term securities at the present prices, but are willing to place their surplus funds

Figure 15.3
Yield Curves of Treasury Securities, Various Dates

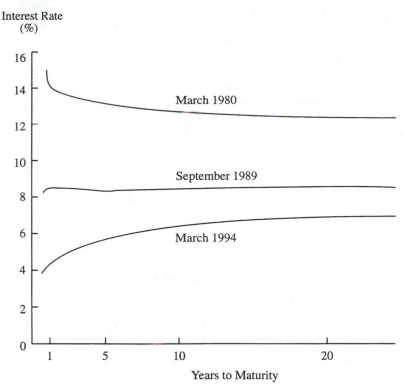

in short-term issues. Thus a premium is paid for short-term maturity outlets in the form of lower yields, while sellers and issuers of long-term securities are forced to offer more favorable yields to attract buyers.

From the preceding discussion it follows that when the shape of the yield curve is upward-sloping, banks following a flexible investment policy place available funds in short-term issues. As the economy recovers and the expansionary phase of the cycle sets in, the proceeds of maturing short-term securities will be available to take advantage of lending and investing opportunities as these arise. To do otherwise—that is, to buy long-term issues during recession—would adversely affect the liquidity of the portfolio and undermine its profitability.

Figure 15.3 shows a flat yield curve for U.S. government securities for September 1989. A flat yield curve indicates a fairly even distribution in investor preferences among instruments of different maturities. It is generally observed during transitional periods—that is, either as the economy proceeds out of a recession into a cyclical peak and increased tightness, or vice versa. Because this stage is usually short-lived, no investment strategy may be devised.

Figure 15.3 illustrates a decreasing or downward-sloping yield curve for U.S. government obligations for March 1980. This curve, also referred to as an inverted yield curve, is typical of a period of monetary tightness. As business expansion approaches a peak, investors expect rates at all maturities to decline. Investing in short-term securities—even at present high rates—will only entail opportunity losses later, since at maturity investors will have to reinvest the funds at the going lower rates. By contrast, investing in long-term bonds will permit investors to "lock in" some of the prevailing high long-term yields and realize capital gains when interest rates fall and bond prices increase. This expectation will induce investors to adjust their portfolio and will affect the supply of funds in the money and capital markets accordingly. As investors become active sellers of short-term securities, they will drive the prices of these instruments down, thus contributing to an increase in their yields. This development, along with a reduced flow of short-term funds and a tight monetary policy, will push short-term rates above long-term rates. At the same time, as investors shift to longer-term maturities, the supply of funds will exceed the demand. Prices for bonds will thus be driven up and yields will consequently fall.

As is evident, when the shape of the yield curve is downward-sloping, banks following a flexible investment policy invest in long-term securities. Although the availability of investable funds at the peak of the cycle is minimal, downward-sloping curves usually persist for several months because of the protracted state of cyclical tightness. Thus, until economic activity begins to slow down and interest rates to decrease, portfolio managers may invest funds generated from loan repayments and declining liquidity needs in long-term securities. To avoid entering the market prematurely, alert managers should monitor certain key financial indicators. These include a decreasing reliance of banks on Federal Reserve borrowing, a drastic decline in short-term interest rates (which usually precedes a drop in long-term rates), and increases in the rates of growth of bank reserves and money supply, which signal an easy money policy by the Federal Reserve.

Barbell Maturity Structure

This strategy provides for the splitting of the portfolio into two parts—the very short maturities and the very long. The resulting two "bulges" at the ends of the maturity spectrum give this strategy its name.

The purpose of this strategy is to ensure the average performance of the portfolio. The short end of the portfolio provides the necessary liquidity, and the long end generates the high yields that come from investing in long-term issues. This approach requires short-term securities to be rolled over as they mature, and long-term issues to be sold as they approach the midpoint of the maturity schedule. The proceeds from this sale are reinvested at the long end of the maturity spectrum. To lock in the necessary high yields in the long end of the portfolio, the purchase of the long-term securities must be made in tight-money periods, when the yield curve is downward-sloping. If interest-rate forecasts prove wrong and rates continue to rise, the long end of the portfolio will fail to produce as expected and will suffer significant depreciation. However, as short-term securities mature and their proceeds are reinvested at the prevailing higher market rates, the profitability of the portfolio will increase. If, on the other hand, interest-rate forecasts prove correct and rates decline, the high income (and potential capital gains) on the long portion of the portfolio will offset the low income on the short portion, where maturing securities are reinvested at the prevailing low yields.

In a strict sense the barbell strategy calls for the splitting of the portfolio into two equal parts. In practice, however, advocates of this strategy recognize that the relative importance of each part will vary, depending upon the emphasis that different institutions place upon their need for supplementary liquidity and income. Banks using the barbell approach tend to trade portfolios depending upon the prevailing economic conditions. In tight-money periods these banks allow a higher concentration of long-term bonds in order for the portfolio to produce a higher level of current income. This process is reversed in periods of monetary ease, as long-term bonds are sold to reap capital gains and the proceeds are invested in the short end of the portfolio.

As implied by the preceding discussion, the barbell approach requires the same degree of sophistication and expertise as the flexible investment policy, since part of the portfolio is shifted to take advantage of expected major movements in interest rates. For bank managements that possess the necessary competence, either of these two approaches is preferable to the space portfolio. For banks lacking such competence, the spacing of maturities outperforms a haphazard or intuitive approach.

ORGANIZATION OF THE INVESTMENT FUNCTION

A bank's investment policy should provide for the internal organization to carry out the investment function. The size and form of such organization exhibit significant variation from one bank to another, reflecting, among other things, differences in the size of the bank, the type of securities purchased and held, involvement in underwriting activities, and the latitude of the authority delegated by the board of directors.

As with lending, the legal responsibility for bank investing rests with the entire board of directors. Here, too, however, it is customary for the board to assign the responsibility for supervising the investment function to a senior management member or to an investment committee, which will ensure that investments are made in accordance with legal prescription and the bank's own policies.

In small banks, where the relative importance of the investment portfolio is limited, the investment function is likely to be part-time. In such instances this function is usually delegated to the leading full-time executive officer, the president, who may also be the principal lending officer. In such banks a number of alternative approaches may be used to overcome the lack of proficiency in investment portfolio management. One approach is to concentrate on risk-free securities—that is, to invest in and hold U.S. government securities. On many occasions such holdings may be combined with local municipals. Another approach is to include nongovernment securities, on the basis of the information available from rating agencies. Obviously the availability of such information substitutes for the lack of individual knowledge and judgment. Such reliance can be detrimental, since ratings trail market developments, cannot claim to be faultless, and do not include very small issues that may be of high quality. A final, and in all respects better, approach is to use the services of the large-city correspondent, which ordinarily has the specialized staff to effectuate its investment policy. Reliance upon correspondent expertise will complete transactions at opportune times and generally provide important guidance in the management of the portfolio.

In large banks there is usually more delegation of authority. As with lending, it is customary for the board to assign responsibility for effecting the investment policies of the bank to an investment committee. In the larger of these banks, the investment committee serves as the liaison between the board of directors and the bank's investment or bond department, which carries out the investment function. In such banks the investment department gathers, records, and analyzes data with the objective of determining the degree of risk (credit and interest-rate risk) among alternative investment opportunities and evaluating the bank's ability to assume such risk. This information is made available to investment officers, who are customarily authorized to trade in securities. Like loan officers, investment officers are assigned maximum dollar trading limits that give them the authority to purchase or sell securities up to a certain amount independent of the investment committee. However, they are required to report periodically to this committee about the bank's investment position.

Once securities are bought and become part of the bank's investment portfolio, the investment department is expected to assess these securities on a continuing basis. This aspect of the investment function, and the research and analysis aspects mentioned above, are carried out by a group of individuals specializing in the various phases of the investment program. The investment department staff, however, is small compared with the staff of the credit department. This is to be expected, since a bank's investments are the obligations of a few, while loans are made to thousands of individuals, business firms, and others. Furthermore, bank investments, and especially national bank investments, are generally limited by legal prescription to specified classes of issues, of which default-free federal government obligations have been a long-time favorite and convenient holding.

Whatever the form of organization of the investment function, the execution of portfolio policy should not be overburdened with constraints and limitations. An excess of either of these, whether it pertains to quality, maturity, or income, can negate the benefits of a flexible policy. Flexibility in investment policy, therefore, must be understood to extend to the working aspects of a portfolio policy and not just to its broader perspectives. Failure to realize this may render the portfolio manager a passive spectator of market developments as they shape and influence the financial world around him.

SUGGESTED REFERENCES

Berguist, Lizbeth S. "Trends in Investment Portfolio Management." *Bank Management*, January 1991, pp. 64–67.

An Examiner's Guide to Investment Products and Practices. Washington, D.C.: Comptroller of the Currency, December 1992.

Fabozi, Frank, and T. Dessa Fabozi. *Bond Markets, Analysis and Strategies*. Englewood Cliffs, N.J.: Prentice-Hall, 1993.

French, George E. "Tax Reform and Its Effects on the Banking Industry." *Issues in Bank Regulation*, Summer 1987, pp. 3–10.

Koch, Timothy W. "Municipal Securities." In *Handbook of Modern Finance*, ed. Dennis Logue. 4th ed. Boston: Warren, Gorham & Lamont, 1994, pp. A6.1–32.

Platt, Robert. *Controlling Interest Rate Risk: New Techniques & Applications for Money Management*. New York: John Wiley & Sons, 1986.

Rodrigues, Anthony. "Government Securities Investments of Commercial Banks." Federal Reserve Bank of New York, *Quarterly Review*, Summer 1993, pp. 39–53.

Part V

Special Topics

Chapter 16

International Banking

Perhaps the most remarkable development that the banking industry has experienced since the end of World War II has been the internationalization of its services. The banks that took the lead and embarked on multinational banking were major commercial banking institutions, located principally in Western Europe and the western hemisphere. Unhampered by geographical restrictions, these banks embarked upon the creation of worldwide networks of outlets and became actively engaged in foreign markets. The international expansion of these banks has brought about the effective linkage of national financial markets and the increasing integration of worldwide banking systems. Despite apparent differences in the patterns of their international expansion, these banks have become a truly multinational set of competing financial institutions.

Banking is becoming an increasingly international business. Although the nationality of the leading international banks has changed from time to time, the overall trend of international banking has been the same—rapid expansion in the type and volume of services offered and in the number of banks providing these services. This chapter reviews the development of international banking, the vehicles used, and the services offered in building a multinational banking network.

DEVELOPMENT OF INTERNATIONAL BANKING

For several centuries the financing of interregional or international trade was controlled by European institutions. From the twelfth to the fifteenth century, Italian, especially Florentine, banks were supreme in the area of international finance because of their dominance in foreign trade. German banks then became important, only to be succeeded during the seventeenth century by the Dutch by virtue of their control over maritime trade with southern Asia.

Rise of British Banking Houses

The end of the Napoleonic Wars ushered in a period of political stability and created an environment conducive to the growth of international trade and investment. Large-scale industry and capitalistic enterprise, which had begun to flourish in Great Britain in the early eighteenth century, grew very rapidly and contributed to the expansion of commerce with European, North American, and Asian markets. A number of merchant-banking houses rose to prominence by specializing in the financing of particular branches of trade. Export-led growth provided the momentum for the development of the British economy and the rise of London to be the leading financial center of the world.

Since Great Britain enjoyed significant savings and balance of payment surpluses, a large number of foreign borrowers—both private and government—floated debt and equity securities in London to finance a wide variety of industrial and infrastructure projects (e.g., railways, canals, factories, mines). British banks rose to a position of leadership in international finance that they maintained until World War I.

Internationalization of U.S. Banks

The United States entered World War I as a debtor nation and emerged as a creditor. The growing needs of the Allies and neutral nations generated the necessary momentum for the growth of exports. At the same time this war stimulated the influx of flight capital from Europe and thus contributed to the rise of New York as an international financial center.

In the postwar period, the United States experienced greater demand for its manufactured products, increased its investments abroad, and generally was transformed into an industrial and financial power. In fact, by 1929 it was the world's outstanding manufacturing power and its largest creditor. Foreign government bond issues in the United States outstripped those in London, and New York replaced London as the most important financial center.

The banking collapses during the Great Depression, together with the huge foreign loan defaults, triggered a wave of protectionism and economic nationalism that affected the world economy until World War II. The period immediately following this war laid the foundations for the development of modern international banking. The establishment of new international organizations (such as the World Bank, the International Monetary Fund, and the General Agreement on Tariffs and Trade), and a more favorable international economic and political environment were conducive to the reemergence of international banking.

The United States resumed its prewar role of principal capital exporter in the world. It extended assistance to Europe to help the reconstruction efforts and provided foreign aid to developing countries to promote development of agriculture and industry. More important, it opened its markets to foreign goods and simultaneously exported a great deal of long-term capital. Some of this capital was raised by foreign borrowers who were attracted to U.S. financial markets because they were a cheaper and more convenient source of funds. A more sizable portion, however, was raised by U.S.-based corporations seeking to expand their operations internationally. As these corporations began to establish networks and develop global operations during the 1950s and 1960s, they created a natural incentive for expanding the foreign activities of U.S. commercial banks. Thus, large money-center banks, following their corporate and commercial customers abroad, expanded their international operations and presence overseas. A key consideration in this move was the introduction, in the mid-1960s, of capital-control measures aimed at curbing foreign borrowing and at diverting multinationals to foreign markets to finance their growing investments abroad.*

The international expansion of U.S. banks is exemplified in the following data. In 1960, 9 U.S. banks had a physical presence overseas, consisting of 139 branches and subsidiaries. By 1970, 80 U.S. banks operated abroad through 540 branches and subsidiaries. And by 1982, almost every large and medium-sized bank in this country engaged in international banking; 162 banks had 900 branches and 758 subsidiaries operating abroad. Their combined assets amounted to close to $471 billion; about half of this amount was held in major European centers, with London accounting for the largest share. U.S. banks were in active competition not only among themselves but also with the major international commercial banks, and merchant/investment banks, in loan syndications and Eurobond underwriting.

The energy crisis, brought about by the quadrupling of oil prices in late 1973, created a great need for the global financial intermediation of the surplus oil revenues of the Organization of Petroleum Exporting Countries (OPEC). U.S. banks were in the forefront of this intermediation, recycling petrodollars from oil-exporting to oil-importing nations. Their international eminence contributed to attracting a large share of petrodollars in the form of deposits that were then loaned to various borrowers, including less-developed countries (LDCs). Bank lending to these countries grew rapidly until the early 1980s. Pursuit of a tight U.S. monetary policy to curb inflationary pressures led the country into a deep recession that reduced the demand for imports and adversely affected world commodity prices. Similar conditions in other industrialized countries accentuated these trends and contributed to the collapse of the export markets of debtor nations, with drastic consequences for their ability to service their debts to major

---

*These measures were the Interest Equalization Tax (IET) of 1963, the Foreign Direct Investment Program (FDIP) of 1964, and the Voluntary Foreign Credit Restraint (VFCR) Program of 1965. Reference to these measures is made in the Eurodollar section of Chapter 7.

banks around the world. In the summer of 1982, when Mexico announced its inability to meet scheduled payments, it set off the *international debt crisis*. This announcement produced a chain reaction, and within a year 30 countries— including Poland and many Latin American countries—followed suit. With the onset of the debt crisis, new lending to LDCs dried up and many U.S. banks took large losses.

International Expansion of Japanese Banks

As American banks were retreating from international lending, Japanese banks were filling the gap they left. Following the lead of their corporate clients (manufacturing companies and trading firms), Japanese banks began to expand their international operations and presence overseas in the late 1970s. Flush with the proceeds of Japan's trading surpluses, they set out to penetrate foreign markets and build market share at the expense of profits. In 1980, Japanese banks had a foreign network of 139 branches and subsidiaries with assets of $189 billion; by 1989, this network had grown to 300 and $1.4 trillion, respectively. Lending at low profit margins enabled Japanese banks to capture a sizable market share worldwide; it reached 40 percent of total international lending by 1989.

The early 1990s saw the international retrenchment of Japanese banks because of adversity at home. Financial market deregulation, combined with higher interest rates, raised the cost of funds and put pressure on banks to increase earnings. This pressure prompted Japanese banks to abandon their low-cost lending practices abroad in favor of loans that generated higher returns, boosted profits, and added to bank capital.

The new focus on profit was consistent with the need for Japanese banks to improve their capital adequacy ratios, in accordance with the Basel agreement, by 1993. The Basel capital requirements, though fair and consistent in their application to different countries, were significantly higher than the ones Japanese banks had had to comply with at home. Under the circumstances, during 1988 and 1989 Japanese banks had undertaken significant capital-raising activities through issuance of new equity and convertible bonds and realization of gains from the sale of their shareholdings in other Japanese companies. But some of the improvement in the capitalization of Japanese banks was undone by the ensuing sharp stock market decline of the 1990–92 period. This decline made it difficult for banks not only to raise additional equity but also to liquidate their shareholdings to bolster their capital positions. The depressed value of their shareholdings affected bank capital in another way. Japanese banks were allowed to count as part of their capital base (Tier II capital) 45 percent of the unrealized capital gains from their stock portfolios. With stock prices drastically reduced, the contribution of these shareholdings to bank capital suffered accordingly.

The worldwide recession and the collapse of Japan's speculative economy put further pressure on Japanese banks in the form of substantial losses from international and domestic operations. In the United States most of their losses were on real estate in the depressed Northeast and California markets. In the domestic market, too, the drastic drop in real-estate prices magnified the size of problem loans, which by some estimates exceeded $1 trillion in 1995. These developments prompted an international downsizing of the operations of Japanese banks.

Trends of the 1990s

Just as the 1960s and 1970s belonged to the U.S. banks, and the 1980s to the Japanese banks, so the 1990s may be the decade of East Asian and European banks. The 1980s were a period of fast growth for the East Asian "tigers": Hong Kong, Taiwan, Singapore, and South Korea. Development and growth of high-tech manufacturing enabled the technological transformation of their economies within a decade—a process that took Japan 50 years. As exports of high-tech products expanded rapidly, the Asian "tigers" realized significant trade surpluses that were funneled into the Eurocurrency market, the standard source of funds for major corporations. A large part of these funds went to finance corporate restructurings in the United States and Europe, where the pace of consolidation was gaining momentum.

European banks are strong contenders for global dominance. Their strengths include solid capital bases, strong balance sheets, and control of the home market. The Second Banking Directive of 1989, which went into effect on January 1, 1993, permits banks to operate throughout the European Community (EC) with a single banking license issued by the bank's EC home country. Economic integration and the move toward a monetary union by the turn of the century are creating important incentives for the consolidation of the financial sector. Banks are seen as the catalysts for this consolidation. The model for banking under the EC regime is the universal banking system of Germany—fully integrated financial conglomerates that provide their customers with commercial and investment banking, leasing, and insurance services. With many European countries having no effective regulatory barriers to a comprehensive coverage of financial services, European banks are rapidly becoming universal. Leading universal banks within the EC are Germany's Deutsche Bank, France's Credit Agricole, and Britain's Barclays Bank. Notable universal banks outside the EC countries are Union Bank of Switzerland, Swiss Bank Corporation, and Swiss Credit Bank.

ENGAGING IN INTERNATIONAL BANKING: OBJECTIVES AND STRATEGY

Key Objectives

A bank's decision to engage in international banking may involve the pursuit of one or more objectives. Although factors such as bank size and degree of international sophistication may affect individual perspectives, most institutions active in international banking seek to attain certain broad objectives. A principal objective is to provide international banking services to domestic corporate customers who expand and improve the scope of their activities abroad. The emergence of multinational corporations in the United States and Japan sharply increased the demand for international financial services in the respective countries and induced the expansion of banks' international operations and presence abroad. The initial ventures of banks overseas were defensive in nature, designed to accommodate the needs of their domestic customers. In time, however, increased competition and narrowed profit margins abroad prompted many banks to seek new markets, among them the large and medium-size local companies.

Profit, too, has been a key objective in the initiation of international services. Entry into new markets often entails greater profit potential than is available in the domestic market. A bank may extend to foreign markets the expertise it has developed in its home market for the purpose of generating additional income. U.S. penetration of foreign consumer-banking markets is a case in point. With their consumer lending experience in this country dating from the 1920s, U.S. banks enjoy a competitive advantage in this field abroad. Indeed, personal financial services constitute an attractive niche in foreign markets, and many U.S. banks have gained a major share of the consumer-loan and deposit markets of Europe and Asia.

Escaping burdensome regulation has been another important reason for banks' international expansion. Just as burdensome regulation has been a cause for financial innovation, so it has also been a spur to international banking. Restrictive domestic regulation offered both U.S. and Japanese banks limited opportunities for growth; international banking was a substitute. Indeed, U.S. banks have faced considerable restrictions regarding securities, insurance, and commercial activities, and their operations at home are subject to a host of regulatory controls. Expansion abroad allowed banks to circumvent some of these controls (particularly reserve requirements, ceiling rates on deposits, and deposit-insurance premiums), and in certain offshore locations to benefit in addition from a favorable tax treatment.

Diversification is still another reason for international banking. As with expansion in domestic markets, international activities potentially enhance the opportunity for a bank to improve diversification of its assets and earnings flows. Domestic earnings flows from financial services are linked to the state of the economy. With the economies of the world growing at different rates and subject to different business cycles, international expansion holds the potential for greater earnings diversification.

Other objectives in international expansion include the increased visibility and prestige associated with such a move, and taking advantage of improvements in technology and communications that have allowed the extension and maintenance of real-time control over overseas operations at a decreasing cost.

Branches

A foreign branch is a banking office owned by the parent bank, and therefore does not constitute a separate legal entity. It is subject to two sets of regulations—those of the home country and those of the host country. Although branching abroad calls for a sizable investment, it enables a bank to offer more personalized services than through a representative office or a correspondent relationship. Thus, it can provide full banking services, including large loans based on the size of the parent bank's capital. Deposits are a legal obligation of the parent bank, not of the branch. From the customer's viewpoint, the branch organization is most accommodating because branch services are based on the worldwide value of the customer relationship rather than on the relationship to any specific office.

Foreign branches constitute the principal vehicle used by U.S. banks in the conduct of their international activities; they account for the largest concentration in foreign assets. Most of the foreign branches of U.S. banks are located in Latin America, Asia, and the Caribbean. However, the majority of foreign assets (47 percent) are held by branches in Europe (particularly in the United Kingdom, because of London's preeminence as the center of the Eurodollar market) and in the Caribbean (28 percent). The two primary Caribbean banking centers are the Bahamas and the Cayman Islands. Since the early 1970s, the Federal Reserve has allowed U.S. banks to establish *shell branches* (also known as "brass plate" branches) in these islands for the purpose of "booking" offshore transactions that took place on the U.S. mainland. Since the Fed's intention was to promote competition among U.S. banks in international markets, all offshore-booked transactions are exempt from reserve requirements, ceiling rates on deposits, and other regulations.

Subsidiaries and Affiliates

When entry into a foreign market through a branch or other facility is restricted or too costly, a bank may choose to enter that market by acquiring stock in a local institution. If the acquisition results in a majority ownership position, the acquired institution is referred to as a *subsidiary*; if it results in a minority ownership position, it is known as an *affiliate*. In essence, then, the difference lies in the size of equity investment in—and, hence, extent of control of—the foreign institution, which otherwise operates with its original name, charter, and personnel.

Purchase of complete or partial interests in foreign institutions has been an important avenue in the international activities of U.S. banks. In general, as vehicles for implementing an international banking program, subsidiaries and affiliates provide the parent bank with an entry into foreign markets with only minimal demands on its manpower resources while adding international expertise to the domestic experience of the nationals managing the subsidiary or affiliate. The major advantage for the parent bank, however, is that the potential

Strategy

Strategy refers to the measures a bank may take to realize the established objectives. In weighing entry into a foreign market, a number of factors must be taken into account, including the bank's financial resources, volume of international business, knowledge of—and experience with—foreign markets, banking structure and regulation in the countries targeted for entry, and customer profile. A key variable of the decision process is the vehicle to be used in the delivery of international services. Major banks around the world have used any one or a combination of vehicles to expand their international operations. These vehicles, some of which were identified in Chapter 3 in connection with the operation of foreign banks in the United States, are described below.

Correspondent Banks

U.S. banks that actively engage in the provision of international services may have international banking departments or a staff of specialists who offer services related to trade finance—collections, letters of credit, and foreign exchange. The majority of U.S. banks engage passively in international banking by relying on correspondent banks for the provision of international services. The correspondent banks providing such services may be U.S. banks or foreign banks located in the country's national or regional money centers.

Banks that engage actively in international banking also make use of correspondent banks; in fact, they may rely on a network of correspondent banks abroad to handle their foreign transactions. Under this arrangement a U.S. bank, for example, may have a prior agreement with a foreign bank to the effect that each will function as the agent of the other in their respective countries. Correspondent banking entails no foreign investment, no salaries for staff or any other related expenses. The banks may carry deposit accounts with one another or charge direct fees for the services rendered. Correspondent services include accepting drafts, honoring letters of credit, collecting or paying funds, furnishing credit information, and buying or selling securities for the account of the U.S. bank or its customers.

Representative Offices

A bank establishes a representative office in a foreign country primarily to assist its clients that conduct business in that country or in neighboring countries. A representative office cannot engage in general banking activities; that is, it cannot accept deposits nor make loans, but it can generate business for the head office. Some banks establish representative offices as an interim step prior to direct establishment of a full-fledged branch. These offices are also utilized for entry into countries where the presence of foreign commercial banks is either limited or prohibited (People's Republic of China, Saudi Arabia, and India).

for developing new business and fruitful connections in the foreign country is far greater than might be possible through the establishment of a branch or the de novo formation of a banking institution.

Subsidiaries constitute the second most important vehicle used by U.S. banks. Most of their assets (60 percent) are held in Europe, particularly in the United Kingdom.

One special type of subsidiary is an *Edge Act corporation*. Drawing its origin from a 1919 amendment to the Federal Reserve Act, an Edge Act corporation is a domestic subsidiary that may be owned by a U.S. bank or (since enactment of the IBA in 1978) by a foreign bank. An Edge Act corporation may function as a commercial bank accepting deposits and making loans to companies engaging in international business. Moreover, it may function as an investment company, taking equity positions in foreign financial organizations, such as merchant banks and finance companies. Because Edge Act corporations can be located anywhere in the United States, they have become an established vehicle for banks to engage in interstate banking. Some Edge Act corporations operate offices overseas. The state-chartered and -supervised counterparts to Edge Act Corporations are known as *agreement corporations* because they must agree to the same restrictions that govern Edge Act corporations.

A special type of affiliate is a *consortium bank*. A group of banks, not necessarily of the same nationality, may establish abroad a joint venture, known as a consortium bank, to undertake activities they are restricted from engaging in, in their respective countries. The consortium bank has its own name and functions as an independent corporate entity in the framework of the policies developed by its shareholding banks represented on the board. Its activities include medium- and long-term credits, facilitating corporate mergers and acquisitions, taking equity participations, and performing underwriting or private placements of public and private issues. Since their heyday in the 1960s and early 1970s, consortium banks have declined in importance. Antagonism with their bank owners has led to the restructuring of many consortia into single-parent banks (subsidiaries). Some of those in existence today operate as merchant and investment banks and are often located in offshore tax heavens.

International Banking Facilities (IBFs)

Like shell branches, IBFs were created by the Federal Reserve to encourage American banks to do more international business in the United States rather than abroad. To this end, IBFs have been exempted from regulatory costs (reserve requirements and deposit-insurance premiums) and many states have exempted them from state and local taxes. An IBF is a record-keeping entity (accounting entity) similar to an offshore shell branch; that is, a separate set of asset and liability accounts segregated from the regular bank books. As such, IBFs may be maintained by a U.S. bank, an Edge Act corporation, or U.S. offices of a foreign bank. IBF facilities are limited to time deposits (negotiable CDs are prohibited) that must be in minimum amounts of $100,000 and may originate from non-U.S. residents and other IBFs. Deposits so obtained cannot be used domestically but may be used to make foreign loans. Of the nearly 500 IBFs in this country, about half are located in New York and the rest in regional financial centers that actively engage in international banking.

Export Trading Companies

A new horizon on international banking for U.S. banks was the establishment or participation in export trading companies (ETCs), made possible by the Export Trading Company Act of 1982. Clearly, the objective of this legislation was to boost U.S. export activity. The rationale behind bank ownership of, or participation in, trading ventures was that U.S. banks are already in the business of researching foreign markets, evaluating risks, and understanding the subtleties of international finance. ETCs offer such services as international market research, export insurance coverage, transportation and warehousing of goods, and trade financing. According to Federal Reserve regulations, at least half of ETC revenues must come from activities associated with the export of goods and services from the United States. A number of bank holding companies have established ETCs, following the precedents set by banks in Brazil, France, Great Britain, and Japan.

INTERNATIONAL SERVICES OF U.S. BANKS

Continued growth of the international economy in the postwar decades has contributed to an ever-increasing demand for international financial services. Responding to this demand, U.S. banks have focused not only upon developing an extensive network of international banking facilities but also upon expanding the different types of international services offered and increasing the volume of these services. U.S. banks offer some of these services directly, while others are offered indirectly through subsidiaries and affiliates operating abroad. In the latter instance, as indicated earlier, the wider scope of activities permitted local banks abroad has induced U.S. banks to acquire equity interests in foreign banks and other financial institutions, and to offer a variety of ancillary services to meet the needs of their multinational clientele.

Of the international services that U.S. banks offer directly, some are an extension of those they provide in the domestic market (such as transfer of funds and acceptance of deposits), while others are unique to international banking (such as purchase and sale of foreign exchange, and letter of credit financing). Because of the variety of services that U.S. banks extend to their customers, discussion here will be limited to the more traditional ones. These include transfer of funds, financing international trade, collections, purchase and sale of foreign exchange, and international loans.

Transfer of Funds

One of the basic services offered by banks engaging in international banking is the transfer of funds between parties residing or traveling in different countries. This transfer can be effected in any of three ways: airmail remittance, cable remittance, or foreign drafts. A customer wishing to transfer funds via air mail to a party in another country would pay the bank, in cash or by a check drawn on his account, the stated amount plus a fee covering the expenses of the transaction. The bank then would send an airmail letter to its correspondent bank in the country where the beneficiary resides, specifying the amount of payment, the name and address of the beneficiary, the name of the sender, and authorized signatures. Upon receipt of these instructions, the foreign bank would verify the authenticity of the signatures and contact the beneficiary. After payment of the funds (in local currency), the account of the instructing bank would be charged for the amount of the payment.

If speed is important, the transfer can be effected by cable or by telephone. The process will be the same, except that the message is cabled or telephoned to the correspondent bank. The authenticity of the instruction is verified by code or test key arrangement. Clearly, the code or key issued would be prearranged, and would change daily for purposes of security.

Unlike the airmail and cable remittances, which are bank-to-bank instructions, a foreign draft is a negotiable instrument drawn by a bank on its foreign correspondent bank. A draft is issued when a client wants to have an actual instrument to mail to the beneficiary abroad. In such a case it is customary for the issuing bank to send its foreign correspondent a nonnegotiable copy of the draft, or a letter of advice that includes all the necessary details, as a protection against fraud.

One of the most widely known and used means of transferring funds abroad has been traveler's checks, a negotiable instrument of worldwide acceptability. Though few banks issue these checks, virtually every bank maintains a large inventory to accommodate the needs of its traveling customers. Traveler's checks have generally come to be accepted by tourists as a safe and easy instrument for the transfer of funds from one country to another.

Financing International Trade

Letter of Credit

One of the safest and most common ways to finance a transaction between international trading parties is the commercial letter of credit, or simply letter of credit. This instrument, depending upon the party to which reference is being made, is also referred to as an import letter of credit or an export letter of credit.

A letter of credit is a financial instrument issued by a bank at the request of a customer, whereby the bank undertakes to accept and/or pay drafts drawn upon it by a designated party, provided certain conditions are met by this party. In essence, the letter of credit provides for the substitution of a bank's strength for that of its customer, and assures the exporter payment against delivery of documents rather than of the actual merchandise. The exporter is also protected against government restrictions preventing payment by the importing firm. Experience shows that cases in which governments have prevented banks from honoring already issued letters of credit are limited (if there have been any). The importer is assured that the exporter will not be paid until the documents that transfer title to the merchandise are carefully examined by the bank and are found to be in order.

Issuance of a letter of credit by the importer's bank (*issuing* or *opening bank*) is the product of a process that usually begins with the exchange of correspondence between two parties located in different countries and interested in entering into a transaction. Once agreement is reached, a merchandise contract is concluded between the seller (exporter) and the buyer (importer). Two important features of this contract are the currency of payment and the means through which it is to be effected. If the invoice is to be expressed, and hence be paid, in the exporter's currency, the importer will have to bear the foreign-exchange risk of this transaction. On the other hand, if the invoice is to be stated in the importer's currency, the exporter will have to bear the foreign-exchange risk. In either case this risk can be reduced by hedging in the foreign-exchange market (see Chapter 9, section "Foreign-Exchange Risk"). The means of payment is another important aspect of this contract. If it is agreed that the transaction is to be paid by means of a letter of credit, the importer will contact his local bank and file a formal application for a letter of credit, which comes in a standardized printed form. The importer's bank will want to know the amount of money involved, the terms of payment, the documents that the bank should receive to effect payment, the time period for which the credit will be valid, and other conditions.

Processing a letter of credit request is similar to processing a loan. The bank will seek to determine the ability and willingness of the importer to provide the funds necessary to honor the letter of credit and to pay the required fees. A well-established importer already has access to a substantial line of credit at the bank, in which case issuing a letter of credit entails no difficulty. The amount to be drawn under the letter of credit is charged against the total available under the credit line. Small and less-known importers, on the other hand, have to provide some type of security, such as a cash deposit (for part or all of the credit) or other collateral.

Once the bank is satisfied with the creditworthiness of the importer, it will proceed to open a letter of credit in favor of the exporter, guaranteeing its payment subject to the terms and conditions contained in the credit (see Figure 16.1). The letter of credit is then forwarded to a bank in the exporter's country (that is, to a correspondent bank or to the exporter's bank), which is instructed to advise the beneficiary of the establishment of a letter of credit in its name. This bank (*advising bank*) has no financial responsibility, nor does it receive fees. After receipt of the letter of credit, the exporter arranges for the shipment of the goods to the importer, to fulfill the conditions of the credit.

Once the goods are shipped, the exporter draws a draft against the issuing bank and attaches it to the required documents, which are submitted to the

Figure 16.1
Letter of Credit

MANUFACTURERS HANOVER INTERNATIONAL BANKING CORPORATION
100 NORTH BISCAYNE BOULEVARD. MIAMI, FLORIDA 33132

DATE *June 6, 1996*

IRREVOCABLE COMMERCIAL LETTER OF CREDIT	OUR CREDIT NO. *AB-100140*	ADVISING BANK NO.

ADVISING BANK

APPLICANT

ADVISING BANK
MANUFACTURERS HANOVER TRUST COMPANY
Gran Via Carlos III, 140-142
Barcelona 34, Spain

APPLICANT
VENCO IMPORT COMPANY
Post Office Box XXXX
South Miami, Florida 33133

BENEFICIARY
A & M MANUFACTURERS
Apartado de Correos 44 CX
Barcelona, Spain

AMOUNT
U.S. $46,000.00 ***

EXPIRY DATE
September 6, 1996

GENTLEMEN:

YOU ARE AUTHORIZED TO VALUE ON *Us*

BY DRAWING DRAFTS AT *Sight*   FOR FULL INVOICE VALUE WHEN ACCOMPANIED

BY THE FOLLOWING DOCUMENTS:

- *Commercial Invoice, signed in Original and Four (4) Copies.*

- *Customs Invoice, in Original and Two (2) Copies.*

- *Insurance Policy or Certificate for Invoice value plus 15% covering Marine, War, and All Risks.*

- *Certificate of Origin issued by Chamber of Commerce, in Original and Three (3) Copies.*

- *On Board Ocean Bills of Lading (full set required if more than one original has been issued) issued to order of: Manufacturers Hanover International Banking Corporation, Miami, marked: NOTIFY Venco Import Company, Post Office Box XXXX, South Miami, Florida 33133. Freight Prepaid.*

COVERING *LADIES DRESSES, C.I.F.*

SPECIMEN

SHIPMENT FROM *Barcelona, Spain* TO *Miami, Florida* LATEST	PARTIAL SHIPMENTS *Permitted*	TRANS-SHIPMENTS *Prohibited*

DOCUMENTS MUST BE PRESENTED TO PAYING BANK WITHIN 15 DAYS AFTER THE DATE OF ISSUANCE OF DOCUMENTS EVIDENCING SHIPMENT BUT WITHIN THE VALIDITY OF LETTER OF CREDIT.

SPECIAL CONDITIONS:

THE AMOUNT OF ANY DRAFT DRAWN UNDER THIS CREDIT MUST BE ENDORSED ON THE REVERSE OF THE ORIGINAL CREDIT. ALL DRAFTS MUST BE MARKED, "DRAWN UNDER MANUFACTURERS HANOVER INTERNATIONAL BANKING CORPORATION LETTER OF CREDIT NUMBER *AB-100140* DATED *June 6, 1996*

WE HEREBY ENGAGE WITH THE DRAWERS, ENDORSERS AND BONA FIDE HOLDERS OF DRAFTS DRAWN UNDER AND IN COMPLIANCE WITH THE TERMS OF THIS CREDIT THAT SUCH DRAFTS WILE BE DULY HONORED ON DUE PRESENTATION, IF NEGOTIATED ON OR BEFORE THE EXPIRATION DATE OR PRESENTED TO US TOGETHER WITH THIS LETTER OF CREDIT ON OR BEFORE THAT DATE, Yours very truly,	ADVISING BANK'S NOTIFICATION
AUTHORIZED SIGNATURE	

EXCEPT SO FAR AS OTHERWISE EXPRESSLY STATED, THIS CREDIT IS SUBJECT TO THE "UNIFORM CUSTOMS AND PRACTICE FOR DOCUMENTARY CREDITS" (1974 REVISION) INTERNATIONAL CHAMBER OF COMMERCE (PUBLICATION NO. 290)

Source: Manufacturers Hanover International Banking Corporation.

exporter's bank along with the letter of credit. Assuming that the documents are found to be in order, the exporter's bank forwards them to the issuing bank for payment. If the draft and accompanying documents comply with the terms and conditions of the letter of credit, the issuing bank pays the exporter's bank, which then makes the funds available to its client, the exporter. The issuing bank, in turn, collects from the importer against release of documents that are essential for the latter's physical possession of the merchandise.

The great majority of the letters of credit issued are *irrevocable*—that is, once the beneficiary is notified, the letter of credit cannot be canceled prior to the expiration date or altered in any way without the prior consent of all parties to the transaction, including the beneficiary. If the letter of credit is *revocable*, the credit is subject to cancellation or modification at any time before payment and without notice to the beneficiary. Not infrequently the exporter may request the advising or notifying bank to add its own liability to that of the opening bank. In such a case the letter of credit becomes *confirmed*, meaning that both the issuing and the confirming bank are obligated to honor drafts drawn in compliance with the credit. If both the irrevocable and the confirmed features are combined in the same letter of credit, such a letter is virtual guaranty of payment once the conditions of the credit are fulfilled, and is referred to as an *irrevocable and confirmed letter of credit*.

Over the years, because of particular needs of importers and/or exporters, there have been other important variations of the basic document to accommodate different conditions. Thus, a letter of credit may provide for advances to the exporter prior to shipment (*red clause letter of credit*); call for payments not at the time of shipment but later, in accordance with scheduled dates over the life of the credit (*deferred-payment letter of credit*); make possible the transfer of proceeds by the beneficiary (a trading intermediary) to another party (a supplier) in the transaction (*transferable letter of credit*); permit the exporter to seek the most favorable foreign-exchange rate among those quoted by different banks or exercise its judgment as to the bank that would be most desirable to effect collection (*negotiable letter of credit*); or cover more than one transaction through successive reinstatements of the letter of credit, renewing the amount involved and extending the expiration date (*revolving letter of credit*).

Whatever the specific features of the letter of credit, the terms and conditions should be clear and simply stated. Reference to the quality or condition of the merchandise and other details are not customarily included in the letter of credit. No one would expect bank employees to open and examine the contents of boxes or crates—and even if they did, they would hardly be qualified to express an opinion on the state of these goods. If the exporter is dishonest, a letter of credit will not prevent shipment of inferior goods, or even rocks. Since banks deal only in documents, they cannot be held liable in such instances. However, the bank can withhold payment from the exporter if there is some irregularity in the necessary documents (those covering shipment and insurance of goods) or if some of the terms and conditions stated in the letter of credit have not been met.

Drafts and Acceptances

The final phase in the letter of credit financing process is the actual payment, which is effected by means of a *draft* or bill of exchange. A draft is a written order to pay, signed by the drawer, requiring the party to which it is addressed to pay on demand, or at some future date, a stated sum of money to the order of a named party or to the bearer. As follows from this definition, there are three parties to a draft: the *drawer*, the *drawee*, and the *payee*. The drawer or maker is the exporter, who, after the goods are shipped, originates the draft and presents it—along with the required documents—to its bank for payment of what is due. The drawee is the party to which the draft is addressed—the importer or its bank—and which is asked to pay the stipulated amount in accordance with the terms of the document. The payee is the beneficiary in favor of whom the draft is payable—that is, the exporter or the exporter's bank.

Another feature of the draft is the time of payment, often called a draft's tenor. Depending upon the prior agreement between importer and exporter, a letter of credit may call for a sight or a time draft. If the letter of credit provides for a sight draft, the issuing bank will make immediate payment once the draft and certifying documents are received and are found to be in accordance with the terms of the letter of credit. If provision is made for a time draft, payment by the importer is due 30, 60, 90, or some other specified number of days after the date of the draft. As this implies, the main purpose of a time draft is to provide the importer with sufficient time to claim and dispose of the goods, and meet the maturity of the underlying draft.

Issuance of a time draft calls for an additional step in the financial transaction, its acceptance by the importer's bank and, hence, the creation of a *banker's acceptance*. The draft is changed into an acceptance by a stamp across the face of the draft that includes the word "accepted," the date, the signature of an authorized officer, the name of the bank, and other information. Clearly, the accepting bank will charge its client a commission for creating this acceptance. The banker's acceptance may be returned to the exporter, to be held until maturity and then collected.

Alternatively, the exporter may discount (sell) the draft to its bank or to an investor, receiving payment immediately. When the accepting bank is a U.S. bank, foreign exporters usually favor authorizing the U.S. bank to sell its dollar-denominated acceptance in the domestic money markets. This is because the U.S. money markets are generally more liquid and have lower transaction costs than is true for markets in most other currencies. Such a request presents no problem, especially if the accepting bank has a strong reputation in international trading circles. The stature of the accepting bank makes it a prime asset—that is, a high-quality investment for banks and other institutional investors interested in holding liquid assets of this type. The selling of the acceptance will be at a discount from the face amount, based on the going discount rate for bankers' acceptances. Since the importer may have agreed in advance to pay for this discount, the accepting bank will remit the exporter's bank the full amount of the draft for payment to the exporter. The investor, in turn, will hold the accepted draft until its maturity, then present it to the bank for payment. The accepting bank will then look to its customer for reimbursement.

In many cases, businesses well known to each other may find use of a letter of credit unnecessary, and instead agree on payment through drafts to be collected through banking channels. In other words, the banks involved act only as agents in performing a collection function, thereby earning a collection fee. Specifically, after shipment of the merchandise, the exporter draws a draft on the importer (rather than on its bank), in accordance with the terms agreed upon by the two parties, and submits it, along with the other documents necessary for the transaction, to its bank for collection. The exporter's bank then forwards them to its correspondent in the importer's country, which arranges for collection of the funds due the exporter. If the draft is a sight draft, the documents are turned over to the importer upon payment of the draft. If the draft is a time draft, the documents are released to the importer when the latter accepts the draft liability, which is then known as a *trade acceptance*.

In either case the collecting bank may choose to time the presentation of the drafts to the importer—for payment or acceptance—when the merchandise arrives in the importer's designated port. On the basis of an exporter's letter of instruction to the collecting bank, the latter collects from the importer the stipulated amount (plus any fees) and remits it to the exporter's bank for payment. Clearly, should the importer fail to make any payment or go into bankruptcy after accepting the draft, the collecting bank has no obligation or commitment to pay. The risk of nonpayment is carried by the exporter.

Documents

Whether drafts are part of a letter of credit transaction or merely items for collection, documents are an integral part of the transaction. These documents generally certify title to the goods and the condition of shipment. With banks functioning as intermediaries between exporters and importers, it is only natural that they be concerned about these documents and make every effort to assure that they are in good order. Following is a list of the documents required in most international transactions.

Commercial Invoice. Once a merchandise contract is concluded, the exporter issues an invoice in the name of the buyer, describing the merchandise and its attributes, unit prices, the terms of sale, and the total value of the transaction. The invoice includes information pertaining to shipping terms and charges, such as CF (cost and freight), CIF (cost, insurance, and freight), FOB (free on board), and FAS (free alongside). The data contained in the invoice should be consistent with the corresponding data on the letter of credit.

Bill of Lading. A key document in the financing of a foreign-trade transaction is the bill of lading. This document, issued by steamship companies, airlines, railroads, and other common carriers, provides a description of the terms and conditions under which a shipment is accepted. It is a receipt from the carrier that it has accepted goods for transportation; a contract with the shipper for the transport and delivery of goods to a designated party or its order; and a transferable title to the goods, provided it is negotiable (made out "to order"). These attributes of the bill of lading render it the principal document supporting the exporter's draft and, hence, its claim for payment.

Insurance Certificate. Depending upon the terms of the merchandise contract, insurance may be placed by the exporter for his account or for the account of the importer; or it may be placed by the importer with his own underwriting firm. Active importers and exporters usually maintain open or floating policies on the basis of which they issue insurance certificates for individual shipments; these certificates accompany the required title documents. Marine insurance policies cover the normal hazards of a voyage, usually referred to as *shipping risks*. These risks range from total loss of goods through sinking of the vessel to losses resulting from fire, collision, or fuel oil or water damages.

In addition to sea perils, there are a number of other real risks that can interrupt the commencement and/or the completion of the voyage: strikes, riots, civil commotion, and war. Of these risks, strikes are the most common faced by traders today. Strikes can prevent the transfer of the shipment from the dock to the vessel or vice versa. This can be especially disastrous for the importer when the shipment consists of perishables. The same is true for seasonal items— for example, Christmas ornaments are landed in time for the season but are delayed by a longshoremen's strike. If insurance is desired to cover against strikes or any of the other risks, it can be included in the marine insurance policy by endorsement. The exception is war risk, which requires a separate contract.

Upon arrival of the vessel at the port of import, and after the shipment is unloaded at the docks, it is exposed to added risks that include theft and pilferage, which are usually referred to as *dockside risks*. These are also subject to a marine insurance coverage.

Other Documents. Other documents that may be required by a letter of credit are a *certificate of origin*, which certifies the country where the goods are grown or manufactured; a *weight list*, which itemizes the weight of each package or bale; *a packing list*, which identifies the contents of individual packages, especially when these are numerous; and an *inspection certificate*, which is usually issued by a third or independent party to verify the contents or quality of the shipment. Since banks deal only in documents, this certificate assures the importer that it is receiving what it ordered.

Collections

Collection, the presenting of an item for payment, is essentially the same internationally as domestically. The major difference is the absence of an international clearinghouse for checks and other negotiable items drawn on the banks of one country and deposited in the banks of another. Correspondent relationships are therefore established between commercial banks that also serve as agents, collecting negotiable items for exporters.

These collections may be either *clean* (without documents attached) or *documentary* (with documents attached). Clean items are usually checks, traveler's checks, and money orders, which, drawn on banks in the currency of one country, are exchanged for local currency in another country. American tourists abroad using traveler's checks to pay for services received or goods purchased, represent an example of clean collections. Recipients of these checks turn them over to their local banks for settlement. These foreign banks collect by sending the clean items, usually by airmail, to their correspondent American banks, either for immediate credit or as a collection, with the amount of the item to be credited only after payment is made by the maker's bank. Clean items are thus presented for collection in exactly the same manner internationally as they are domestically.

More complicated and, at this time, more important to international trade are documentary collections. If the risk of nonpayment is relatively small, an exporter may opt for the less costly collection approach instead of a letter of credit. In such a case, the exporter, after shipment of the merchandise, will turn over to the bank all the related documents, along with a draft that directs the importer to make payment for the goods. The exporter's bank will send these documents to its correspondent bank in the importer's country for presentation and payment. Once the importer has made payment to the bank, all the documents are turned over to him and he proceeds to claim the goods. The correspondent bank in the importer's country acts only as an agent and performs a collection function. This collection approach is known as "documents against payment."

In the above situation, the exporter must give his bank precise instructions pertaining to presentation of the collection for payment, the party that will pay the fees, the method for transferring payment, and the steps to be taken if the collection is not made. Any deviation from these explicit instructions and any action initiated by the collecting bank are at the risk of the latter.

The principal international clearing center in the United States is New York. In the mid-1960s a committee composed from the New York Clearing House banks was given the task of putting in place a settlement mechanism to handle the clearing of interbank money transfers and to facilitate international transactions (e.g., foreign-exchange and Eurodollar trades). The result was the Clearing House Interbank Payments System (CHIPS). A private electronic transfer system, CHIPS currently has a membership of more than 100 banks, a large number of which are branches and agencies of foreign banks. CHIPS daily processes a little over $1 trillion of interbank transfers arising from international movements of funds. CHIPS must be distinguished from SWIFT, a global funds-transfer system linking major banks all over the world and owned by a cooperative venture, the Society for Worldwide Interbank Financial Telecommunications.

Foreign Exchange

One activity conducted by a bank's international department that has no domestic parallel is foreign-exchange trading. No matter what the nature of an international business transaction, as long as it involves foreign payment, it will entail the exchange of one currency for another. There is no one physical, central marketplace for this kind of transaction (equivalent, for example, to the New York Stock Exchange for bonds and stocks). Rather, there is an electronically linked network of banks and foreign-exchange brokers and dealers who are located in the principal financial centers of the world and whose function is to bring together buyers and sellers of foreign exchange. The foreign-exchange market is thus very informal, with no official setting of rates or trading rules, and is generally guided by a code of ethics that has evolved over time.

Most U.S. commercial banks engaging in international banking consider foreign exchange as one of the services they provide to customers, but they do not regard it as central to their product mix. These banks participate in the *retail* portion of the market. They do not maintain inventory positions in foreign currencies but rely on their correspondent banks who are active in this market to execute their orders.

A number of internationally active U.S. banks trade currencies on a continuing basis with the largest banks headquartered abroad; they are participants in the *wholesale* or *interbank foreign-exchange market*. These banks are *market makers* in the currencies in which they specialize; that is, they are prepared to buy and sell these currencies with other banks at any time. To effect foreign-exchange trading, U.S. banks hold dollar balances and foreign-currency-denominated deposits with banks abroad. At the same time, foreign banks maintain offices in the United States to manage the accounts of their foreign clients (businesses and governmental agencies). Trading is generally done by telephone, telex, or the SWIFT system that electronically links all brokers and traders. Terminals display up-to-the-minute information concerning buy and sell orders, which, carried on an anonymous basis, are visible to all market participants and may be executed anywhere in the world at the press of a few buttons. Before the local financial market opens for business, traders communicate with their counterparts in other parts of the world where trading is already in progress. The information received, combined with their own technical analysis, give traders a better feel for market direction and developing trends, and prepares them for subsequent market trading activity. Since thousands of transactions are executed each day, a bank's working balances in foreign currencies are inevitably affected. To even out temporary surpluses and shortages, traders must continuously buy and sell various currencies to adjust the bank's position in individual currencies. This is all the more important because prices in the market are sensitive and can change quickly.

Although transactions in the interbank market are effected directly between banks, a sizable number are conducted through foreign-exchange brokers. Brokers maintain instant access to dealers worldwide; this enables them to locate quickly an opposite party with whom a client can enter into a transaction while earning a commission for their efforts. Besides dealer and nondealer banks, broker services are used by businesses and governments. Brokers thus contribute to the efficient operations of the foreign-exchange market.

With the foreign-exchange market spanning the globe, the prices and currencies traded can change in the course of the day. Changes in foreign-exchange rates affect market participants throughout the world. Because these changes can be sudden, significant losses can be realized. Dealer banks have a risk exposure when they hold foreign-currency positions. Such exposure can be managed by imposing dollar limits on positions in a certain currency, on regions of the world, or on particular customers. Alternatively, a bank may use hedging techniques to control its exposure.

Exchange-rate risk is inherent in all international commercial and financial transactions. As long as rates fluctuate, even within a narrow range, risk is involved for those who expect to convert one currency to another. Whether it is a multinational corporation, an institutional investor, or an exporter, taking on foreign-exchange risk can undermine its viability as a going concern. For an American exporter, for example, who sells goods abroad for payment in a foreign currency, a drop in the value of the foreign currency will reduce profits or cause losses, thereby undermining his ability to compete effectively in international markets. Hedging in the foreign-exchange market reduces the exchange-rate risk. The exporter can cover his position through a forward, futures, or options contract, whatever best suits his needs. Commercial banks earn fee income from arranging for such coverage (hedging against foreign-exchange risk was discussed in Chapter 9).

International Loans

As in domestic activity, the largest source of income from international operations is lending. Usually the banks most active in international lending are those that maintain branches abroad or other types of vehicles that ensure a presence in foreign markets. Banks that have only international departments generally limit themselves to lending funds or giving credit to their domestic customers, thereby helping to finance international trade by making possible both the production of goods for export and the purchase of foreign goods for domestic use.

International loans are extended to such foreign borrowers as business firms, banks, and governments. In many ways the loans that banks make to these borrowers are similar to domestic business loans. Funds are loaned for both short- and medium-term maturities, are made at floating rates, and borrowers are of moderate to high quality. There are, however, important differences with regard to one or more of the following aspects: funding, pricing, collateral, syndication, and risk.

Funding

International loans are funded in the Eurocurrency market. Banks operating in this market employ their time deposits to fund short- and medium-term loans to other international banks and nonbank borrowers. The interest paid to depositors generally reflects the prevailing home-country interest rate for the currency in question; the lending rate covers the borrower's perceived riskiness and the bank's expenses for lending.

Pricing

The most important feature of Eurocredits is that they are made on a floating-rate basis. Interest rates on loans are tied to LIBOR, which is the rate banks charge each other in London. Alternatively, interest rates on loans to borrowers in the Pacific Basin are tied to SIBOR, the Singapore Interbank Offered Rate. Loans to governments and their agencies, corporations, and nonprime banks are priced at a fixed margin over LIBOR for the specified period and currency of choice. Although periods of one or three months may be used for repricing purposes, the period most frequently used is six months. Whatever the period of choice, the interest charged on the loan for the coming period is calculated at the same fixed margin over the new LIBOR at the beginning of the period. By pricing loans on a rollover basis, banks avoid exposure to the interest-rate risk inherent in medium-term, fixed-rate loans. Over the years, spreads have ranged from slightly below 0.5 percent to over 3 percent.

Collateral

Most international bank loans involve no collateral. Because procedures for taking security interest against specific assets of borrowers usually require special on-site legal assistance, and perhaps other costs, foreign loans are usually made without specific collateral. The loan recipients are generally large, creditworthy multinational corporations and official borrowers (governments and their agencies).

Syndications

Although some Eurocurrency loans take the form of a line of credit or a note issuance facility, most loans are *syndicated*. Several banks are assembled by a lead bank, or syndicate manager, to participate in the financing of a loan to a multinational corporation or a sovereign entity. This process enables the participating banks to spread the risk involved in making large specialized loans, and it permits the borrower to obtain funds well in excess of a single bank's lending limit. The syndicate manager originates the transaction, structures it, assembles the syndicate, supervises the documentation, and in most cases services the loan after signing. Its position is the most crucial and, from a legal perspective, the most exposed. It owes a duty to the borrower to arrange a syndication, and a duty to the other banks not to mislead them or misrepresent any aspect of the credit. Management fees, payable by the borrower, range from 0.5 to 2 percent of the total amount of the loan; participation fees of lesser amounts are paid, normally by the manager out of the total fee, to very large participants in proportion to the size of their participation.

Syndicated credits vary in maturity from approximately three to ten years and are made at floating rates (some premium over LIBOR). Throughout the 1970s and early 1980s, syndicated bank credits were the single most important financing vehicle in international financial markets. The onset of the debt crisis caused a drastic decline in the volume of syndicated credits from $100 billion in 1982 to $25 billion in 1985. The subsequent rejuvenation of the syndicated loan market was due to the new direction in Eurocurrency credits—corporate borrowers in industrialized countries. Most of the syndicated credits of the late 1980s and early 1990s were directed to U.S. and U.K. corporations and provided for the financing of mergers and acquisitions.

Risks

The risks involved in international lending are both common to domestic lending and unique to the international function. Default (or credit) risk is clearly the same type of risk faced in domestic lending; its evaluation entails use of the same principles. However, two risks unique to international lending are the foreign-exchange risk and country risk. Foreign-exchange, or currency, risk arises from loans denominated in a foreign currency and involves the likelihood of losses to the bank because of a drop in the value of that currency in the course of the loan (e.g., repayment will be with fewer dollars). If the tenor of the loan is short and the foreign currency has a well-developed market, hedging will effectively reduce the bank's exposure. A frequent practice is to fund loans in the bank's home currency. For example, U.S. banks, by lending primarily in dollars, shift the foreign-exchange risk to the overseas borrower. This practice does not eliminate currency risk. The bank still has an exposure, in that the borrower may not be able to obtain the dollars to service his debt. A bank may avoid this possibility by sourcing the loan funds in the borrower's home-country currency. Loan repayment will not then be subject to the foreign-exchange rate; only the loan's profit margin in terms of the bank's home currency will be.

As was stated in Chapter 12 in connection with project loans, country risk refers to the political, economic, and social conditions of a particular country that have unfavorable effects on the repayment of the loan (or the recovery of an investment made in that country). A country-risk evaluation process encompasses several elements. From a political perspective, country evaluation seeks to ascertain the degree of political stability in the borrower's country (e.g., threat of war, civil unrest, political tensions, nationalization, and changes in regulatory philosophy). On the economic side, the evaluation process considers factors including inflation, wage-price controls, profit controls, taxation, and the country's balance-of-payments situation. Social problems are equally important because they may lead to political and economic pressures that will affect the timely service of the loan. A component of country risk is *transfer risk*, which denotes borrower inability to convert local currency into foreign exchange due to foreign-exchange controls.

If the borrower is a national government or a government entity, the bank's hazard is identified as *sovereign risk*. This risk occurs because under international law, official borrowers enjoy sovereign immunity—that is, they cannot be sued without their consent; the courts of one country cannot sit in judgment on the acts, or omissions, of another country; and the property of a government or its agencies is immune from any attachment, arrest, or execution.

Several methods are available to banks for assessing country risk. They range from fully qualitative to scoring systems and discriminant analysis. Whatever the method used, it enables the bank to determine appropriate loan limits, or concentrations, in particular countries. Banks can further control exposure to country risk through diversification—by spreading these loans over several countries or regions.

The international debt crisis of the 1980s stressed the importance for banks to keep country exposures under control. With a large share of banks' international credits concentrated among nonoil-producing LDCs, the debt crisis severely impacted the quality of loan portfolios. As the recession of the early 1980s spread throughout the industrialized countries, it resulted in lower commodity prices worldwide and drastically reduced the capacity of LDCs to service their debts. Deterioration in borrowers' debt-service capacity accordingly affected the quality of LDC debt. The prospect of holding uncollected loans prompted banks to respond to a rapidly escalating demand for debt reschedulings. Rescheduling refers to the rolling over of a loan, often capitalizing accrued interest or extending the maturity of the loan. Between 1982 and 1990, while the International Monetary Fund (IMF) provided temporary financial assistance to debtor nations, over $140 billion worth of debt was rescheduled in response to the repayment problems of LDCs. Alternatively, banks added billions to their loan-loss reserves to absorb the necessary loan write-downs. Some banks carried out exchanges of debt paper between themselves to reduce their concentrations in particular countries, and others sold loans in the secondary market at substantial discounts. A few banks engaged in debt-for-equity swaps, exchanging debt held for equity in state-owned enterprises in the debtor countries. Mexico offered bank creditors a debt-for-debt conversion in early 1988. Under this plan, bank loans were swapped for bonds issued by Mexico and collateralized by U.S. Treasury zero-coupon bonds.

The Brady Plan of 1989, initiated by Secretary of the Treasury Nicholas Brady, provided for the negotiation of comprehensive packages of debt restructuring that offered debtor countries debt and debt-service relief and required them to embark upon economic reforms to cure their problems. The Brady restructurings enhanced the quality of the debt held by bank creditors and contributed to genuine economic reforms in debtor countries. The adoption of free-market policies in countries such as Mexico and Chile had led others to follow suit and has contributed to restoring their creditworthiness in international capital markets.

LOAN INSURANCE AND GUARANTEE PROGRAMS

Banks can reduce the risks associated with foreign loans when lending to exporters who insure their trade credits. Export credit insurance is available in the United States through the Foreign Credit Insurance Association (FCIA), an unincorporated association of about 50 private insurance firms. FCIA offers short-term policies involving payment terms up to 180 days and medium-term policies with payment terms from 181 days to 5 years. Coverage up to seven years may be arranged on a case-by-case basis for selected capital goods. Coverage applies to goods produced and shipped from the United States during the policy period. Protection against commercial risk (e.g., insolvency or protracted payment default of buyer) ranges from 90 to 95 percent, and against political risk (actions of foreign governments beyond the control of buyer or seller) from 90 to 100 percent.

An institution that guarantees certain foreign loans made by commercial banks is the Export-Import Bank, or Eximbank. Created in 1934, the Eximbank is an independent agency of the U.S. government empowered to finance and facilitate U.S. exports. To this end, the bank extends credit to foreign buyers, offers assistance to commercial banks and other financial institutions that are supporting export sales, and provides various guarantee and insurance programs. Eximbank guarantees repayment of medium-term (181 days to 5 years) and long-term (5 years to 10 years) export loans made by U.S. banks to foreign borrowers. Most Eximbank guarantees provide comprehensive coverage of both political and commercial risks.

SUGGESTED REFERENCES

Aliber, Robert Z. "International Banking: A Survey." *Journal of Money, Credit and Banking*, November 1986, pp. 661–78.

Eiteman, David K., and Arthur I. Stonehill. *Multinational Business Finance*. 7th ed. Reading, Mass.: Addison-Wesley, 1995.

Eng, Maximo V., Francis A. Lees, and Laurence J. Mauer. *Global Finance*. New York: HarperCollins, 1995.

Hirtle, Beverly. "Factors Affecting the Competitiveness of Internationally Active Financial Institutions." Federal Reserve Bank of New York, *Quarterly Review*, Spring 1991, pp. 38–51.

Hultman, Charles W. *The Environment of International Banking*. Englewood Cliffs, N.J.: Prentice-Hall, 1990.

Liepold, Alessandro. *International Capital Markets: Developments and Prospects*. Washington, D.C.: International Monetary Fund, May 1991.

Pavel, Christine, and John N. McElravey. "Globalization in the Financial Services Industry.'' Federal Reserve Bank of Chicago, *Economic Perspectives*, May/June 1990, pp. 3–18.

Roussakis, E. N. ''Role of Commercial Banks in Postwar Japan.'' *Academia* no. 13 (1994): 67–80.

Shapiro, Alan C. *Multinational Financial Management*. 5th ed. Upper Saddle River, N.J.: Prentice-Hall, 1996.

Stern, Richard L. ''(Dangerous) Fun and Games in the Foreign Exchange Market.'' *Forbes*, August 22, 1988, pp. 69–72.

Index

About the Author

EMMANUEL N. ROUSSAKIS is professor of finance and director of the certificate programs for bankers at Florida International University, Miami. He holds degrees from the University of Athens, Atlanta University, College of Europe, and the Catholic University of Louvain, where he received his doctorate in economics. He has taught at American universities in the United States and Europe, worked for American and European banks, and served in an advisory capacity to government agencies, both in the United States and abroad. He participated in the negotiations for Greece's admission to the European Economic Community in the area of commercial banks and banking policy. He was corecipient of a Florida State Research (STAR) grant for the study of international banking legislation and taxation; study recommendations were the basis for legislative changes implemented in Florida in July 1979 and June 1980. He has published widely on banking subjects, his articles having appeared in academic and professional journals in the United States, Europe, and Latin America.

Dr. Roussakis is the author of *Friedrich List, the Zollverein and the Uniting of Europe* (1968), *Managing Commercial Bank Funds* (Praeger, 1977), and *Miami's International Banking Community: Foreign Banks, Edge Act Corporations and Local Banks* (1981). He is also the editor of, and contributor to, *International Lending by U.S. Commercial Banks: A Casebook* (Praeger, 1981), *International Banking: Principles and Practices* (Praeger, 1983), and *Cases in Commercial Bank Management* (1994). His book *Commercial Banking in an Era of Deregulation*, 2nd edition, was translated into Chinese and published in China in 1992.